THE RELUCTANT SUPPLIER

The Reluctant Supplier

Supplier

U.S. Decisionmaking
For Arms Sales

Paul Y. Hammond
University of Pittsburgh

David J. Louscher
University of Akron

Michael D. Salomone
Carnegie-Mellon University

Norman A. Graham
The Futures Group

 Oelgeschlager, Gunn & Hain, Publishers, Inc.
Cambridge, Massachusetts

International Standard Book Number: 0-89946-149-2

Library of Congress Catalog Card Number: 82-22514

Printed in the U.S.A.

Library of Congress Cataloging in Publication Data
Main entry under title:

The Reluctant supplier.

Bibliography: p.
Includes index.
1. Military assistance, American—History—
20th century. 2. Munitions—United States—
History—20th century. 3. United States—Foreign
relations—20th century. 4. United States—Military
relations—Foreign countries. I. Hammond, Paul Y.
UA12.R44   1983   355'.032'0973   82-22514
ISBN 0-89946-149-2

Contents

List of Figures

List of Tables

Preface and
Acknowledgments

The national security issues surrounding U.S. arms sales policies have been the subject of our research for the past five years. David Louscher has examined these issues for more than a decade, and Paul Hammond for more than two decades. Our interests in the subject coalesced around common skepticism concerning the wisdom, rationale, and prospects for success of the bold arms transfer restraint policies and initiatives of the Carter administration. This book grew from our observations of that period and our agreement concerning the key issues confronting the U.S. government as it formulates and implements its security assistance policies today. Many misconceptions about past and present U.S. arms sales policies, programs, and procedures abound in the current scholarly and popular literature. The book addresses these misconceptions and assesses arms transfers as a primary instrument of U.S. foreign policy.

Much of our information came from extensive interviews (nearly 300) and other field work from 1978 to mid-1982. We wish to thank all those who generously gave their time and cooperation; without their assistance this book could not have been written. Hammond, Louscher, and Salomone interviewed senior U.S. government civilian and military officials who were, or had been, involved with the formulation and implementation of U.S. security assistance policies and programs. The responsibilities of the respondents covered every region of the globe, and nearly every nation with which the U.S. government has or had an arms transfer relationship. These interviews were conducted in Washington, D.C., in Europe, and in Latin America. They involved officials of the Office of the Secretary of Defense; Office of the Joint Chiefs of Staff; military departments and services, including U.S. regional and unified commands; Department of State; Arms Control and Disarmament Agency; Central Intelligence Agency, National Security Council Staff; Congressional Research Service; General Accounting Office; and nongovernment elites in Great Britain, France, and the Federal Republic of Germany concerning European economic, security, and export policies regarding arms sales.

Some of this work has been published previously as articles, and has been adapted, updated, and enlarged for the present volume. We specifically wish to thank the following scholarly journals for their permission to use or reprint parts of these articles: The Foreign Policy Research Institute, Philadelphia, Pennsylvania, for permission to use material from David J. Louscher, "The Rise in Military Sales as U.S. Foreign Assistance Instrument," *Orbis* 20,4 (Winter 1977); Paul Y. Hammond, David J. Louscher, and Michael D. Salomon, "Controlling U.S. Arms Transfers: The Emerging System," *Orbis* 23,2 (Summer 1979); The Inter-University Seminar on Armed Forces and Society, Chicago, Illinois, for permission to use material from Paul Y. Hammond, David J. Louscher, and Michael D. Salomon, "Growing Dilemmas for the Management of Arms Sales," *Armed Forces and Society* 6,1 (Fall 1979); The International Institute for Strategic Studies, London, England, for permission to use material from Michael D. Salomon, David J. Louscher, and Paul Y. Hammond, "Lessons of the Carter Approach to Restraining Arms Transfers," *Survival* 13,5 (September-October 1981); and The Naval War College, Newport, Rhode Island, for permission to use material from David J. Louscher and Michael D. Salomon, "Conflicting Trends for Arms Transfer Restraint," *Naval War College Review* 33,6 (November-December 1980) and "New Directions and New Problems for Arms Transfers Policy," *Naval War College Review* 35,1 (January-February 1982).

Some of the ideas and analyses for other parts of this manuscript were initially presented as papers before several scholarly conventions. These included David J. Louscher and Michael D. Salomon, "American Arms Deliveries to the Third World: An Examination of Trends in Supplies, 1950 to 1980" delivered before the Western Political Science Association and International Studies Association/West, San Diego, March 1982; Norman A. Graham, "Trans-Atlantic Arms Transfers: The

Search for Security, Industrial Cooperation, and Transfer Coordination"; and Paul Y. Hammond, David J. Louscher, and Michael D. Salomon, "The Failure of CATT: Bureaucratic Perspectives on Policy Innovation," papers presented to the International Studies Association Annual Convention in Los Angeles, 1980.

We also wish to thank those who generously assisted our research. At the Department of Political Science, University of Akron, James Nixon provided excellent research assistance and was valuable in providing computer tests for our ideas. E. J. Hurd also provided excellent research assistance, and Bonnie Ralston typed the first draft of the manuscript.

At the Dean's Office, College of Humanities and Social Sciences, Carnegie-Mellon University, Dorthea Marsh and Susan Ritchie entered various portions of a much-revised manuscript into the word processor, and Kathleen Confer undertook the monumental task of preparing the final copy of the manuscript. John Roppo entered the data base into the CMU computer and constructed figure graphics on Tellagraf software and a Xerox 9700 laser printer. Thanks to the support of these staff members, we took maximum advantage of this technology.

We also wish to acknowledge the support provided by our respective institutions, The University of Pittsburgh, The University of Akron, Carnegie-Mellon University, and The Futures Group of Glastonbury, Connecticut. These institutions have created the research environments necessary to make such an extensive project possible. We owe special thanks to the Department of Political Science of the University of Akron for providing research and secretarial assistance, as well as computing support; and special thanks also to the College of Humanities and Social Sciences of Carnegie-Mellon University for providing research and secretarial assistance as well as computing, computer printing, graphics, and word processing support. We wish also to thank the Institute on Western Europe of Columbia University and the Institute for the Study of World Politics, New York, for providing grants to Norman Graham to undertake field research on Western European arms transfer policies; and the James Madison College, Michigan State University for helping compile and prepare the initial bibliography.

Chapter 1

Introduction

Many readers will find it puzzling that a book about American arms transfer activities and decisionmaking processes should be entitled *The Reluctant Supplier*. In recent years many articles and more than a few books have been written on the subject. The vast majority of these writings have decried what their authors perceived as the enormous growth of arms transfers, citing the dangers and charging that U.S. arms transfers have gotten out of hand. Various instruments for reestablishing "control" over arms transfers have been proposed. Often scholars have recommended that the United States attempt to become "a more reluctant supplier".[1]

In the early 1960s, a distinguished political scientist, Ralph Huitt, admonished students of the Congress, who were at that time suggesting numerous reforms of the institution, that before we change an institution we should know its functions. Huitt persuasively argued that basic descriptions of a phenomenon are central to an explanation of it, and prudent prescription depends on sagacious description. Huitt's basic but wise advice has rarely been followed by analysts of arms transfers.

Prescriptions for future uses of arms transfers are not in scarce supply; but misperceptions abound about the past and present direction of U.S. arms transfer programs, about the goals and functions they serve, and about the control process for arms transfers within the U.S. government.

Our purpose in this volume is to replace mistaken perceptions, where they exist, with more accurate ones. Our thesis is not optimistic, although it may appear to be. We demonstrate that the trends in arms transfers have not been rising as steeply as many authoritative voices have claimed. On the other hand, we note the endemic strength and persistence of arms transfers as a phenomenon in international affairs. Suppliers, including the United States, find arms transfers a convenient and necessary instrument of foreign and domestic policy. Recipients likewise perceive the acquisition of arms, of associated military hardware (sometimes called "nonlethal" hardware), and of supporting equipment and services to be essential to national programs for a variety of reasons. We attempt to describe these reasons in general and associate them with the aggregate data about transfers in order to understand the phenomenon of arms transfers.

If our picture of trends, by deflating common claims about the rate of increase, appears to be optimistic, then it is offset by a more than usually pessimistic picture of the intractability or at least the persistence of the arms transfer phenomenon. The phenomenon is widespread and deeply rooted in the international system. Yet we offer an additional, relatively optimistic picture of U.S. behavior, from which we take the title of this volume: the United States as a *reluctant supplier*. There have always been influential elements of the Executive Branch and Congress who were reluctant to supply arms to other countries—sometimes for narrow reasons of national interest, and sometimes in pursuit of broader and more lofty goals, such as the reduction of arms transfers through a ceiling limitation during the Carter administration.

Yet, again, this picture has a darker side, at least for the reformer whose main objective is to reduce the volume of arms transfers, expenditures, and inventories. Supporters as well as critics of arms transfers have long been at least generally aware that modern arms are burdensome, that they can be used for purposes the U.S. government as supplier and American public opinion would condemn, and that the resort to their use often produces human and material costs out of all proportion to the original purpose for employing them.

This volume is not a defense of the present or past security assistance programs of the United States. Nor does it attempt to make a case for arms transfers. Indeed, in the past the authors have published criticisms of many aspects of American arms transfer activities.[2] This book, simply put, is an effort to clarify and specify the issues, processes, and trends concerning this major instrument of U.S. foreign policy. We seek more accurate descriptions and explanations as aids to sounder diagnosis and prescription.

This chapter identifies a number of common misperceptions and methodological errors made by observers of arms transfers. It also discusses the basic research questions that guided the construction of this volume. Before these items are identified, however, it is important to place arms transfers within the broader perspective of U.S. foreign policy since World War II, because of continued concern about the proper relationship of security assistance to the broader national interest over the past forty years.

The modern era of American arms transfers began with the so-called Lend-Lease arrangements in 1940 for supplying arms to Great Britain and the Soviet Union. For more than two decades, until the early 1960s, arms transfers usually took the form of grant aid—conditional gifts— rather than credit or cash sales. During these twenty-odd years, grant military and economic assistance were major instruments of U.S. foreign policy, employing the preeminent economic power of the United States to promote national economic development and national and regional military security.

Perhaps the first significant arms transfer from the U.S. government to another government in this era was the delivery of fifty over-aged destroyers to the British navy in 1940, in exchange for certain British bases in the Atlantic. President Franklin D. Roosevelt and the interventionist wings of both political parties wanted to act but were reluctant to run political or legal risks in order to do so. The U.S. Navy was particularly reluctant to act because it needed the ships, too, and because the legality of transfer turned on the navy's endorsement of a particularly broad interpretation of national security. To comply with the law, the Chief of Naval Operations had to certify that turning these ships over to the British would promote the national security of the United States. For two decades the navy had been starved for ships, and it now suffered from a powerful impulse to hoard. To give up even these old vessels was to put aside old habits of thought and to rest the future of the navy on a long-delayed shipbuilding program that had only begun.

In the Roosevelt Library at Hyde Park one can see the original letter that made the transfer possible, signed by Admiral Harold R. Stark, the navy's chief at the time, and addressed to President Roosevelt. It certified that the destroyers were not essential to the United States in view of the national security value of the bases obtained through the exchange.[3] The letter brought the transfer into compliance with a federal statute barely seventy days old.

More than forty years làter it would be difficult to find anyone who thinks the transfer was a bad idea. The British desperately needed warships to protect their trade routes and to defend against an anticipated German invasion. The United States was not as yet directly involved in the war and would soon be building new ships in record-breaking speed and numbers. Whatever America's military needs were in the late summer of 1940, Britain's were more urgent.

Stark's letter marked the end of a long and painful process of deliberation that had begun in mid-May, more than a month before the legislation in question had gone into effect. Stark at first had opposed the transfer.[4] Indeed, Roosevelt had also doubted that the United States could spare the ships, but that was before the fall of France, which came in June. As late as mid-August the Secretary of the Navy believed that congressional approval would be required to legalize the transfer, which would have superseded the requirement for Stark's certification. Yet Stark did sign it, and in the margin of his letter to Roosevelt he wrote: "This is when a fella needs a friend."

In his final hesitation over the Destroyer Deal, Stark showed a lingering concern about stripping arms from the services at the very time their perceived need for arms was growing. By the end of August 1940, for instance, it was not yet entirely clear what had happened to the French navy. On the other hand, Army Chief George C. Marshall had evidently certified the transfer of small arms to the British with less trepidation. When the same problem occurred again only nine years later, the service chiefs reacted in a like manner. The Mutual Defense Assistance Program, which began in 1949, gave priority to the reconstitution of European military forces over the needs of U.S. forces. The services resisted. The principal voice in behalf of the Europe-first priority was the Secretary of State, George C. Marshall.

In the forty years that have passed since the Destroyer Deal, security assistance—the government's transfer of military equipment and services to other countries—has been a' persistent feature of U.S. foreign relations. The question whether to engage in the transfer of arms that concerned the Roosevelt administration in 1940 has been asked repeatedly since then in many different circumstances. The Mutual Defense Assistance Program, authorized by Congress in 1948, was designed as a grant arms transfer program for the NATO allies of the United States to strengthen their military forces without requiring them to postpone or abandon the milestones for economic recovery established under the Marshall Plan.

Barely two years later the Truman administration plunged into the Korean War. Involvement in an Asian war changed the expectations of the U.S. government about arms transfers, and also changed their use. (Involvement in another Asian war fifteen years later would change them again in a different direction.) Grant aid had started in Europe in 1940 under considerable time pressure and had resumed in Greece and Turkey in 1946 and in Western Europe in 1948 with the same sense of urgency. The opening of the Korean War created a similar sense of urgency, but the problems of national security among developing countries outside Western Europe were of a different order from Western Europe's in the late forties. Military assistance could, in the context of economic recovery, buy time in Europe while a planned process of recovery took place. No such finite goal existed in most developing countries. Despite this difference, the Trumann administration proceeded to extend its arms transfer programs to the developing countries around the periphery of the Soviet bloc (then considered to include the People's Republic of China) from Korea to Turkey. The Eisenhower administration completed the extension of grant military aid to these "forward-area" countries and to others in Latin America, Africa, the Middle East, and indeed Westen Europe (Spain and Portugal).

Grant arms aid predominated during the 1950s and into the 1960s. Few states that wanted American arms had the foreign exchange to buy them even on credit. During the 1960s, grant aid was gradually displaced by sales that were promoted at first to earn foreign exchange in Europe, which would in turn forestall pressure in the United States to withdraw U.S. troops from Europe. As grant aid programs were extended in time and became a regular or established part of U.S. government activities with established mechanisms for their annual appropriation and implementation, they changed further in actual purpose and form. During the Eisenhower administration (1953-1960), a Cold War perspective became imbedded in the routine procedures for implementing arms transfer programs. A perceived worldwide Soviet conventional military threat served to define arms transfer objectives even where the supporters of arms transfers, to say nothing of their critics, considered such a threat to be remote. It is scarcely a surprising conclusion at this time of writing that the Cold War was overused as a reason for arms transfers, but it is important in dealing with the phenomenon of arms transfers to understand how.

Quite simply, the idea of a generalized Soviet conventional military threat became an administrative convenience for implementing military alliance programs, including arms transfer programs. It is true that the forward-area countries were singled out as a matter of priority. They were perceived in Washington to be under the more direct threat of military attack by the Soviet Union or their communist regime neighbors backed up by Soviet military power. But the same rationale for U.S. military grant assistance was also applied to countries with as different geographic and strategic situations as Brazil, Spain, and

Ethiopia. The conventional threat to these countries was stated with manifestly less conviction than with respect to the forward areas, as well it might be. The fact that this rationale was applied at all is a striking indicator of the convenience and utility of Cold War concepts. Wherever the United States extended grant military aid, its justification was to strengthen the common or combined capability of grantor and recipient to defend the region against conventional military attacks by the Soviet Union and its allies. Usually the military planners described the threat of such attacks in the context of a general war. This was the case whether the recipients were countries that bordered the Soviet Union or other states in the Soviet bloc, or countries that were geographically remote from the bloc.

The Joint Strategic Operations Plan (JSOP), a policy-planning instrument used extensively in the 1950s and 1960s, illustrates how, at the working level of U.S. military planning, grant military assistance fit into the standard operating procedures of U.S. defense policy. The JSOP consisted of planning documents designed to relate military requirements to military capabilities. They described the military threat from the Soviet bloc, and then described U.S. force capabilities in terms of how U.S. forces would meet that threat. Annexes to the documents described what each country that was a recipient of U.S. arms would be able to do to supplement U.S. force capabilities and thus help meet the stated conventional war threat.

This perspective for military planning prevailed throughout the 1950s and, in altered form, throughout the 1960s. While it was by no means the only way that arms transfers were viewed by the Eisenhower administration, or by the next three presidential administrations, it was important because it guided the routine implementation of these programs toward missions and force capabilities for aid recipients that mirrored U.S. missions and forces.

During the 1950s, bilateral arms transfer programs were usually initiated at the cabinet level, often in response to requests for help from the potential recipient government. Usually the Secretary of State and sometimes the Secretary of Defense and the Chairman of the Joint Chiefs of Staff played a direct role in instigating arms transfers to a new recipient country. Sometimes the President became directly if briefly involved—for example, in direct communication with the head of state or chief of government in the other country.[5]

Commitments made at the cabinet level then became guidelines for a program that might last five to ten years. These programs were too numerous to command much attention from the President or his cabinet officers. They acquired a momentum of their own, guided in the abscence of steady cabinet-level attention by such middle or upper-middle management devices as the JSOP.

In effect, the JSOP assumed that allied states and client states were appropriately viewed from the standpoint of U.S. military planning as supplements to U.S. forces that would (or might) contribute to the achievement of U.S. force-planning objectives. The identification of U.S. interests with its allies, when expressed in terms of mutual defense alliances and grant military and economic aid, was an American claim of shared interests with arms transfer recipients that offered and delivered far more than America asked or required. It was manifestly ideological, first, in its claim to free-world (non-communist) leadership and, second, in casting all aid recipients into the same role, namely, to deter war by preparing to fight a general conventional war with the Soviet bloc. It was imperious, though inadvertently so, because military plans that served as guidelines for arms transfer programs treated the national security policies of recipient states as appendages to U.S forces and missions and because these plans guided the day-to-day implementation of bilateral arms transfer programs. These administrative mechanisms provided no formal—that is, explicit—recognition that military grant recipient states might have national security interests separate and distinct from U.S. interests. This military planning perspective survived until the beginning of the seventies, when the Nixon doctrine replaced it with the premise that regional allies had their own regional interests that would be distinct from yet could be compatible with U.S. interests in the same region.

The Truman and Eisenhower administrations usually stated alliance policies in terms of a general common interest or parallel interest—"mutual security", for instance. The practice in joint operational planning to assume a comprehensive parallel interest or an identical interest with the grant aid partner was consistent with this concept of mutuality or commonality. The claim of identical common interest became strained when its application shifted from the North Atlantic region to the new developing states. The north Atlantic states had many political and economic values in common with the United States. They are states that, in Dean Acheson's justification of economic and political aid to Western Europe, were missing only one component in order to be viable, a component that the United States could supply in the form of economic assistance. Military assistance in these terms was a temporary arrangement that enabled the economic recovery program to remain on track.

The situation in the new and developing states of Asia, the Middle East, Africa, and Latin America was quite different. Usually these states had fewer values in common with the United States, and they were usually further away from political stability and political and economic viability than were the North Atlantic states. In Acheson's

Euro-centered conception, they lacked several components vital to political and economic stability, and many, if not all of these components, could not be supplied by the United States.

Acheson's concept of the missing component was submerged in a tide of concern about security in the developing world triggered by the Korean War and pursued by his successor as Secretary of State, John Foster Dulles. Dulles set about to build an alliance system that would contain Soviet military power in a quite literal sense. Under his leadership, the Eisenhower administration established or expanded military assistance programs with over twenty less developed states outside of Europe.

Economic and military assistance often bolsters the political and economic status quo in the short run. In the domestic politics of the Western European countries that participated in the Marshall Plan, it was not without political effects. Yet dissent on the grounds of partisan advantage, as well as over the details of national fiscal and economic policy, was muted by the economic success of the Marshall Plan. When the United States turned to aiding the developing countries outside Europe in the early fifties, the precedent had already been established that the United States could provide economic and military aid assistance without addressing internal political conditions. The United States, by intervening to defend Korea in 1950 (and later Vietnam), became involved in assuring the survival of the existing government in a very direct way. The South Korean government was a narrow authoritarian regime ruled by an aging nationalist, Syngman Rhee. Washington did not subject the Rhee regime to strong reformist pressures, although it quietly went about protecting Rhee's Vice President when it became obvious that the old man did not want him waiting in the wings.

The questions of what kinds of governments we are aiding and what our aid is enabling them to do, however, could not remain ignored when a recipient of arms transfers was conspicuously authoritarian—as was the case with the martial law regime in Pakistan in the late fifties—or when U.S. aid could be seen to enable a colonial power, such as France, to hang on in Vietnam or Algeria while its own government drifted toward a military coup. John F. Kennedy siezed upon these issues during the late 1950s as he sought to demonstrate his stature. As a result, he staked out a position favoring more support for groups interested in change and less identified with the status quo in the new and developing states. The effects of the Kennedy administration's efforts to modify military and economic aid policy in pursuit of this goal are instructive.

In 1961, when the Kennedy administration came to office, it was aware of an intent to deal with many of the issues and charges about military assistance that had dominated this policy sector in the previous decade. These issues included concerns (1) that military assistance tends to push recipient governments rightward in the political spectrum; (2) that U.S. foreign policy had relied too heavily on military instruments; and (3) that military assistance was a waste of resources for both supplier and recipient. But efforts to correct these perceived faults in arms transfers were diverted by a sustained concern for security goals and high expectations about nation-building, two factors that were less prominent in the succeeding decade.

The Kennedy administration denied that security assistance should support forces preparing to defend South America against a conventional military threat from the Soviet Union. Instead, reflecting a mood of self-confidence about nation-building as a foreign policy goal, it directed that the main goal of security assistance in Latin America and other non-forward areas be to strengthen the capacity for counterinsurgency. The intention was to apply this criterion broadly and in such a way as to encourage more political participation and the utilization of the armed services in political and economic development, but that required a delicate handling of incentives and a fine steering of programs that was often well beyond the capacities of existing U.S. military or economic assistance mechanisms. In fact, the shift to counterinsurgency as the main aim of military assistance to less developed countries (LDCs) usually enabled and sometimes encouraged recipient regimes to resist change. Viewed from the vantage point of this complication, the earlier policy of holding recipient regime's military plans on a somewhat artificial course toward conventional external war now appears to have had the merit of limiting U.S. involvement in internal politics by enabling the U.S. government to avoid dealing with political questions made to look like internal security questions.

In short, the administrative mechanisms through which arms transfer programs were run on a year-to-year basis had advantages as well as drawbacks. The standard military planning procedures that forced arms transfer request justifications onto a procrustian bed of U.S. military mission requirements also had at least two advantages. First, it provided U.S. Defense Department officials who administered these programs with a familiar measure of military utility. Using an American measuring stick to assess the utility of Pakistan's or Taiwan's military forces was hardly the best way to evaluate the grant arms transfer requests of those countries, but it was better than nothing. Second, the more conspicuous weakness of this measuring stick for aid recipient countries was that it dealt with security issues on a global scale consistent with the power position of the United States. It thus gave short shrift to regional security issues and neglected internal security issues, but this approach also enabled the United States to avoid embarrassing involvement in regional and internal political issues.

The Johnson administration did not make a fresh start in foreign relations, but in dealing with military and economic aid it quickly altered the course of the Kennedy administration's program in Latin America, the Alliance for Progress. Political and economic assistance and diplomacy—in fact, all the tools of foreign policy—had been enlisted in a combined effort to achieve democratic political and economic development. At least that was the goal of the Kennedy administration. The Johnson administration became convinced that it was not working. Initially resolved to limit his commitments to foreign relations, President Johnson lowered the expectations about structural political and economic change in Latin America that had been associated with the Alliance for Progress. Once again, the question that had arisen at the beginning of the postwar period concerning the utility of arms and economic aid to Europe was, with regard to Latin America, answered by lowering expectations.

Vietnam became a sharp contrast to this Latin American experience for the Johnson administration. Johnson inherited in Vietnam a recipient regime in political chaos. A military coup had occurred in what became the last months of the Kennedy administration, and political instability coutinued while the United States built up its military and economic commitment to the Republic of Vietnam (South Vietnam). The failure to defeat the insurgent and invading forces in South Vietnam or to strengthen the regime in South Vietnam sufficiently to ensure its survival became the most conspicuous test for American political leaders concerning the validity of arms and economic aid as instruments of U.S. foreign policy. This led to an extensive and searching review throughout nearly all sectors of attentive American political life concerning the utility of foreign assistance, and particularly military assistance.

The Nixon administration, facing these serious questions about military and economic aid, adopted a policy somewhat like Johnson's abandonment of the ambitious reformist goals of the Alliance for Progress. The Nixon Doctrine shifted the attention of U.S. policy away from internal conditions to national independence and regional stability. U.S. assistance would be aimed at assisting recipient states to stand on their own, without U.S. grant aid, and to be able to cope with regional security issues without the continuing involvement of the United States in their region. The Nixon Doctrine was in effect a repudiation of the commonality and mutuality principles as they had come to be applied throughout the previous twenty years and that had been imbedded in standard planning and operational procedures for screening and implementing arms transfer agreements in the Defense Department. It could also be described as a return to the first conceptions of security assistance, as a temporary measure that would end when the recipient

became self-reliant. It answered the question "How entangling sho
America's involvement with other governments be?" with a Delp
answer: "As little as possible!"

Opposition to arms transfers as an encouragement of militarism and
war, never absent among critics of U.S. foreign policy, began to appear
in the form of congressional ceilings on the dollar value of grant aid to
Latin America as early as the mid-1960s, but was enhanced by the
experience of the U.S. involvement in Vietnam. We have traced and
described congressional opposition to arms transfers elsewhere.[6] Our
purpose here is to note that opposition became articulated around the
classic themes of liberal internationalism, i.e., to antidemocratic governments, promotion of peace and of peaceful change to democracy. This
image of America's role in world affairs, always present in the 1950s and
1960s,[7] was increasingly articulated in the post-Vietnam angst. Containment advocates appeared reluctant to challenge this image because they
themselves had increasingly become uncertain concerning both the
effectiveness of security assistance, and the means by which this
effectiveness was measured.

The difficulty with measuring the effectiveness of security assistance
evident in the 1950s and 1960s became more acute in the 1970s. This is
revealed by the emergence of three major policy questions related to the
use of arms transfers. The first policy question was the most generally
significant: how to move the recipient regime toward the long-run
solution of its security, economic, and political problems when U.S. aid
almost invariably reduced in the short run the pressure to achieve long-
run solutions.

The second question had to do with the mutuality of the interests and
goals of the United States as supplier and those of the recipient. From
the standpoint of U.S. policy, how much must the objectives of the
recipient coincide with those of the supplier to justify supplying arms?

The third question concerns the capacity of the United States to set
goals and effectively pursue them in the arms transfer relationship.
Given the plurality and openness of the U.S. political process, how can
arms transfers be used to promote the national interest without being
unduly effected by direct pressures from special interests both at home
and abroad?

These policy questions have, for the last several years, represented the
major focus of most of the literature on arms transfers as well as the
many policy prescriptions relating to the control of arms transfers. Yet
these questions have often been discussed with less illumination than
may be possible because of certain standard misconceptions about arms
transfer activities. Regrettably, standard misconceptions about arms

transfer activities often possess a kernel of truth and a core of incorrect, naive, or simplistic assumptions, creating in the aggregate a generally distorted picture of U.S. arms transfers.

For example, examination of foreign military sales has led many critics of U.S. arms transfer policies to conclude mistakenly that arms transfers have grown at an alarming rate, especially since the Nixon Doctrine was promulgated in 1969. In a recent book for the Council on Foreign Relations, Andrew Pierre, for example, concluded that "U.S. foreign military sales had increased fourteenfold in the previous five years to over $15 billion in new sales per year by 1975 and appeared to be heading upward."[8] Using current-dollar figures that he obtained from official government documents, Pierre displayed U.S. arms sales from 1970 to 1980 as having sharply increased on a steady incline from $1.8 billion in 1970 to $17 billion by 1980?[9] Citing statistics reportedly provided by the Defense Security Assistance Agency, the *Defense Monitor* reported that arms sales to foreign countries would total over $25 billion in fiscal year 1981 and that exports "in Fiscal Year 1982 may exceed $30 billion, surpassing by a substantial margin those of any previous year in U.S. history."[10]

This book challenges these assertions. Too often analyses of arms transfers focus only on sales agreements, which indeed have grown, but which constitute only a portion of U.S. arms transfer activities. Indeed, when all arms transfer programs of the United States over a 30-year period are reviewed, there is a remarkable stability in the level of U.S. export delivery patterns. (This is demonstrated in Chapter 5.) Furthermore, it should be noted that yearly comparisons of growth rates cannot be conducted with current dollars. The motion picture industry, in comparing current with past per-picture costs of production and promotion, and with gross and net revenues, deals in non-constant-dollar values as a promotional expedient. New pictures can be said to have broken all box office records, or have cost a record-breaking sum to produce. We should expect better handling of facts about arms transfers. This book uses constant dollars!

Another misconception about arms transfers is that they will continue to expand because the demand for arms worldwide is growing. Pierre, in particular, does not believe the "arms boom" of the 1970s is over,[11] yet he fails to consider the constraints on supplier production or effective demand. The capability of suppliers to deliver at the rates demanded is likely in the future to diminish, as are the abilities of recipients in the developing world to finance and absorb ever-increasing amounts of modern weaponry. Currently, the United States alone has a "pipeline"—promised but undelivered weapons—worth more than $50 billion, which is expected to continue to grow. Throughout this volume we present evidence of a real structural limitation on the U.S. ability to deliver arms at rates significantly greater than current delivery schedules.

A third major misconception is that there are few or no controls on arms exports from the United States. Leslie Gelb, who later became an important architect of the Carter administration arms transfer restraint policy, charged in the winter of 1976 that the Ford and Nixon administrations had a "policy of selling virtually anything to virtually anybody."[12] This view was prominent in the widely read *Controlling Future Arms Trade*, which was written for the Council on Foreign Relations, 1980s Project.[13] The Carter administration initiated its policy of arms transfer restraint because the President and several of his key advisors—Secretary of State Cyrus Vance and Arms Control and Disarmament Agency Director Paul Warnke—believed that the U.S. arms transfer program had "run amok." While partially correct as a description of Executive Branch decisionmaking during Henry Kissinger's tenure as Secretary of State, it fails to acknowledge the existence of strong controls initiated through congressional action and mandated by law as well as a number of coordination and control experiments attempted by several administrations.

Andrew Pierre argues that the Reagan administration, seeking a more flexible security assistance instrument, abandoned all U.S. restraint and "ran the risk of becoming overly permissive".[14] The charge that the Reagan administration, in reversing Carter's restraint policy, has abandoned careful policy review and policy coordination of arms transfers is simply not true.

A fifth prevalent misconception about arms sales is that they are not critical to the economies of Western suppliers. This misconception has resulted in naive proposals for limiting arms exports from industrial suppliers to Third World recipients. A failure to comprehend the national political and economic importance of arms sales for America's European allies was a major reason for the collapse of the Carter administration's multilateral effort to restrain arms transfers. Despite this evidence, the notion persists that arms transfers are not critical to the economies of Western suppliers. For example, the Pierre book concludes that the domestic economic benefits of arms sales to suppliers are minimal. According to Pierre, military exports are not critical because they amounted to only 0.9 percent of total exports of France, 0.8 percent of total exports of Great Britain, and only 4.5 percent of the total exports of the United States.[15] Furthermore, continues Pierre, national employment is not seriously affected by military exports because "foreign military sales provided 277,000 jobs in 1975. Since total employment in the United States comes to 80 million arms exports accounted for only 0.3 percent of national employment".[16] This evidence not withstanding, an examination of the role of arms transfers for critical high-technology industries suggests quite different conclusions about the economic impact of arms transfers.

Related to simplistic economic analyses is the proliferation of naive proposals for limiting arms transfers from the industrial nations to the developing nations through a multilateral agreement of suppliers. Among the proposals that Pierre finds particularly attractive is a "market sharing approach" among Western suppliers to limit or control sales to the Third World.[17] Accordingly, the major suppliers would be assigned specific regions of predominance. Thus France could be assigned Africa, the United States could be assigned Latin America, and so on. This proposal completely ignores the importance of supply relationships to the maintenance of bilateral relations and common, shared defense goals that arms transfers support. Another dimension ignored by this proposal is that many Third World recipients have become particularly keen about avoiding dependence on suppliers especially through "sole supply relationships," the very phenomenon that would result from "market sharing" agreements among industrial suppliers. Finally, the Soviet Union has few incentives to participate in or condone a supplier-organized restraint regime, as the experience of the Carter administration proves.

Too often analyses of arms transfer policies of the United States or other suppliers fail to assess the interrelationship between NATO goals of rationalization, standardization, and interoperability (RSI) and total arms sales policies. This omission results in an inadequate understanding of the role of inter-allied sales in the total arms transfer policy of the United States. The arms sales decision process, the goals of U.S. arms sales, and the dilemmas involved in arms transfers are greatly affected by NATO's RSI objectives and the efforts of European members to meet those objectives. This volume addresses many of the problems that are created for the United States by European sales efforts and the objectives of RSI.

The major questions this volume addresses are summarized in the questions below. Chapter 2 focuses on questions related to the basic determinants of arms transfers. Why do nations sell arms? Why is there such a large demand for arms? How large and how extensive is the demand? What are the domestic and international pressures on suppliers to sell arms? What are their major pressures to limit the transfer of arms?

Chapter 3 addresses questions related to the rise of foreign military sales as a major instrument of U.S. foreign policy. Why did foreign military sales become a major foreign policy instrument of the United States? How did economic factors affect the increased use of this instrument? Were anti-foreign aid attitudes in Congress a factor in the increased use of arms sales? How did European rearmament questions influence U.S. arms sales practices? How did the Nixon Doctrine affect the rise of arms transfers?

Chapter 4 focuses on the United States' decisionmaking process for arms transfers and on internal control. How are arms sales decisions made? What are the functions of the decision process? Who has responsibility for these functions? How are these policymakers and their responsibilities integrated? What coordination devices exist? How well do they work? How integrated are arms sales decisions with general foreign policy goals? What are the instruments for control? How influential is Congress in limiting arms sales? What problems currently exist in management and control process? What problems can be anticipated? What solutions are available for dealing with coordination and control problems?

Chapter 5 addresses the directions and magnitude of U.S arms transfers over the decades of the 1950s, 1960s, and 1970s. What are the various arms transfer programs? Who have been the recipients of these programs? Have there been major changes in the direction of these programs since 1950? When military deliveries are isolated from security assistance agreements, what conceptual judgments may be made about how the phenomenon of arms transfer is measured?

Chapter 6 examines questions related to the Carter administration's effort at unilateral and multilateral arms transfer restraint. Why did the Carter administration attempt an arms transfer restraint policy? What were the features of the restraint policy? How were these features convergent with other foreign policy goals? How did the major suppliers react to the Policy? How did recipients react? Why did the unilateral restraint effort fail? Why did the multilateral restraint policy fail? How did the Reagan administration perceive the Carter effort? What changes did the Reagan administration make to the Carter policy? How interested is the Reagan administration in restraint? What factors in the international system restrict the expansion of arms sales regardless of the intent of suppliers and recipients?

Chapter 7 addresses the major problems confronted by the United States in dealing with European allies about NATO defense policies. What are European defense policies? How do they affect arms transfer policy? What is the extent of transatlantic arms transfer cooperation? What is the extent of such competition? How have NATO rationalization, standardization, and interoperability (RSI) goals influenced arms transfer policies of the allies? What are the patterns of arms procurement among major European states? How have these procurement practices affected sales policies? What are the prospects for allied cooperation in supplying arms to other nations?

NOTES

1 Anne Hessing Cahn et al., *Controlling Future Arms Trade* (New York: McGraw-Hill, 1977), p. 31.
2 Paul Y. Hammond, David J. Louscher, and Michael D. Salomon, "Controlling U.S. Arms Transfers: The Emerging System," *Orbis* 23,2 (Summer 1979); Paul Y. Hammond, David J. Louscher, and Michael D. Salomon, "Growing Dilemmas for the Management of Arms Sales," *Armed Forces and Society* 6,1 (Fall 1979); David J. Louscher, "Constancy and Change in American Arms Sales Policies," *Selected Papers of the Mershon Center* (Columbus: Ohio State University Press, 1978); David J. Louscher, "The Rise of Military Sales as a U.S. Foreign Assistance Instrument," *Orbis* 20,4 (Winter 1977), pp. 933-964; David J. Louscher and Michael D. Salomon, "New Directions and New Problems for Arms Transfers Policy," *Naval War College Review* 35,1 (January/February 1982); David J. Louscher and Michael D. Salomon, "Conflicting Trends for Arms Transfer Restraint," *Naval War College Review* 33,6 (November/December 1980), pp. 82-88; Michael D. Salomon, David J. Louscher, and Paul Y. Hammond, "Lessons of the Carter Approach to Restraining Arms Transfers," *Survival* 23,5 (September/October 1981); Michael D. Salomon and David J. Louscher, "Conventional Arms Sales in the Carter Administration: Dilemmas of Restraint," *Arms Control Today* 10,8 (September 1980).
3 Stark to Roosevelt, September 3, 1940, *Roosevelt Papers*, Secretary's File, Box 59, Franklin D. Roosevelt Library, Hyde Park, N.Y.
4 See also William L. Langer and S. Everett Gleason, *The Challenge to Isolation, 1837-1940* (New York: Harper & Brothers for the Council of Foreign Relations), pp. 742-776.
5 A detailed examination of the interactive process between the U.S. government and the government of Pakistan that initiated grant arms transfers to Pakistan in the mid-1950s can be found in Paul Y. Hammond's "Military Aid and Influence in Pakistan: 1954-1963," (Santa Monica, Calif.: The Rand Corporation, RD-5505/1-ISA, June 1971).
6 See Chapters 2, 3, and 4.
7 Charles O. Lerche, *The Uncertain South* (New York: Quadrangle, 1964), pp. 58-94.
8 Andrew J. Pierre, *The Global Politics of Arms Sales* (Princeton, N.J.: Princeton University Press, 1982), p. 46.
9 Ibid., p. 47.
10 "U.S. Weapons Exports Headed for Record Level." *The Defense Monitor* 11,3 (1982).
11 Pierre; *Global Politics of Arms Sales*, p. 276.
12 Leslie H. Gelb, "Arms Sales," *Foreign Policy* 25 (Winter 1976-1977), p. 3.
13 Cahn et al., *Controlling Future Arms Trade*, p. 41.
14 Pierre, *Global Politics of Arms Sales*, pp. 62-68.
15 Ibid., p. 26.
16 Ibid.
17 Ibid., p. 298.

Chapter 2

The Demand for Arms, the Pressure to Supply, and the Urge to Control

In 1933 the great military analyst B. H. Liddell Hart ended a series of lectures with the following words of advice:

We live in a time when war is on everyone's lips; when everything contemporary is dated in relation to the last war; when those, who dislike the subject most, talk about it most—if their talk be only about the prevention of war.

That volume of talk is proof of their subconscious realization of the part that war has played in . . . their lives, and in the life of modern Europe. Subconscious, because they give astonishingly little recognition, in a practical sense, to the importance of the subject. They talk much about war, but rarely do they talk of it—as a subject so serious as to be worth the serious study of every thinking man and woman.[1]

However, governments talk seriously of war. Worldwide, governments prepare for war. They do so either to promote national objectives or to protect their national security. With minor exceptions, all states in the international system maintain modern armed forces. Those forces vary in size, strength, and the degree to which they use—and therefore demand—advanced weaponry; but all of them (again, with only insignificant exceptions) use modern equipment to promote or secure their objectives.

Arms transfers since World War II reflect a serious concern among governments relating to means of promoting national objectives. The phenomenal expansion of arms transfers worldwide, in part reflects a disparity in industrial capabilities. Some nations have major capabilities for producing instruments of violence; others have limited capabilities. Nearly all, however, have a determined commitment to the utility of the devices of war. A brief review of that commitment is imperative for understanding American arms transfer and security assistance activities.

THE DEMAND FOR ARMS

Figure 2.1, in part, reveals the level of governmental commitment to armaments throughout the world.[2] The figure shows a gradual increase in world military expenditures since 1969 measured in constant dollars, that is, dollars discounted for the effects of inflation. By 1978 developed country[3] expenditures had reached $345 billion in constant 1977 dollars. By 1978 developing countries were spending about $102

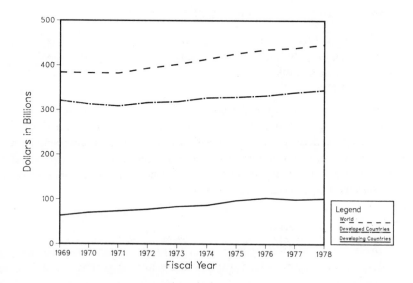

Figure 2.1. World military expenditures, 1969-1978.

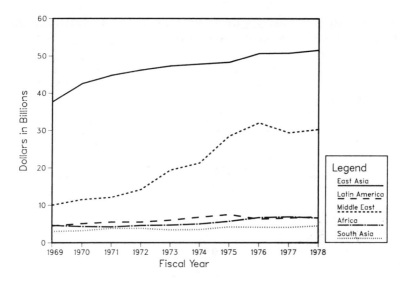

Figure 2.2. Developing country military expenditures by region.

billion annually. For the developed countries this represented an increase of 8 percent in constant dollars. For the developing nations during the period, however, expenditures grew by 62 percent.

Figure 2.2 displays military expenditures by regions. Again, there was a gradual but substantial increase in military expenditures for most regions, measured in constant dollars. In South Asia such expenditures increased from $3.0 billion to $4.5 billion, a growth of 50 percent in the ten-year period from 1969 through 1978. Defense expenditures increased from $4.6 billion to $6.6 billion in Africa, an expansion of 43 percent. In Latin America for this period, military costs increased from $4.5 billion to $6.9 billion. This constituted an expansion of 53 percent for the ten-year period.

Figure 2.2 reveals that Middle East and East Asia expenditures are much greater and that the increases for the period have also been greater. East Asian expenditures have increased from $37.7 billion to $51.6 billion, a growth of 37 percent. The largest increases in military expenditures throughout the world have occurred in the Middle East. In 1969 such expenditures were just $10 billion, but by 1978 they had more than tripled, to $30.3 billion.

The vast commitment to armaments throughout the world is further revealed in Table 2.1. This table displays military expenditure as a percentage of gross national product and as a percentage of central government expenditure. For example, in 1978 developed countries, on

Table 2.1. Military Expenditure as Percentage of Gross National Product and Central Government Expenditure, 1978

Area	Military Expenditure as Percent of GNP	Military Expenditure as Percent of Central Government Expenditure
World Totals	5.4%	22.4%
Developed	5.3	22.5
Developing	5.5	22.1
Africa	3.1	10.2
East Asia	3.9	22.5
NATO Europe	3.6	13.6
Warsaw Pact Europe	10.8	39.3
Other Europe	2.4	11.0
Latin America	1.6	10.9
Middle East	13.4	24.3
North America	4.8	22.6
Oceania	2.5	8.4
South Asia	3.3	15.0
NATO, All	4.3	18.1
Warsaw Pact, All	10.8	39.3

Source: United States Arms Control and Disarmament Agency, World Military Expenditures and Arms Transfers, 1969-1978, December 1980.

the average, expended 5.3 percent of their gross national product on military items. The developing countries each, on the average, spent 5.5 percent of their gross national product on military costs. However, there are wide variations among nations and regions concerning the relative military expense burden each nation is willing or capable of sustaining. Latin American nations, for example, generally spend only 1.6 percent of their GNP on military hardware and personnel. Regions such as Africa, East Asia, NATO Europe, other European countries, Oceania, and South Asia have military expenditures that constitute no more that 4 percent of their gross national product. The Warsaw Pact has sizable defense expenditures consituting 10.8 percent of those nations' GNPs. However, the countries most willing and/or capable of placing major burdens on their economy are in the Middle East. The region as a whole spends 13.4 percent of the GNP on the military. Some countries, such as Israel, spend 24.3 percent of their GNP on armaments and military personnel.

A significant indicator of government commitment to instruments of violence is military expenditure as a percentage of central government budgets. Worldwide, governments spend 22.4 percent of their total budget on military items. Africa and Latin American nations are among the lowest spenders. Warsaw Pact nations spend the highest percentage of their budget on armaments. East Asian, Middle Eastern, and North American nations devote about 22 to 24 percent of their budgets to such costs.

The figures in Table 2.1 reveal quite clearly that, for whatever purposes, a broad international demand for armaments exists. The frequency of civil wars, border wars, and actual interventions, suggests why there is such a worldwide demand for arms. In the last two decades there have been scores of border conflicts, and on many occasions bordering states and/or superpowers, or allies of various regimes, have found it necessary to support one faction or another in a civil conflict. Finally, numerous countries have experienced outright invasions, and the numerous additional threats and crises that did not escalate to violence have also given rise to major decisions to purchase armaments.

Governments procure armaments for essentially three purposes: to enhance national security, to promote regime stability, and to expand economic growth. For example, armaments are seen as a means of promoting national objectives relative to other nations. They may protect trade routes, resources, and populations. They may be used to acquire resources. They may be used to solve border conflicts favorably or to prevent conflicts from occurring in the first place.

All states refer to military expenditures as defensive in purpose. To nearly all, preparation for war is preparation for peace. Ideally, each state wishes to have enough arms to prevent all enemies from challenging it. Prior to World War I, Sir John Fisher, the head of the British navy, expressed this idea for countless government leaders:

> My sole objective is PEACE in doing all this! Because if you rub it in both at home and abroad that you are ready for instant war with every unit of your strength in the first line and intend to be "first in" and hit your enemy in the belly and kick him when he's down and boil your prisoners in oil (if you take any!) and torture his women and children then people will keep clear of you.[4]

The consequences of universal acceptance of theories of peace similar to Sir John's is extensive defense preparation and major arms development and procurement competition. That competition can become quantitative; developing, procuring, and deploying *more* of some weapon system or capability. That competition can be qualitative: developing, procuring, and deploying a *new* and technologically superior weapon system or capability. These two types of competition are widespread and have altered international systems from the inception of armed states.[5]

George Rathjens has argued that a major consequence of adherence to deterrence theory in an era of contant technological breakthroughs is a development called the "action-reaction" syndrome.[6] Competitors attempt to anticipate the technological advances of each other. They prepare for the worst; they overestimate each other's capacity to develop or procure new weapons systems. While the Rathjens thesis concerning increased defense expenditures or "arms races" has been challenged in explaining U.S.–USSR competition in the 1960s and 1970s,[7] it seems highly suggestive for understanding some procurement practices in less developed areas. For example, procurement of the McDonnell F–15 combat aircraft by Saudi Arabia complicates all air defense systems in the Middle East. In its air interceptor role, the F–15 in the hands of a Saudi or other Arab pilot will become a major new form of threat in the region. It has speed, agility, and a sophisticated fire-control system and air-to-air ordnance that makes it capable of destroying in the air all other aircraft presently deployed in the region. For the first time Israel's air superiority, the central factor in its territorial defense, has been challenged. For the Middle East, this truly is a "technological breakthrough" requiring a major reaction from countries who may perceive Saudi Arabia as a threat. Israel's response has been to request additional F–15s to add to its current arsenal of fifteen, and to attempt, unsuccessfully, to lobby in the U.S. Congress to prevent Saudi Arabia from acquiring sophisticated auxiliary equipment such as Sidewinder air-to-air missiles and long-range fuel tanks for the sixty-three F–15 fighters sold to the Saudis in 1978.[8] Israel had been offered forty F–15s during the Carter administration. The Reagan administration offered Israel an additional fifteen fighters.[9] Israeli acceptance would sizably enhance defense expenditures for the region. F–15 fighters and supporting hardware and services cost about $20 million each. If Saudi Arabia takes delivery of all sixty-three ordered and Israel takes delivery of all fifty-five offered, the region will have increased defense expenditures in excess of $2.3 billion for this one weapon system alone.

But nations procure weapons for many reasons other than to acquire superiority or remain equal in an arms competition. Often military systems are procured for the status they confer externally and the prestige that results at home. In explaining the expanded emphasis on nuclear energy research in Brazil, a nuclear energy administrator made this comment in Brazil's official military journal, *A Defesa Nacional*: "The Brazilian people need to be proud of their country for other, more serious reasons than football and carnival. International prestige is, evidently a national objective ... "[10]

Governments procure arms for domestic political and economic reasons as well. Major military forces may promote regime stability. The current regime may find such expenditures necessary to defeat domestic opponents. In nations where there is little consensus concerning the instruments for acquiring political office, military expenditures are essential for coalition building. The current incumbents may find the military to be one of the few sources of support, or potential organized opposition, and are willing to procure new equipment as a means of maintaining this support.[11] Large military expenditures also may be necessary to counter massive public opposition to a regime, as was the case for the Shah of Iran.[12] In many instances the military assumes control of a government and appropriates large sums for its own purposes. Often competition within factions of the military will necessitate even greater defense expenditures as the leaders attempt to maintain a coalition.[13] The military rulers may find large expenditures necessary in order to counter opposition to their rule,[14] and often a regime will seek support from the military for a specific policy by offering a substantial military expansion program. Charles De Gaulle, for example, was able to reduce military opposition to the French withdrawal from Algeria by promoting the concept of a national French nuclear force, the *force de frappe*.[15]

In less structurally differentiated societies, military organizations often represent the most modern and stable institutions. They can become an instrument of political and economic development, generating a sense of nationalism, and they can perform tasks beyond protecting the current regime, such as road building, dam construction, and education.[16]

Civil war has also contributed to the demand for arms. Many analysts have argued that the pervasiveness of civil war since the turn of the century is the result of psychological and social dislocations caused by rapid economic growth, and the inability of governments to satisfy rapidly rising social expectations of the mass populace.[17] Concerns about domestic upheaval in the developing world have predisposed many governmental leaderships there to acquire arms to insure regime stability. Additionally, the incidents of civil strife and regime instability in the developing world may further stimulate a worldwide demand for arms as there are no guarantees that civil wars will be localized within the particular national boundaries where they erupt. As the research of Small and Singer demonstrates, between 1946 and 1977, approximately one-fourth of the civil wars begun during that period were internationalized.[18]

Some regimes may expend large sums on armaments for domestic economic reasons. As extensive review of the economic determinants of weapons procurement or an attempt to establish the validity of economically determined procurement practices is beyond the purview of this chapter, but a brief review is necessary to understand arms transfer trends.

Whether or not the costs of arms outweigh their positive economic contributions, military expenditures do create jobs and do protect industries central to the economic health of many nations.[19] The French arms industry employs nearly 4.5 percent of that nation's industrial sector. In 1977 nearly 280,000 people were employed there, which contributed to an annual product of 35.8 billion francs.[20] Michael Reich, in a study of U.S. industrial dependence on military spending, discovered that certain industrial sectors had high job dependence upon military expenditures. Industrial employment attributable to defense expenditures in 1967 were 26.1 percent for the electronic and electrical components industry; 59.1 percent for the aircraft and parts industry; 23.3 percent for the machine shop products industry; and 11.5 percent for the engines and turbine industry.[21]

James Kurth has argued that industrialized nations often procure weapons according to the "follow-on" imperative and the "bail-out" imperative.[22] According to Kurth, national decisionmakers are quite determined to maintain production lines of critical industries as an important national resource. Weapons systems production requires thousands of personnel with rare skills who must learn to work as a team. Should production lines be stopped, it would take years to reassemble these personnel. According to Kurth, then, a new contract will be awarded to a firm whenever its previous contract is about to expire. He found that there are eight major aerospace "production lines" in the United States, but they do not compete for contracts that are dictated by national strategic needs. Rather, the Department of Defense seems to award contracts so that all eight production lines are actively maintained at all times. The follow-on imperative, said Kurth, "would have predicted and can perhaps explain the production line and the product structure of eleven out of twelve major contracts awarded from 1960 through 1972...."[23] A related aspect is the "bail-out" imperative, whereby "the government comes to the aid of corporations in deep financial trouble" by offering them expensive rescue contracts.[24] Kurth identified twelve major contracts in the period 1960-1972 that seemed to be more motivated by a desire to restore health and reliability to a defense contractor than by any strategic need.[25]

Scholars investigating the increased tendency of underdeveloped countries to create their own defense industry or to negotiate "coproduction" arrangements with industrial suppliers point to perceptions by such governments of the economic benefits of indigenous arms production. The economic incentives for Third World nations may be that arms industries can become a "leading sector" for a state's modernization process by providing critical skills for an industrial base from which nonmilitary production may eventually emerge.[26]

Another explanation for extensive defense expenditures and new weapons acquisition has been referred to by David Ziegler as the "ripening plum" argument: "Just as we pick ripe fruit whether we are hungry or not, so states order new technologies whether they need them or not."[27] He argued that the development of the Poseiden submarine missile was a salient case:

Although intended to overcome a possible Soviet ABM system with its greater range it also had greater accuracy, which would threaten to destroy Soviet missiles in their silos and thus make it possible for the United States to consider striking first in a nuclear war. This greater accuracy was not needed to fulfill the basic mission of Poseidon, which was simply to deter a Soviet strike, but, as one expert testified, "The technology is available—why not use it?"[28]

The "ripe plum" phenomenon was perceived by the Carter administration in 1977 to be a serious problem in the Third World. The President and many members of his administration were convinced that in the past U.S. military assistance field personnel and U.S. defense industry representatives in the country or dispatched from the U.S. on sales expeditions were too eager to demonstrate the value and availability of new weapons systems to military leaders in the Third World. Once their appetites were "whetted," they became eager buyers. The Carter administration thus adopted a number of policies and procedures designed to limit these practices.[29]

These pressures have created an enormous demand for arms throughout the world. However, only a few states have the capital and skills to produce the increasingly sophisticated weapons systems demanded. Those states are for the most part the twenty-eight developed countries. For many of these producers, the pressures to supply are as great as the demands for arms. Increasingly, however, some developing countries have begun to produce weapons of one kind or another to avoid dependence upon sole-suppliers, to create industrialized infrastructures, and to balance international payments problems. As many as thirty developing countries have initiated indigenous defense production capabilities,[30] although the level to which these production capabilities are self-sufficient varies widely. This variation includes:

1. Maintenance and overhaul capability.
2. Domestic assembly under license of unassembled kits from major suppliers.
3. Coproduction, in which basic components are produced indigenously while major items such as engines and electronics are imported.
4. Modification of coproduced or unassembled weapons with larger proportions of domestically produced components incorporated.
5. Production of indigenously designed systems with minimum dependence on foreign components.
6. Domestically designed and domestically manufactured weapons systems utilizing all domestic components.

Few developing states have indigenously designed and produced weapons systems of any sophistication. According to A. L. Ross, no developing nation has indigenously produced armored vehicles, military aircraft, or naval vessels. Israel has designed and produced missiles and small arms and ammunition. Brazil and India have autonomously designed and produced small arms and ammunition.[31] Countries such as Argentina, Brazil, the Republic of China, Colombia, Egypt, India, Indonesia, Iran, Israel, North Korea, South Korea, Libya, Mexico, Pakistan, Peru, the Philippines, and Venezuela do produce military aircraft, but such production is either under license from a major supplier or utilizes design and critical components such as engines from major suppliers.[32] Five developing countries are capable of producing aircraft engines: India, Israel, South Africa, Brazil, and Argentina.[33] By 1977, only three developing countries—Argentina, Brazil, and Israel—were producing missiles that were indigenously designed and had a minimum of foreign parts. Developing country dependence on industrial suppliers is most saliently displayed in the area of small arms and ammunition production. In 1977, only three countries—Brazil, Israel, and India—were designing and producing even these weapons systems.[34]

Thus, clearly, the arms export market is dominated by a few industrialized suppliers. In 1978, for example, 33 percent of all arms exported were from the United States, 34 percent from the Soviet Union, 5 percent from the United Kingdom, 7 percent from France, and 4 percent from Germany.[35] In sum, 83 percent of all arms exported in 1978 were produced in these five industrialized states. Other suppliers with more limited shares of the export market included Italy, Poland, the People's Republic of China, and Canada. As countries such as Israel, India, Brazil, Taiwan, Argentina, and Yugoslavia have developed an indigenous production capability, so too have they launched export programs. The weapons produced by these minor suppliers are primarily at the intermediate level of sophistication and, for the most part, have relatively simple maintenance and operational requirements. But there is a high demand for such equipment in Latin America and Africa. Reflecting that demand, Third World exports increased from $49 million in 1969 to $707 million in 1978.[36]

Despite increased competition from minor suppliers in the Third World, the industrialized nations of the West continue to dominate the world armaments market. Sizable proportions of that market include the industrialized nations themselves. Table 2.2 reveals that among the major armaments exporters, about one-fifth of the value of arms exported is to other developed countries. Primarily such exports are to other NATO countries by NATO suppliers and to other Warsaw Pact countries by Warsaw Pact suppliers. Sizable proportions of total world arms exports are, however, from major industrial suppliers to the Third World. For example, according to the U.S. Arms Control and Disarmament Agency (ACDA), from 1974 through 1978 there were $80.7 billion

Table 2.2.   Percentage of Value of Arms Transfers by Major Suppliers to Developed Countries, Cumulative 1974-1978

Country	%
United States	21
Soviet Union	23
France	17
United Kingdom	17
Federal Republic of Germany	18
Czechoslovakia	74
Italy	7
Poland	69
Canada	63

Source: The raw data is published in United States Arms Control and Disarmament Agency, World Military Expenditures and Arms Transfers, 1969-1978 (Washington, D.C.: USGPO, December 1980), pp. 159-166.

in arms exported. Of that total, $19.0 billion, or 24 percent, went to developed countries. The remaining $61.7 billion worth (76 percent) were exported to the Third World.

Using a much less conservative definition of armaments than ACDA uses, a recent report by the Senate Foreign Relations Committee showed even greater amounts of arms being transferred to the Third World. Table 2.3 reveals total sales agreements with Third World recipients from 1974 to 1979. The report suggests that the total value of arms exported to the Third World from 1974 through 1978 is $118.8 billion rather than the $61.7 billion reported by the ACDA.

Table 2.3 also reveals changing market shares among Western suppliers during the 1970s. While United States exports to the Third World have remained constant at about $11 billion, other major suppliers have been expanding their exports to the Third World. French exports have expanded from about $2 billion in 1974 to $4 billion by 1979. United Kingdom exports, too, have more than doubled in this period, increasing from $760 million in 1974 to $2.4 billion by 1979. When European exports are compared as a whole to United States exports to the Third World, the growth of European exports is even more striking. Table 2.4 compares United States and European exports to the Third World from 1976 through 1979, during which period European exports more than tripled.

Table 2.3. Arms Sales to Third World, by Suppler (in Millions of Current U.S. Dollars)

	1974	1975	1976	1977	1978	1979
TOTAL	23,521	22,329	21,394	27,356	24,198	29,978
Non-communist	16,581	17,979	14,254	17,606	20,458	19,258
Of which:						
United States	11,921	11,614*	10,669	9,976	11,268	10,388
France	2,030	2,300	1,025	2,800	2,500	4,000
United Kingdom	760	1,400	630	1,550	1,800	2,420
Germany	725	790	360	1,170	2,220	400
Italy	425	990	220	960	1,360	360
Other free world	720	885	1,350	1,150	1,310	1,690
Communist	6,940	4,350	7,140	9,750	3,740	10,720
Of which: USSR	(5,900)	(3,600)	(5,900)	(9,000)	(2,900)	(9,800)
Dollar Inflation Index (100 = 1974)	100	109	118	127	136	148

Source: United States, Senate, Committee on Foreign Relations, *U.S. Conventional Arms Transfer Policy*, 96th Congress, 2d Session (June 1980), p. 3.

Note: Foreign data are for the calender year given. U.S. data are for the fiscal year given (and covers the period from July 1, 1973, through September 30, 1979). Statistics shown for foreign countries are based on the estimated selling prices. Prices given include sale of weapons, construction, military assistance, and spare parts. The Third World category excludes Warsaw Pact countries, NATO countries, Europe, Japan, Australia, and New Zealand. All data are current as of January 1, 1980, and reflect the termination of all sales contracts other than those with Iran. The value of Iranian contracts, cancelled by fiscal year, are as follows: fiscal year 1974, $359,000,000; fiscal year 1975, $1,133,000,000; fiscal year 1976 and transition quarter, $206,000,000; fiscal year 1977, $2,478,000,000; fiscal year 1978, $1,823,000,000; fiscal year 1979, 0.

* The U.S. figure excludes $2,667,000,000, which represents the transition quarter for fiscal year 1976.

Soviet exports to the Third World are displayed in Tables 2.3 (Senate Foreign Relations Committee estimates) and 2.5 (ACDA estimates). It should be noted that ACDA figures are much lower than other arms transfer statistics because that agency employs a very restricted definition of arms transfers. Only deliveries are estimated; construction, training, and technical services as well as other items that are deemed to have a dual role or possible civilian applications are excluded. Many

Table 2.4. U.S. and European Arms Exports to Developing Nations (in Billions of Dollars)

Years	United States	Europe*
1976	10.7	2.2
1977	9.9	6.5
1978	11.3	7.9
1979	10.4	7.2

Source: Compiled from data provided in United States, Senate, Committee on Foreign Relations, U.S. Conventional Arms Transfer Policy, 96th Congress, 2d Session (June 1980).

*Note: Includes France, United Kingdom, West Germany and Italy.

Table 2.5. Arms Exports of the United States and the Soviet Union, 1969-1978 (Millions of Constant 1977 dollars)

Year	United States	Soviet Union
1969	5,685	1,786
1970	4,788	2,317
1971	4,997	2,355
1972	5,787	4,093
1973	6,542	7,076
1974	5,489	5,001
1975	5,233	4,453
1976	6,242	5,607
1977	6,900	6,500
1978	6,237	6,609

Source: United States Arms Control and Disarmament Agency, World Military Expenditures and Arms Transfers, 1969-1978 (Washington, D.C.: USGPO, December 1980). ACDA data is not isomorphic with the data in Chapter V. The data in Chapter V were drawn from the Defense Security Assistance Agency, and were converted to constant dollars using Department of Defense deflators. The issue of data appropriateness and congruence is addressed in Chapter V.

analyses, including the authors', view this practice as peculiar. An F-15 fighter, for example, is lethal only if it has proper runways, if the pilots have proper training, and if the ground crews have been trained and provided with major technical services. Despite the disparities between the data sets in absolute amounts, the relative figures are about equal for the two major suppliers. United States exports have remained steady over the periods assessed. Soviet exports have varied from year to year, but by 1979 they equaled those of the United States. Table 2.3 shows each supplier to be exporting about $10 billion. Table 2.5 reveals each as exporting about $6 billion.

The competition among industrialized nations to supply arms to the Third World is further revealed by a brief examination of types of weapons delivered there. Table 2.6 lists major weapons delivered to the Third World. The Soviet Union exports mainly tanks, self-propelled guns, and surface-to-air missiles (SAMs). Artillery is a major export item of the United States, the Soviet Union and Western Europe. Prior to 1977 the United States was the major exporter of helicopters; however, since 1977 the Russians and Europeans have rapidly expanded their helicopter exports. The United States has dominated the export market of naval vessels, although European suppliers and the Soviet Union have increased their shares of that market since 1977.

Patterns of arms exports from the industrialized to the developing world are clear, as Table 2.7 reveals. Certain recipients or regions receive most of their equipment from one supplier over another. The table also reveals the patterns of competition among suppliers in various regions. As is shown, the United States has been the primary supplier in East Asia during the 1974-1978 period. Most U.S. arms to the region

Table 2.6. Weapons Delivered to the Third World*

Weapons Category	U.S.A.	USSR	Major West European
1973-77:			
Tanks and self-propelled guns	4,921	7,300	1,610
Artillery	3,546	3,140	510
APCs and armored cars	7,104	5,510	1,685
Major surface combatants	73	5	12
Minor surface combatants	134	50	204
Submarines	18	5	16
Guided missile boats	0	44	13
Supersonic combat aircraft	996	1,670	315
Subsonic combat aircraft	793	325	55
Helicopters	1,202	410	980
Other aircraft	750	200	670
Surface-to-air missiles (SAMs)	4,459	14,870	890
1977-79:			
Tanks and self-propelled guns	2,086	5,265	785
Artillery	795	2,535	465
APCs and armored cars	6,957	5,035	1,740
Major surface combatants	16	2	12
Minor surface combatants	28	85	60
Submarines	1	4	8
Guided missile boats	0	38	17
Supersonic combat aircraft	456	1,280	160
Subsonic combat aircraft	131	255	2
Helicopters	150	530	520
Other aircraft	223	185	275
Surface-to-air missiles (SAMs)	4,476	4,625	55

Source: United States, Senate, Committee on Foreign Relations, U.S. Conventional Arms Transfer Policy, 96th Congress, 2nd Session (June 1980), p. 4.

*The Third World category excludes Warsaw Pact countries, NATO countries, Europe, Japan, Australia, and New Zealand. All data is current as of January, 1, 1980.

have been exported to South Korea, Cambodia, and South Vietnam. Soviet transfers to that area have been to North Vietnam and North Korea. Throughout this period the United Kingdom has been the primary supplier for the People's Republic of China (PRC), exporting over $270 million to that country. The PRC's exports in that area, while the fourth largest, were almost entirely to North Korea.

The Near East has been the largest regional recipient of arms produced by industrial nations. The region also is an area of intense competition among suppliers. From 1974 through 1978, the United States was a large, but not dominant, supplier in the region. Iran, Israel, and Saudi Arabia have been the major recipients of U.S. Arms, whereas Iraq and Syria were the major recipients of Soviet arms. West European exports to the region have been sizable, amounting to over $5 billion. West European nations have provided much competition to the Soviet Union, selling large amounts of equipment to Syria and Iraq, the traditional Soviet clients.

Table 2.7. Value of Arms Transfers to the Third World Regions Cumulative 1974-1978, by Major Supplier (Million Current Dollars)

REGIONS

Major Suppliers	East Asia	Near East	South Asia	Africa	Latin America	All Regions
United States	5,200	13,800	170	480	700	20,350
USSR	975	7,500	2,000	7,400	1,300	19,175
France	80	1,800	280	1,500	430	4,090
United Kingdom	350	2,100	80	160	625	3,315
West Germany	100	950	20	575	360	2,005
Czechoslovakia	5	340	30	230	---	605
Italy	70	575	5	550	190	1,390
Poland	5	30	40	240	---	315
PRC	280	40	240	120	---	680
Canada	20	50	---	50	20	140
Others	490	1,900	200	1,800	500	4,890
TOTAL	7,575	29,085	3,065	13,105	4,125	56,955

Source: Created from data included in United States Arms Control and Disarmament Agency, World Military Expenditures and Arms Transfers, 1969-1978 (Washington, D.C.: USGPO, December 1980), pp. 159-164.

Note: These data are not isomorphic with those in Chapter V. Chapter V uses DSAA data which were derived from different regional compositions of natons, and from different counting rules.

Exports to South Asia have also been dominated by the Soviet Union, with Soviet exports amounting to two-thirds of all transfers there. India, the major buyer in the area, has purchased $1.6 billion from the Soviet Union of its total of $1.9 billion in purchases. The United States ranks below France and the People's Republic of China as a supplier to South Asia.

The Soviets are clearly the dominant supplier of arms to Africa. The major recipients there have been Libya, Ethiopia and Algeria, although the Soviet Union supplied over twenty African nations from 1974 through 1978 with arms and equipment. In contrast to the $7,400 million in exports from the Soviets, the United States has exported only $480 million to nine African countries. Most U.S. transfers were to Morocco and Ethiopia. France appears to be the Soviets' major competition within the region.

The Soviet Union also was the major supplier of arms to Latin America although they had only two clients, Cuba and Peru, which received almost equal dollar amounts between 1974 and 1978. The United Kingdom has established a very strong market in Latin America, equaling U.S. transfers to the region. French, German, and Italian exports to the area constitute a sizable market for these countries as well. U.S. and Soviet clients in Latin America have been, for the most part, mutually exclusive. But U.S. reticence to sell in Latin America, as well as Latin American desires to avoid excessive dependence on the United States, has provided West European suppliers with considerable market opportunities.

THE PRESSURES TO SUPPLY

Just as the demand for arms transfers is great, so too is the pressure to sell. Those pressures vary with suppliers. They can be grouped into two types: (1) domestic economic and (2) international. Among suppliers, the Soviet Union and the United States have more complex motivations for arms sales than other nations, and both countries view arms transfers primarily as instruments of their own broader global and regional security objectives. As James L. Buckley, Under Secretary of State for Security Assistance, Science and Technology, in the Reagan administration, has stated, "This administration believes that arms transfers judiciously applied, can compliment and supplement our own defense efforts and serve as a vital and constructive instrument of American foreign policy."[37]

Since the mid-1960s successive administrations have reiterated the diplomatic and strategic uses of arms transfers in support of U.S. policy objectives.[38] Former Secretary of State Cyrus Vance, in his 30 June 1977 report to Congress, summarized these as follows:

To support diplomatic efforts to resolve major regional conflicts by maintaining local balances and enhancing our access and influence vis-a-vis the parties;

To influence the political orientation of nations which control strategic resources;

To help maintain regional balances among nations important to us in order to avert war or political shifts away from us;

To enhance the quality and commonality of the capabilities of major allies participating with us in joint defense arrangements;

To promote self-sufficiency in deterrence and defense as a stabilizing factor in itself and as a means of reducing the level and automaticity of possible American involvement;

To strengthen the internal security and stability of recipients;

To limit Soviet influence and maintain the balance in conventional arms;

To enhance our general access to and influence with government and military elites whose political orientation counts for us on global or regional issues;

To provide leverage and influence with individual governments on specific issues of immediate concern to us; and

To secure base rights, overseas facilities, and transit rights to support the development and operations of our forces and intelligence systems.

Secretary Vance's report concluded:

> There is little disagreement that, on balance, conventional arms transfers have contributed to U.S. national interests in a number of important ways. U.S. Arms transfers have enabled friends and allies to defend themselves and deter aggression, have cemented good relations and enhanced our influence with recipients, and have denied hostile powers the opportunity to gain positions of influence in a number of developing Third World countries.[39]

Soviet strategic and political motives for arms transfers, it appears, could easily be the same. An additional motive for the Soviet leadership would be to penetrate traditional regions of U.S. influence. This is demonstrated by the kinds of agreements they entered into with Third World nations in the mid-1960s. The USSR offered free training and maintenance services, major financial inducements such as discount prices, and low payments options up to nineteen years, and they sometimes accepted local goods as repayment.[40] Since the mid-1970s these concessions have been eliminated. Robert Harkavy has argued that the Soviet leadership has also used arms transfers as a means of expanding its access rights for naval and air bases,[41] and Avigdor Haselkorn has argued that the Soviet leadership uses arms transfers as a way to warehouse arms within a region for its own contingent use.[42]

The importance of international pressures affecting other suppliers' sales motives is more difficult to discern. The British seem to face a set of negative pressures more related to domestic political embarrassment than concern about strategic questions. As Martin Edmonds has argued in exploring whether or not the United Kingdom had an arms sales policy related to international criteria, "The ultimate criteria, arguably, are expediency and pragmatism: the expediency of not embarrassing the British government and the practicality of being as flexible as possible in order to be able to respond to new challenges."[43]

The British policy is, then, a "disposition to export arms"[44] with few public statements as to their international implications. Yet the record of actual sales suggests a concern for military power balances. After the

1967 and 1973 Arab-Israeli wars, Britain attempted to supply both sides. As a foreign ministry official noted, "In doing so we have tried to maintain a balance which would give some sense of security to each country, but which would not tempt either to launch a war against its neighbor."[45] Nevertheless, many members of Parliament thought that the refusal to sell Israel Chieftain tanks and that successive sales of British equipment to Libya, Saudi Arabia, and Jordan from 1967 to 1973 seemed to challenge the argument that Britain's purpose in selling arms to the region was to maintain a power balance.[46] British officials also argue that the government's arms sales program promotes a basic principle of the charter of the United Nations, namely, "the right of each state to ensure its own sovereignty and defense."[47] Britain traditionally has also enjoyed a special relationship with members of the Commonwealth, with whom it has alliances. These represent military commitments that, increasingly, Britain can support only through arms sales.

France appears to be even less inclined than Great Britain to impose international criteria on its arms sales decisions. Some authors have argued that French arms sales are solely directed by and compelled by domestic economic considerations.[48] Yet Edward Kolodziej has insisted it would be a mistake to argue that French arms sales are entirely for economic motives: "French arms transfer behavior reflects a more basic demand for an independent arms production capability as a means by which to provide some maneuver and leverage in bargaining with other states, particularly the superpowers."[49] Thus arms sales provide France with the international prestige and influence similar to that provided by its nuclear weapons.

Another point particularly important for understanding arms sales motivations of non-superpower nations is that these nations often face critical economy-of-scale problems in their defense industries. They do not have a domestic market or a domestic need for weapons in quantities sufficient to produce them at viable economic costs. Thus the development of weapons for which there is an external market is a necessary condition for several NATO members.

France and Britain in particular, as will be shown in Chapter 7, have economy-of-scale problems. Nearly 60 percent of all defense equipment produced in France is exported; defense equipment produced for export in Great Britain may be as high as 35 percent. Some European defense industries are highly dependent on arms exports. For example, Dassault-Breguett is the manufacturer of the primary fighter aircraft of the French Air Force, the Mirage F-1, and the soon-to-be-deployed Mirage 2000. Yet, of the 162 fighter aircraft produced by Dassault-Breguett in 1977, only 44 were produced for France. The other 118 were exported.[50]

For all suppliers, arms exports hold out the promise of reducing research and development costs, reducing fixed costs, and creating a longer production run. In 1976, the Congressional Budget Office studied the budgetary cost savings from exports of seven modern aircraft (E2C, F-14, F-15, F-16, F5E/F, AWACS, and F-4E). The study concluded that sales of $9.95 billion had accrued budgetary savings to the Department of Defense of $1.3 billion. Nearly $600 million of this savings was based on research and development. It was further concluded that $726 million was saved by exporting $3.32 billion in ground equipment. The export of the M60A1 main battle tank constituted 63 percent of these savings to the Department of Defense.[51] The more sophisticated the equipment, the greater the savings in R & D costs by exporting. The U.S. Air Force reportedly encouraged the $1.2 billion sale of the Airborne Warning and Control System (AWACS) to Iran for the dual purpose of keeping the Boeing production line open and recouping some of the systems R & D costs.[52] Each AWACS unit with ancillary equipment and training costs approximately $400 million. The Reagan Administration's April 1981 proposal to sell five to Saudi Arabia—at a projected cost of $2 billion[53]—will compensate for the loss of the Iranian sale. One trend is clear: as weapon systems become more technologically sophisticated, the pressure to export grows. European producers face similar problems, as Chapter 7 will demonstrate.

All major suppliers experience greater employment levels as a consequence of arms export programs. Yet some analysts have argued that the economic benefits of arms exports have been exaggerated. Andrew Pierre constantly emphasizes this point throughout his most recent book on arms sales. In particular, he repeatedly cites a Bureau of Labor Statistics study which indicates that foreign military sales provided only 277,000 jobs in 1975 from an entire labor force of 80 million.[54] To Pierre this represents only 0.3 percent of national employment. But many other studies suggest the employment benefits of arms exports are much greater. Some officials have calculated that an estimated 400,000 jobs are related to military exports.[55] The Defense Security Assistance Agency (DSAA) calculates that the entire security assistance program creates fifty new jobs and maintains fifty existing jobs for each $1 million of exports.[56] This would suggest a much higher employment impact of about 1 million Americans.

It is somewhat naive to conclude that the economic benefits of arms exports are limited by dividing employment derived from such exports by the entire American work force. Many key electronics, communications, and transportation industries depend upon military exports a great deal. In 1977, for example, the top ten U.S. contractors depended for an average of 12 percent of their total sales on arms exports. One company, Northrop, depended upon arms exports for 25 percent of its total sales.[57] When, in 1977, the Carter administration proposed a ceiling on all arms exports (see Chapter 4), the Electronics Industry Association commissioned a study to determine its impact on industry profits and jobs. The study concluded that by 1977 the communications-electronics industries and the transportation equipment industries exported about $27 billion providing employment to some 600,000 individuals. The study also concluded that reducing military equipment exports as prescribed by the President's ceiling would in the near term result in a loss of some 100,000 jobs in these two critical industries alone.[58] Suppliers who have economy-of-scale problems for their own defense industries are under considerable pressure to have ambitious export programs, since export programs help maintain employment. Our discussion of transatlantic arms transfers in Chapter 7 examines in greater detail the employment and economic benefits for European suppliers. Briefly, it should be noted that 28 percent of all the workers in France's armaments industry are employed in the production of equipment for export. Nearly 67 percent of naval construction workers are employed producing products for exports. In the French aerospace industry 50 percent of all workers are involved in export production.[59]

Arms transfers are also an instrument by which industrialized nations may attempt to balance international trade deficits. For many suppliers, arms exports are a major instrument for offsetting petroleum costs or for avoiding higher petroleum costs. Though arms were sold to Iran and Saudi Arabia for a variety of reasons, the $8 billion plus in arms delivered to Saudi Arabia and the $10 billion in arms delivered to Iran played a major role in deferring increased oil import costs from those countries. Indeed, in September 1976, the Senate Foreign Relations Committee reversed its position of opposition to the sale of 650 Maverick missiles to Saudi Arabia after Secretary of State Henry Kissinger testified before the committee that such action might result in higher oil prices. As a Carter administration Department of Defense official involved in arms sales decisionmaking stated, "Why did we sell to Iran? Because they wanted the weapons and we needed the oil." The nearly $17 billion in foreign military sales and commercial sales abroad of defense equipment represents one of the largest industrial sector contributions to balancing the U.S. international payments deficit, a deficit largely created by $30 to $40 billion of oil import costs per year.

The contribution of arms sales toward creating favorable trade balances for the Soviet Union is also sizable. In 1976, for example, the Soviet Union had a currency trade deficit outside the Soviet bloc of $6.4 billion. The $3 billion in arms deliveries to the Third World did a great deal to reduce that deficit.[60]

The pressure to sell arms to offset oil costs is particularly acute in France. In November 1980, France sold its SA365 Dauphin naval helicopter to Saudi Arabia as part of a $3.5 billion package of naval frigates and missiles. It was the largest contract ever signed by France. In explaining the sale, one observer noted:

> It is hardly coincidental that France's best arms customers are Saudi Arabia, Iraq and other Mid-East producers that supply the bulk of France's petroleum imports. In the early 1970s, the French government made a conscious decision to offset its mounting oil import bill with arms shipments—and France has since pursued its goal with what rival arms salesmen describe a zealous efficiency.[61]

It has been estimated that by 1977 arms deliveries from France balanced one-third of France's oil bill.[62] To offset its growing oil costs, France will be compelled to sell at greater-than-current levels or find some substitute export item. But the French commitment to an autonomous arms industry makes it unlikely that France will find that substitute export product.

THE URGE TO CONTROL

Since World War II, there has been an increased worldwide demand for arms, and the pressures on suppliers to sell have become more severe. At the same time there has existed a continuing, if modest, interest within the international community toward controlling the quantity and the quality of arms transferred. For example, there have been international initiatives toward developing legal norms banning the export of weapons judged inhumane. Individual suppliers have embargoed specific equipment or specific regimes. The United States, for example, imposed an embargo on arms shipments to combatants in the 1965 war over Kashmir and the 1967 Middle East conflict. Both embargoes were an attempt to support efforts to impose a regional settlement on the conflict. There are few instances of multilateral embargoes on arms transfers, although in 1962 the United Nations General Assembly passed a resolution imposing an embargo on South Africa.

Most suppliers have official lists defining arms, combat equipment, or controlled articles and have regulations that control industries who may wish to export such items. These regulations vary from country to country and often vary from year to year. Moreover, the extent of government control varies. All major suppliers require export licenses from industries, but here, too, reporting requirements vary. Some supplier governments require only industrial manufacturing licenses, while others require constant supervision. This can range from prior approval of industry-recipient negotiations for sales to transit verification of sold items, to end-use restrictions on the recipient. It should be noted, however, that only in the United States has the issue of limiting arms transfers, controlling the conditions under which transferred arms are used, or maintaining control of retransfer of "end use" been a significant political issue. As Chapter 7 will demonstrate, the pressures to sell arms by Western European countries are very strong while the political and especially legislative opposition to them is relatively weak.

As discussed in greater detail later, interest in multilateral attempts to control arms transfers has been greatest in the United States. Apart from the arms embargo on South Africa, the one arms transfer restraint proposal to be given serious multilateral attention has been the registration of international arms transfers. While the proposal has received support from Britain and the United States, it has not been supported by the Soviet Union, France, or most Third World nations. Proponents state that public knowledge of arms transfer activity would create an international constituency to oppose them. They believe that most nations arm because of misperception of external threat and exaggeration of potential opponents' capabilities, which disclosure could ameliorate. The Third World opponents of the proposal state that publishing details about supplies threatens their security. The Soviets have argued that this is not a disarmament proposal at all, but merely a ruse by the United States to gain more information about Soviet activities in the Third World.[63]

Occasionally, proposals have been entertained that provide for multilateral regional restraint of conventional arms transfers. The United States, for example, made a limited effort toward encouraging regional agreements at the United Nations Special Session on Disarmament in 1978. Indeed, a group of Latin American leaders meeting in Mexico City that same year discussed the possibility of a Latin American multilateral regime to limit arms imports there. But these discussions shifted to a more fundamental concern, expressed by Mexican Foreign Secretary Santiago Roel, that such a regime might provide instruments by which the industrial nations "would try to form a club of suppliers in the future."[64]

The major existing multilateral forum for arms export control is the Coordinating Committee (COCOM) consisting of fifteen nations, including all members of NATO (excluding Iceland) and Japan. COCOM represents a mechanism by which the Western nations can prevent sensitive technology from being compromised through transfers to the Soviet Union or Soviet bloc nations. The members have no treaty but have agreed to consult each other on items to be exported, and they have a previously agreed munitions list.[65] COCOM was the result of U.S. concerns about the danger of arms transfers. Set up as a consequence of the Mutual Defense Assistance Control Act ("Battle Act") of 1951, its principal enforcement authority was to withhold U.S. foreign assistance from countries trading restricted items to members of the Soviet bloc. Later, COCOM posed the threat of restricting shipment of critical components of transferrable systems produced in the United States, of which the critical and sensitive technology was a part.

Interest in controlling arms transfers is most significant in the United States. The greatest pressures for control emerged in the Congress in the late 1960s, as it reviewed the relationship between U.S. intervention in South Vietnam and prior U.S. military assistance activities in Southeast Asia. An extensive and sometimes agonizing reappraisal of U.S. foreign policy goals, objectives, and methods for their achievement by strategic analysts and the attentive public contributed to congressional concern about the consequences of arms sales.

While these issues had been latent in the U.S. political scene for some time, they were made manifest in the searching reappraisal of the country's role in world affairs generated by the Vietnam War. This reappraisal was instituted not just among the political left or liberal intellectual community, but also by former government officials and others who have been labeled the "foreign policy establishment." Key members of the Council on Foreign Relations increasingly spoke out against the assumptions that governed use of the instruments of foreign policy. Writing in *Foreign Affairs* in 1970, former Deputy Assistant Secretary of Defense and Under Secretary of the Air Force Townsend Hoopes asked the question so central for attentive students of foreign policy in that period: "Why did so many intelligent, experienced and humane men in government fail to grasp the immorality of our intervention in Vietnam and the conscious diversion it was producing at home long after this was instinctively evident to their wives and children?"[66] Hoopes and many others concluded the major error could be labeled the "Cold War syndrome."[67] In 1972, Hamilton Fish Armstrong, then editor of *Foreign Affairs*, in a widely read article, "Isolated America," decried the loss of influence of the United States and blamed it on "mistaken beliefs" about the proper instruments for peace.[68] Containment, the central theme of U.S. foreign policy since the Truman presidency was increasingly challenged.[69] Its premises, and the central premises of the U.S. foreign policy consensus that operated from Truman to Johnson, were (1) that the Soviet Union is motivated to be the dominant world power; (2) that since in another world war the United States would quickly become a prime target of mass destruction, peace must be pursued through the avoidance of situations that would compel or induce a Soviet strategic attack; (3) that since containment of the Soviet Union is central to peace, the United States should make its power available to friends and allies attempting to dissuade or block Soviet expansionism; and (4) that a Communist success in any part of the world would critically undermine the power of the non-Communist world to dissuade the Soviets from further advances.[70] In sum, the balance of power defined as a distribution of power in the international system favorable to the status quo was critical to American survival. The United States could implement deterrence of Soviet aggression through containment by having a strong military posture of its own, by providing military power to allies, and by convincing friends and enemies alike of the credibility of the American commitment.[71] Direct intervention on behalf of friendly regimes or military assistance in the form of grants, credits, sales, training, advisors, and economic develop- ment assistance become central instruments of this policy. A review of the causes of the Vietnam War or identification of the "mistaken beliefs" about U.S. foreign policy involved, not surprisingly, a critical assessment of U.S. security assistance policies and activities. The prom- inent U.S. foreign policy journals were replete with reappraisals of the containment doctrine and its instruments. Townsend Hoopes, Arthur M. Schlesinger, Jr., Paul Warnke, Thomas L. Hughes, Leslie Gel, Richard Holbrooke, Richard H. Ullman, Adam Yarmolinski, and Marshall Shul- man led the reappraisal.[72] George Kennan, a major architect of the containment doctrine, who had long been uncomfortable about the prominence of military measures in implementing it, now became one of is most important critics. As Shahram Chubin has succinctly noted, the Vietnam debate accelerated a crisis of confidence in the United States as well as raised doubts about the morality of American intentions.

It is small wonder, then, that in the aftermath of Vietnam the attitude of the United States towards the Third World was conditioned by a debate that bore its scars and that generated much fervour but little clarity as to this core of strategic interest and the criteria for and scope of involvement or the appropriate instruments for influence.

The emergence of a new school of influential analysts reinforced the inclination of many who had been transformed by the bitterness of the Vietnam war to interpret the world in new and comforting terms, to deny the centrality of military power in interstate relations and to argue, for example, that oil was safe because the producers "can't drink it," or that allies would remain loyal "because they have nowhere else to go."[73]

This group decried what they perceived as an excessive dependence of successive American administrations on military solutions to political or diplomatic problems. They saw in U.S. foreign policy a predisposition to intervention. American militancy and excessive concern with perceived Soviet advantages, argued many, had actually provoked the Soviet leadership into an arms race. Excessive concern about Soviet power projection and presence in the Third World had alienated the United States from countless millions there, because the United States frequently found itself supporting repressive, unpopular, authoritarian, and frequently unstable regimes, as long as they were "anti-Communist." The United States, in short, had become insensitive to major changes in the international system, including a diminished Soviet threat to U.S. security interests. Though their prescriptions varied, these writers advocated replacing containment with a number of "non-collision" strategies. Detente and arms control were major themes of what conservatives called the "neo-isolationists." Others referred to them as the "new foreign policy establishment."

Reflecting in many ways the consensus of the "new establishment," the Council on Foreign Relations, in a 1980s project study on arms transfers, documented trends in worldwide arms transfers, cited the dangers, and proposed control techniques and negotiation strategies for the United States in seeking multilateral restraint among suppliers.[74] The major theme of the study was to demonstrate that arms transfers had become a major foreign policy instrument and arms control problem requiring a considerable diplomatic and administrative commitment if it was to be controlled. This study had a substantial impact on key members of the future Carter administration, as did a similar study by the United States United Nations Association, which reached similar conclusions. The latter was endorsed by soon-to-be Secretary of State Cyrus Vance and ACDA Director Paul Warnke.

Before joining the Carter administration as Director of Politico-Military Affairs, prominent *New York Times* journalist Leslie H. Gelb declared that previous administrations had attempted to use arms sales for too many purposes without seriously considering the impact of the sales on international security. Said Gelb of Secretary of State Henry Kissinger, "He has been too preoccupied with his purposes in selling rather than with their purposes in buying.... [and] he seems to have consistently over-estimated the diplomatic leverage accruing to the United States from arms sales."[75]

A growing concern about the impact of arms transfers was reflected in the words of candidates Jimmy Carter and Walter Mondale during the 1976 presidential campaign. Mondale stated "The unrestrained competition among nations to build more arms, to sell more weapons, to deploy more forces is senseless, wasteful, but above all, dangerous to our security." It was Carter's belief that the United States could not be "both the world's leading champion of peace and the world's leading supplier of weapons of war." Apart from Carter's stark comment, however, not even the more ardent critics of the Nixon and Ford arms sales policies who were to join the Carter administration were convinced that the United States should stop transferring arms to other countries.[76] Rather, they advocated greater policy control of the arms transfer decisionmaking process, greater concern for the impact of arms transfers on regional and global security, more careful assessment of the dilemmas and dangers of over reliance on this instrument of foreign policy, and more imagination or initiative in finding agreement among suppliers to limit arms transfers worldwide.[77] In short, they advocated that the United States become a more reluctant supplier than in the past.

The urge to control arms transfers, so evident among liberal congressmen and apparent in the academic journals of the time, was also highly salient in the early months of the Carter administration. Upon assuming the presidency, Carter ordered an interagency review of arms sales and held up approval in nearly $6 billion in sales pending the review. In addition to considering the international and foreign policy implications of arms transfers, the interagency group tasked with the review considered the impact that reduced U.S. arms transfers would have on the balance of payments, trade, employment, and weapons procurement.

The fears and hopes of those concerned about arms transfers were well expressed by Secretary of State Cyrus Vance in his 30 June 1977 report to the Congress. In arguing for a restraint policy, he cited the following purposes of reduced arms sales:

To encourage a general reduction in both world arms transfers and reliance on military might as an essential element in a more peaceful and stable world order;

Through a lower level of armament, to curtail the potential for arms races and limit the intensity of conflict if it occurs;

To reduce the potential and pressure for U.S. involvement in local conflicts to the extent this follows from various arms supply relations;

To moderate superpower competition and the prospect for conflict in regional situations (if multilateral initiatives are successful);

To reduce reliance on arms transfers as a means of implementing our diplomacy, to the detriment of alternative nonmilitary instruments;

To protect U.S. Military capabilities by limiting the dispersion of military technology that could be used against us and our allies;

To distance ourselves from regimes that do not respect and observe basic human rights and fundamental freedoms;

To limit the diversion of monies and skills in developing nations away from fundamental economic development needs;

To permit U.S. resources to be shifted from financing arms transfers to supporting economic development;

To minimize the risk of diversion of destructive weapons to terrorists; and

To build U.S. domestic support for our foreign policy objectives in the developing world.[78]

The Congress

Concomitant with and reflecting in large measure the post-Vietnam debate over the direction of U.S. foreign policy was a congressional desire to control and limit the military dimensions of foreign policy, including arms transfers. Congress has displayed a longstanding interest in, and concern about, this and other aspects of the U.S. government's security assistance program. Since 1948, for example, as much as one-third of the Congress has at any given time opposed grants, training, or credit sales to foreign governments. Yet, until the early 1970s there remained a significant consensus favoring these foreign policy instruments, as well as a general recognition in Congress that security assistance was an important and positive instrument supporting U.S. foreign policy objectives. Certainly, a large aspect of this consensus lay in the bipartisan coalition which had supported U.S. foreign policy since 1941, and which was to summarily collapse through the political and social angst of the Vietnam years. Yet, a more fundamental dimension of opposition to, or concern about, the U.S. security assistance program and its implementation by the Executive Branch had been growing since the decade before Vietnam. Thus, while Congress often encouraged the increased use of the security assistance as a foreign policy instrument, its expanded use seemed simultaneously to generate added concern that the United States was becoming the arsenal of the world.

The growth of arms sales can be traced to a search by the Congress for a "cheaper" aid instrument, for no sooner had the U.S. government begun foreign aid programs than opposition developed against grant (non-reimbursable) aid. Congressmen searched for more "businesslike" aid. They emphasized a switch from grants to loans, and repayment first in soft currency and then in hard currency. Furthermore, Congressmen began to demand that loaned funds be used to buy American goods. The PL480 program (the Agriculture Trade and Development Act of 1964) illustrated the congressional search. Here was a program that established a precedent from the idea that the sale of an item to a country constituted "aid."[79]

Grant Assistance. Concern over the balance-of-payments deficit and the contribution of economic grant assistance and military grant assistance to that problem produced greater pressures to reduce the Military Assistance Program (MAP) during the second term of the Eisenhower presidency. Indeed, while the Eisenhower administration attempted to reduce defense costs in Europe, the Senate Foreign Relations Committee at the same time was insistent that MAP in Europe be terminated and that America's NATO allies be encouraged to adopt an increasing share of the Western defense burden. The Military Assistance Program, once the backbone of many European acquisition programs, had significantly dwindled to that region by 1962. By calender year 1966, Belgium, Denmark, France, West Germany, Italy, Luxembourg, the Netherlands, Norway, and the United Kingdom had received their last MAP authorizations.

The major results of these congressional pressures toward increased burden-sharing was a proliferation of logistics problems and an increase in standardization problems within the NATO alliance.[80] An additional, and not surprising, result was the generation of considerable European arms purchases, which accompanied the growth in sales to non-NATO countries. While prior to fiscal year 1962, arms sales to Europe had constituted a considerable proportion of the U.S. Foreign Military Sales (FMS) program, Table 2.8 illustrates that the impact of the decline of MAP on United States sales within the alliance was to raise their total volume. As Table 2.9 reveals, the decline of MAP to Europe was directly related to the increase in FMS and commercial arms sales deliveries to the region. The European situation, however, was but one element of a continuing divergence between the Executive Branch and Congress

Table 2.8.   Impact of the Decline of MAP on U.S. Sales within NATO (Current Dollars × $1,000)

Fiscal Year	Worldwide U.S. FMS Agreements	FMS Agreements With NATO Cohort*	%
1962	645,761	520,460	80.6
1963	1,501,807	805,657	62.3
1964	1,410,245	1,081,699	76.7
1965	1,779,091	543,459	30.5
1966	1,457,650	1,006,775	69.1

*Belgium, Denmark, France, Federal Republic of Germany, Italy, Luxembourg, Netherlands, Norway, United Kingdom.

Source: Defense Security Assistance Agency, Fiscal Year Series, 1980.

Table 2.9. Comparison of MAP and FMS/Commercial Deliveries of Arms to Europe and Canada (in Constant 1977 Dollars)

Year	MAP Delivered	FMS & Commercial Delivered
1950	$ 121,174,000	$ 4,694,000
1951	1,750,272,000	43,461,000
1952	2,728,722,000	128,113,000
1953	6,963,975,000	62,675,000
1954	5,970,043,000	236,247,000
1955	3,945,521,000	224,795,000
1956	4,456,400,000	178,379,000
1957	3,252,480,000	191,245,000
1958	2,564,689,000	573,296,000
1959	1,858,075,000	338,674,000
1960	1,697,728,000	542,873,000
1961	912,045,000	513,822,000
1962	750,313,000	555,452,000
1963	867,263,000	1,430,883,000
1964	717,750,000	818,283,000
1965	961,337,000	1,150,609,000
1966	519,708,000	991,487,000
1967	391,936,000	993,758,000
1968	348,683,000	1,037,342,000
1969	318,036,000	1,332,043,000
1970	249,238,000	1,456,961,000
1971	266,548,000	1,259,619,000
1972	202,177,000	1,302,724,000
1973	128,605,000	1,128,105,000
1974	105,534,000	1,311,743,000
1975	77,993,000	1,491,548,000
1976	4,291,000	2,197,891,000
1977	2,662,000	1,777,379,000
1978	27,552,000	1,503,775,000
1979	33,270,000	1,185,952,000
1980	73,218,000	2,343,604,000

Source: Defense Security Assistance Agency, Fiscal Year Series, 1980.

concerning MAP,[81] which is partially reflected in the large congressional cuts in the Executive Branch MAP authorization request displayed in Table 2.10.

Throughout the late 1960s and early 1970s, while FMS was not without congressional critics, it was generally more acceptable than MAP. Congressional attitudes of disapproval toward MAP were central to the shift from grant assistance to military sales as the primary instrument of the U.S. government's military "assistance" program. Curiously, the Nixon Doctrine, one of the major elements of this shift, was favored by the Senate Foreign Relations Committee even though it

Table 2.10. Congressional Cuts in Executive Branch MAP Request (Current Dollars in Millions)**

Fiscal Year	Executive Branch Request	Appropriated	% Cut
1952	$ 6,303	$ 5,744	9
1953	5,425	4,219	22
1954	4,274	3,230	24
1955	1,778	1,192	33
1956	1,959	1,022	48
1957	2,925	2,017	31
1958	1,900	1,340	29
1959	1,800	1,515	16
1960	1,600	1,300	19
1961	2,000	1,800	10
1962	1,885	1,600	15
1963	*	1,325	*
1964	1,405	1,000	29
1965	1,055	1,130	+7
1966	1,170	1,470	+26
1967	917	792	14
1968	620	500	19
1969	420	375	11
1970	425	350	18
1971	690	690	0
1972	705	500	29
1973	780	553	29
1974	685	450	34
1975	985	475	52
1976	790	252	68
1977	279	264	5
1978	230	220	4
1979	133	83	38
1980	160	110	31

Source: United States, Department of Defense, Congressional Presentation: Security Assistance Programs, FY 1982.

*The Foreign Assistance Act of 1961 authorized $1,700,000; no Executive Branch authorization was required. $1,325,000 was ultimately appropriated.

**Fractions of millions of dollars have been dropped.

meant that other nations would be aided by the United States through the sale of arms. Likewise, since MAP was being reduced, a strong group in the House promoted an expansion of FMS to help friends and allies overseas adjust to a reduced U.S. military presence.

By the late 1950s, Congress increasingly intervened in MAP decision-making, giving detailed instructions as to whom military grants should be given, and as to what the conditions of aid would be. A salient threshold of congressional oversight was the 1959 vote of the Senate Foreign Relations Committee to cut aid off progressively to countries "capable of providing and maintaining their own defense." In 1960, Congress voted to prohibit new military grant commitments to West

Germany, the United Kingdom, and Luxembourg; in 1961 new commitments to France were prohibited. In 1963 MAP was prohibited for any "economically developed nation capable of its own defense burden"; that same year MAP was denied to any country trading with Cuba. In 1967 Congress ordered President Johnson to terminate MAP deliveries to any country that diverted its resources to military spending that was "unnecessary." In 1968 Congress directed the executive not to use grant funds to furnish "sophisticated weapons" to any "underdeveloped country" and placed ceilings on the amount of military assistance that could be given to Latin America and Africa. During consideration of the 1969 aid bill, members of Congress demanded a review of military training programs. The House Foreign Affairs Committee was committed to a reduction of U.S. military missions abroad, to prohibiting aid to governments that denied freedom to their people, and to cutting all aid to Greece. Congress voted to limit the number of officers brought to the United States for training. During consideration of the 1970 Military Sales bill, further restrictions were placed on the Executive Branch as to quantities, types, and recipients of military aid.

By 1971 opposition to military aid had become reinforced by the association of military aid issues with larger questions surrounding the Vietnam War, including the War Powers Amendment, concern about "creeping commitments" and executive secrecy in making commitments, the Cooper-Church Amendment forbidding combat forces and advisors in Cambodia, repeal of the Formosa Resolution, and even with such issues as administration support of the Greek military government. Congress failed in 1971 to complete action on the Military Assistance Program, and the Senate rejected a House appropriation bill for funding economic and military aid in fiscal years 1972 and 1973. This represented the first outright defeat for grant assistance in twenty-four years. Liberals in particular were disenchanted with MAP. However, military aid was continued through congressional budget resolutions.

The fiscal 1973 military aid authorization action revealed further congressional opposition. The Senate Foreign Relations Committee warned of the rise in arms transfers and threatened to place country-by-country ceilings. It did place a ceiling on MAP to Cambodia. Many on the committee became convinced that military assistance had caused wars in Latin America and South Asia. The committee voted to prohibit all MAP and FMS to India and Pakistan. This proposal was sustained by the Senate, 43-41. But the foreign aid bill was caught up in the Mansfield Amendment to cut off funding for the Vietnam War and thus was rejected. A signal of the growing opposition to various aspects of military aid occurred when Senator J. William Fulbright, Chairman of the Foreign Relations Committee and a previous supporter of aid, refused to be the floor manager of the revised Senate Bill. He stated:

I do not believe it is any longer in the interest of the United States to carry on the bilateral foreign aid program, especially military aid....

I am particularly opposed to military aid. I feel it is wrong for a big and powerful country to inject itself into the military affairs of these smaller and weaker countries.... If we give them these things and at a cheap rate, we create a market we would not otherwise have.

A House-Senate dispute over military bases and the issue of the separation of the military aid bill from the economic aid bill resulted in a deadlocked conference. Congress again failed to authorize military aid in the normal way, and funded it instead by interim resolutions, a procedure that permitted actual supporters to minimize their political exposure.

By 1973, Senate defeats, conference disagreements, emergency funding resolutions, and ever-increasing congressional criticisms of MAP were commonplace. This increased criticism of military aid must be placed within the context of a change in congressional roles in defense policymaking which was considerable, if not permanent. Many factors explain this change, the Vietnam War being the most obvious. Others include decreased public perception of external threat, continuing debate on national priorities, and the rise of a bloc of nearly thirty "anti-defense" senators.[82]

The Senate Foreign Relations Committee became the nucleus of this block. In 1973 the committee voted to consider a Fulbright military aid bill rather than the one submitted by the Nixon administration. The administration wanted economic and military aid in one bill, but the committee separated them. As Senator Church suggested, the motive was to bring military assistance under greater review and not force people to vote for the military provisions of aid simply because they supported economic and humanitarian aid. The committee also voted to phase out all military aid and military missions overseas by 1977 in order to "lower the American profile abroad and cut down on our overseas involvement and expenditures." Military training programs outside the United States were to be terminated by 1974. By a vote of 48 to 44, however, the Senate did not support either of these committee proposals.

The foreign and military aid package for fiscal year 1974 barely passed the House (188-183). This may be attributed to inflation, devaluation, deficits, and overall disenchantment with "give-away" programs. Military assistance and sales came under considerable attack in the House debate. The next year, consideration of the fiscal 1975 military aid provisions, now separated from the economic aid program, involved countless amendments in each house, including attempts to reduce grants, set overall ceilings, prohibit aid to dictators, and cut off aid to Turkey, Greece, Chile, South Korea, and all OPEC nations. So many amendments were proposed on the floor of the Senate that the members voted (41-39) to recommit the bill to the Foreign Relations Committee. The Senate then supported the committee's proposal to terminate MAP and the Military Assistance and Advisory Groups (MAAGs) by 1977. However, the House bill did not contain this provision, and the conference report did not include the termination requirement. Rather, the conference committee expressed a Congress's sense that MAP and MAAGs should be re-examined and ended as soon as it was compatible with U.S. security interests. The conferees directed the President to provide a detailed plan for the elimination of the program within one year. With all of these expressions of opposition built into the legislation, Congress was unable to complete action on either the authorization or the appropriation bill.

Congress, in 1976, again demanded that it have greater control over military assistance. This led to a major dispute with the Ford administration, which resulted in a veto of S.2662, the military assistance bill. Salient features of that bill included elaborate reporting procedures on arms transfers; a $9 billion ceiling on all sales; prohibition of aid or sales to countries that discriminated on the basis of religion, sex, or race against any U.S. citizen; prohibition of aid to any country that violated human rights; and termination of MAP and the MAAGs by September 1977, except as specifically authorized by Congress. The bill further gave Congress sweeping control to review and reject—by concurrent resolution—proposed commercial and government-to-government arms sales. The Ford administration objected to five features of the bill: (1) the $9 billion ceiling; (2) the proscription against aid for violations of human rights; (3) resumption of trade with Vietnam; (4) termination of the MAAGs and MAP; and (5) the provision that major arms sales could be blocked by concurrent resolution of Congress. The final substitute bill (H.R. 13680) included most of the provisions of S.2662 except the $9 billion ceiling. Congress was undaunted by threats of another presidential veto and kept the MAP and MAAG terminations in the bill. Reluctantly, the President signed the bill. The administration was forced to sacrifice the MAP program, except as authorized country-by-country.

Foreign Military Sales. Congressional efforts to control arms sales decisionmaking were minimal until 1967, and sporadic until 1973. After 1973 they became intensive. Congress increasingly recognized that FMS decisions are major foreign policy decisions and expanded its control over this instrument. In 1967 Congress required that the administration present it with semiannual reports on all credits and guarantees to underdeveloped countries, semiannual reports predicting or forecasting credit sales, annual reports predicting total yearly sales, and semiannual reports of all military exports on the U.S. Munitions List. By 1973 Congress had become sufficiently concerned that it was not being given "up-to-date" information that it supported a proposal by Senator Gaylord Nelson requiring the President to report to both houses of Congress any single arms sale to any one country in excess of $25 million. It further provided that if after thirty days Congress did not object, through concurrent resolution, the sale would be permitted. Agreements with one country amounting to a total of over $50 million were also subject to this procedure. The Nelson Amendment represented a major congressional effort to establish, at a minimum, a policy veto over arms sales transactions. Yet, Congress has never vetoed an arms sale, although many attempts have been made to do so. For example, in 1976 Senator Nelson introduced thirty-seven resolutions and Senator Proxmire introduced twenty-four. Even the proposed sales of AWACS to Iran in 1977 and Saudi Arabia in 1981, which received extensive congressional criticism and challenge, were ultimately not "vetoed" by Congress. In 1976 there were no resolutions of challenge in the House even though the Nelson Amendment was strengthened that year. These amendments provided that a letter of offer for $25 million in sales to any country, or a sale of $7 million of major defense equipment, would be subject to the thirty-day concurrent resolution procedure. These amendments also required quarterly reporting of any sales over $1 million. In addition, Congress attempted to place a $9 billion ceiling on total arms sales. This bill, however, was vetoed by President Ford, and the ceiling was dropped in a revised bill, which was subsequently passed.

Recurrent Congressional Concerns.   Several recurrent and salient congressional criticisms have made concrete the congressional drive to control and limit arms transfers. These may be summarized as follows:

1. *Opposition to all grant aid.* As the preceding analysis has shown, Congress has generally attempted to replace grant aid with sales and credit.
2. *Rejection of all military aid and sales.* A significant group in Congress believes that the United States has become the arsenal of the world and is taking "blood money" from other countries. These Congressmen are part of what Laurance calls the anti-defense bloc.[83]
3. *Opposition to certain military assistance and sales goals.* Many members of Congress think that selling or giving arms to other countries for influence is folly. Others think arms do not help create a balance of power.

4. *Opposition to sales or aid to certain regions.* For several years, Congress placed restrictions or ceilings on sales or aid to Latin America and Africa. Recent House bills initially have called for a ban on all sales or aid to the Near East and South Asia. Some proposed amendments have called for a ban on all military deliveries to the Persian Gulf or the Middle East.

5. *Opposition to military assistance to certain countries.* Many countries have been singled out for one reason or another as nations that should not receive military assistance: some because it was thought they had developed a capability to handle their own defense problems, others because they may have used the weapons in a way displeasing to Congress. Turkey, after its invasion of Cyprus, was proscribed from further aid. Greece, Pakistan, India, and certain dictatorships have also been proscribed from aid. Any country that systematically violates human rights can now be prevented from receiving arms aid.

6. *Opposition to the transfer of certain kinds of equipment.* The proposed sale of AWACS to Iran in 1977 generated considerable congressional opposition because it was thought the weapon was too sophisticated for Iran. Similarly, the Foreign Relations Committee initially objected to the sale of Hawk missiles to Jordan in 1975.

7. *Concern that aid or sales will decrease U.S. preparedness.* This type of criticism usually comes from the pro-defense bloc in Congress. This group generally supports military aid but not at the expense of the services. The proposed worldwide sale of F-16 fighters has been opposed for this reason. Many members felt that the Shah's Iran had higher priority than the Air Force on many types of weapons. In 1977 hearings, Chairman Long of the Appropriations Committee expressed deep concern about the conflict between FMS and the preparedness needs of the U.S. Military.

8. *Opposition to IMET.* Some congressmen believe that training provides foreign officers with the skills to overthrow democracies and to rule by authoritarian means. A more serious criticism is that IMET is really a public relations tactic by which officers are introduced to U.S. weapons. IMET helps create a demand for U.S. equipment.

9. *MAAGs generate demands for U.S. equipment.* This criticism is widespread in congressional hearings. Both the Ford and Carter administrations were aware of this concern and established rules of conduct for the MAAGs. Certainly the congressional attempt to limit the MAAGs or other security assistance organizations in authorized countries to a personnel ceiling of three is a manifestation of this concern. Security assistance field personnel have been

reduced in total numbers to fewer than 20 percent of the FY 1962 level of 6,000, basically as a consequence of this repeated concern of Congress.

10. *Opposition to Commercial Sales.* Congress has generated elaborate controls over the years for commercial sales, fearing that such sales may contradict U.S. national interests or implicate the United States in conflicts. There have been hearings on graft and payoffs by commercial representatives. In the early 1970s Congress sought to restrict arms sales to government-to-government channels. However, by 1974 it wanted the government representatives to get out of the arms trade and turn it over to commercial representatives, thus revealing uncertainty as to what roles should be played by whom.

11. *Concern that security assistance personnel and industry representatives confront the Congress with* **fait accompli.** Congress has attempted to control what it thinks is a *fait accompli* by military assistance field personnel and commercial firm representatives. Once the field people have generated a demand, negotiated a contract, and presented a letter of offer, it is feared that officials in Washington or Congress can reject the proposed sale only at a risk of disrupting relations with the prospective buyer government or regime.

12. *Concern about coordination and control.* Frequently, members of Congress contend that the Executive Branch has no military assistance or sales policy or that the numerous agencies and offices do not consult each other, or that low-level officials make major arms sales decisions. Several hearings have been held to investigate how military assistance and sales decisions are made and who participated in such decisions.

13. *Concern about information flow to Congress.* This has been a major congressional criticism. Many congressmen have become aware that FMS decisions are major foreign policy decisions, but they are not content with the role they have in the decision process. In 1967, in 1973, and again in 1975 and 1976, Congress expanded the requirements for Executive Branch reporting of arms sales to congressional committees.

Future Prospects for Control. Increased congressional concern about the impact of arms transfers both generated and sustained a larger review of the instruments, purposes, and strategies of the United States in world affairs. A central question for the future is how strong will be the urge of Congress and the Reagan administration to control arms transfers. Throughout the 1980 presidential campaign, arms transfer restraint was not an issue. President Carter did not make a campaign issue of his efforts in this area. Candidate Reagan did not dwell on the modest accomplishments of Carter's restraint effort, nor did he indicate how he would use arms sales as a foreign policy instrument. He did, however, mention arms transfers in a positive light. The change of direction on arms transfer policy effected by the Reagan administration was obvious from its earliest days. As early as January 1981, interviews with congressional, State, and Defense Department officials indicated a common belief that President Reagan would be less concerned about the possible dangers of arms transfers than was his predecessor, and that he would focus more on the possible benefits of increased use of arms transfers to further U.S. foreign policy objectives. Many within the Washington foreign policy establishment evidently believed at that time that "arms transfers would no longer be considered an exceptional instrument" of foreign policy and that "this administration's position would be more positive and pragmatic." An official in the Defense Department speculated that while there were positive elements in Carter's restraint policy, such as better review and control of arms sales decisions, during the Reagan presidency "there will be less hand wringing about the moral consequences of arms sales." An industry spokesman stated that "under Carter, it was assumed that arms sales were evil but necessary. Under Reagan, I think greater attention will be given to the importance of strong friends and allies for the national interest." In addition, a member of the staff of the Foreign Affairs committee told the author; "I think you can expect the Reagan people to try to crank up sales the way the Carter people tried to crank them down."

These early expectations of the new administration's approach to arms transfers were confirmed on March 19, 1981. As Secretary of State Alexander Haig and James L. Buckley, Under Secretary of State for Security Assistance, Science and Technology, stated in testimony to Congress, the total program authority for grant military assistance and credit that the administration would request represented a 30-percent increase over FY 1981 levels, and budget authority requested would be 57 percent higher than the FY 1981 level.[84] For FY 1982, the administration was requesting $1.48 billion to support FMS financing of $4.05 billion to be furnished to thirty-eight countries. The most salient features of the proposed Reagan FMS program for FY 1982 were the following:

$2,573 million for loans from the Federal Financing Bank with Department of Defense guarantees of repayment;
$500 million in FMS credits for Israel;
$981.8 million in FMS credits to fifteen countries at reduced interest rates.

In addition, the President requested that Congress permit greater flexibility by authorizing $100 million in unallocated funds for the Military Assistance Program (MAP). And in a major shift from previous requests, the administration requested a Special Defense Acquisition Fund of $350 million for FY 1982. This program was intended to create a special account to procure military equipment for military assistance in "emergencies" without diverting U.S. service stocks.

It is quite clear that the assumptions of President Reagan and his key advisors about the contribution of military power to the maintenance of peace are different from the assumptions held by President Carter and those who initally guided the foreign policy of his administration. Principally, the Reagan administration appears to be committed to military containment of the Soviet Union as a major foreign policy objective, and the President has often expressed a determination to strengthen America's allies militarily and to increase U.S. military presence throughout the world.

Regardless of the Reagan administration's intentions, it is unlikely that security assistance can be easily expanded. Several international and domestic factors will prohibit any extensive expansion. In the international enviroment, these factors include the limited funds available to most potential customers, high interest rates, concern of international lending institutions about growing Third World indebtedness, and expanded sales efforts of European competitors that have increased their market shares in the developing world. Domestic constraints on the expanded use of arms transfers include continued congressional reticence concerning the advisability of arms transfers, congressional and Executive Branch interest in limiting the budgetary costs of foreign aid, industry opposition to increased use of coproduction arrangements, and opposition of the army, navy, and air force to exports of top-line equipment until the procurement needs of the services are fulfilled. Each of these factors will be given greater attention in later chapters.

It is clear that a variety of forces are urging or compelling controls on the use of arms transfers. The Reagan administration, while critical of the Carter efforts, has itself imposed criteria on arms sales decisions which may eventually constitute restraint. In a speech before the Board of Governors of the Aerospace Industries Association, Under Secretary Buckley stated that although requests for arms from members of major alliances who contribute to U.S. efforts to deter Soviet advances would be given highest priority, arms transfer requests would have to meet specific criteria before they would be approved:

> In assessing arms transfer requests, the United States will continue to give due consideration to such factors as the degree to which the equipment requested corresponds to the military threat facing the recipient; the manner in which such equipment will serve to maintain stability

within regions where friends of the United States are on less than the best terms one with the other; and whether the proposed transfer can be absorbed by the recipient without overburdening its military support system or financial resources.[85]

The dilemmas involved in arms sales decisions are so great, the unknowns concerning the impact of arms transfers on national and international security so numerous, and the centrality of arms transfers to basic foreign policy so salient, that it is highly likely that the urge to control will remain as compelling a factor as the demand for arms and the pressure to supply. These three forces and the contradictions they create will be apparent in each of the following chapters.

NOTES

1 Quoted by Theodore Ropp, *War in the Modern Age* (New York: Collier Books, 1962), p. 11.
2 The data used here are from the United States Arms Control and Disarmament Agency, *World Military Expenditures and Arms Transfers, 1969-1978*. (Washington, D.C.: USGPO, December 1980). Although this source is widely used among scholars in the areas of security assistance and world military expenditures, many researchers, including the authors, have found many inconsistencies and methodological problems with this data. In particular, the data tend to understate the value of military expenditures or arms transfers. In this chapter, however, the authors are merely arguing the pervasiveness of military expenditures. That such expenditures may be even higher than shown in no way challenges the general argument. For an analysis of the data problem, see Edward A. Kolodziej, "Measuring French Arms Transfers: A Problem of Sources and Some Sources of Problems with ACDA Data," *Journal of Conflict Resolution* 23 (June 1979), pp. 195-227.
3 Developed countries constitute twenty-eight nations: all those in NATO, except Greece and Turkey; all those in the Warsaw Pact except Bulgaria; Austria, Finland, Ireland, Japan, South Africa, Sweden, Switzerland, Australia, and New Zealand. All other nations are classified as developing. This classification system is widely used both by the U.S. government and by various international organizations. It follows the classification used by the Development Assistance Committee of the Organization for Economic Co-operation and Development (OECD).
4 Quoted by Leonard Wainstein, "The Dreadnought Gap," *United States Naval Institute Proceedings* (September 1966).
5 For an exceptional historical analysis of the impact of armament competition on diplomacy, see Ropp, *War in the Modern Age*.
6 George Rathjens, "The Dynamics of the Arms Race," *Scientific American* 220,4 (April 1969), pp. 15-25.
7 Albert Wohlstetter, "Is There a Strategic Arms Race?" *Foreign Policy* 15 (Summer 1974), pp. 3-20; Albert Wohlstetter, "Rivals, but No Race," *Foreign Policy* 16 (Fall 1974), pp. 48-81.
8 "U.S. May Sell Saudis Radar, Fuel Planes," *New York Times* (April 3, 1981), p. 1.
9 Judith Miller, "U.S. to Offer Israel Jets on Easy Terms," *New York Times* (February 26, 1981), p. 1.
10 Elve Montiero de Castro, "A Energia Nuclear no Brazil," *A Defesa Nacional* (January-February 1974), p. 63; quoted in Norman Gall, "Atoms for Brazil, Dangers for All," *Foreign Policy* 23 (Summer 1976), p. 184.

11 Brian Loveman and Thomas M. Davies, Jr., *The Politics of Anti-Politics: The Military in Latin America* (Lincoln: University of Nebraska Press, 1978).

12 Abdul Kasim Mansur, "The Crises in Iran," *Armed Forces Journal* (January 1979), pp. 26-33.

13 Charles W. Anderson, *Politics and Economic Change in Latin America* (Princeton, N.J.: D. Van Nostrand, 1967), pp. 87-114.

14 James Payne, *Labor and Politics in Peru* (New Haven: Yale University Press, 1965).

15 Edgar S. Furniss, Jr., *De Gaulle and the French Army* (New York: The Twentieth Century Fund), pp. 181-219.

16 Lucian W. Pye, "Armies in the Process of Political Modernization," in *The Role of the Military in Underdeveloped Countries*, edited by J. J. J. Johnson (Princeton, N.J.: Princeton University Press, 1962), pp. 69-89.

17 Mancur Olsen, "Rapid Growth as a Destabilizing Force," in *When Men Revolt and Why*, edited by James C. Davies (New York: Free Press, 1971), pp. 215-227.

18 Melvin Small and J. David Singer, "Conflict in the International System, 1816-1977: Historical Trends and Policy Futures," in *Challenges to America*, ed. by Charles W. Kegley, Jr. and Patrick J. McGowan (Beverly Hills, California: Sage, 1979).

19 This is not as clear as liberal and radical critics of defense expenditures often allege. Stanley Lieberson, for example, found that jobs and other side payments of arms production tended to equal economic societal costs of such production. Stanley Lieberson, "An Empirical Study of Military-Industrial Linkages," in Steven Rosen (ed.), *Testing the Theory of the Military-Industrial Complex* (Lexington: D. C. Heath, 1973).

20 Jean Klein, "France and the Arms Trade," in *The Gun Merchants: Politics and Policies of the Major Arms Suppliers*, edited by Cindy Cannizzo (New York: Pergamon Press, 1980), p. 137.

21 Michael Reich, "Military Spending and the U.S. Economy," in Rosen, *Testing the Theory*, p. 95.

22 James R. Kurth, "Aerospace Production Lines and American Defense Spending," in Rosen, *Testing the Theory*, pp. 135-156.

23 Ibid., p. 141.

24 Ibid., p. 142.

25 Ibid., p. 143.

26 A. L. Ross, "Conventional Arms Production in Developing Countries: An Overview," a paper delivered at the International Studies Association Annual Meeting, Los Angeles, March 1980.

27 David W. Ziegler, *War, Peace and International Politics* (Boston: Little, Brown, 1981), p. 214.

28 Ibid.

29 United States, House, Committee on International Relations, *Conventional Arms Transfer Policy*, 95th Congress, 2nd Session, February 1, 1978, p. 43.

30 Michael Moodie, "Defense Industries in the Third World: Problems and Promises," in *Arms Transfers in the Modern World*, edited by Stephanie G. Neuman and Robert E. Harkavy (New York: Praeger, 1979), p. 294.

31 Ross, "Conventional Arms Production," p. 17.

32 Ibid.

33 *Strategic Survey 1976* (London: The International Institute for Strategic Studies, 1977), p. 22.

34 Ross, "Conventional Arms Production," p. 16.

35 United States Arms Control and Disarmament Agency, *World Military Expenditures and Arms Transfers, 1969-1978* (Washington, D. C.: USGPO, December 1980), p. 9.

36 Ibid., p. 21.

37 James L. Buckley, "Arms Transfers and the National Interest," an address before the Meeting of the Board of Governors, Aerospace Industries Association, Williamsburg, Virginia (May 21, 1981).

38 David J. Louscher, "Constancy and Change in American Arms Sales Policies," *Selected Papers of the Mershon Center* (Columbus: Ohio State University Press, 1978), pp. 29-46.

39 *Report to Congress on Arms Transfer Policy* (pursuant to Sections 202(b) and 218 of the International Security Assistance and Arms Export Control Act of 1976, Public Law 94-329).

40 United States, Central Intelligence Agency, *Communist Aid Activities in Non-Communist Countries, 1979 and 1954-1979* (October 1980), p. 4.

41 Robert E. Harkavy, "The New Geopolitics: Arms Transfers and the Major Powers Overseas Basing Networks," unpublished paper delivered at the 1977 Annual Meeting of the Midwest Political Science Association.

42 Avigdor Haselkorn, *The Evolution of Soviet Security Strategy 1965-1975* (New York: Crane, Russak, 1978).

43 Martin Edmonds, "The Domestic and International Dimensions of British Arms Sales, 1966-1978," in Cannizzo, *The Gun Merchants*, p. 96.

44 Ibid.

45 United Kingdom, Parliamentary Debates (House of Commons), 8861, Col. 421 (October 18, 1973); quoted in Edmonds, "Domestic and International Dimensions," p. 95.

46 Ibid.

47 United Kingdom, Parliament, House of Commons, 5th ser., 815, Col. 457 (April 22, 1971).

48 Felix Fessler, "Weapons Merchant: French Arms Exports Mount as Paris Seeks to Counteract Oil Bills," *The Wall Street Journal* (November 19, 1980), p. 1.

49 Edward A. Kolodziej, "Determinants of French Arms Sales: Security Implications," in *Threats, Weapons and Foreign Policy Behavior: Volume 5, Sage International Yearbook of Foreign Policy Studies*, edited by Patrick J. McGowan and Charles W. Kegley, Jr. (Beverly Hills, Calif.: Sage, 1980), p. 165.

50 United States, Senate, 96th Congress, 1st Session, Committee on Foreign Relations Staff Report, Prospects for Multilateral Arms Export Restraint (April 1979), p. 27.

51 U.S. Congressional Budget Office, *Budgetary Costs Savings to the Department of Defense Resulting from Foreign Military Sales* (Washington, D. C., May 24, 1976).

52 *New York Times* (July 12, 1977), p. 1.

53 *New York Times* (April 12, 1981), p. 1.

54 Andrew J. Pierre, *The Global Politics of Arms Sales* (Princeton, N. J.: Princeton University Press, 1982), pp. 26, 68, 299; see also United States Department of Labor, Bureau of Labor Statistics, *Foreign Defense Sales and Grants, Fiscal Years 1973-1975: Labor and Material Requirements* (July 1977), p. 17.

55 United States, Senate, Committee on Foreign Relations, Hearings on U.S. Arms Sales Policy, 94th Congress, 2nd Session (1976), pp. 53-55.

56 See General F. Michael Rogers, "The Impact of Foreign Military Sales on the National Industrial Base," *Strategic Review* 5 (Spring 1977), p. 18.

57 See "U.S. Arms Sales Abroad: A Policy of Restraint?" *American Enterprise Institute Defense Review* 2 (1978), p. 10.

58 *The Impact on U.S. Industry of a Restricted Arms Control Policy*, A Publication of the Government Division of the Electronics Industries Association, (Washington, D. C., 1977), p. 1.

59 Le Theule report on "Le Projet de loi de finances pour 1976," Assemblee Nationale, No. 1916.

60 Eugene Kozicharow, "How Currency Problems Spur Soviet Export Push," *Aviation Week and Space Technology* (April 11, 1977), p. 17.

61 Felix Kessler, "Weapons Merchants: French Arms Exports Mount as Paris Seeks to Counteract Oil Bills," *The Wall Street Journal* (November 19, 1980), p. 1.

62 Kolodziej, "Determinants of French Arms Sales," p. 142.

63 Stockholm International Peace Research Institute, *The Arms Trade with the Third World* (New York: Holmes and Meir, 1975), p. 313.

64 Foreign Broadcast Information Service VI (23 August 1978).

65 Lewis A. Frank, *The Arms Trade in International Relations* (New York: Praeger, 1969), p. 203.

66 Townsend Hoopes, "Legacy of the Cold War in Indochina," *Foreign Affairs* 48,4 (July 1970), p. 601.

67 Ibid., p. 609.

68 Hamilton Fish Armstrong, "Isolated America," *Foreign Affairs* 1,1 (October 1972), pp. 1-10.

69 For a review of the impact of the containment doctrine of each administration, see especially Seyom Brown, *The Faces of Power: Constancy and Change in United States Foreign Policy from Truman to Johnson* (New York: Columbia University Press, 1968); and Paul Y. Hammond, *Cold War and Detente* (New York: Harcourt Brace Jovanovich, 1975).

70 Brown, *The Faces of Power*, pp. 11-13.

71 A concise summary of containment, as well as a defense of the intervention in Vietnam by a critic, is provided by James Payne, *The American Threat* (Chicago: Markham, 1970).

72 For a review of their impact, see Carl Gershman, "The Rise and Fall of the New Foreign Policy Establishment," *Commentary* (July 1980), pp. 13-24.

73 Shahram Chubin, "The U.S. and the Third World: Motives, Objectives, Policies," in *Third-World Conflict and International Security, Part II*, Adelphi Papers, No. 167 (London: The International Institute for Strategic Studies, Summer 1981), p. 21.

74 Anne Hessing Cahn et al., *Controlling Future Arms Trade* (New York: McGraw-Hill, 1977).

75 Leslie H. Gelb, "Arms Sales," *Foreign Policy* 25 (Winter 1976-77), pp. 4 and 20.

76 Cahn, *Controlling Future Arms Trade*, pp. 39-49.

77 Gelb, "Arms Sales," p. 21.

78 *Report to Congress on Arms Transfer Policy.*

79 Andrew F. Westwood, *Foreign Aid in a Foreign Policy Framework* (Washington, D. C.: The Brookings Institution, 1966). Also see Louscher, "Continuity and Change."

80 See Chapter 3.

81 Harold A. Hovey, *United States Military Assistance* (New York: Praeger, 1965).

82 Edward J. Laurance, "The Changing Role of Congress in Defense Policy-Making," *Journal of Conflict Resolution*, 20,2 (1976), pp. 213-253; see also Norman A. Graham and David J. Louscher, "The Political Control of Weapons System Acquistion: A Comparative Analysis of the Legislative Role in the United Kingdom and the United States" in *Threats, Weapons and Foreign Policy Behavior: Volume 5, Sage International Yearbook of Foreign Policy Studies*, edited by Patrick J. McGowan and Charlie W. Kegley, Jr. (Beverly Hills, Calif.: Sage, 1980).

83 Laurance, "The Changing Role of Congress."

84 Haig's statement was to the Senate Foreign Relations Committee; Buckley's to the Subcommittee on International Security and Scientific Affairs, House Foreign Affairs Committee.

85 James L. Buckley, "Arms Transfers and the National Interest," an address before the meeting of the Board of Governors, Aerospace Industries Association, Williamsburg, Virginia, May 21, 1981.

Chapter 3

The Emergence of Arms Transfers as a Foreign Policy Instrument

Since 1961 revised assessments of the utility and feasibility of grant aid programs have produced dramatic shifts in the foreign assistance policies of the United States. Arms sales have gained increasing prominence as instruments of assistance to other countries. Today, the Foreign Military Sales (FMS) program is much larger, measured in dollar values, than either of the traditional aid programs, the Military Assistance Program (MAP) and economic grants and loans. By 1981, Foreign Military Sales had become the United States' major assistance program. In fiscal year 1979, $15 billion in military equipment was sold to over sixty countries. Figure 3.1 indicates the comparative size of FMS and the economic assistance program, showing the clear decline of the latter and the rise of military sales. Figure 3.1 alone strongly suggests that the United States has altered its foreign aid strategy. Figure 3.2 indicates that as the shift to military aid has occurred, the mix of military aid components has also changed. The United States is now more inclined to sell military equipment than to give it to others.

One additional comment should be made about the changing characteristics of arms sales: as with grant economic assistance and grant military assistance, the list of recipients has changed noticeably over the past three decades. Until 1964 about 80 percent of arms sales each year

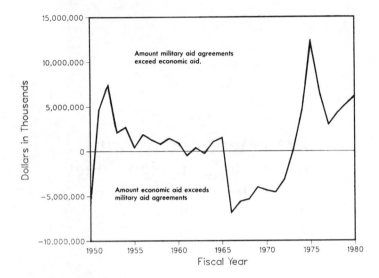

Figure 3.1. The difference between arms agreements and total economic assistance.

were to Europe, Japan, Canada, and Australia. By 1974, however, these countries accounted for only 14 percent of total arms sales[1] and Iran had become the largest recipient of FMS, purchasing 45 percent of the arms sold by the United States.

To explore the meaning of the amplification of arms sales as an instrument of U.S. foreign policy, this chapter illustrates the impressive size and growth of FMS, discusses the attitudes and goals that favored the inception of the program, and examines the factors that contributed to its increased growth.

The first substantial rise in arms sales came in fiscal year 1962, when military sales agreements jumped to almost $1.4 billion (constant dollars). Until this time arms sales had averaged about $200 million per year in the early 1950s and were about $700 million per year in the late 1950s and early 1960s. In April 1962 the concept of military exports as a government activity was institutionalized through the creation of an Office of International Logistics Negotiations (ILN) within the Office of International Security Affairs of the Department of Defense.

Why did foreign military sales emerge as a major foreign policy instrument? What factors led to its dramatic amplification? It is the thesis of this chapter that the enlarged foreign military sales effort developed from three different, but not unrelated, attempts by Congress and the Eisenhower and Kennedy administrations to find solutions to three major policy problems.

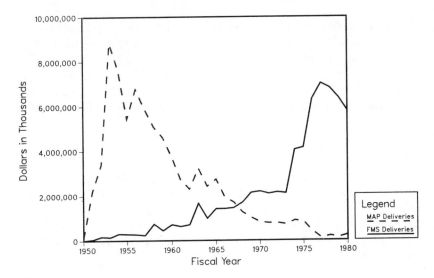

Figure 3.2. MAP and FMS deliveries worldwide (constant 1977 dollars).

The first was a search for an inexpensive economic and military assistance instrument. The second, in the 1950s and early 1960s, was an effort to deal with the United States' adverse balance of payments in the international economy. The third was the concern of the Joint Chiefs of Staff and Secretary of Defense Robert McNamara about problems in logistics cooperation and weapons standardization within the Atlantic Alliance. Related to this third problem was McNamara's attempt to reorient the defense of America's allies toward the doctrine of "flexible response."

A diverse set of actors was involved in each of these activities, and to a limited extent each involved different actors. Certainly military exports were encouraged by diverse groups for different reasons, each perceiving an expanded sales effort as contributing to the resolution of its specific problem. America's mammoth foreign military sales effort, in short, developed from a convergence of preferences regarding effective ways to resolve several policy problems.

GRANT ASSISTANCE: THE SEARCH
FOR AN ALTERNATIVE

The goals of foreign assistance derive mainly from premises legitimized during the Truman administration. One fundamental assumption was that the Soviet Union was an expansive power in world politics that could be contained ultimately only by force or deterrence. This compelled the United States to adopt a strategy of building "situations of strength," in Secretary of State Dean Acheson's phrase, primarily in Europe and secondarily in the rest of the world. Foreign aid was perceived as assisting the preservation of American security in at least three ways, according to Deputy Secretary of Defense Paul H. Nitze:

> (a) by fostering an improved climate of political independence and individual liberty; (b) by improving the ability of free countries and international organizations to deter or, if necessary, defeat Communism or Communist-supported aggression; (c) by facilitating arrangements for individual and collective security and stability in the developing free countries essential to their more rapid social, economic and political progress.[2]

Five administrations in the postwar period, and several congresses, have generally agreed on the legitimacy of these goals.[3] The greatest discussion, disagreement, and variability have focused on the best means of implementing them.

Foreign Military Sales developed out of a search for a "better" aid instrument. Prior to the beginning of the Korean War, most foreign assistance took the form of economic grants (nonreimbursable aid). The authorized funds for 1949, for example, amounted to $6.91 billion. Of this amount, 80 percent was for economic reconstruction and 20 percent for military rearmament. The year 1950 marked a shift in the means of implementing assistance goals, with emphasis now on rearmament rather than reconstruction. This shift was reflected in the aid categories; of the $8.5 billion provided in 1950, $5.7 billion was designated for the rearmament of America's allies.

The Korean War provided the occasion to expand this rearmament of U.S. allies in several ways over the decade of the fifties. While the war itself put pressure on the United States to use its arms inventories for its own immediate needs, this pressure came after the Truman administration had already begun to rearm America's European allies, an effort that was reflected in the 1949-1950 shift just noted. The opening of the Korean War, and the U.S. involvement in it, launched a broad rearmament effort intended to expand and modernize America's armed forces and to further strengthen its allies, particularly its European allies.[4] The war also led to partisan controversy over geographic priorities; for example, Republicans attacked the Truman administration for its preoccupation with Europe.

When President Eisenhower finally terminated the Korean War, several circumstances favored the expansion of military aid. First, the modernization of U.S. armed forces launched in 1950 assured that by 1953 a large stream of surplus military equipment and material could flow into foreign aid channels. Second, NATO had become relatively well organized and in need of—and capable of handling—quantities of modern equipment. Third, the Eisenhower administration's concern for strengthening allies and client states around the rim of Asia from Turkey to Korea and in Latin America assured a demand for surplus equipment. In an oversimplification characteristic of writing on arms aid, one analyst observed that the ending of the Korean War allowed the United States to convert its industrial capacities that had been mobilized during the war to supplying Europe with military equipment.[5] The increased emphasis on military equipment as a way of implementing foreign assistance goals is indicated by the fact that from 1953 to 1961, military assistance usually constituted at least half the funds provided for foreign aid.

During the Eisenhower and Kennedy administrations, the search for an effective foreign aid instrument was compounded by a parallel search for an inexpensive instrument. Although many members of the Eisenhower administration wanted to spend less on foreign aid, this desire conflicted with equally important foreign policy goals, namely, to contain Communist advances throughout the world, which required more, not less, aid. Thus, much of the search for a cheaper instrument was conducted and supported by Congress. Moreover, within Congress opposition to grant assistance[6] was particularly high among Midwestern members of the President's own party,[7] although southern Democratic opposition in the House in the late 1950s rose to as high as 50 percent of Democratic congressmen.[8]

As early as 1954 this extensive congressional sentiment against grant assistance affected the Eisenhower administration's foreign aid program. Evidently sensing congressional disquietude, the administration asked that 10 percent of the nonmilitary funds authorized be in the form of loans rather than grants. The House Foreign Affairs Committee accepted this proposal. However, from the floor of the House the bill was amended to require that 50 percent of the nonmilitary funds be in the form of loans. In the Senate a similar amendment was defeated by a vote of 57 to 53. The compromise reached during the House-Senate conference on the bill provided that 30 percent of the authorized funds should be in the form of loans. This action by Congress marked the beginning of annual attempts to reduce grant assistance and to find some substitute for it. One way for the Eisenhower administration to mollify Congress was to reduce aid funds available to Europe.

Communist advances in Indochina and the Middle East and increased anti-Americanism in Latin America had apparently convinced the administration that it should increase both military and economic aid to these areas, but the Congress seemed intent on reducing aid everywhere, not just to Europe. Noting this, the administration requested only $3.5 billion for foreign aid for fiscal 1955, nearly a billion dollars less than the amount appropriated the previous year. Funds for NATO countries were cut from $1.8 billion to only $800 million, and the cut in funds available to Europe consequently made more aid available for other parts of the world.

These events indicate a pattern of responses that was important for the future of military exports. Each succeeding year the Congress made further demands that aid to Europe (both military and economic) be cut or terminated. The cumulative effect of these demands on America's European allies eventually became considerable. Congressional attitudes also favored aid linked to security interests at the expense of economic development assistance. To justify economic assistance, therefore, the Eisenhower administration relabeled much of its economic aid "defense support" assistance to show its tie to the objectives of arms transfers. Grant military aid also faced a hostile challenge in Congress. Yet NATO countries depended on grants through the Military Assistance Program for the acquisition of modern and sophisticated weapons. Aid cuts by Congress had the effect of reducing the availability of weapons and increasing the desire of Europeans and Defense Department officials such as Henry Kuss for a solution to what Kuss called the "tremendous hiatus" in military supplies to Europe.[9]

Meanwhile, many congressmen discovered what they considered to be a superior form of assistance, Public Law 480. The Agriculture Trade and Development Act of 1954 essentially permitted the United States to transfer its agriculture surpluses to foreign countries who lacked convertible currencies to pay for them. The law makes it possible for the United States to accept inconvertible local currencies in exchange for agriculture surpluses. The currencies accepted are owned by the U.S. government,[10] and the United States may lend back to the foreign country the currency it has received. Such loans are to be used by the recipient country to purchase U.S. equipment and commodities.[11]

The idea of selling surplus agriculture products in this way was encouraged by those who were attempting to alleviate the domestic agricultural crisis. However, many also perceived that PL 480 was "not just a disposal program but a supplement to, and indeed a superior substitute for, 'money' aid as well."[12] It represented another major attempt by the Legislative Branch to compel the Executive Branch to seek alternatives to grant assistance and to search for other forms of "cost-free" aid. PL 480 appears to have created legitimacy for the idea that a sale of a commodity to a country constitutes "aid."[13]

Emphasis on loans rather than grants was given further support in the following years. In 1957 the administration decided that aid for economic development should consist of technical assistance, with the bulk of aid coming from loans for major development projects. These loans would be administered through a new Development Loan Fund (DLF). Those who were opposed to grant assistance greeted the proposal with some enthusiasm, and it was adopted. Many felt that the DLF would finally put aid on a "businesslike" basis. The early loans, however, were "soft"; that is, repayable in a currency other than the dollar. Then, as the adverse balance of payments began to develop, the United States found it necessary to demand that the loans be "hard" and repayable in U.S. currency. In 1959, President Eisenhower was compelled to insist that DLF loans be given to countries under the stipulation that funds would be used to purchase only U.S. goods. In 1961, President Kennedy insisted that all DLF loans be hard. These two presidential actions marked the final stages in the evolution of economic aid from grant assistance in money and commodities to credit assistance for the purchase of U.S. products. The development continued throughout the 1960s. By 1964, for example, the ratio of loans to grants was 70 percent to 30 percent.[14]

Because Congress and the White House were interested in a strategy that would encourage other developed nations to "share" the aid burden, the Eisenhower administration launched a concerted campaign to persuade European countries to enlarge their foreign aid programs. Also, the Senate endorsed in July 1958 a resolution introduced by Senator Mike Monroney urging the administration to consider forming an International Development Association as an institution through which other wealthy nations might share the burden of foreign aid contributions. The Monroney resolution is often cited as an example of congressional initiative in policymaking.[15] It illustrates the demand for an active congressonal role in foreign policymaking that was to become much stronger in the seventies.

Secretary of the Treasury Robert Anderson strongly urged the European nations and Japan to accept the Monroney proposal, primarily because he interpreted it as shifting the aid burden from America's shoulders.[16] In a press conference before his August 1959 trip to Europe, President Eisenhower indicated that one of the primary purposes of his visit was to encourage European leaders to make greater contributions to underdeveloped countries.[17] In September he attended a meeting of the International Monetary Fund especially to urge finance ministers from the advanced countries to give more economic assistance to the less advanced countries. In his State of the Union address in January 1960, he again made known his desire that the European nations assume more responsibility in this area. The Senate Democratic leadership gave enthusiastic support to his call for a more equal sharing of foreign aid costs among NATO allies.[18]

The Kennedy administration also perceived the effort to reduce the U.S. share of economic assistance to be important. It looked mainly to West Germany for relief in carrying the burden of foreign economic aid, pressuring Bonn in a message to NATO's Permanent Council. Simultaneously, President Kennedy reiterated Eisenhower's plea for a more equitable sharing among all developed countries of assistance costs.[19] For example, considerable pressure was put on West Germany to increase its foreign aid from about $600 million in loans tied to German purchases to approximately $1 billion in low-interest loans not requiring the purchase of German products. Moreover, as Franz Josef Strauss, West Germany's Defense Minister, revealed, the Kennedy administration asked West Germany to assume the entire burden of aid to Turkey.[20] U.S. aid to Turkey at that time was about $150 million.

The expanded Foreign Military Sales program did not develop directly from these attempts to reduce the burden of foreign aid on the U.S. Treasury, but resulted instead from the persisting inadequacy of several alternative efforts. In addition, it was facilitated by a persistent and growing skepticism toward foreign assistance within Congress and the administration during the late Eisenhower and early Kennedy years. The above review demonstrates that this skeptical attitude manifested itself in a series of actions directed toward finding a less burdensome way to implement the goals of foreign aid effectively.

INTERNATIONAL BALANCE-OF-PAYMENTS PRESSURES: THE SEARCH FOR RELIEF

By the end of the 1950s, the U.S. balance-of-payments deficit had become a major crisis for the Eisenhower administration and Congress, augmenting the motivation to reduce grant assistance, multinationalize credit assistance, and find a cheap foreign aid instrument. The excess in foreign monetary payments over receipts totaled over $10 billion during the years 1958 through 1960.[21] By 1960 foreign holdings of the dollar had surpassed America's holdings in gold for the first time in American history.[22] Moreover, there was a substantial decline in the nation's gold supply; from the end of 1957 to the beginning of 1960 the gold reserve in the Treasury had declined by nearly $5 billion.[23]

Among the causes of this mounting deficit was increased private investment by U.S. firms in foreign countries, particularly in Europe; from 1956 through 1959 these investments reached $3 billion per year. In 1954 they had totaled only $1.6 billion.[24] Another cause was foreign aid. Economic assistance in the form of grants and credits, although declining from highs in the early 1950s, amounted to about $1.6 billion per year.[25] In the minds of many economists, a third factor, one not easily described, was that the export sectors of U.S. commerce were not as dynamic as they had been in the early 1950s.[26] But by far the greatest contribution to the deficit came from increased military expenditures abroad. Foreign military expenditures had climbed from $576 million in 1950 to an average of $3 billion per year after 1958.[27]

Looking back from a vantage point twenty years later, the reaction of alarm over the adverse trade balance that appeared at the end of the fifties appears as exaggerated, connoting a certain innocence. We have come to live with trade balances much larger, particularly since the oil embargo of 1973. The White House responded to the growing deficit by issuing numerous directives requesting that agencies reduce expenditures in foreign countries. Cabinet members uttered admonitions to industry,[28] and the administration and Congress made attempts to "tie" economic assistance to the purchase of U.S. products.[29] News commentators speculated on what might develop for the security of the West if the deficit problem were not solved and on how the problem would circumscribe U.S. security policy.[30]

This was the beginning of the accumulation of Eurodollars, unrepatriated dollar credits held in Europe and elsewhere by creditors who preferred to hold dollars outside the United States than any other currency. This demand for unrepatriated dollars had not yet been anticipated. Had it been, the Eisenhower administration's resolve to stanch the outward flow of dollars very probably would have been undiminished. America's relations with Europe in the postwar era had been built on surplus trade balances. It was difficult to conceive of economic and military relationships surviving with trade balances reversed.

Faced with this historic reversal, the U.S. Treasury Department launched a concerted diplomatic effort in the fall of 1960, led by Treasury Secretary Anderson with substantial personal support from President Eisenhower, to alter the unfavorable balance-of-payments trend. It was from this particular effort that a number of officials discovered the monetary potential of military sales.

Anderson, who had become alarmed about America'a declining monetary situation, convinced Eisenhower that some form of dramatic action was imperative. On October 8, 1960, the President sent a letter to West

German Chancellor Konrad Adenauer asking that Germany assist the United States in alleviating its balance-of-payments problem. Adenauer's reply on October 21 suggested that the defense and treasury secretaries of the United States meet with those of West Germany. Accordingly, Eisenhower decided to send a delegation to Germany headed by the Secretary of the Treasury, with the assistance of Douglas Dillon, Under Secretary of State for Economic Affairs. Three weeks later the cabinet-level discussions were elevated to a "presidential mission" and expanded to include talks with top officials in London and Paris.[31] In announcing this fact, Anderson stated, "The President has instructed me to pursue with Chancellor Adenauer and other representatives of the German Republic matters of mutual interest in the international financial field, including *the cost of U.S. Troops in West Germany* and assistance to developing countries."[32]

Anderson had been active in getting the President to accept the view that unless the allies, particularly West Germany, made a substantially larger contribution to allied financial costs, the United States would be compelled to reduce its troop strength in Europe. In 1959, reportedly, Treasury and Budget Bureau officials almost succeeded in persuading Eisenhower to withdraw at least two divisions and seven fighter-bomber squadrons. Only strong opposition from General Lauris Norstad, Supreme Allied Commander, Europe, and the Department of State, had dissuaded him.[33] By fall 1960, however, the administration was less opposed to such drastic measures. In a press conference prior to Anderson's departure for Europe, the President uttered a veiled threat to NATO members when he said that a troop cut would be a decision he would not like to make, but "I do think that the time is coming when all of us will have to study very carefully what should be our proper proportion of the load."[34]

Several measures were taken that indicated the administration was serious about decreasing the dollar deficit. A presidential directive was issued limiting offshore expenditures of the federal government. This action was intended to save nearly a billion dollars per year. The Secretary of Defense was instructed to reduce dependents overseas from 484,000 to a limit of 200,000. Military expenditures abroad were to be kept to a minimum. Foreign goods were to be replaced by U.S. goods whenever possible. The Secretary of State was directed to reduce personnel in other countries. Foreign aid agencies were to place "emphasis on financing goods and services of United States origin."[35] Even the Central Intelligence Agency was ordered to cut its overseas personnel.

The most drastic action attempted was Secretary Anderson's proposal that West Germany reimburse the United States $600 million per year for America's troop deployment costs in that country. The Germans reacted negatively. They considered such a direct payment for troop costs to be a "touchy political issue" domestically.[36] Anderson made this proposal during a conference with five German cabinet ministers in Bonn. One member of the U.S. delegation, Henry Kuss, indicated that the Germans interpreted Anderson's proposal to be similar in nature to "reparations."[37] Adenauer and Finance Minister Erhard expressed their willingness to consider other alternatives to "help the dollar." However, Anderson became adamant in demanding direct payments for troop costs; he refused to entertain proposals for "indirect payments."[38] Evidently he sought a form of payment that would reduce total dollar expenditure figures in the annual defense budget and the total federal budget.

It appears that Defense Minister Strauss recognized this budget factor in Anderson's position, although not early enough to deal with it at the November meetings in Bonn. According to Kuss, he pointed out to lower-level members of the American team that the United States and the Federal Republic had complementary problems. Germany had a large requirement for more advanced military equipment, and the United States had a need to increase its exports to Germany. If they developed a system of cooperative logistics, he suggested, the consequence would be to offset the U.S. balance-of-payments deficit.[39] It would also make possible reduced defense expenditures by the U.S. government that would be reflected in annual appropriations. This was the origin of the idea of offset payments as support for U.S. troops in Germany.

Kuss mentioned his discussion with Strauss to Anderson and Dillon during their trip back. "The day after we landed in Washington," he later recalled, "I was ordered to return to Germany and expand on the idea."[40] Accordingly, a five-man delegation of State, Treasury, and Defense personnel arrived in Bonn in early January 1961 for further talks. Again the Germans suggested that, among other things, a huge purchase of American arms might help the dollar.[41] The American negotiators responded by requesting that West Germany agree to purchase $600 million per year in military equipment from the United States.

Initially the Germans were shocked at the magnitude of the request; it was the same figure that Anderson had proposed, and they were reluctant to make such a huge commitment. Throughout the spring and summer of 1961, however, talks concerning other aspects of an "offset agreement" progressed well. In October, when President Kennedy sent U.S. Deputy Secretary of Defense Roswell L. Gilpatric to Germany to encourage the plan, Gilpatric and Strauss quickly reached an agreement for a German purchase of $600 million worth of U.S.-produced military equipment.[42]

The Anderson initiative had the effect of directing American problem-solving efforts to what became the offset arrangement. Seven significant additional measures appear to have been considered and at least partially implemented to ameliorate the dollar deficit. One was for the United States to devalue the dollar. In an election year such an unpopular action seemed infeasible. Moreover, the European nations would not have supported it because they had great quantities of dollars, and to solve the deficit problem, European cooperation was deemed essential.

A second possiblity was to alter tariffs and investment laws to encourage European investors to invest in U.S. industries. However, the probability of success of this option was low because it was anticipated that a considerable time would lapse before it had an impact; in any case, its impact was likely to be small. At the time, investment opportunities were judged more attractive in Europe than in the United States, and U.S. tariff reductions were considered unlikely to alter much their relative attractiveness.

A third possibility was to liberalize international trade through *mutual* reductions in tariffs. The Eisenhower administration had attempted to do this. Its efforts had failed, due largely to domestic opposition in the United States. While support for reciprocal tariff reduction negotiations remained strong, and the setback from protectionist interests was considered temporary, it was clear that a long and tedious path lay ahead that would require a concerted fight to get congressional approval for the needed authority to negotiate,[43] followed by extended negotiations.

Another option, discussed earlier, was to encourage Europeans to increase their own foreign aid programs and to grant credit assistance not tied to the purchase of the donor's products. The Germans, after considerable pressure from the United States, did increase their foreign assistance from $600 million in 1960 to $800 million in 1961. Increased European aid would enable the United States to reduce its aid in the future. For the time being, however, it would have no direct effect on the balance-of-payments problem. It would contribute to lower U.S. assistance costs and lower expenditure totals only in the future. Many European nations already contributed more economic assistance than did the United States, relative to population and gross national product. It was considered unlikely that they could be persuaded to increase their contributions further, particularly if those increases became the occasion for further U.S. reductions.

International monetary reform was also among the tools considered. The deficit problem had developed in part because interest rates were higher in Europe than in the United States, making it attractive for U.S. private investors to send their dollars overseas. In 1959, Great

Britain and France, in an effort to discourage the private dollar flow to Europe, actually made reductions in the official discount rates of interest. But this action also had little impact in reducing U.S. private investment on the continent,[44] and therefore little affect on the net outward flow of dollars from the United States.

A sixth possible measure, one that was also adopted, consisted of direct actions to reduce current U.S. government and private expenditures abroad. Measures were taken to reduce operations and maintenance dollar payments for U.S. military forces in Europe and to reduce dollar payments in Europe by U.S. military and civilian officials and even by tourists. It was hoped that in the first year these measures would save a billion dollars. But this approach, too, had limited potential, for it was essentially a stop-gap measure. It was doubtful that the reductions could be sustained without severe adverse consequences for the effectiveness of U.S. programs in Europe, and even more doubtful that they could be expanded. The problem was that nonmilitary expenditures abroad were relatively small, and that a substantial reduction of military expenditures would require troop cuts. In the administration and Congress, it was feared that such withdrawals would destroy NATO's efficacy by setting a precedent for other allied countries to do likewise. NATO already was 20 percent below its troop strength goals. President Kennedy was adamantly opposed to this option and made his views about quite clear.

A seventh way to decrease the trade deficit was to make U.S. industry more competitive in export trade. The administration issued a few admonitions to private industry to expand its export trade but took little effective action to bolster the competitive position of American business abroad.

None of the preceding options offered much prospect of obtaining immediate relief from balance-of-payments pressures. In comparison, the sale of military equipment had considerable potential for reducing the trade deficit, for as military grant assistance was gradually curtailed by Congress, Europeans—especially West Germans—were willing to obtain new equipment and supplies by purchasing them from the United States, where much of the sophisticated equipment desired by other states was produced. Here, at least, the United States had a favorable market advantage. In addition, the military offset agreement was a tool administrators could control; rather than relying on industry to initiate the export of military items, they could themselves intervene by arranging for increased sales through diplomatic negotiations.

Kennedy viewed a program of expanded exports generated by government initiatives as a primary way to solve the deficit problem. In a message to the Congress in February 1961, he said: "In seeking overall equilibrium, we must place maximum emphasis on expanding exports ... and the Government must play a more vigorous part in helping to enlarge foreign markets for American goods and services."[45] In order for the government to play a "vigorous part" in export expansion, he directed the Secretary of Defense to "urge the purchase of new weapons and weapons systems by those of our allies who are financially capable of doing so."

An expanded military sales program, moreover, interested not only those concerned with the international monetary position of the nation. Defense officials encouraged the effort because it appeared necessary to increase the collective military strength of America's allies and implement a revised strategy for NATO that relied more heavily on conventional forces in case of war. Political leaders, concerned about public support for defense policies and expenditures also supported it as a way to redistribute the burden of defense costs with our allies, particularly within NATO, and to reduce or forestall the growing demand for the withdrawal of U.S. troops stationed in Europe.

ALLIED LOGISTICAL PROBLEMS: THE SEARCH FOR COORDINATED WEAPONS SYSTEMS

While officials in the Executive Branch and Congress were searching for alternatives to grant assistance, and for solutions to the balance-of-payments deficit, others were becoming concerned about the lack of integration among the several different logistical systems of America's allies. The most salient manifestation of this concern developed out of events surrounding the 1961 Berlin crisis. On July 25, 1961, President Kennedy responded to Soviet Premier Nikita Khrushchev's threat to turn over the access routes to Berlin to East German officials by, among other actions, calling the reserves to active-duty status and announcing a troop strength increase of 25 percent. The mobilization during the crisis compelled officials to obtain information about allied logistics.

Defense Secretary McNamara requested of the Joint Chiefs of Staff a report on the state of NATO's logistics system as well as a report on what weapons would be needed to augment the forces of America's allies should it become imperative to do so quickly. The chiefs replied that they were unable to determine precisely what the allies had in terms of weapons systems. Only in Turkey and South Korea did the United States have adequate information about its allies' logistics.[46] During the crisis it became apparent that each nation in the Atlantic Alliance had different kinds of equipment, with different specifications, to perform similar functions. One NATO member was using no fewer than nine different rifles.[47] Each nation had its separate supply depots. Consequently, one allied army would have a shortage of an item while another would have surplus. The chiefs perceived this lack of integration to be dangerous in the event of war.

But how did this lack of integration develop, and why did the United States have so little information about the logistical systems of its European allies? Primarily because each ally had a large variety of supply sources. In the early and middle 1950s, the lack of standardization had been minimal simply because the Europeans depended to a great extent on the U.S. Military Assistance Program for their supplies of major weapons systems—for example, in 1953 MAP deliveries to NATO countries, excluding Turkey and Greece, exceeded $2.4 billion, but by FY 1962 this sum had declined to less than $170 million.

Military grant assistance to Europe declined rather precipitately in the late 1950s, since Congress was intent on reducing military assistance to that area, as noted in Chapter 2. To reiterate, in 1959 the Senate Appropriations Committee added to the FY 1960 Military Assistance appropriation a provision for the administration "to cut off military assistance progressively to countries capable of providing and maintaining their own military forces."[48] In 1960 Congress prohibited new commitments of military grant assistance to West Germany, the United Kingdom, and Luxembourg; in 1961 new commitments to France were prohibited.

As long as the United States had been the major supplier of weapons to these countries, the Department of Defense had had relatively adequate information on what weapons the allies had, their quantity, and their state of usefulness. American grant assistance to Europe also provided for standard weapons throughout the alliance. Defense Department spokesmen thus interpreted the 1961 logistics problem to be a consequence of congressional attempts to reduce MAP for Europe. Said Deputy Assistant Secretary Kuss, "The cooperative logistics problem actually developed from the gap that resulted from congressional pressure to reduce grant assistance. When it was reduced, then we didn't know what our allies had—we no longer had logistics cooperation."[49] To remedy the situation, the Joint Chiefs of Staff recommended to McNamara that an office be organized to deal with the "coordination of allied logistics."

Kennedy gave further impetus to the creation of an office to coordinate and monitor logistics among America's allies. The President was disturbed when France, in 1961, sold Mirage fighters to Australia. He questioned how the United States had allowed a situation to develop whereby an ally as friendly as Australia would procure its weapons from

France. He asked McNamara to have the problem studied.[50] Accordingly, in the summer of 1961 a task force was appointed, headed by the President's Special Assistant for National Security Affairs, McGeorge Bundy. It included Paul Nitze, Assistant Secretary of Defense for International Security Affairs, Henry Kuss, who served under Nitze, and several members of an interest group for defense industries, the National Security Industrial Association. This task force recommended that an office be organized to handle logistics coordination. In April 1962, as noted earlier, the concept of foreign military sales was institutionalized through an Office of International Logistics Negotiations formed within the Defense Department. Kuss was appointed its head and became a conspicuously aggressive promoter of arms sales to Europe.

FACTORS IN THE CONTINUED GROWTH OF FOREIGN MILITARY SALES

This explanation of how military sales were amplified from under $350 million a year in the 1950s to a program overshadowing economic or military grant assistance would be incomplete without consideration of the factors that sustained the program once it was institutionalized. Basically, those factors that led to the program's inception continued to encourage its growth. The balance-of-payments deficit remained substantial throughout the 1960s, compelling decision-makers to develop and use a variety of instruments to reduce it. Congress continued to reduce military grant assistance and to press for alternatives to grant assistance. Senator Frank Church expressed a typical congressional sentiment of the early 1960s when he said, "For three years now I have been trying to get the bill amended to provide that no further grants of aid shall be made to countries that the President finds are fully capable of purchasing, without undue burden to their economies, the aid proposed to be given."[51] Similarly, in 1967, looking retrospectively at her support for the sales effort in the 1960s, Representative Edith Kelly, a member of the Foreign Affairs Committee, said, "I should say at this point that one of the key considerations which influenced my actions in these instances [congressional votes to expand the authority of FMS] and which I am certain was also in the mind of other members of the Committee on Foreign Affairs, was our desire to achieve a more equitable distribution of the burden of our mutual defense undertaking."[52] Congressional demands for equalization of defense costs among America's allies were a primary force in the expansion of the sales effort.

Another contributing factor was the Kennedy administration's revision of the basic defense strategy for the West. The Secretary of Defense, in particular, feared that the Atlantic Alliance had relied too heavily on nuclear weapons for deterrence of aggression. Wanting to expand the means of responding to a Soviet challenge to Europe, McNamara proposed that the United States and Europe increase their conventional forces to provide for a more "flexible response."

In October 1961 Roswell Gilpatric was sent to Europe to convince the NATO members of the wisdom of McNamara's strategy and to encourage them to increase their conventional forces. He also made it clear that Washington would not pay for this buildup, but that it would welcome purchases of weapons produced in the United States.[53] It is difficult to measure precisely how many European purchases of American arms resulted from this revision of strategy. From FY 1962 to FY 1966 they exceeded $3.5 billion, while sales to Europe in the FY 1950-FY 1961 period had never exceeded $400 million per year and in more than half of those years were less than $100 million. Thus, European purchases of American arms were significantly higher than their pre-1961 levels.

The Nixon Doctrine and Beyond

By 1968, the Guam Doctrine, or Nixon Doctrine, gave even further impetus to the growth of FMS. In a speech in Guam that became the primary reference point for the Nixon Doctrine, President Nixon states, "In cases involving other types of aggressive (other than nuclear) attacks, we shall furnish military aid and economic assistance when requested in accordance with our treaty commitments. But we shall look to the nation directly threatened to assume the primary responsibility of providing the manpower for its defense."[54] Somewhat later, in his 1970 State of the Union message, Nixon said: "The nations of each part of the world should assume the primary responsibility for their own well-being; and they themselves should determine the terms of that well-being."[55] In testimony before Congress in 1970, Deputy Secretary of Defense David Packard declared that these two statements of the President required that "we must continue, if requested, to give or to sell them [i.e., allies] the tools they need for this bigger load we are urging them to assume."

Associated with the Nixon Doctrine was Congress's continued drive to encourage more "burdensharing" by America's allies and to find a substitute for grant assistance. The Senate Foreign Relations Committee declared the Foreign Assistance Bill of 1973 to be a "major overhaul" of foreign aid. Reported by a vote of 14 to 3, the bill provided that military grant assistance would be phased out in four years. In addition, during those four years all grant recipients would be required to pay 25 percent of the amount of the total grant to the United States. The local currency generated would be used by the United States to meet its aid costs in the recipient country.[56] This reform, Committee Chairman J. William Fulbright explained, was designed to require "true burden sharing which is the basic meaning of the Nixon Doctrine."[57] The Senate sustained the Foreign Relations Committee's move to replace grants with sales by a vote of 50 to 42. The House also voted 210 to 193 to replace grants with sales.

Even though President Carter committed his administration early and conspicuously to arms transfer restraint, and placed rigid limitations on his administration's use of arms sales, they remained an important instrument of U.S. foreign policy during his administration. The puzzling dichotomy between intentions and practice can be explained on the basis of the review presented in this chapter of persistent trends in U.S. foreign policy since the fifties that have loaded on arms sales more and more of the functions previously performed by other instruments of U.S. policy. These trends have been reinforced by trends in the external world, the international system, that have reduced the U.S. government's ability to control external events: (1) an increased number of nations with security problems that were only marginally related to the East/West confrontation; (2) the emergence of nonindustrialized economic superpowers without the industrial capability to prodce sophisticated weapons systems but with large amounts of capital and resources with which to bargain with arms producers; (3) arms supply competitors in Western Europe vulnerable to the nonindustrial economic superpowers and compelled by domestic economic considerations to sell arms; and (4) a perceived reduction in the U.S. government's ability to respond to friends' and allies' assessments of threats to them except through arms transfers.

The Nixon Doctrine, or what it came to mean, had become a central element of U.S. foreign policy that the Carter administration did not in practice repudiate. The United States, for a variety of reasons, was unwilling or unable to respond to perceived threats to friendly governments in any way other than through arms sales. Having all but abandoned grant military assistance and having abandoned the practices of bolstering allies with new deployments of U.S. forces and new collective security alliances, the United States had few measures available to it to assist them militarily, even to assist them to assist themselves. Without a corresponding decrease in threats perceived by friendly powers or in the worldwide demand for arms, increasingly the main way the United States could demonstrate commitment to Iran, Saudi Arabia, Israel, Egypt, Jordan, South Korea, Taiwan, Spain, and other friendly countries was through arms sales. The main way the United States could get agreement among conflicting nations was to promise arms as compensation for concessions made. An example was the aid promised Egypt and Israel after the Camp David accords. A major instrument by which the United States could encourage moderation in oil-pricing policy was to deliver arms to those nations with the power to limit prices. The United States could offset international payments deficits with oil-producing countries by trading items those countries desired for the oil the United States desired. Lacking a desire for more direct involvement in Asia or Africa, arms transfers remained an available measure to counter Soviet penetration in those continents for President Carter as well as for his predecessors, even thought he and his spokesmen might state the nature of the threat and of the desire of response in different terms. Increasingly, also, arms transfers had become a means for discouraging certain nations from developing nuclear weapons. Political and interest group leaders in the United States and in Western Europe—and, we may presume, their equivalents in the Soviet bloc—favor arms production and exports for economic reasons. Arms transfers have been supported as an important instrument for generating employment and a means of reducing technology costs and weapons development costs. Despite its goal of arms transfer restraint and its public and diplomatic support of that goal, the Carter administration found that because of the limited number of instruments available to it for dealing with international problems, arms transfers were simply too useful for too many purposes to be extensively curtailed.

In effect, the Nixon Doctrine, by any other name, may be a continuing and is a major impetus toward the continued use of arms transfers by the Reagan administration. President Carter attempted to use arms transfers as an "exceptional instrument" of foreign policy. It is clear that President Reagan intends to use arms transfers as a primary instrument of foreign policy, particularly as an instrument of containment. Commitment to the containment of Soviet power has been a constant theme of the Reagan administration, as Secretary of State Alexander Haig stated:

A major focus of American policy must be the Soviet Union, not because of ideological preoccupation but simply because Moscow is the greatest source of international insecurity today. Let us be plain about it: Soviet promotion of violence as the instrument of change constitutes the greatest danger to world peace ... Soviet policy seeks to exploit aspirations for change in order to create conflict justifying the use of force and even invasion.[58]

Haig noted that Soviet goals could be frustrated by strengthening America's friends and allies. In testimony before the Senate Foreign Relations Committee, he indicated how useful arms transfers could be for containment:

As we strengthen these states, we strengthen ourselves, and ... we do so more effectively at less cost. Friendly states can help to deter threats before they escalate into a world shaking crisis. The issue is not whether a local state can singlehandedly resist a Soviet assault. Rather, it is whether it can make that assault more costly, more complicated and therefore potentially less likely to occur.[59]

Speaking in May 1981 before the Board of Governors of the Aerospace Industries Association, Under Secretary of State James L. Buckley insisted that the arms transfer policies of Congress in the past ten years and the Carter administration in the past four years had prompted "an American withdrawal from world responsibilities that contributed to a dramatic shift in global power relationships."[60] Buckley charged that the previous administration had failed to see the importance of strong allies and friends and had "adopted policies toward the transfer of arms to friends and allies that substituted theology for a healthy sense of self-preservation."[61] The Reagan leadersip was convinced that the Carter restraint policy had undermined U.S. influence, undermined the credibility of U.S. commitments, made the U.S. appear as an unreliable and fitful partner of those countering Soviet influence, and undercut "the capabilities of strategically-located nations in whose ability to defend themselves we have the most immediate and urgent self-interest."[62]

To implement the containment of the Soviet Union through arms transfers, the Reagan administration, in its first five months, promised Saudi Arabia sixty-two F-15 Eagle fighters as well as the Airborne Warning and Control System (AWACS). It offered Pakistan a $3 billion aid package that included an offer to sell that country a F-16 fighter to counter the threat posed to Pakistan as a result of the Soviet presence in Afghanistan. By June 1981 the administration also indicated it was considering a reversal of the long-standing U.S. policy of attempting to prevent sophisticated arms from being introduced into Latin America: it prepared to sell F-16 fighters to Venezuela. Officials of the Reagan administration said that the Venezuelan request was being viewed sympathetically because of President Lois Herrera Campin's full support for efforts to counter Soviet and Cuban advances in Central America.[63] Secretary Haig, in Peking on June 16, 1981, announced another important change in U.S. arms transfer policy in declaring that the United States would consider requests from China to purchase such items. This declaration reversed U.S. policy against sales of "lethal" weapons to China.

These and other actions by the Reagan administration indicate that it is willing and eager to expand arms sales for a variety of reasons— certainly including the variety of reasons previously invoked, such as balance of payments, standardization, and the support of regional autonomy and stability. There are forces that may act as serious constraints on an expanded use of arms transfers by the Reagan Administration. They will be considered later. In mid-1982, however, it appeared that the Reagan commitment to the use of arms transfers for containment would be sufficiently high to assert that arms sales, having emerged as a primary foreign policy instrument in the late 1960s, would remain a key instrument in the 1980s.

NOTES

1 United States Arms Control and Disarmament Agency, *The International Transfer of Conventional Arms: Report to Congress, Committee on Foreign Affairs*, 93rd Congress, 2nd Session, 1974; for 1974 figures, see *Congressional Quarterly Weekly Report*, March 29, 1975, p. 657.

2 United States, Senate, Committee on Banking and Currency, Hearings on 9, 1155: *Export-Import Bank Participation and Financing in Credit Sales of Defense Articles*, 90th Congress, 1st Session, 1967, p. 25.

3 Some roll-call studies have shown a slow decline in congressional support for the goals of foreign assistance. See, for example, Charles O. Lerche, *The Uncertain South* (New York: Quandrangle, 1964), pp. 58-94.

4 This point is elaborated in Paul Y. Hammond's "NSC-68: Prologue to Rearmament," Part III of W. R. Schilling, G. H. Snyder, and P. Y. Hammond, *Strategy, Politics and Defense Budgets* (New York: Columbia University Press, 1962).

5 Harold A. Hovey, *United States Military Assistance* (New York: Praeger, 1965), p. 10.

6 Differentiated from other forms of assistance in that it is nonreimbursable aid.

7 Leroy N. Rieselbach, *The Roots of Isolationism: Congressional Voting and Presidential Leadership in Foreign Policy* (Indianapolis: Bobbs-Merrill, 1966), pp. 105-139.

8 Lerche, *The Uncertain South*, p. 62.

9 United States, House, Committee on Foreign Affairs, *Hearings on the Foreign Assistance Act of 1964*, 88th Congress, 2nd Session, 1964, p. 509.

10 For a discussion of this arrangement, see Robert E. Asher, *Grants, Loans and Local Currencies: Their Role in Foreign Aid* (Washington, D.C.: Brookings Institution, 1961), pp. 10-13.

11 Memorandum submitted by C. Douglas Dillon, Under Secretary of State for Economic Affairs, U.S. Congress, House, Committee on Appropriations, *Hearings on Mutual Security Appropriations for 1960*, 86th Congress, 1st Session, 1959, pp. 364-376.

12 Andrew F. Westwood, *Foreign Aid in a Foreign Policy Framework* (Washington, D.C.: Brookings Institution, 1966), p. 51.

13 Ibid. p. 52.
14 United States, Senate, Committee on Foreign Relations, *Hearings on the Foreign Assistance Act of 1965*, 89th Congress, 1st Session, 1965, p. 103.
15 A major study of it is James A. Robinson's *The Monroney Resolution: Congressional Initiative in Foreign Policy Making* (New York: Henry Holt, 1959).
16 *New York Times* (September 30, 1959), p. 36.
17 Ibid. (August 26, 1959), p. 16.
18 Ibid. (January 8, 1960), p. 2.
19 Ibid. (January 17, 1961), p. 2.
20 Speech before the Overseas Press Club, New York, January 17, 1961; for the text, see *New York Times* (January 18, 1961).
21 "Statement of President Eisenhower," *Department of State Bulletin* (December 5, 1960), p. 860.
22 Richard N. Gardner, "Strategy for the Dollar," *Foreign Affairs* (April 1960), p. 433.
23 "Statement of President Eisenhower," p. 860.
24 William B. Dale, *The Foreign Deficit of the United States* (Stanford, Calif.: International Industrial Development Center, Stanford Research Institute, 1960), p. 46.
25 Robert B. Anderson, "The Balance of Payments Problem," *Foreign Affairs* (April 1960), p. 424.
26 Gardner, "Strategy for the Dollar," p. 433.
27 Statistics are from U.S. Department of Commerce; cited by Dale, *Foreign Deficit*, p. 46.
28 See, for example, Anderson, "The Balance of Payments Problem," p. 429.
29 See Westwood, *Foreign Aid in a Foreign Policy Framework*, p. 81, and Gardner, "Strategy for the Dollar," p. 433.
30 See, for example, C. L. Sulzberger, "Mr. Eisenhower's last and Cruelest Dilemma," *New York Times* (November 22, 1960).
31 *New York Times* (November 15, 1960), p. 25.
32 Ibid. (November 16, 1960), p. 1 (emphasis added).
33 Sulzberger, "Mr. Eisenhower's Dilemma," p. 5.
34 Text of press conference, *New York Times* (November 15, 1960), p. 25.
35 "Statement of President Eisenhower," pp. 860-863. For an examination of these measures, see Walter S. Salent, et al., *The United States Balance of Payments in 1968* (Washington, D.C.: Brookings Institutin, 1963), pp. 193-204.
36 *New York Times* (November 22, 1960), p. 1.
37 Personal interview with Henry J. Kuss, former Deputy Assistant Secretary of Defense for International Security Affairs, April 1, 1970.
38 *New York Times* (November 24, 1960), p. 1.
39 Kuss interview.
40 Ibid.
41 *New York Times* (January 9, 1961), p. 64.
42 Ibid. (October 29, 1961), p. 1.
43 Ibid. (November 13, 1960), p. 31.
44 Ibid.
45 United States, House, Document 84, 87th Congress, 1st Session, February 6, 1961.
46 Kuss interview; see also James L. Trainor, "Can the U.S. Maintain the Momentum of Its Export Sales?" *Armed Forces Management* (January 1967), p. 36.
47 George Thayer, *The War Business: The International Trade in Armaments* (New York: Simon & Schuster, 1969), p. 183.
48 Quoted by Hovey, *United States Military Assistance*, p. 77.
49 Kuss interview; see also *Hearings on the Foreign Assistance Act of 1964*, p. 509.

50 Kuss interview.
51 United States, Senate, Committee on Foreign Relations, *The Foreign Assistance Act of 1963*. 88th Congress, 1st Session, 1963, p. 130.
52 *Congressional Record* (July 27, 1967), p. 20515.
53 *New York Times* (October 30, 1961), p. 30.
54 *Hearings on H.R. 15628: To Amend the Foreign Military Sales Act*, p. 2.
55 Ibid.
56 United States, Senate, Report No. 93-189: *Foreign Military Sales and Assistance Act*, 93rd Congress, 1st Session, June 1973.
57 *Congressional Record*, (June 25, 1973), p. S.11900.
58 Address by Secretary Haig before the American Society of Newspaper Editors in Washington, D.C., on April 24, 1981, printed in *Current Policy* (No. 275), United States Department of State.
59 Statement of Secretary of State Alexander Haig before the Senate Foreign Relations Committee, March 19, 1981.
60 Address of James L. Buckley, Under Secretary of State for Security Assistance, Science and Technology, before the Meeting of the Board of Governors Aerospace Industries Associations, Williamsburg, Virginia (May 21, 1981.)
61 Ibid.
62 Ibid.
63 Philip Taubman, "U.S. Considering Venezuelean Bid for Jet Fighters," *New York Times* (June 3, 1981), p. 1.

Chapter 4

Decisionmaking for Arms Transfers

In this chapter we assess the dynamics of the decisionmaking process by which the U.S. government chooses to sell or not sell arms to other nations. We focus here on the control mechanisms that have emerged within the agencies processing arms sales decisions. This concentration on the decision-and-control process is important for several reasons. First, the U.S. government has increasingly relied on arms sales as a major foreign policy instrument in recent years. Second, most of the limited but growing academic literature on arms transfers assumes a "state-as-actor" approach;[1] thus, U.S. government activity is assessed solely in terms of decision outputs. Third, considerable popular and political discussion assumes that there are no controls on U.S. Arms exports, when in fact there are fairly strong ones. President Carter's early campaign speeches, for example, understated the control machinery already in place. During his administration, restraining controls were much strengthened. Yet, recent discussions make the same mistake that candidate Carter made about the restraints on arms sales that are a legacy of the Carter administration. While the development of better controls over conventional arms transfers may be desirable, pursuit of this objective should be informed by knowledge of the control procedure now functioning—of its strengths, weaknesses, and frustrations.

To describe the decision process as it actually works, we found it necessary to do two things that, in retrospect, were obvious yet conspicuous for their previous neglect. The first was to draw together and state in an orderly way the extraordinary number of formal constraints—in the form of criteria and procedures—that register previous congressional and Executive Branch concern about arms transfers. The second was to determine from participants how the remarkably complex processes of control mandated as a result of these concerns actually work. To this end, from February 1978 through January 1982, we interviewed over one hundred officials in the U.S. State Department, the Arms Control and Disarmament Agency, the National Security Council Staff, The Office of The Secretary of Defense, and the various services, as well as officials of the unified commands headquarters and department of Defense field personnel in twenty-seven countries in the military advisory groups. Here we describe the U.S. system of arms sales decisionmaking, identify the actors and the roles they perform, and describe the stages of the arms transfer decision process. We assess current trends and problems of the present control system and assess how the arms sales decisionmaking process might be improved.

The U.S. security assistance supply system functions in a high-demand environment externally. Recent trends in U.S. politics, however, have created domestic pressure to restrain the use of this instrument. More and more members of Congress have become critics of security assistance. Some have opposed security assistance to specific regions or countries; many oppose the transfer of certain weapons. Considerable numbers feel that the Department of Defense and the Military Assistance Advisory Groups (MAAGs)[2] "push" arms worldwide and that the Executive Branch arms transfer decisionmaking process is "out of control." Moreover, there has been great concern about the activities of commercial sales representatives. In addition, Congress has voiced displeasure with the management, control, and coordination of security assistance organizations.

In contrast, then, to the high-demand international environment, the U.S. security assistance system operates domestically in an environment that accentuates the pressures for restraint. A fundamental problem for the system is to adapt to this conflict. In the late seventies, the Carter administration and the Congress directed considerable attention to providing strict control of U.S. public- and private-sector activities that might encourage a demand for arms. (Congressional action had actually begun somewhat earlier.) An attempt was also made to induce other major arms suppliers to undertake similar efforts at limiting supply to restrain demand-inducing activities. The main theme of the Carter administration's approach toward managing security assistance, however, was self-control. To understand how that approach was applied, and to what effect, we shall now turn to a description of functions and actors.

THE SECURITY ASSISTANCE SYSTEM

The decision to sell or grant U.S. military hardware, supplies, and support services to foreign governments is the result of a complex process involving various elements in the U.S. government. Those elements perform different functions and become involved at different points in the process. From the identification of a need or want on the part of the potential buyer or grant recipient (which itself is the result of an elaborate process of determining what the United States is willing to provide), to the delivery of hardware and the commodities and services that will support absorption of the new equipment into the recipient's armed services, and finally to monitoring (where appropriate) the recipient's use of that equipment, elements of the Defense and State departments and other agencies, in Washington and in the field, perform many tasks.

Six Functions of Arms Sales Decisionmaking

To provide security assistance as a goal-directed activity, the U.S. government, or any provider, must accomplish certain minimal, basic functions. They may be performed by several actors within the provider government at the same time, and some may shift over time from one group of actors to another. It is important to emphasize, however, that no matter who performs the following functions, they must be accomplished if a security assistance program is to be effective. (1) recognition of a recipient's needs and wants, (2) initial review of a government's request for information about a weapon system or a service, (3) policy review of a purchase request; (4) negotiation and development of an agreement; (5) execution of an agreement, and (6) "feedback" and evaluation concerning recipient use of the assistance received.

1. Recognition of a country's wants and needs begins the security assistance process. Wants may be equated with the expression of a foreign government that it desires certain equipment or services from the United States. Need, on the other hand, can be defined as an estimation of what another government ought to have in order to meet certain minimal (or other) defense requirements deemed in the United States' interest. Sometimes the United States advises allies or friends of basic deficiencies in their defense plans or posture.

2. The second function—initial review—was performed informally in the past, but the Carter administration placed it within a more formal process. All U.S. government personnel and, under certain circumstances, commercial representatives who deal with foreign states—other than with NATO members (except Iceland, Portugal, Greece, and Turkey), the developed countries of Western Europe (except Spain), Japan, Australia, or New Zealand—must obtain prior approval from the State Department before responding either to a request for information about a weapon system (including planning data) or to a request to negotiate a weapon-system agreement.
3. The third function consists of a policy review of the impact of the proposed security assistance on international security, on the potential recipient, on the immediate regional balance of power, and on U.S. security. This function involves the greatest diversity of actors.
4. Security assistance, when in the form of cash or credit sales, involves considerable bilateral negotiation. Intricate arrangements take place as each party determines its responsibilities for payment, for delivery, and for operation of the equipment or utilization of the services. In the case of grants, less negotiation occurs. The fourth function, then, negotiating and developing a contract, determines the nature of the assistance to be transferred or acquired and the conditions under which this will occur.
5. The fifth function, of course, consists of performing the agreed responsibilities. This includes not only responsibilities of the supplier for delivery, but also for service, training, infrastructure, and spare parts, where applicable. The recipient may also have certain responsibilities concerning end item utilization, prohibition against retransfers, and so forth.
6. Finally, feedback and evaluation have to do with observing, reporting, and analyzing end uses; establishing and maintaining familiarity with the recipient's plans and objectives; and reporting on the impact of security assistance transfers. It should be noted that the current ability of the system to perform these tasks is limited.

Primary Actors in Security Assistance

Many actors, playing varied roles, are involved in performing these six basic functions. Many of these actors participate at several stages of the decision process and contribute to the performance of two or more of the six functions listed. Others have very limited tasks and are involved in only one stage. Collectively, they constitute the system.

For the convenience of the reader, we will merely identify the primary actors at this point; we will explain their roles as each function is examined. It should be recognized that the system is dynamic; the actors' roles and responsibilities change over time and with the issues.

In some arms transfer cases, certain actors may have broad discretion, while in other cases those same actors may be bypassed. The fact that such variations occur in the way the security assistance system within the U.S. government operates is scarcely surprising. Any functional system of any complexity would have similarly dynamic qualities. However, understanding how these variables work—for instance, to reinforce or frustrate the goals of policy control—is crucial to understanding the policy control that system is intended to effect.

The principal field personnel in the recipient countries are the ambassadors and their political counselors; Military Assistance Advisory Groups; defense attaches; temporary field teams that survey, train, manage, and negotiate; and privately employed sales representatives of commercial firms. In addition, industries may send specialists to perform services or to provide advice similar to the counsel provided by the temporary teams of the Department of Defense. On certain construction projects, the Army Corps of Engineers may be in the field. At the regional level, the security assistance staffs of the regional unified commands (in Stuttgart, Pearl Harbor, and Panama) monitor and support the country team missions.

Within the Department of State, a number of officials are involved in security assistance. The Secretary of State has primary authority; the Under Secretary for Security Assistance, Science and Technology has the task of constant supervision; and the Director of the Bureau of Politico-Military Affairs is more directly involved in day-to-day decisions. But the Office of Security Assistance and Sales (PM/SAS) and the Office of Munitions Control (OMC), within the Bureau of Politico-Military Affairs, are the actors having continual contact with the field personnel. Each may request a specific analysis from the regional bureaus in State, which in turn may request an opinion from the country desks, or from the embassy.

The director of the Arms Control and Disarmament Agency (ACDA) and the Bureau of Nuclear and Weapons Control (NWC) in that agency are also involved. More immediate daily tasks are performed by the Arms Transfer Division in ACDA/NWC.

A great many actors within the Department of Defense perform security assistance roles. Only primary actors—those frequently involved in policy administration—will be identified here. The Secretary of Defense sometimes meets with the President and the National Security Council (NSC) to consider assistance questions. More immediate policy decisions are made by the Assistant Secretary for International Security Affairs, whose office (ISA) is divided into regional and functional desks, considering primarily the political-military implications of transfers. The Assistant Secretary for International Security Policy has primary responsibility in NATO and European affairs, while the Under Secretary of Defense for Policy has overall policy responsibilities. The Defense Security Assistance Agency (DSAA) is the focal point for information exchange within the Department of Defense, although it also engages in extensive analysis. Often the initial policy justification for "36(b) cases" (cases that require congressional review) is written in the Operations Directorate of DSAA.

The Joint Chiefs of Staff also have input. The Joint Staff, particularly J-5 (Policy and Plans), gives advice or logistic information on the military dimension of certain cases, especially when a case involves two or three of the armed services. The staff also supports the Department of Defense field personnel (MAAGs). The regional unified commands have a number of staff personnel who monitor security assistance and provide accounting and budget-data support to the MAAGs. The commanders-in-chief normally will become interested in a proposed transfer only if it appears that it will have a significant impact on their regional responsibilities.

The individual services—army, navy, and air force—have sales-and-assistance divisions. The U.S. Army Security-Assistance Center (USA-SAC) has regional, country, and functional offices. Similarly, the Security-Assistance Division (OP-63) of Naval Operations has regional and functional offices. Within the Air Force, the Office of the Chief of Staff for Systems and Logistics has a subdivision, the Military Assistance and Sales Office, which also has functional divisions.

Various officials within the Office of the Under Secretary of Defense for Research and Engineering (USDR&E) maintain close contact with industry. They are able to provide advice concerning production timetables and on proposed modifications for weapons systems. USDR&E is also interested in questions relating to the transfer of highly sophisticated or sensitive equipment.

The Treasury Department, the Central Intelligence Agency, the Agency for International Development, and the Office of Management and Budget are less directly involved, but their roles are not insignificant. The General Accounting Office frequently reviews the process, as do the staffs of the House Foreign Affairs Committee and the Senate Foreign Relations Committee. In some cases, the Congress plays a central role in arms transfer decisions.

Several interagency groups have arisen to coordinate sales-and-assistance decisions overall. The formal instruments include the Security Assistance Program Review Committee (SAPROC) in the Ford administration, the Arms Export Control Board (AECB) in the Carter administration, and the Arms Transfer Management Group in the Reagan administration. In addition, during the Carter administration, the Policy Review Committee (PRC) of the NSC played a significant role. NSC staff involvement in security assistance decisions has been minimal in the Reagan administration, however. Finally, various manufacturers, industry salesmen, and lobby groups also perform important functions.

The Six Functions: A System Description

1. Recognition of Wants and Needs. Recognition of a government's wants and needs requires two things. First, elements of the U.S. government must receive and forward to policymakers in Washington requests to discuss the provision of U.S. equipment and services. Second, there must be a calculation of what equipment or services a government should have in order to meet U.S. estimates of minimal defense or collective-security obligations.

The function of recognizing a nation's wants has in the past been performed in a variety of ways, through several channels, and at many levels. Most of these functions are still performed in the way described, although the recently diminished strength of the MAAGs has undoubtedly reduced the preeminence of their role in phase 1 as well as in later phases. The several ways are:

1. Frequently, the host military may ask the MAAG in the country about a weapon system in the U.S. inventory, or the host military may seek information about training, credits, grants, or other services the United States might provide.
2. Host government officials may ask the U.S. ambassador about a weapon system or service.
3. The host government or military may request information or ask to purchase weapons from a U.S. commercial representative who may be in the country; or its attache in Washington may seek information from a variety of actors in Washington who are involved in security assistance. Those asked may include PM/SAS, the various service sales desks, the regional bureaus of the Department of State, officials within the Defense Security Assistance Agency, or staff members and princpals of the National Security Council.
4. A government may have a supply or purchasing mission located in Washington that frequently will deal directly with a number of U.S. government organizations responsible for security assistance, such as PM/SAS, DSAA, OP-63, USASAC, or the U.S. Air Force sales directorate.
5. Sometimes a foreign government leader may make a direct request to the President or to the Secretary of State.
6. An attache, or officials of a nation's Washington supply mission, may make a direct request of industry representatives with regard to weapons.

There is another aspect to this functon. It has to do with the process by which the United States informs a given government of basic deficiencies in its posture and urges it to request specific items from the United States. By a variety of means, Washington formulates its view of the other country's needs. First, an MAAG, while observing host military activities, may perceive, and so inform the host, of technical or training deficiencies in its military structure. During the Carter administration, the MAAGs were required to obtain prior approval from Washington to do so; this requirement, however, always difficult to monitor in practice, has been significantly eased under the Reagan administration. Second, the U.S. Embassy may determine whether the host govermnent needs a particular weapon system. Such a determination would be coordinated among the ambassador, the embassy's political officer, and the MAAG. After approval from Washington, the host may be informed of a perceived deficiency. Third, the MAAG, the embassy, and the regional command, as well as other field personnel, play an important role in the preparation of the Joint Strategic Planning Document Supporting Analysis (JSPDSA). Preparation of the document is a planning exercise intended to determine the basic military capabilities of the United States and another, friendly state. Recommendations to a government may emerge from this analysis. The Joint Procedures Assessments Memorandum (JPAM) addresses worldwide "prioritization" based on fiscal constraints in accordance with the U.S. government's budget cycle. The JPAM, which has a security assistance annex, is used to assign priorities to governments in regard to their contributions to collective security. It should be noted, however, that normally these planning documents are used as a basis on which to assess country requests. A nation is not approached and directly informed: the JPAM or the JSPDSA merely suggests that a country should purchase certain equipment.

In September 1977, U.S. diplomatic and military group personnel in-country were instructed that they "should not convey to host government officials information, including planning data, which might elicit or influence a foreign request to purchase significant combat equipment unless such an approach has been fully approved by the Executive Branch."[3] Field personnel were instructed not to give any advice about whether or not a request for sale of significant combat equipment might be approved or about how to get such a request approved.

2. Initial Review. Prior approval of arms transfers varies with the type of the recipient and with the type of equipment or service. Nations eligible to purchase defense items and defense services were formally divided into two categories by the Carter administration. Although these distinctions existed in practice before President Carter and continue in practice under President Reagan, the Carter administration's labels of Category A and Category B have been abolished.[4] Stated one official, "We don't use the labels anymore, but as before, NATO need but ask." We will use the labels here, though, for clarity since the Reagan administration retains the distinction in practice. Category A consists of all NATO countries (except Iceland, Portugal, Greece, and Turkey), the developed countries of Western Europe (except Spain), Japan, Australia, and New Zealand. Category B consists of all other nations eligible for Foreign Military Sales (FMS). Commercial-sale and FMS items are themselves divided into "significant combat equipment"[5] and "all other defense articles and services."

Both FMS and commercial sales are subject to the initial review process. FMS review occurs with any request to purchase significant combat equipment. If the reqest comes from a Category B country, it will be forwarded through diplomatic channels to the Department of State for review, to determine whether further discussion is merited.

The primary manager of initial reviews of requests for significant combat equipment from Category B countries is the Office of Security Assistance and Sales (PM/SAS), within the Department of State. Such requests are also sometimes sent to the ACDA Weapons Evaluation Control Office, which reviews about one-third of the 3,600 yearly transfer cases. Frequently, ISA, DSAA, and the armed services sales offices are asked to state their views. Each provides input in accordance with its special interests. For example, ACDA/WEC views a request from the perspective of how it will affect regional balances. The sales offices of the armed services would consider the request in terms of the proposed sale's impact on availability of equipment for the U.S. military. USDR&E views requests vis-a-vis technology release, the introduction of new classified equipment into a region, and the impact on U.S. production. If these various offices wish to present an opinion, that opinion will be forwarded to the DSAA Operations Office. The regional desks within DSAA Operations and the regional desks within PM/SAS maintain daily contact in any discussions about an initial review. The recommendation that PM/SAS sends back to the U.S. Embassy or to the agency dealing with a given foreign government will normally reflect the impact of the various participants.

The channels of communication and the initial review process are different in the case of Category A countries. These are perceived as close allies, and sales to them are less controversial; thus, the decision process is rather routine if the proposed transfer amounts to $7 million or less for "significant combat equipment" or $25 million or less for "all other defense articles and services." Communication is generally directed between the relevant service's sales office and the field; DSAA, PM/SAS, the appropriate unified command, and ACDA usually receive copies. Initial review normally takes place within the service sales office, although certain weapon systems may warrant greater interagency review if DSAA, PM/SAS, ACDA, the Unified Command, or others believe such a review will be useful.

3. Policy Review of Transfer Requests. Because arms transfers have important policy implications, elaborate review processes concerning them have developed over the years.[6] Because actors play different roles in the system, they use different criteria for evaluating the utility of a proposed transfer. Typically, it is assumed that these multiple clearances will add up to joint calculation of whether a transfer is in the national interest or not. As enumerated by the former director of DSAA, General Howard M. Fish, the factors considered in determining the U.S. national interest are (1) the relationship of the recipient country to the security interests of the United States, its allies, and its close friends (e.g., the presence of bases or other security installations); (2) the recipient country's relationship to U.S. financial, commercial, and resource interests (e.g., oil); (3) the strength of U.S. bilateral relations with the recipient country (e.g., obligations or other historical responsibilities, as in the case of Israel); (4) the role of the recipient in advancing U.S. global objectives (e.g., peaceful settlement of regional disputes, nuclear nonproliferation, human rights); and (5) the importance of the particular case to the United States' overall relationship with the recipient country. Each case is also examined in terms of its possible effect on the regional military balance in order to ensure that the security interests of the United States, its allies, and its close friends are not adversely affected.[7]

Among the agencies, however, there exist differences in interpretation of the national interest—differences that the review process may not resolve. As a consequence, several review committees have emerged to consider such problems. Although the utility of a transfer will have been evaluated by many agencies, and although such reviews have been informally coordinated, certain problems can still develop. In a report to Congress in July 1977, Secretary of State Cyrus Vance discussed those problems. Noting that the system had been "essentially ad hoc and fragmented," with myriad decision channels and without "a single document or coherent series of documents on policy planning and procedures," Vance went on to say that there had been "difficulty in controlling all significant decision points" as well as problems stemming from "inadequate planning."[8] To correct this perceived deficiency, the Carter administration created the Arms Export Control Board. The AECB was designed to provide coordination and policy guidelines for the review process. Its successor in the Reagan administration, the Arms Transfer Management Group, serves the same purpose.

Before delineating the review function, we should give close attention to the classes of arms transfer, since different types of review occur for each class. In a broad sense, there are two types of arms exports: (1) grant aid and (2) sales for credit or cash. Sales may be divided into FMS and commercial. In addition, as noted earlier, there are the "significant combat equipment" types and "all other defense articles and services." We may further speak of "major defense equipment" (MDE) cases and "nonmajor defense equipment" cases. An MDE can be defined as "any item of significant combat equipment on the United States munitions list having a nonrecurring research and development cost of more than $50,000,000 or a total production cost of more than $200,000,000."[9] Subdivisions are also made into dollar groups, describing transfers of (1) $25 million and over, (2) $7 million and under, and (3) $7 to $25 million. Finally, as described earlier, there are two categories of recipients. Again, the review process varies according to type.

All these transfer types have emerged because of (1) the congressional desire for an optional voice in significant transfers and (2) the U.S. government's desire to differentiate among recipients. Nonmajor defense equipment worth $25 million or less does not require congressional notification or review before a letter of offer and acceptance can be presented. Likewise, major defense equipment costing $7 million or less does not require congressional notification or review. Commercial sales and sales to Category A nations involve different review processes; neither was included in President Carter's ceiling of $8.6 billion in arms transfers. Figure 4.1 depicts the review processes for the various cases.

a. Commercial Export Cases. Review of commercial export cases differs somewhat. A request for sale of an item on the U.S. munitions list is first reviewed by the Office of Munitions Control (OMC). The OMC director, who manages a variety of reviews, forwards all requests to the appropriate regional bureau of Department of State, to its counterpart element in ISA, and to ACDA.

Within each receiving agency there is a specialization of function. For example, once a request is sent to the Department of Defense, it will be forwarded to DSAA, ISA, UDSR&E, or the army, navy, or air force sales office, depending on the weapon. This specialization can be illustrated by focusing on a single example: USASAC.

The clearance process within USASAC usually involves the following procedures. The director of USASAC delegates the review request to one of the relevant regional desks. The desk officer immediately consults the army "item manager" or program manager (if the item is a large system still in development). The item manager, who is in charge of monitoring a specific weapon system, is an expert on that system (or service). The item manager's report is considered heavily in the final

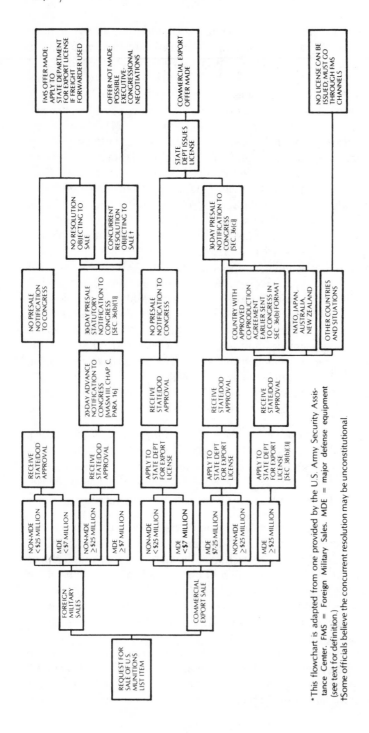

*This flowchart is adapted from one provided by the U.S. Army Security Assistance Center. FMS = Foreign Military Sales. MDE = major defense equipment (see text for definition.)
†Some officials believe the concurrent resolution may be unconstitutional.

Source: Paul Y. Hammond, David J. Louscher, and Michael D. Salomon, "Controlling U.S. Arms Transfers: The Emerging System," *Orbis* 23, 2 (Summer 1979), p. 330. © 1979 by the Foreign Policy Research Institute, reprinted with permission.

Figure 4.1. Arms Export Control Act Review Process.

position paper of the regional desk. Essentially, though, the desk makes decisions on the basis of NATO's standards for rationalization, standardization, and interoperability (RSI),[10] or, in other cases, on the basis of whether or not such a transfer will undermine army procurement schedules or compromise the weapon's technological security. Once regional and technical opinion is received, the program management director will write an opinion which, with rare exception, will become the official army view. This opinion is sent to the Director of International Programs, within the Office of the Under Secretary of Defense for Research and Engineering (USDR&E), which evaluates proposed transfers from the perspective of the technological security of the weapon. Finally, the opinion is sent to the Office of the Assistant Secretary of Defense for International Security Affairs and then transferred to Munitions Control.

Returning to a more general discussion, we should mention that Munitions Control will disapprove a request if the regional bureau in the Department of State or any of the service sales offices objects. Again, most commercial cases are routine and are handled by Munitions Control and the relevant service sales office, with the regional desks in State, the Bureau of Economic Affairs, the Office of Scientific Affairs, and ACDA acting as primary reviewers should they wish to provide input. Occasionally, when appropriate, NSA, the Department of Energy, other agencies, or the NSC staff is consulted.

Congress may provide the final review of a case. License requests for the export of major defense equipment amounting to $7 million or more, and any other defense articles or services amounting to $25 million or more, must be reported to Congress. In its report, the State Department must indicate the recipient, the dollar amount, and the item to be exported at least thirty days before a license is issued. Congress may also request a report on the capabilities of a weapon being exported through this channel. However, Congress has not yet provided itself a "veto power" through concurrent resolution over commercial cases [Section 36(c)] as it has over some FMS cases [36(b)].

b. Foreign Military Sales. The review process for Foreign Military Sales involves a great many more actors and stages than does the process for commercial sales, largely becaues many FMS decisions are perceived to have greater strategic and political import. Again, FMS cases are generally divided into Category A and Category B, as previously stated. Category A involves sales to allies, such as NATO countries (except Iceland, Portugal, Greece, and Turkey), the developed countries of Western Europe (except Spain), Japan, Australia, and New Zealand; such sales do not require as much policy review as sales to Category B. Sales of defense items and services to Category A countries are routinely processed by the Departments of State and Defense, and sale is directly authorized. The service sales offices are also actively involved in the decision. ACDA, ISA, ISP, and the NSC staff are informed, but only occasionally do they play roles in Category A case reviews.

Category B recipients receive more extensive review. Here, the initial traffic manager is PM/SAS, but a number of traffic managers subsequently emerge. In State, an initial review is conducted by the regional bureau. Concomitantly, PM/SAS analyzes the request, and when the issue is perceived as political, it will be reviewed by the staff of the Under Secretary for Security Assistance, Science and Technology. Specialized offices in the Treasury Department, Commerce, the CIA, the Office of Management and Budget (OMB), and the Agency for International Development (AID) will be made aware of the review and may create position papers for the later stages of interagency coordination. The Arms Transfer Division in ACDA will initiate an analysis, and the request for a foreign military sale will be sent to the Office of the Secretary of Defense (OSD) and DSAA, where a variety of specialized reviews take place. In both ISA and DSAA, the transfer request will be assessed by one of the regional desks. Frequently, each service sales office will receive a request from DSAA to provide an analysis of the proposed sale. If the proposed transfer is a matter of interest to the Joint Chiefs of Staff, each of the service sales offices may be asked to do an analysis also.

Finally, a position paper is presented to the Assistant Secretary for International Security Affairs, in Defense, who will then forward his opinion to the Department of State. The process within State is very similar. An analysis will be conducted by PM/SAS, which will also request an opinion from the appropriate regional bureaus. The regional bureaus will have briefs presented by the country desks. The opinions of other agencies, together with the views of the regional bureaus, are then forwarded to the Director of the Bureau of Politico-Military Affairs, who acts on behalf of the Secretary of State in most roles decisions. If the issue is politically sensitive, it will be forwarded to the Under Secretary of State for Security Assistance, Science and Technology, as previously noted, or to the Secretary of State himself. Sensitive cases are occasionally forwarded for presidential approval, at which time the involvements of the NSC staff and Advisor to the President for National Security Affairs increases. During the Carter administration the involvement of the National Security Advisor and NSC staff in arms transfer decisions was much more persuasive than it is today. That involvement is now usually limited to those arms sales decisions involving presidential approval such as those of AWACS to Saudi Arabia and F-16s to Venezuela and Pakistan.

c. Formal Interagency Coordination.   The AECB was created early in 1978 to improve the coordination of all security assistance decisions. It was created from the Ford administration's Security Assistance Program Review Committee (SAPRC), which had been responsible for coordinating the Military Assistance Program (MAP), credit decisions, International Military Education and Training (IMET), and security-supporting assistance. Besides handling the already existing SAPRC functions, the AECB was "concerned with policies and procedures for conventional arms transfers under MAP, FMS and commercial sales." It was designed to be an "advisory body with policy planning and review functions" which would "serve to assist the Under Secretary of State for Security Assistance in carrying out delegated responsibilities and in advising the Secretary of State on policy matters." As was stated in materials submitted to Congress by then Under Secretary of State Lucy Benson on February 1, 1978:

> It [the AECB] will review, consult, and hear recommendations on security assistance and arms export control policy on: procedures for implementing the Arms Transfer Policy conveyed by the Presidential statement on May 9, 1977; guidelines and criteria for setting priorities and making decisions; means for systematically collecting, analyzing and utilizing pertinent data, and for exchanging views of interested agencies; transfers of defense articles and services as they relate to policy; preparation and submission of all security assistance plans, programs, budgets and legislative proposals.[11]

According to then Under Secretary Benson, the AECB did in fact accomplish the following tasks that it was designated to accomplish:

> To provide the Secretary of State with a reliable mechanism for carrying out his responsibility for continuing supervision and general direction of the country's arms transfer activities; to ensure that all the agencies involved in the arms transfer business are aware of the provisions and requirements of the policy and that they apply them consistently; and to set orderly procedures for handling day-to-day arms transfer operations and for reconciling policy differences, and for making decision.[12]

The AECB was chaired by the Under Secretary of State for Security Assistance, with representatives of State, Defense, and the Treasury; the Joint Chiefs of Staff; ACDA; the National Security Council; the

CIA; the Agency for International Development; and the Office of Management and Budget. Typically, meetings of the AECB were gatherings of up to fifty people, with discussion usually taking place among the agency directors and the assistant secretaries, who would present their agency's position papers on a particular issue. Attempts were made to reach consensus, but since the AECB was an advisory body, consensus was not necessary. The Under Secretary would declare a "sense of the meeting" and forward the position of the group to the Secretary of State; any dissenting views were also forwarded. The Secretary would then forward his recommendation to the President. It should be noted that while only politically sensitive sales cases were actually discussed at AECB meetings, most of the bargaining or discussion related to the creation of general security assistance policies or guidelines. During its existence, the AECB also devoted considerable time to organizing the Carter administration's ceiling on the dollar volume of U.S. arms sales. Specific cases were discussed primarily in terms of their meaning for the ceiling.

Although the Reagan administration abolished the ceiling, the structure of the AECB remains, recast as the Arms Transfer Management Group (ATMG); it is still chaired by the Under Secretary of State for Security Assistance, Science and Technology. Organizationally, the ATMG is divided into two working groups. The Security Assistance Operations Committee deals with policy issues and is chaired by the Director of the Bureau of Politico-Military Affairs. Budget issues and the security assistance program budget are the responsibility of the Security Assistance Program Review Committee (SAPROC), which is chaired by the Deputy Director of PM. Each spring, country team estimates of necessary budget authority for security assistance are solicited for review by the SAPROC, and during the summer months security assistance priorities by regions are established in the State Department following SAPROC review.

The imposition of an enduring managerial discipline over an ad hoc, fragmented, and sometimes chaotic decisionmaking structure was probably the major accomplishment of the Carter administration, although this was not the primary objective. Routinizing the process, ensuring that a broad and stable group of primary actors is involved in all cases, and providing substantially the same bases for review has permitted a consistency by which the Reagan administration can claim that sales are made on the basis of policy review in accordance with established policies and procedures, and in accordance with an assessment of the administration's foreign and national security policy objectives.

d. Congressional Notification. Certain Sales cases require congressional notification, and some others are subject to congressional veto. The various reporting requirements provide Congress—especially the

Senate Foreign Relations Committee and the House Foreign Affairs Committee—an opportunity to monitor security assistance decisions. Congress receives quarterly reports of all letters of offer on any major defense equipment worth $1 million or more.

Section 36(b) of the Arms Export Control Act provides Congress with a policy veto for certain kinds of arms transfers. Before any letter of offer can be made for defense services or items costing $25 million or more, or for major defense equipment amounting to $7 million or more, the Foreign Affairs Committee and the Foreign Relations Committee must be notified thirty days in advance. By agreement with the Executive Branch, Congress is provided an additional twenty-day advance notice before submission. During the thirty-day period, Congress, by concurrent resolution, may object to the sale and thus block it. Since 1974, however, when the procedure was adopted, Congress has never passed a concurrent resolution against a sale—although there have been many opportunities to do so, as Table 4.1 shows. Many officials in the Executive Branch feel that the concurrent resolution is unconstitutional. Hearings have been held on some proposed sales. Occasionally, after considerable Executive-congressional bargaining, or alteration of the proposed letter of offer and resubmission to Congress, the Foreign Relations Committee or the Foreign Affairs Committee has dropped its objections.

During the Carter administration, it was a presidential requirement that all 36(b) notifications be approved at the White House before being submitted to Congress. The President would then review and personally approve and initial each one, more than 300 cases. This example elucidates both Carter's penchant for micro-level management in foreign affairs and the fact that during his presidency the Special Assistant for National Security Affairs and the NSC staff held far-reaching authority in arms transfer policy. Things have changed under President

Table 4.1. Arms Sales Agreements Requiring Prior Notification to Congress under Section 36(b) of the Arms Export Control Act

Fiscal Year	Number of 36(b) Cases
1975	40
1976*	58
1977	92
1978	99
1979	150
1980	123
1981 (through May 1981)	125
Total	796

*Includes transition quarter.

Reagan. In politically sensitive or controversial cases, other than those requiring presidential decision, the NSC staff and White House are informed of the decision and subsequent implementation procedures. In some cases, such as the AWACS sale to Saudi Arabia, the White House serves as both the locus of decision and as the primary political agent coordinating the public relations and political arm-twisting aspects of the sale as presented to the Congress. But this is the exception. The NSC no longer routinely clears cases as the Policy Review Committee did during the Carter years, and the Assistant for National Security Affairs and his staff no longer play a central role in arms transfer policy or decisionmaking.

4. Negotiation and Development of Agreements. Once the appropriate agency, the President, or Congress (depending on the case) has approved the proposed transfer, a letter of offer and acceptance (LOA) is developed. The service sales offices of the Army, Navy, and Air Force, working closely with DSAA, are the primary actors here. It frequently takes from sixty to ninety days to obtain the price and availability data.

Negotiation with the recipient often takes place during this period, although it can also take place after presentation of the LOA. Negotiations take place through numerous channels and at a variety of levels. Sometimes the host government negotiates with the MAAG, at other times, with an ambassador; sometimes the Secretary of State becomes involved. More sophisticated weapons systems may require U.S. survey teams to determine in detail the host's needs and capabilities. It may also be necessary for the sales officers of the Army, Navy, or Air Force to send special technical teams to negotiate with the recipient. Occasionally, when negotiations are at a stalemate, a special briefing team may be sent to provide information about some specific aspect of the negotiations. Some nations send negotiating teams to the United States to examine equipment, talk with producers, or visit test facilities. A few have supply missions in Washington that may talk directly with the sales office of one of the services or with officials in PM/SAS.

The issues that must be resolved in security assistance negotiations will also vary. When the request is merely for an item currently being procured by the U.S. military, a standard agenda guides the discussions: the type within a family of weapons systems; price, including procurement, handling, accounting, and delivery costs; availability; delivery dates; expiration dates; supply and support arrangements; guarantees for each party; and special conditions of use. Coproduction negotiations are even more complex.

Considerable time and energy are expended at this stage in order to establish reliable price and availability estimates. Unexpected and substantial price increases and delivery delays could cause a recipient government to become disillusioned with the U.S. security assistance system. Foreign customers must be warned that the price quotations contained in the sale request or in the final letter of offer are only estimates and that, by law, the United States must be reimbursed for all actual costs of equipment and services. The negotiators work closely with DSAA and the armed services to assure accuracy in price and availability information.

5. Performance of Agreed Responsibilities: The Execution of Agreements. In commercial cases, this fifth function is performed when the Office of Munitions Control provides an export license to an industry that has negotiated a contract with a foreign government. The execution function for FMS cases, however, is much more complicated. After review and approval, a letter of offer and acceptance is sent to the recipient, and discussions take place. If the LOA is accepted, the execution stage is implemented.

Each service has a sales division that handles requisitions, ensures that the material is shipped, tracks shipments, and has responsibility for some of the fiscal aspects of FMS. Offices such as the Security Assistance Accounting Center (SAAC) monitor payment and ensure the receipt of funds from foreign governments. When funds or credits are provided, procurement can begin. Procurement of materiel from industry and stocks is the central task here. DSAA and the service divisions must ensure that plans are provided for support (including logistic support) of the transfer. Records must document the number and types of items delivered under various contracts. In the case of FMS, accounting procedures must ensure that the United States is fully reimbursed for the work of procurement. Because it must be determined that the materiel shipped is of the same quality as that provided to the U.S. military, most items are subject to preshipment inspection. In addition, field personnel monitor the shipments to their hosts; they frequently discover problems in the delivery process.

6. "Feedback". "Feedback" refers to information about the impact of a military transfer or service. The information may bear on U.S. management of a service (e.g., whether deliveries are timely or whether proper accounting techniques have been used), or it may relate to a foreign government's use of delivered equipment or services. The acquisition of such information is principally performed by the MAAGs, which are required by law to monitor the condition and use of equipment provided through MAP, and which are often directed by the regional commands or by the Joint Chiefs of Staff to do the same for FMS items. Each year a report on the quality, condition, and current use of MAP materiel is produced. The volume of MAP transfers had declined, but the magnitude of the reporting task diminishes slowly because it pertains to equipment in inventory, not simply to current transfers. Even though reporting requirements for FMS are not mandated by law, a great deal of effort is expended in the field monitoring and reporting on end item utilization.

In the past, the Joint Strategic Objectives Plan (JSOP), a coordinated assessment of a given nation's security capabilities, provided the MAAG and others with an opportunity to cite problems that might be emerging in MAP or FMS transfer programs. The JSOP has now been replaced by the Joint Strategic Planning Document Supporting Analysis (JSPDSA) and the Joint Procedures Assessment Memorandum (JPAM), both of which address security priorities. Evaluation of the host's utilization of weapon services is part of that task; that is to say, while the JSOP has been replaced, the reporting opportunity it once offered the MAAGs is now provided through the JSPDSA exercise.

Feedback is also generated by foreign governments when they complain, as they sometimes do, about equipment malfunctions, delayed deliveries, and logistic or support problems. Host governments usually make such complaints to the MAAG. Another form of feedback occurs in requests for "follow-on" sales or service. Occasionally, survey teams are sent to assess host problems in adapting a weapon or weapon system into its force structure. In the embassy, of course, the political counselor or the defense attaché receives, and may report, information on the host government's use of equipment or services. In addition, the CIA may evaluate host capabilities.

Security assistance programs may also be assessed by the General Accounting Office as it evaluates program decisions, assesses security assistance management structure, or conducts field audits of operations as requested by Congress. Occasionally, congressional staff members will themselves evaluate security assistance activities, both in the field and in Washington. While the information thus acquired may be intended primarily for the use of Congress, other actors in the security assistance administrative system usually pay attention to such information when it becomes available.

PROBLEMS OF THE SECURITY ASSISTANCE SYSTEM

The new mechanisms of policy and management control in the security assistance system are designed to correct perceived failings in that system. The general direction of those changes has been to reduce the strength of the field offices, to concentrate functions in Washington, and to subject arms transfer decisions to an extensive clearance process within the Executive Branch and Congress. What has emerged is a complex and counterbalanced system of procedures and policy guide-lines. Some problems can be anticipated in the operation of this new system.

Diminished Field Capabilities

A serious emergent problem is the growing disparity between the reduced capability of the security assistance administration in the field and the increased need of information for policy review and implemen-tation in Washington. Military Assistance Advisory Groups are the principal field monitors for the system, yet their strength and functions have been drastically reduced. Corresponding declines have occurred in "in-country" field capabilities (1) to monitor host-government use of MAP and sale-acquired materiel and (2) to monitor and expedite MAP and FMS deliveries.

Increasingly, the President, members of the strategic elite, and a growing number of congressmen have become concerned about the reduction in U.S. presence in friendly governments. One instrument for establishing this presence has traditionally been the Military Assistance Advisory Groups. Until 1976, their advisory and representational func-tions were sizable and highly valued by host governments, for their presence was perceived as a tangible symbol of U.S. interest in the host's security requirements. In addition, MAAGs provided the U.S. govern-ment with information from the field and with assistance in managing actual arms transfers. Partially as a result of a breakdown of the foreign policy consensus in the United States, however, certain elements perceived the MAAGs as a serious problem. The Congress and signifi-cant parts of the foreign affairs bureaucracy became concerned about the autonomy of field personnel and the extent to which they precipitat-ed expanded U.S. commitments or promoted unnecessary arms sales. The result was a concerted attempt to reduce MAAG presence abroad and to restrict MAAG activities. These reductions and restrictions, however, have undermined both the field information functions and the military presence or representation functions performed by the MAAGs, including providing needed information, maintaining contact with host military, and restraining and rationalizing the weapons acquisitions decisions of the host government.

The use of field personnel generally is a basic dilemma for policymak-ers. Providing field personnel with too much autonomy might precipitate situations or commitments that may not be desired by central decision-makers. On the other hand, extensive control and restrictions or major reductions in strength may undermine the initiative and the ability of field personnel to gather timely information for rational policymaking. The dilemma is as dangerous for policymakers as the narrow channel was for sailors in Homer's *Odyssey*: Charybdis, a giant whirlpool in which no ship could survive, was imagined to be in a narrow channel opposite a monster called Scylla, who seized and destroyed ships. The problem for sailors, and for central decisionmakers, is to avoid one danger without becoming the victim of the other. Our research suggests that whereas the Congress and the Carter administration avoided the monster, perhaps they did not avoid the whirlpool.

Traditional MAAG Functions. Prior to the 1976-77 restrictions placed on them by the Congress and the Carter administration, MAAGs had quite extensive roles to perform. These roles were of three types: representational, informational, and managerial.

Representational roles were broad and were generally an effort to demonstrate U.S. presence and concern for host military and security problems by giving advice and assistance; by maintaining liaison between the U.S. defense establishment and that of the host country; and by establishing and maintaining a relationship of mutual trust and confidence with the host country's military establshment.

Informational roles were highly dependent upon success in performing representational roles. Access to key host-government military and government personnel was highly instrumental for gathering information about country needs, wants, fears, or attitudes, as well as internal domestic developments that might affect U.S. security interests. MAAGs reported on host government's plans and programs relevant to the Unified Command; provided specifically requested reports for the Office of the Secretary of Defense, the Defense Secretary Assistant Agency, the Joint Chiefs of Staff, and the military departments; regularly reported on the host government's utilization of defense articles provided as grant aid; and often reported on any problems with recently purchased arms services and training.

Managerial roles included assisting host governments in arranging the purchase of U.S. weapons and services; assisting DSAA and the military departments in foreign military sales negotiations; assisting U.S. commercial representatives who wished to sell defense articles and services to host governments; assisting U.S. military departments in delivering security assistance to recipients; assisting host governments in meeting contractual obligations related to grant aid, foreign military sales, or excess defense articles; providing training or advice to host governments concerning plans, programs, budgets, or military resources; assisting DSAA or ISA on matters relating to joint research and development with a host country; and preforming other tasks if specifically requested by competent authority.

Concerns about MAAGs and Restrictions on Their Activities. Over the years major concerns emerged about the MAAGs' performance of their functions. Some critics believed that the MAAGs were too large, too visible, too autonomous, and too costly. They questioned the access and influence MAAGs claimed, or the utility of this access and influence.[13] Others were concerned that certain MAAG contingents might make a commitment to a host country not consistent with other U.S. government policies or objectives.

Congress was particularly concerned about MAAG functions; by 1976 its interest had become noticeably stronger. It perceived a lack of control of field operatives, as well as a lack of coordination among those agencies and departments involved in security assistance. But more importantly, Congress expressed a growing concern that military personnel in the field were generating demands for U.S. military equipment either by assisting representatives of the uniformed services or of U.S. commercial firms, or by actively promoting the acquisition of American defense equipment in their consultations with host military personnel. A fear existed that the MAAGs, through these activities, were creating situations in which the policymakers in the Executive Branch and Congress were being presented with *fait accompli* concerning sales requests from foreign governments—which could be disapproved only at the risk of endangering U.S. bilateral relations. These fears were only heightened by the traditional congressional concerns over the perceived lack of information provided Congress by the Executive Branch concerning security assistance programs, as well as by more recent fears of disorganization within the Executive Branch concerning implementation of its own security assistance policies.[14]

The record is unclear concerning the extent to which these congressional concerns were valid, at least prior to the signing into law of the International Security Assistance Act of 1977 (PL95-92). For example, a 1972 Department of Defense directive states that MAAG chiefs, along with their other responsibilities, will "assist the host government in arranging for purchase of defense articles and services to meet valid country requirements through foreign military sales (FMS) and commercial sales, and cooperate with and assist representatives of U.S. firms in the sale of U.S. defense articles and services to meet valid country requirements."[15] Moreover, it had been the traditional role of the MAAGs to provide their hosts with advice on force structure, force planning, stragegy, and doctrine, as well as to provide administrative and fiduciary services at the end of the security assistance pipeline.

In addition to a concern about those activities, a perception of lack of coordination and control within the Department of Defense organization for security assistance led some congressmen and Department of State personnel to conclude that the MAAGs had created semi-autonomous positions for themselves "in-country." As such, they would be in a position to frustrate the lines of authority flowing from both the ambassador and the Department of State. These concerns were enhanced by both the perception of a closed military chain of command running through the regional commanders and the military communications system and the "military-to-military" relationship enjoyed by the MAAGs and their host counterparts.

On the other hand, the contention that the MAAG activities promote arms sales has been vigorously denied by representativs of the Department of Defense.[16] In addition, recent testimony before Congress has indicated that at least one senior Arms Control and Disarmament Agency official saw certain MAAGs as serving arms control interests by advising foreign governments that certain sales were "ill advised" or "inappropriate" for the country considering them.[17] Finally, a review of the hearings on foreign and military assistance for the last three fiscal years underscores agreement among both State and Defense Department representatives that

1. the Department of State holds both statuatory and de facto authority with respect to the continuous supervision and general direction of the military assistance program, including whether or not there shall be a program for a particular country and the composition of that program. In this process the Department of Defense serves as implementor of the policy and also provides State with advice on host-country needs and capabilities, price and availability of the equipment in question, and so forth.
2. in-country, the MAAGs are under the direction and supervision of the Chief of the U.S. Diplomatic Mission.[18]

Nonetheless, a desire for tighter controls over the MAAGs was prevalent at the Department of State and Congress as well. In the FY 1977 foreign assistance legislation, Congress responded to its own concerns as well as to those of the MAAG critics.

Restrictions on MAAG Functions. In the International Security Assistance and Arms Export Control Act of 1976, Congress placed definite restrictions on the organization and implementation of the security assistance function. In Section 104 of that act, Congress amended the Foreign Assistance Act of 1961 by adding a new subsection, which specified that "after 30 September 1977, all securty assistance field organizations must be authorized by the Congress and, with the exception of 34 countries, all other security assistance organizations were limited to three man teams."

The following legislative season produced further amendments to the Foreign Assistance Act of 1961 in the International Security Assistance Act of 1977 (PL95-92). The major intent of that law was to redefine

MAAG functions. Henceforth, their primary functions were to be limited to logistics management, transportation, fiscal management, and contract administraton of country programs. Except for MAAGs in the Republic of Korea, Panama, Brazil, Morocco, Iran, Kuwait, and Saudi Arabia, all military groups providing security assistance in-country were to have no more than three personnel each unless the Chief of Mission specifically requested three additional personnel. A ceiling of 865 security assistance field personnel was established.

After initial and sometimes heated battles between elements of the State Department and elements of the Defense Department over the meaning of certain provisions of PL95-92, traditional MAAG roles were altered. To reiterate, their primary functions were to be logistics management, transportation, fiscal management, and contract administration. Limited advisory or training functions could be performed as long as they did not distract from the primary functions. MAAGs were prohibited from discussing matters related to host requests for information about significant combat equipment without prior approval from the State Department. MAAG chiefs were required to clear any meetings with host military or host governments with the Chief of Mission and to route all their communications through the embassy message center and State Department communications channels. MAAGs were instructed to avoid any activity that would stimulate host-country requests for significant combat equipment or "convey the impression that the United States Government would respond favorably to such requests." Further, in the September 1977 so-called leprosy letter from the State Department, MAAGs were forbidden to assist representatives of U.S. commercial firms who might wish to sell defense equipment or services to a host government.

Restrictions on MAAG Personnel. The impact of the restrictions on MAAG functions was not nearly as great as the sizable reductions in field personnel. In fiscal year 1960, over 7,000 United States personnel were assigned to overseas security assistance organizations. By fiscal year 1978, however, that figure had been reduced to under 1,000. Military personnel alone have been reduced by more than 64 percent since fiscal year 1974; from 2,109 in fiscal year 1974 to 854 in fiscal year 1978. Figure 4.2 displays the reduction over time. Such drastic reductions are certain to have had a major impact on traditional MAAG roles in host governments. But the reductions have been greater in some countries than in others. A review of authorized military strengths in the MAAGs, or equivalent organizations, from fiscal year 1974 through fiscal year 1978 revealed five basic types of military personnel patterns. These patterns are shown in Table 4.2.

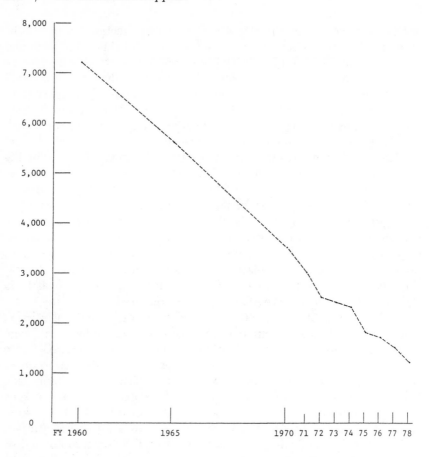

Figure 4.2. Decline of Authorized U.S. Personnel, Military or Civilian, in Overseas Security Assistance Organizations, 1960-1978

First, in five countries—Korea, Saudi Arabia, Thailand, Turkey, and Brazil—sizable MAAG strengths were reduced to more than the six staff members specified for most missions. Substantial reductions in these missions left them still relatively large.

A second group consisted of thirteen countries with moderately sized missions that were drastically reduced to either three- or six-person teams in fiscal year 1977 or fiscal year 1978.

A third group of thirteen nations had MAAG missions of comparatively small size, but these also were reduced to six or fewer military personnel. Commonly, the reduction in fiscal year 1977 or fiscal year 1978 was from a nine-person to a six-person management team.

A fourth group of nations was scarcely affected by military personnel reductions. Some countries such as Iran, the Philippines, Greece, and Morocco had fairly large missions stationed within them, and these missions were not reduced. Others, such as Peru and Japan, lost one person. Still others, such as Costa Rica and Nigeria had no change in representation in fiscal year 1977 or fiscal year 1978.

In a fifth group of nations, the number of MAAGs stationed actually grew. In fiscal year 1977, the MAAGs in Spain were expanded from twenty-five to thirty; in Panama from nine to thirteen; in Portugal from eleven to twelve; and in Jordan from nine to ten.

Table 4.2. Types of Authorized Strengths for Military Personnel Processing MAP, FMS, FMS Credit, Commercial Sales, 1974-1978

	1974	1975	1976	1977	1978	Reduction Since Fiscal Year 1976
			Fiscal Year			
Type 1 Large missions reduced						
Thailand	258	169	166	117	40	126
Saudi Arabia	133	140	184	167	80	68
Turkey	146	146	113	85	64	49
Korea	397	159	155	154	130	25
Brazil	40	40	38	38	32	6
Type 2 Medium missions drastically reduced						
Indonesia	45	55	55	54	6	48
Taiwan	166	46	43	30	6	37
Venezuela	36	31	30	19	6	24
Bolivia	29	29	29	29	6	23
Argentina	29	27	27	22	6	21
Germany	26	22	22	3	6	16
Colombia	24	24	22	21	6	15
Guatemala	19	19	15	12	4	11
Paraguay	15	14	14	3	3	11
Nicaragua	17	17	15	11	6	9
Italy	11	11	11	3	3	8
Chile	15	15	15	7	6	7
Uruguay	13	13	13	3	3	10
Type 3 Small missions reduced to six or fewer personnel						
Honduras	11	11	11	11	6	5
El Salvador	10	10	10	6	5	5
Netherlands	8	8	8	3	3	5
Zaire	20	10	10	10	6	4
Denmark	7	7	7	3	3	4
Liberia	16	12	9	9	6	3
Tunisia	8	9	9	9	6	3
Pakistan	5	8	9	9	6	3
Dominican Republic	11	8	8	8	5	3
France	7	7	6	3	3	3
Norway	6	6	6	3	3	3
Ecuador	-	6	8	6	6	2
Belgium	7	7	7	3	5	2

Table 4.2. *continued*

	1974	1975	Fiscal Year 1976	1977	1978	Reduction Since Fiscal Year 1976
Type 4 Relatively stable missions						
Iran	192	191	191	185	185	5
Philippines	50	45	39	37	34	5
Greece	46	27	29	29	28	1
Morocco	18	18	19	19	16	3
Peru	7	7	7	7	6	1
Japan	7	7	7	7	6	1
Kuwait	-	9	9	9	9	0
India	4	4	4	2	2	2
Australia	3	3	3	3	2	1
Costa Rica	4	2	2	2	2	0
Austria	2	2	2	2	2	0
United Kingdom	-	-	2	2	2	0
Nigeria	1	1	1	1	1	0
Haiti	-	-	-	1	1	0
Mexico	1	1	1	1	1	0
Yemen	-	-	-	1	1	0
Singapore	1	1	1	1	1	0
Malaysia	-	1	1	1	1	0
Khmer Republic	77	82	-	-	-	-
Ethiopia[1]	80	79	46	46	0	-
Type 5 Expanded missions						
Panama	9	9	9	13	13	+4
Spain	38	31	25	30	27	+3
Jordan	8	9	9	10	10	+1
Portugal	11	11	11	12	12	+1

[1] Inactivated May 10, 1977.

Source: Paul Y. Hammond, David J. Louscher, and Michael D. Salomon, "Growing Dilemmas for the Management of Arms Sales", *Armed Forces and Society* Vol. 6, No. 1. (Fall, 1979).

MAAG Perceptions. Our interviews with MAAG personnel revealed significant frustration concerning the restrictions placed on them. It is quite apparent that they believe that they work in a highly restrained environment. Indeed, field personnel must work under a significant number of constraints. Their host counterparts view their own security problems as separate and quite different from the U.S. concern about the East-West confrontation.

Since a significant number of host governments have considerable amounts of capital with which to purchase arms from a variety of sources, many MAAG respondents noted a significant increase in foreign suppliers in-country, specifically salesmen from Britain, France, and Germany. Finally, many of our respondents suggested that their hosts had assessed post-Vietnam U.S. foreign policy to be one of limited capability to respond directly to them, thus necessitating increased arms purchases for self-defense, and often from other suppliers. As a consequence, MAAGs have been placed in a high-demand environment. They experience considerable pressure from host governments for information about, as well as assistance in, acquiring military services and weapons. A considerable number of industry salesmen and third-country sales teams are active in these countries, with the result that MAAG officials are increasingly asked their views on arms purchases.

Recent trends in U.S. politics, however, have created a domestic pressure to restrain the activities of MAAGs. Many of our respondents felt that as a consequence of the restrictions on their representational, planning, and informational activities, reductions in their numbers, and increased administrative work required by their congressionally mandated functions of logistics management, fiscal management, transportation, and contract administration, their lives have become extremely complicated. Many complained that they simply did not have the staff to perform all the administrative functions. Further, the MAAGs perceived themselves as being bypassed by both host governments and Washington, as security assistance negotiations and decisions have increasingly been transferred to Washington. Host representatives go to Washington or create Washington-based supply missions that deal directly with U.S. officials and private industries.

Yet, there remains considerable commitment to the implementation of congressional intent in the MAAGs. Further, the MAAG chiefs are well informed of the changing political environment for security assistance. Even though they are intent upon adapting to this new environment, the cumulative impact of the varied restrictions, reductions, and trends has resulted in significant frustration. First, many are frustrated about their reduced capability to act as "field monitors." Several contended that as the U.S. government has decreased MAAG strength, it has also diminished the capability of the security assistance system to monitor absorption and end item utilization.

MAAG personnel generally perceived their reduced number as inconsistent with the changing roles of the United States and its friends and allies. They are cognizant of the limits of American power, and that increasingly the United States has become dependent upon other countries to perform security functions. MAAG personnel perceive themselves as providing a field monitor role for Washington in determining the extent to which the United States can rely upon other nations to perform security functions for it. They can also reassure host governments of U.S. concern for their security.

Second, many of our respondents felt they had become "parts managers." Several respondents contended that management functions, basic accounting functions, and recordkeeping should not be an MAAG task. They felt that the MAAGs should be military advisors who talk philosophy, strategy, and military tactics with their host counterparts and not be "parts managers" for the Department of Defense. As one respondent said:

> The Problem with a small MAAG detachment that is tied down with the task of counting items and checking serial numbers is that it really doesn't have an opportunity to talk three or four hours about philosophy or several hours about strategy with the host military. Thus, the MAAGs never get to know the military host and, more importantly, the host military and host government never gets to know how an American thinks.

The diminished representational roles of the MAAGs, the restrictions on their joint military planning activities with host military officials, and their increasing administrative burden are perceived as having the long-term consequence of isolating the United States from future leaders, both military and political. This is potentially dangerous, for increasingly the United States does not have the resources to meet all its security objectives alone. Stated one MAAG respondent:

> The utility of the MAAG having a close working relationship with the host was revealed to me about a month ago when I was in France. We were touring French military installations and a political military officer [POL-MIL] of the American Embassy said to me that he found it amazing that the senior French officers were quite pro-American and quite positive toward American objectives. But he found middle-level French officers were very anti-American. The POL-MIL continued to express his surprise about that. I told him that I wasn't at all surprised. The fact is that senior officers had lots of contact with Americans through the MAP program. But the middle-level officers have had scarcely any contact with American personnel.

Third, most of our MAAG respondents contended that restrictions on the discussion of sophisticated weapons systems are unrealistic. In particular, they place the MAAGs in an embarrassing position. As one respondent said, "To tell us not to talk to our host about sophisticated weapons systems is to undermine our credibility and make us look silly before our host." Or, as another respondent stated: "We just look ridiculous when a host asks us about a new weapon system, and we have to tell them that we don't know anything about it, or that we are not authorized to discuss the matter. Many times the host government is an ally of ours or on very friendly terms. In any case, they have information sources beyond the MAAG in learning about new weapons systems." And still another MAAG chief said, "That particular guideline reeks of paternalism, and the host military in the country where I was stationed told me that."

The proscription against discussing new weapons systems in certain countries was prompted by a desire to prevent new, sophisticated systems from entering a region. Yet, many respondents claimed it could have the opposite effect. Said one, in speaking of a Latin American country in which he had been stationed during the Carter administration:

> People in Washington have the impression that through our restraint we will hold down arms races in Latin America. But if you look at my host's recent purchases of SU-22 fighters, the T-55 tank, the APC, all of which are Russian, the M22 guided missile, and the Mirage fighter, which was French, you will see that on each occasion they came to the United States first; came to the MAAGs and requested an opportunity to purchase somewhat equivalent weapons from the United States. Each time we said no. We might have been able to convince them to buy a less sophisticated system if we had not been so ideological about the problem.

Our Washington respondents, however, did not agree with MAAG contentions that field personnel could more adequately and flexibly deal with host-government requests. Said one:

> There is a basic conflict of view between a number of the MAAGs and people here in Washington. The MAAGs are still under the impression that as field personnel they are the most expert people on a question, and as a consequence they should have maximum authority to perform whatever tasks need to be performed. We don't feel that way, however. We feel that a field person can get caught up in the pressures of the situation; he can't see the broad picture. MAAGs are frustrated because they are unable to identify with this position which in recent years has become the prevailing one.

Other Washington respondents contended that the MAAG frustration concerning reduced autonomy is part of an anachronistic view of what the function of field personnel should be. One highly placed official stated "The MAAGs must come to understand that technology has caught up with them. Modern communication, in particular, makes it less necessary for decentralization and autonomous field behavior. The advent of sophisticated communication systems has undermined their freedom. We no longer have to take the risk of an autonomous MAAG making decisions that precipitate certain situations for Washington."

Fourth, most of our respondents were distressed that they were accused of promoting arms sales in their particular country. Many said that on a number of occasions they were able to discourage their host governments from purchasing particular weapon systems, or they were willing to persuade them to buy less sophisticated weapon systems, that would be less upsetting to regional balances of power. Most of the MAAGs we interviewed cited several situations in which they felt they had performed restraining roles with regard to host military purchases. MAAGs do generate arms sales decisions. This view is being increasingly accepted by officials of the Reagan State and Defense departments.

The most prevalent problems for the MAAGs, however, seem to be small technical problem cases or specialized training cases. As a former MAAG chief related:

> The most common arms sales I generated were small technical problem cases. An example occurred while I was visiting an air base of my host. They had F-86 fighters. While touring the base, I saw a bubble on a wing. I asked my sergeant to look at it. He stabbed the bubble with a screwdriver and determined that it was intergranular-exfoliation corrosion. It is caused by diurnal variation as well as suspended sand and moist air which collects between the wings and creates gas. Well, we didn't have experts there to determine the extent of the damage to the F-86s, so we asked for a mobile team to inspect it. Well, this generated a sales case. They recommended repairs; this generated another case. Yet, both cases really involved basic flying safety.

Conclusion. A serious, emerging problem is the growing disparity between the reduced capability of the security assistance administration in the field and the increasing need for information for policy review and implementation. MAAGs are the principal field monitors for the security assistance system, yet our MAAG respondents complained that limited staff and new reporting requirements seriously limited their efficiency. By law, MAAGs are required to report on the quantity and current utilization of Military Assistance Program equipment. They are also regularly asked to provide information to the Joint Chiefs of Staff, the Office of Secretary of Defense, Politico-Military Affairs/Security Assistance and Sales, Defense Security Assistance Agency, and others. Most of the MAAGs we interviewed, however, indicated that they were unable to meet the reporting requirements placed on them while continuing to perform their primary functions of logistics management, fiscal management, transportation, and contract administration. These claims should not be wholly discounted. We discovered the emergence of a self-fulfilling prophecy with regard to MAAG reports. Under the new system MAAGs are asked to provide more information, but, because of limited staff, Washington officials tended to deprecate the quality of MAAG reports.

The problems that result from such limited capabilities and confidence in the sources of information from the field were illustrated during the Carter Administration by what was a particularly demanding requirement: "ceiling management." The policy clearance and ceiling management processes needed information to make sound decisions. When the participants in ceiling management attempt not only to assess the need and assign a priority to a nation's request, but also to anticipate, sometimes months in advance, what the request will be (as sound management of the ceiling required), they needed field access to the general planning efforts of the military buyers in question. MAAGs were usually, though not always, in the best position to perform this task.

MAAGs may not have the influence and access they often claim, but if decisions about arms sales are to be centralized in Washington, then serious consideration must be given to what timely and accurate information can and should be acquired from the field and how to acquire it. This may require more security assistance experts in the field, different arrangements within the country teams, or heavier reliance on temporary or mobile teams.

The reduced field capabilities have been the result of concern that the MAAGs generate arms sales. The two principal control measures employed have been reductions in strength and detailed instructions or guidelines that proscribe MAAG activities deemed likely to encourage host countries to buy more arms. Our interviews suggest that the restrictions placed on MAAG activities have generated uncertainties among host-government officials about the ability of the MAAGs to solve foreign military sales problems. Doubts about the utility of the MAAGs among recipient governments extend beyond their former, and now proscribed, advisory role to include much of their present management role as well. There was a concern among our MAAG chief respondents that without an unambiguous mandate to talk with senior host military personnel in the country, the United States would not have a reliable means of estimating independently the future military needs of friendly nations.

The policies and decisions that are the products of the security assistance administrative system described in the previous section are no better than the information upon which they are based. The MAAGs, of course, are not the only source of information about the military plans and programs of their host governments, and field representatives are in any case subject to special biases. The MAAGs, nevertheless, have been and are a potentially valuable source of information which can improve the quality of U.S. security assistance policies and decisions. If, as presently constituted and organized, they do not deserve the confidence necessary to make them effective, then it would seem advisable to alter their organization until they are able to command the confidence needed to permit their utilization in performing needed feedback and evaluation functions.

Another fundamental conclusion of our extensive interviews is that reduction in the numbers of permanent security assistance field personnel, as well as the extensive regulations provided for them, leaves little room for concern that they are preempting foreign policy decisions. Indeed, our interviews with not only current and former field operatives but also with many officials responsible for overseeing the security assistance process in Washington suggest that, over the years, security assistance decisions have increasingly been centralized in Washington. Former and current directors of the Defense Security Assistance Agency have noted before the Congress that the roles that the MAAGs have been increasingly required to play have moved them toward technical support, management, and administration at the end of the security assistance pipeline. The congressional testimony of the former directors of DSAA has been substantiated through our interviews. Several respondents complained that they were reduceed to being "accountants" or "parts managers."

The position of the MAAGs in the host country, however, seems to be changing. Our evidence is that, to a significant degree, over the past few years MAAGs have become more closely integrated into country teams. They enjoy better access to the ambassadors than previously, and they are less troubled by conflicting or competitive demands through unified command channels. This trend has little to do with statutory authority or recent changes in administrative authority. Rather, it results in part from the State Department signalling ambassadors that they must take charge and in part from MAAG chiefs responding to changes in their authority and resources. Those who emphasize that the ambassadors have long been recognized as heads of the country teams are missing an important point. That long-recognized position has only recently become effective with respect to arms transfers. For better or worse, the U.S. government has increased its capability to control its in-country interface with the host government.

Foreign Purchasing Missions

A common view of arms transfer critics has been to favor the shifting of activities to Washington, where they will be performed either by U.S. personnel or by purchasing missions or attache offices from the host or recipient country. By one count, eleven countries have established such offices in the United States. Congress's intent in PL95-92 was obviously to reduce the number of people involved in military assistance work overseas and to eliminate certain activities previously included in that work. The reduction in personnel and the shift of many operations previously performed by MAAGs in the field to the recipient country purchasing missions in Washington involves important considerations regarding the conduct of bilateral relations, specifically:

1. shifting the location of transfer activities from the seat of the host government and under the oversight of the U.S. Embassy there to Washington and away from the oversight of any one U.S. agency or official; and

2. shifting the performance of some former MAAG activities from U.S. officials to officials of the recipient government.

The shifting of tasks in this case from the U.S. government to host government agencies is a nontrivial change, even when the tasks involved are labeled "procedural." Many of the tasks and duties involved are mechanisms of control to assure the U.S. government that it has carried out its commitments under foreign military sales and other military supply agreements and to ascertain something about the effects of performing military supply activities. The U.S. government can scarcely turn these monitoring activities over to the recipient government. We need to know from our own information how well we are managing. To acquire such information does not require that U.S. officials become deeply involved in the host military logistics system, but it does require a U.S. monitoring effort for each recipient country. At the very least, the intent of Congress and the Carter administration was to increase U.S. control over the arms transfer process. Shifting control processes into the hands of the recipient country would obviously reduce U.S. control.

Encouraging or inducing the expansion of a recipient government's representational facilities in Washington is very likely to weaken, or at least make more difficult, U.S. government control over arms transfers to that country. Foreign purchasing missions that are able to deal directly and conveniently with Department of Defense and with army, navy, and air force sales offices and that also have convenient access, through their diplomats, to every level of the U.S. government, including Congress, make it extremely difficult for the U.S. government to track and control its contacts with these governments. From the government's standpoint, the control problem is much greater when the main contacts take place in Washington than when they take place in Riyadh, Tel Aviv, Teheran, Seoul, or Manila. This is not simply a matter for speculation. There is a record of difficulties with such purchasing missions that supports this point.

U.S. influence over buyer military policies, assuming that Washington wants to exercise such influence, is more likely if the U.S. government speaks with one voice, makes credible statements, and ensures that it has not been unduly influenced in the first place by buyer-government contacts with specific elements of the U.S. government. This is by no means a trivial problem, although we found that several of our interviewees dismissed it. Compared with buyer governments, the U.S. government is usually bigger, more complex, and more pluralistic, and the extensive clearance procedures now followed in the security assistance system give full play to that size, complexity, and pluralism. These qualities can be advantageous, but they also can be vulnerabilities. To shift the performance of some functions from U.S. officials to foreign officials manning the purchasing missions, and from their capitals to Washington, makes it more difficult for the U.S. government to evaluate its programs, establish coherent purposes, speak with one voice, take coordinated action, and monitor and control its own activities. At the policy formation or decisionmaking stage, the U.S. administrative system would be rendered more vulnerable to the initiatives of other governments and of private interests whose objectives are not shared by Washington. At the policy declaration stage, it would be similarly vulnerable because more foreign representatives making more contacts with security assistance system actors would obtain more versions of U.S. policy.

One of the claimed advantages of recipient countries establishing procurement offices in the United States or of vesting purchasing authority with their attachés in the United States has been that these countries are better able to keep abreast of changes in U.S. security assistance policies. Recipient countries may want their own administrators and observers in Washington, because they want to know as much as they can about those policies, but the U.S. government cannot count on these participant-observers to report what we want reported to their governments. Recipient country acquisition teams and attachés in Washington are no substitute for our own spokesmen. On the contrary, the buildup of foreign acquisition teams in Washington further complicates the problem for the United States of speaking with a harmony of voices (if not a single voice) in foreign relations.

Rigidity of Security Assistance Policies

We have already discussed several problems associated with the formality or complexity of the administrative processes related to security assistance. One aspect of that formality is the growing rigidity of security assistance policies. That rigidity is revealed by the increasing number of congressionally mandated restrictions relating to who can receive security assistance and how such assistance can be used. Some of the restrictions are quite valuable; others are well intended. The cumulative result, however, is a system increasingly incapable of flexible response to changing world conditions.

The following list of restrictions reveals the extent of the system's rigidity. It is by no means a complete list, and the restrictions noted here are merely summarized. A more thorough description of each restriction can be found in the 1961 Foreign Assistance Act, as amended, or in the analysis of that act done by the Congressional Research Service.[19] The following list includes restrictions on MAP and on FMS:

1. The President must determine that MAP will strengthen the security of the United States and promote world peace.
2. Receipt of U.S. military assistance does not imply a defense commitment to a nation.
3. A recipient must use the aid solely for internal security, self-defense, or participation in collective-security activities consistent with the charter of the United States.
4. A Recipient country will prevent defense items from being used by anyone other than an official agent of that country and will not permit transfer of the items to another nation.
5. The President cannot permit third-country transfers to nations other than those to which the United States would itself transfer the weapon.
6. Military assistance is prohibited to nations that fundamentally violate human rights.
7. Congress shall determine which nations receive military grant assistance.
8. No assistance may be provided to countries that discriminate against U.S. citizens who may be involved in furnishing aid to that government.
9. No military assistance may be provided to Communist nations.
10. No military assistance may be provided to countries where a U.S. citizen has been denied legal recourse in collecting debts from the government.
11. No security assistance may be provided to a nation that the President determines is engaging in aggression against the United States or against a recipient of U.S. aid.
12. No military assistance may be provided to a country that has nationalized or seized property of a U.S. corporation.
13. No funds may be provided for police training.

14. No funds may be provided for any country that aids or abets terrorist groups.
15. No military assistance may be provided to a country that receives "nuclear enriched equipment" that is not controlled through multilateral management under the safeguards of the International Atomic Energy Agency.
16. No military assistance may be provided to a country that explodes a nuclear device.
17. No assistance may be provided that will aid Angola.
18. No assistance may be available to Chile.
19. Only $40 million may be provided in military assistance for Africa.
20. Countries that have bases constructed or managed by the United States must permit U.S. news correspondents to enter those bases.
21. No MAP funds for a country may be used for CIA activities.
22. No aid may be provided to Zaire unless a detailed explanation is presented to Congress.
23. No military assistance funds may be used to compensate the owners of expropriated property.
24. No security assistance funds may be used to finance nuclear power plants.
25. No funds may be used to purchase new automotive vehicles outside the United States.
26. All contracts must contain a provision authorizing termination of the contract at the convenience of the United States.
27. No military assistance may be provided to a country in default of its loan payments for a period longer than one year.
28. Dollar limits for military assistance must be approved by Congress.
29. The President may consider terminating aid to any nation that fails to prevent mob damage to U.S. property.
30. The President may terminate aid to any nation failing to provide investment guarantees against expropriation.
31. The President may terminate aid to any country that imposes penalties against U.S. fishing vessels for activities in international waters.
32. The President may terminate aid to any nation that fails to prevent illegal drug traffic.
33. The President may terminate aid to any government in which an official receives improper payment from a U.S. company.
34. No more than twenty flag officers may be stationed in any country receiving security assistance.
35. No MAAGs may be established unless specifically authorized by Congress.
36. Elsewhere, up to six-man teams are authorized.

37. The primary function of MAAGs must be logistic and physical management, transportation, and contract administration of country programs.
38. All advisory and training roles must be performed by temporary teams.
39. All MAAGs are under the control of the Chief of Mission.
40. Export-Import Bank credit may be used for sales of defense items only to developed nations.
41. Sales of defense items or services that would have an adverse effect on U.S. combat readiness will be kept to an absolute minimum.
42. No sale or credit shall be provided to a country that is diverting PL480 funds for the purpose of military expenditures.
43. FMS funds may not be used for procurement outside the United States unless the President determines that such procurement is not adverse to U.S. interests.
44. No credit may be provided for the sale of sophisticated weapon systems to any underdeveloped country other than Greece, Turkey, Iran, Israel, the Republic of China, or the Philippines unless the President determines such financing is necessary to the national interest.
45. Credit for coproduction agreements is strictly limited.
46. Congress may forbid credit assistance to any nation.
47. Congress can prohibit or limit cash or credit sales to any nation.
48. Any cash sale agreement may be cancelled by the United States at its discretion at any time.
49. No military personnel can perform combat duties related to an FMS case.

Conclusion: Continued Reliance on Formal Procedures

The new security assistance system relies heavily on organizational formality—formal assignment of tasks and procedures, and formal statements of principles and goals. It seeks to minimize the problems perceived in the old system by means of an overlay of monitoring and policy-clearance procedures, as well as by other changes, such as a reduction in the strength and role of the MAAGs. This reliance on formal mechanisms may indeed accomplish many of the objectives sought; but there is also a danger of introducing new problems into security assistance administration, and in some cases problems have already been introduced.

The formal mechanisms of the Carter administration's system make it less easy to put pressure, discreetly and inconspicuously, on another government with regard to security assistance. The elaborate process set up as the control mechanism for security assistance administration minimizes the prospects that the United States can influence without being obvious. On the other hand, the new system makes some gains in Washington's capacity to exercise influence, and those gains, to be sure, need to be recognized. It can be helpful for U.S. officials who must deal on a day-to-day basis with buyer governments, and who are in a position to exercise influence discreetly, to have rules or guidelines that limit their ability to accommodate the buyer. In this respect, the new system has built-in arrangements that can facilitate U.S. Influence. Specifically, when Washington states broad policies and then sticks with those policies consistently, they become facts of life with which host governments must live. Other governments now recognize—at least some of them do—that the U.S. government is going to behave in a certain way.

At the same time, the new system employs a conspicuous process of broad clearances that applies explicit decision principles. These characteristics of the clearance process (1) reduce the ability of U.S. officials to bargain with other governments and (2) limit discussions of possible contract terms with a prospective buyer country. These difficulties can be circumvented, most obviously, by having the Secretary of State or the President act as spokesman: some bilateral arms transfers involve sufficiently important policy stakes to bring them in anyway. But involving the President and the Secretary of State is itself a cost, given their limited time and the fact that their involvement makes the case more conspicuous.

As a clearance mechanism, the AECB and its successor, the ATMG, have so far absorbed more problems than they have generated by serving as a consensus-building forum. Since the ATMG serves only in an advisory capacity to the Secretary of State, the Secretary is officially free to act contrary to the sense of the ATMG's deliberations. Neither group was organized to resolve disagreements over policy among the principal actors in the security assistance administrative system. The ATMG can, however, operate smoothly in the manner that it now operates only as long as it does not have to handle major disagreements among its principal participants. Presently, those disagreements are forwarded as options through the Secretary of the State to the President if the case is sufficiently politically sensitive. As matters now stand, the system depends mainly on the mutual interpersonal confidence of the main participants in security assistance. These personal relations carry the ATMG, not the other way around. The system also depends on the fact that no one among the principal participants challenges current applications of arms transfer policy.

NOTES

1 See Anne Hessing Cahn et al., *Controlling Future Arms Trade* (New York: McGraw-Hill, 1977) and, for the state as a rational actor, Graham T. Allison, *Essence of Decision* (Boston: Little, Brown, 1971).

2 The term MAAG used here includes those organizations that are by statute designated MAAGs, and also those referred to as Military Groups (MILGPs), Offices of Defense Cooperation (ODCs), and Military Logistics Organizations (MLOs). It does not include DAOs (Defense Attache Offices), even when these are authorized to perform security assistance functions.

3 "Munitions Control Newsletter, No. 47"; reprinted in United States, House, Committee on International Relations, *Review of the President's Conventional Arms Transfer Policy*, 95th Congress, 2nd Session, March 21, 1978, p. 78.

4 Countries frequently become eligible for Foreign Military Sales after a presidential determination is made in accordance with Section 3(a) of the Arms Export Control Act.

5 Items designated as "significant combat equipment" are listed in International Traffic in Arms Regulation (ITAR), Title 22, Code of Federal Regulations, pp. 121-128. Generally, such equipment includes the following types of weapons: (1) nonautomatic and semiautomatic firearms to caliber .50 incusive, automatic firearms and all components to caliber .50, insurgency-counterinsurgency weapons if in quantity; (2) guns over caliber .50, howitzers, mortars and recoilless rifles, flame throwers; (3) ammunition for the above weapons; (4) rockets, bombs, grenades, torpedoes, mines, guided missles, missile-vehicle power plants, military-type explosive excavating devices; (5) military explosives if in quantity; (6) warships, landing craft, turrets and gun mounts, nuclear propulsion plants; (7) military-type armed or armored vehicles, tanks, self-propelled guns, amphibious vehicles; (8) aircraft, including helicopters designated or modified for military purposes, spacecraft, military aircraft engines, ground-effect machines, some types of inertial systems; (9) military body armor; (10) chemical, biological, and nuclear radiation agents used to incapacitate; (11) nuclear weapons and related design and test equipment; (12) items that are classified; and (13) submersible vessels designed for military purposes.

6 The policy review function of arms sales is considered here. We shall not discuss the decisionmaking process for the Military Assistance Program, which now represents a small proportion of security assistance as a whole.

7 *Review of the President's Conventional Arms Transfer Policy*, p. 82.

8 United States, House, Committee on International Relations, *United States Arms Transfer and Security Assistance Program*, 95th Congress, 2nd Session, March 21, 1978, p. 75.

9 PL95-105, Arms Export Control Act (Foreign Relations Authorization Act, Fiscal Year 1978, H.R. 6689, 91 Stat. 844 to 846, approved August 17, 1977), Section 47(c).

10 *Rationalization*: Any action that increases the effectiveness of alliance forces through more efficient use of defense resources committed to the alliance. Rationalization includes consolidation, reassessment of national priorities to higher alliance needs, standardization, specialization, mutual support, interoperability, and greater cooperation. Rationalization applies both to weapons-material resources and nonweapons materiel. *Standardization*: The process by which member nations achieve the closest practicable cooperation among forces, arrive at the most efficient use of research, development, and production resources, and agree to adopt on the broadest possible basis (1) common or compatible technical operational, administrative, and logistic procedures, (2) common or compatible technical procedures and criteria, (3) common, compatible, or interchangeable supplies, components, weapons, or equipment, and (4) common or compatible tactical documents with corresponding organizational compat-

ibility. *Interoperability*: The ability of systems, units, or forces (1) to provide services to, and accept services from, other systems, units, or forces and (2) to use the services so exchanged in such a way as to operate practically together. (Interviews conducted in USASAC, February-June 1978).

11 *Review of the President's Conventional Arms Transfer Policy*, p. 2.

12 Ibid., pp. 48-50.

13 Paul Y. Hammond, "Gauging the Long Term Value of Military Assistance and of Military Advisory Groups," statement before the Subcommittee on National Security Policy and Scientific Developments, Committee on Foreign Affairs, House of Representatives, October 6, 1970.

14 See United States, House, Committee on International Relations, Arms Transfer Policy: Background Information, 95th Congress, 2nd Session, 1978, pp. 72-76; and David J. Louscher, "The Rise of Military Sales as a U.S. Foreign Assistance Instrument," *Orbis*, 20, 4 (Winter 1977); pp. 933-964.

15 *Department of Defense Policy and Responsibilities Relating to Security Assistance*, Department of Defense Directive 51323, December 20, 1972.

16 United States, House, Committee on International Relations. *Hearings on Foreign Assistance Legislation for Fiscal Year 1978* (Part 2), hearings before the Subcommittee on International Security and Scientific Affairs, 95th Congress, 1st Session, pp. 15-17.

17 Ibid., pp. 95-96.

18 In addition, see *Hearings on Foreign Assistance Legislation for Fiscal Year 1978*, Appendix 1. See also the Foreign Assistance Act, as amended, Sections 622c and 623.

19 *United States Arms Transfer and Security Assistance Program.*

Chapter 5

The Directions of Security
Assistance Programs,
1950–1980

This chapter provides a comprehensive description of trends in the U.S. security assistance program. It details U.S. arms sales and grant assistance in terms of agreements and actual deliveries of equipment, training, services, and credits over a thirty-one-year span from fiscal year 1950 through fiscal year 1980. Costs are stated in current and FY 1977 constant U.S. dollars. The adjustments used to generate 1977 constant dollars were extrapolated from the Department of Defense deflator "total military non-pay," the measure that DOD officials identified as most relevant to the measurement of security assistance costs.[1] The base year 1977 was chosen for two purposes. First, arms sales studies and scholarly works from the academic community that use data to support their analysis most often rely on data generated by ACDA. It is readily available, and most recently has used 1977 constant-dollar figures to measure various worldwide arms sales activities. Second, FY 1977 was the budget year in which the Carter administration's policy arms transfer restraint was initiated. And it is the failure of this policy and the Reagan administration's departure from it that frames both the reluctant supplier theme and the continuing debates over arms sales. The nonspecialist may find more detail here than he cares to know. In that event, we recommend skipping to the closing summary, which provides the basic argument that the body of this chapter documents.

United States security assistance has been provided under several broad programs: the Foreign Military Sales program (FMS), the Military Assistance Program (MAP), the Military Assistance Service Fund (MASF), and the International Military Education and Training (IMET) program. In addition, commercial arms sales have recently grown at a rapid rate.

Frequently in congressional hearings, Security-Supporting Assistance is considered concurrently with these other instruments. It is not addressed here, however, because it is neither an arms transfer nor a military service training instrument. Rather, it is an economic instrument, the purpose of which is to promote the economic and political stability of recipients through budgetary support. A recipient nation is usually provided foreign exchange to purchase imports that improve some economic activity. Sometimes the recipient is provided funds to release its own revenues from mandated activities so that new programs may be instituted. Security-supporting assistance was designed to provide economic assistance to countries whose economies were heavily burdened by defense costs. In principle, security-supporting assistance enables the recipient to overcome its defense problem without being subjected to a simultaneous deterioration in its economy. But security-supporting assistance cannot be considered more than an indirect financing program with respect to military assistance, and the same view applies to all credit assistance, economic grants, international loans, agricultural subsidies, preferred trade, or tariff concessions. If a nation has a military supply relationship with the United States, these forms of credit or assistance may indirectly release funds to purchase U.S. military equipment or services. However, to include these forms of exchange in a discussion of military assistance or security assistance would be misleading and inaccurate.

Presently Foreign Military Sales (FMS) and the related direct financing tools that support it consitute the largest arms transfer program. Through FMS the U.S. government sells military equipment or services to a recipient government. The equipment sold and transferred is sometimes taken from U.S. government stocks; on other occasions the U.S. government acts as the procurement agent for the recipient and acquires weapons and services from U.S. manufacturers. The recipient must deposit U.S. dollars in the foreign military sales trust fund for the materials to be procured from manufacturers or for items sold from any of the military department's stocks. Payment must be made in advance.

Arms transfers through FMS are sometimes financed through one of three U.S. government programs: Department of Defense Guaranteed Credit, Direct Credit, or Waived Credit. In addition, in the past the Export-Import Bank provided credit to developed countries to purchase defense items from the United States. However, Section 32 of the Arms Export Control Act specifically prohibits the Export-Import Bank from using its resources to help finance a sale of defense equipment or services to developing countries. While no such prohibition exists for financing arms sales to developed countries, the Export-Import Bank has chosen not to provide such assistance in recent years, owing to the controversy that arose in Congress over the subject during the late 1960s.[2]

The Department of Defense Guaranteed Credit program is a financing instrument by which the Department insures individuals, corporations, and financial institutions against credit risks and nonpayment by a recipient nation for equipment or services purchased through FMS channels. Since 1974, the Federal Financing Bank has been the exclusive source of DOD guaranteed financing. In the Direct Credit program, credit is provided through funds specifically appropriated by Congress. In the past, U.S. government policy directed that only developing countries be eligible for direct credit. This instrument is used almost exclusively to provide credit for sales to Israel. Funds for these financing programs are authorized and appropriated annually by Congress. The funds are not specifically designated by Congress for individual recipients; rather, Congress establishes a ceiling for the sales credit programs. The exception is Israel, however. Through waived credit, the U.S. government has absolved Israel of nearly $5 billion worth of debts for FMS equipment and services.

The Military Assistance Program (MAP) was a substantial program in the 1950s but has been less used in recent years. MAP is a grant of military equipment, services, training, and administrative support to a foreign recipient. As indicated in Chapter III, MAP originated to assist the military recovery of Western Europe after the Second World War. Presently MAP funding must be authorized by Congress on a country-by-country basis.

The Military Assistance Service Fund (MASF), another grant program, originated in 1966 to aid South Vietnam and other Southeast Asian countries participating in the Vietnam War. Appropriations for this grant program were provided through regular Department of Defense armed services appropriations, rather than as a part of the international security assistance legislation. In FY 1968, aid to Laos and Thailand was provided through MASF. By 1973, grant aid to Thailand was transferred by the MAP. In 1975, grant aid to Laos was returned to MAP and grant aid to South Vietnam was terminated.

The International Military Education and Training (IMET) program was established initially as a grant program for military training of foreign personnel. IMET was intended to be a low-cost, low-risk foreign policy instrument by which the United States could create valuable channels of communications with emerging Third World military leaders.[3]

Increasingly, commercial sales of military equipment and services have become a major element of U.S. security assistance. Commercial sales are not a government program, and no government expenditures are involved in such transactions. They are agreements between domestic private corporations and foreign governments or foreign defense manufacturers. Payment and financing are privately arranged by the foreign buyer and the U.S. private-sector supplier. They are subject to strict regulation, however. The Arms Export Control Act (AECA) and The International Traffic in Arms Regulations (ITAR) create extensive rules and elaborate review processes before arms may be delivered to a foreign recipient.[4] Most commercial export deliveries are to NATO and the developed countries. Often, commercial sales channels are more favorable than FMS channels because commercial channels provide: (1) faster delivery; (2) newer equipment; (3) more flexibility in pricing; (4) fewer penalties for late payment or late delivery; and (5) less bureaucratic red tape.[5]

FOREIGN MILITARY SALES

FMS, the current U.S. government security assistance program, has expanded steadily since the early 1960s. Table 5.1 displays United States FMS agreements measured in both current and constant dollars. Figure 5.1 graphically displays these data. Worldwide, the value of FMS agreements in constant 1977 dollars has grown from $132 million in 1950 to $11.5 billion in 1980. Until 1962, FMS agreements constituted less than $1 billion worth of security assistance, and not until 1972 was FMS used extensively. In that year FMS agreements jumped from $2 billion to $4.4 billion. In 1974, agreements reached $13 billion, and in 1975 such agreements reached $19 billion 1977 constant dollars. Agreements then began to decline to around $10 billion from 1977 through 1980.

The rise of FMS is not nearly as dramatic, however, when measured in terms of actual deliveries to recipients. Indeed, while much analysis, both for Congress and in the scholarly literature, focuses on agreements measured in current dollars, little attention has been devoted to the great differences between FMS agreements and *actual deliveries*. Deliveries, of course, lag behind agreements. The lag time is often nontrivial. Sometimes it is as long as five years and even more. For the thirty-one-year period assessed here, it is quite obvious that many agreements were

Table 5.1. FMS Agreements Worldwide

In Current and Constant 1977 Dollars

==

Fiscal Year	Current Dollars	Constant 1977 Dollars
1950	$ 50,797,000	$ 131,940,000
1951	78,598,000	194,309,000
1952	98,992,000	248,100,000
1953	77,816,000	190,445,000
1954	91,578,000	231,784,000
1955	84,194,000	205,051,000
1956	133,104,000	310,918,000
1957	347,323,000	788,833,000
1958	313,522,000	705,813,000
1959	347,792,000	777,710,000
1960	241,851,000	532,008,000
1961	421,985,000	917,957,000
1962	645,761,000	1,383,971,000
1963	805,657,000	1,702,572,000
1964	1,410,245,000	2,902,933,000
1965	1,779,091,000	3,576,781,000
1966	1,457,650,000	2,767,515,000
1967	1,091,231,000	1,992,752,000
1968	1,173,592,000	2,056,048,000
1969	1,172,820,000	1,978,775,000
1970	1,110,756,000	1,823,602,000
1971	1,390,361,000	2,162,640,000
1972	2,950,017,000	4,389,906,000
1973	4,847,920,000	6,783,154,000
1974	10,343,461,000	13,281,280,000
1975	16,053,447,000	19,043,235,000
1976	14,673,701,000	16,019,324,000
1977	8,304,674,000	8,304,674,000
1978	11,038,575,000	10,173,802,000
1979	13,013,516,000	11,075,333,000
1980	15,276,995,000	11,503,761,000

never completed and U.S. arms sales volume is not as large as it often appears.

There are several reasons for this. Recipients often change their minds about some weapons or service purchase. Frequently, the United States has renegotiated agreements with recipients. It has been estimated by some officials that the "pipeline" of agreed but undelivered systems and services, some portion of which may later by cancelled, as were billions of dollars' worth in the pipeline to Iran, is as large or long as $65 billion. Patently, the value of weapons systems and services delivered to recipients over the past thirty years has been substantially less than the value of agreements to do so.

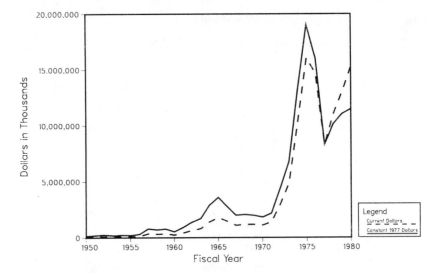

Figure 5.1. FMS agreements worldwide.

Foreign military sales deliveries throughout the 1970s did not equal agreements by any means. The greatest disparities between sales and deliveries occurred in the 1974–1980 period, when agreements ranged from 8 billion constant dollars to 19 billion constant dollars while deliveries only ranged from 4 billion to 7 billion constant dollars. Table 5.2 displays actual FMS deliveries both in current and constant dollars; Figure 5.2 displays the data in graphic form.

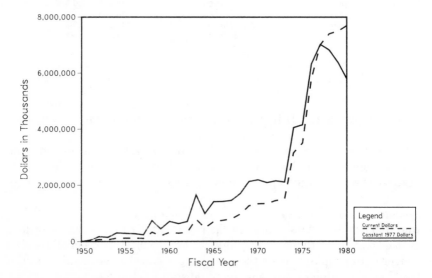

Figure 5.2. FMS deliveries worldwide.

Table 5.2.   FMS Deliveries Worldwide

In Current and Constant 1977 Dollars

Fiscal Year	Current Dollars	Constant 1977 Dollars
1950	$ 2,000,000	$ 5,195,000
1951	19,024,000	47,031,000
1952	69,238,000	173,529,000
1953	60,394,000	147,807,000
1954	120,451,000	304,862,000
1955	118,015,000	287,421,000
1956	117,675,000	274,877,000
1957	104,467,000	237,263,000
1958	328,557,000	739,660,000
1959	201,527,000	450,642,000
1960	323,149,000	710,843,000
1961	290,498,000	631,930,000
1962	330,152,000	707,570,000
1963	781,852,000	1,652,265,000
1964	481,271,000	990,677,000
1965	703,384,000	1,414,121,000
1966	746,556,000	1,417,422,000
1967	797,473,000	1,456,306,000
1968	966,705,000	1,693,597,000
1969	1,267,211,000	2,138,031,000
1970	1,336,453,000	2,194,144,000
1971	1,346,153,000	2,093,876,000
1972	1,450,109,000	2,157,900,000
1973	1,509,733,000	2,112,401,000
1974	3,159,348,000	4,056,687,000
1975	3,501,740,000	4,153,903,000
1976	5,798,492,000	6,330,231,000
1977	7,022,408,000	7,022,408,000
1978	7,407,670,000	6,827,346,000
1979	7,506,286,000	6,388,329,000
1980	7,698,334,000	5,796,938,000

The Near East and South Asia

The rapid expansion of FMS in the 1970s is mostly explained by increased purchases of arms by Near East and South Asian nations.[6] Indeed, as Tables 5.3 and 5.4 indicate, sales to the Near East and South Asia were modest until 1970, when they began to constitute a sizable proportion of all FMS agreements and deliveries. For example, as shown in Table 5.3 and Figure 5.3, agreements for FMS to the Near East and South Asia in constant dollars did not exceed $100 million until FY 1965, when they rose to over $1.4 billion. From FY 1966 to FY 1970,

Table 5.3. FMS Agreements with the Near East and South Asia

In Current and Constant 1977 Dollars

Fiscal Year	Current Dollars	Constant 1977 Dollars
1950	$ 0	$ 0
1951	5,000	12,000
1952	773,000	1,937,000
1953	25,908,000	63,407,000
1954	7,079,000	17,917,000
1955	16,200,000	39,454,000
1956	15,084,000	35,235,000
1957	24,694,000	56,084,000
1958	43,146,000	97,132,000
1959	11,200,000	25,045,000
1960	8,922,000	19,626,000
1961	10,086,000	21,940,000
1962	8,347,000	17,889,000
1963	12,683,000	26,803,000
1964	5,387,000	11,089,000
1965	711,826,000	1,431,094,000
1966	234,898,000	445,981,000
1967	346,647,000	633,030,000
1968	452,551,000	792,836,000
1969	353,637,000	596,654,000
1970	408,607,000	670,837,000
1971	710,569,000	1,105,256,000
1972	1,190,191,000	1,771,118,000
1973	3,482,142,000	4,872,173,000
1974	8,563,431,000	10,995,674,000
1975	8,661,964,000	10,275,165,000
1976	11,248,148,000	12,279,638,000
1977	5,515,406,000	5,515,406,000
1978	7,164,538,000	6,603,261,000
1979	8,311,931,000	7,073,984,000
1980	8,151,512,000	6,138,187,000

agreements remained between 400 and 800 million constant dollars, but began to expand rapidly in FY 1971. In FY 1974, FY 1975, and FY 1976, agreements were approximately 11.0, 10.3, and 12.3 billion dollars respectively, then stabilized at between $5 billion and $7-plus billion after 1977. For the ten-year period from 1971 through 1980, FMS agreements with Near East and South Asian nations constituted the bulk of all FMS agreements. In that period, over $103 billion (constant dollars) worth of agreements were negotiated, of which over $67 billion in agreements were with Near East countries. This represented 65 percent of all FMS agreements.

Table 5.4. FMS Deliveries to the Near East and South Asia

In Current and Constant 1977 Dollars

Fiscal Year	Current Dollars	Constant 1977 Dollars
1950	$ 0	$ 0
1951	3,000	7,000
1952	455,000	1,140,000
1953	9,757,000	23,879,000
1954	15,200,000	38,471,000
1955	10,031,000	24,430,000
1956	23,154,000	54,085,000
1957	3,184,000	7,231,000
1958	51,501,000	115,941,000
1959	7,078,000	15,827,000
1960	21,338,000	46,938,000
1961	13,775,000	29,965,000
1962	4,177,000	8,952,000
1963	3,719,000	7,859,000
1964	9,362,000	19,271,000
1965	41,017,000	82,463,000
1966	95,439,000	181,202,000
1967	108,744,000	198,583,000
1968	149,721,000	262,300,000
1969	253,428,000	427,582,000
1970	469,259,000	770,414,000
1971	477,238,000	742,321,000
1972	583,144,000	867,774,000
1973	677,200,000	947,530,000
1974	1,982,151,000	2,545,135,000
1975	2,084,453,000	2,472,661,000
1976	3,768,801,000	4,114,412,000
1977	5,157,877,000	5,157,877,000
1978	5,385,453,000	4,963,551,000
1979	4,924,230,000	4,190,834,000
1980	4,051,871,000	3,051,108,000

But just as worldwide deliveries have not equaled worldwide agreements, so too have deliveries to the Near East not equaled agreements for that region. In the period 1971 to 1980, the United States delivered 47 billion constant dollars' worth of FMS equipment and services worldwide. Of this total, about $30 billion in deliveries were to the Near East, or about 61 percent of all FMS deliveries. Figure 5.4 displays deliveries to the Near East and South Asia for the thirty-one-year period.

Figure 5.3. FMS agreements with the Near East and South Asia.

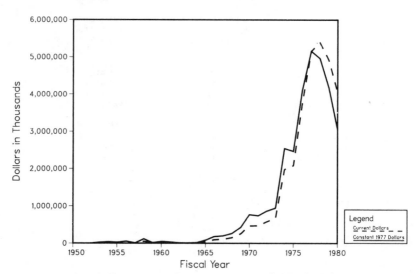

Figure 5.4. FMS deliveries to the Near East and South Asia.

Europe and Canada

European nations and Canada are the second largest recipients of FMS. Table 5.5 presents FMS agreements to these nations over a thirty-one-year period measured in current and constant dollars, and Figure

Table 5.5. FMS Agreements with Europe and Canada

In Current and Constant 1977 Dollars

Fiscal Year	Current Dollars	Constant 1977 Dollars
1950	$ 49,223,000	$ 127,852,000
1951	55,444,000	137,068,000
1952	79,034,000	198,080,000
1953	26,167,000	64,041,000
1954	72,573,000	183,683,000
1955	51,159,000	124,596,000
1956	94,644,000	221,079,000
1957	285,541,000	648,515,000
1958	216,894,000	488,280,000
1959	313,414,000	700,836,000
1960	159,521,000	350,904,000
1961	353,562,000	769,115,000
1962	545,662,000	1,169,443,000
1963	687,913,000	1,453,747,000
1964	1,181,895,000	2,432,884,000
1965	655,794,000	1,318,444,000
1966	1,105,418,000	2,098,762,000
1967	525,867,000	960,312,000
1968	549,656,000	962,957,000
1969	632,609,000	1,067,334,000
1970	499,337,000	819,795,000
1971	455,119,000	707,916,000
1972	1,318,561,000	1,962,144,000
1973	872,076,000	1,220,199,000
1974	1,242,368,000	1,595,234,000
1975	6,491,489,000	7,700,461,000
1976	1,378,426,000	1,504,832,000
1977	1,276,922,000	1,276,922,000
1978	1,760,490,000	1,622,571,000
1979	2,110,509,000	1,796,178,000
1980	4,719,086,000	3,553,529,000

5.5 displays the trends in graphic form. As shown, agreements were small in the early 1950s, when most security assistance to Europe and Canada was in the form of MAP. As MAP to the region declined, however, FMS grew. In 1962, FMS agreements exceeded 1 billion constant 1977 dollars but only once did they exceed $2.5 billion until FY 1980. This exception was in FY 1975, when the U.S. concluded 7.7 billion constant dollars' worth of FMS agreements with nations in the region.

During the period FY 1971 to FY 1980, over 22 percent of all FMS agreements were with nations in Europe or Canada.

Table 5.6 and Figure 5.6 reveal trends in actual deliveries to Europe and Canada; it can be seen that deliveries have lagged substantially behind agreements. For example, even though agreements in FY 1975 exceeded 7.7 billion constant dollars, deliveries for that year and in succeeding years never passed $2 billion. In fact, FMS deliveries to Europe and Canada have never exceeded $2 billion. Yet, it should be noted that in the period FY 1971 to FY 1980, 24 percent of all United States FMS deliveries in the world were to Europe and Canada.

Table 5.6.   FMS Deliveries to Europe and Canada

In Current and Constant 1977 Dollars

Fiscal Year	Current Dollars	Constant 1977 Dollars
1950	$ 1,807,000	$ 4,694,000
1951	17,580,000	43,461,000
1952	51,117,000	128,113,000
1953	25,609,000	62,675,000
1954	93,341,000	236,247,000
1955	92,301,000	224,795,000
1956	76,364,000	178,379,000
1957	84,205,000	191,245,000
1958	254,658,000	573,296,000
1959	151,455,000	338,674,000
1960	246,790,000	542,873,000
1961	236,204,000	513,822,000
1962	259,174,000	555,452,000
1963	677,094,000	1,430,883,000
1964	397,522,000	818,283,000
1965	572,313,000	1,150,609,000
1966	522,216,000	991,487,000
1967	544,182,000	993,758,000
1968	592,115,000	1,037,342,000
1969	789,502,000	1,332,043,000
1970	673,083,000	1,105,045,000
1971	644,981,000	1,003,237,000
1972	667,492,000	993,292,000
1973	552,385,000	772,891,000
1974	744,945,000	956,529,000
1975	961,929,000	1,141,078,000
1976	1,407,626,000	1,536,710,000
1977	1,114,096,000	1,114,096,000
1978	933,060,000	859,963,000
1979	1,500,536,000	1,277,052,000
1980	2,316,414,000	1,744,288,000

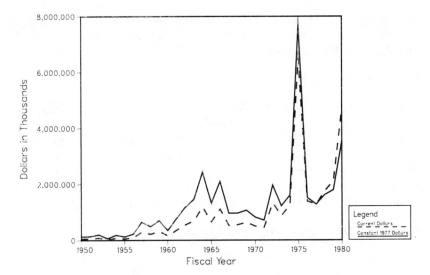

Figure 5.5. FMS agreements with Europe and Canada.

A special point should be made concerning the FMS program for Europe and Canada and the Near East and South Asia. While FMS agreements and deliveries to other areas of the world have not been insignificant in the period from 1971 to 1980, when FMS experienced the

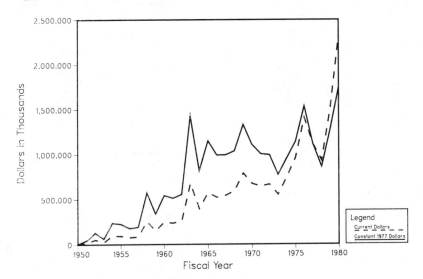

Figure 5.6. FMS deliveries to Europe and Canada.

greatest growth, about 85 percent of all agreements and 87 percent of all deliveries measured in constant dollars have been to Europe, Canada, and the Near East and South Asia.

East Asia and the Pacific

Tables 5.7 and 5.8 show FMS agreements and deliveries for East Asia and the Pacific, and Figures 5.7 and 5.8 display these data in graphic form.[7] Until FY 1975, only once did FMS agreements in the region exceed 500 million constant dollars. The exception was FY 1965, when just over $733 million of agreements were concluded. After FY 1975, however, agreements with countries in the region expanded quite rapidly, reaching a high of 1.86 billion cònstant dollars in FY 1976.

Table 5.7. FMS Agreements with East Asia and the Pacific

In Current and Constant 1977 Dollars

Fiscal Year	Current Dollars	Constant 1977 Dollars
1950	$ 420,000	$ 1,091,000
1951	13,552,000	33,503,000
1952	9,016,000	22,596,000
1953	8,085,000	19,787,000
1954	3,798,000	9,613,000
1955	4,798,000	11,685,000
1956	2,723,000	6,361,000
1957	14,721,000	33,434,000
1958	31,175,000	70,182,000
1959	14,874,000	33,260,000
1960	37,739,000	83,016,000
1961	38,583,000	83,931,000
1962	33,631,000	72,077,000
1963	26,500,000	56,002,000
1964	183,929,000	378,611,000
1965	364,983,000	733,782,000
1966	74,721,000	141,866,000
1967	154,257,000	281,696,000
1968	131,186,000	229,828,000
1969	154,467,000	260,616,000
1970	140,942,000	231,394,000
1971	145,230,000	225,898,000
1972	300,161,000	446,668,000
1973	296,332,000	414,624,000
1974	303,246,000	389,376,000
1975	666,158,000	790,223,000
1976	1,704,929,000	1,861,276,000
1977	1,257,772,000	1,257,772,000
1978	1,712,252,000	1,578,112,000
1979	1,914,525,000	1,629,383,000
1980	2,235,338,000	1,683,236,000

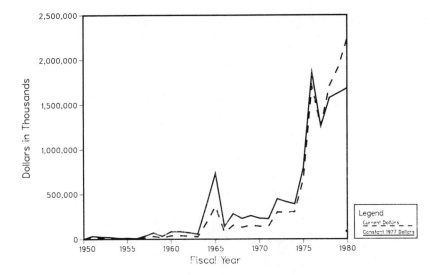

Figure 5.7. FMS agreements with East Asia and the Pacific.

FMS deliveries to East Asia and the Pacific region for the entire thirty-one-year period were substantially fewer than agreements. Indeed, not until FY 1974 did deliveries to this region exceed $300 million per year.[8] For most of the period, deliveries were less that $200 million per year in constant dollars.

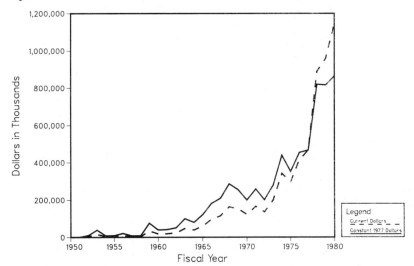

Figure 5.8. FMS deliveries to East Asia and the Pacific.

Table 5.8. FMS Deliveries to East Asia and the Pacific

In Current and Constant 1977 Dollars

===

Fiscal Year	Current Dollars	Constant 1977 Dollars
1950	$ 84,000	$ 218,000
1951	352,000	870,000
1952	4,106,000	10,291,000
1953	15,754,000	38,556,000
1954	3,163,000	8,006,000
1955	3,732,000	9,089,000
1956	8,948,000	20,902,000
1957	3,420,000	7,767,000
1958	3,569,000	8,035,000
1959	33,632,000	75,206,000
1960	17,902,000	39,380,000
1961	19,033,000	41,403,000
1962	23,726,000	50,849,000
1963	46,854,000	99,015,000
1964	38,712,000	79,687,000
1965	60,229,000	121,088,000
1966	96,098,000	182,453,000
1967	114,422,000	208,952,000
1968	163,203,000	285,920,000
1969	151,513,000	255,632,000
1970	121,816,000	199,993,000
1971	166,184,000	258,491,000
1972	135,237,000	201,246,000
1973	199,538,000	279,191,000
1974	341,918,000	439,032,000
1975	296,844,000	352,128,000
1976	416,502,000	454,697,000
1977	466,355,000	466,355,000
1978	889,250,000	819,585,000
1979	958,737,000	815,946,000
1980	1,147,617,000	864,169,000

The limited nature of the FMS program for East Asia and the Pacific as a program supporting military forces in developing countries is further revealed when industrialized states such as Australia, Japan, and New Zealand are excluded from the regional totals. For example, in the period FY 1975 to FY 1980, the period that has seen the largest expansion of FMS to the region, agreements totaled more than $9.4 billion (current dollars). Of this total, more than $3.2 billion in agreements, or 34 percent, were with Australia, Japan, and New Zealand.

A substantial amount of actual deliveries to the region have also been made to Australia, Japan, and New Zealand. These three countries received military equipment through FMS channels exceeding $800 million, whereas FMS deliveries to the region as a whole were about $4 billion. This represents 19 percent of all FMS deliveries to the region.

Latin America

Measured in constant dollars, FMS agreements with Latin American nations have always been relatively minor compared to other regions of the world.[9] Tables 5.9 and 5.10 present FMS agreements and deliveries to Latin America measured in both current and constant dollars; Figures 5.9 and 5.10 display the yearly totals for the region graphically.

Table 5.9.   FMS Agreements with Latin American Republics

In Current and Constant 1977 Dollars

Fiscal Year	Current Dollars	Constant 1977 Dollars
1950	$ 1,154,000	$ 2,997,000
1951	9,597,000	23,726,000
1952	10,071,000	25,241,000
1953	17,575,000	43,013,000
1954	7,769,000	19,663,000
1955	11,930,000	29,055,000
1956	19,999,000	46,716,000
1957	22,112,000	50,220,000
1958	22,147,000	49,858,000
1959	8,208,000	18,354,000
1960	30,165,000	66,355,000
1961	7,341,000	15,969,000
1962	18,047,000	38,678,000
1963	11,939,000	25,230,000
1964	16,547,000	34,061,000
1965	42,748,000	85,943,000
1966	24,512,000	46,539,000
1967	51,891,000	94,761,000
1968	26,197,000	45,895,000
1969	23,365,000	39,421,000
1970	24,269,000	39,844,000
1971	48,205,000	74,981,000
1972	104,806,000	155,961,000
1973	107,765,000	150,784,000
1974	209,687,000	269,244,000
1975	179,277,000	212,665,000
1976	86,583,000	94,523,000
1977	83,547,000	83,547,000
1978	84,065,000	77,479,000
1979	33,116,000	28,184,000
1980	32,441,000	24,428,000

Table 5.10.   FMS Deliveries to Latin American Republics

In Current and Constant 1977 Dollars

==================================

Fiscal Year	Current Dollars	Constant 1977 Dollars
1950	$ 109,000	$ 283,000
1951	1,088,000	2,690,000
1952	13,545,000	33,947,000
1953	9,198,000	22,511,000
1954	8,602,000	21,772,000
1955	11,596,000	28,242,000
1956	8,618,000	20,131,000
1957	13,586,000	30,856,000
1958	18,787,000	42,294,000
1959	9,342,000	20,890,000
1960	35,806,000	78,764,000
1961	19,992,000	43,489,000
1962	11,700,000	25,075,000
1963	19,888,000	42,029,000
1964	10,399,000	21,406,000
1965	16,855,000	33,886,000
1966	25,229,000	47,900,000
1967	24,337,000	44,443,000
1968	46,361,000	81,221,000
1969	36,425,000	61,456,000
1970	34,854,000	57,222,000
1971	28,395,000	44,167,000
1972	42,001,000	62,501,000
1973	52,645,000	73,660,000
1974	65,487,000	84,087,000
1975	114,751,000	136,122,000
1976	149,716,000	163,445,000
1977	163,768,000	163,768,000
1978	63,883,000	58,878,000
1979	61,227,000	52,108,000
1980	75,999,000	57,228,000

From FY 1972 through FY 1975, agreements were at a relatively high level for the region. From FY 1976 to the present, however, agreements have declined dramatically, reaching 1950s levels by FY 1979. This reflects in large measure the view within the Carter administration that arms sales have been a major source of conflict. It also reflects the economic stagnation of national economies within the region.

Table 5.10 and Figure 5.10 portray FMS deliveries to the region in both constant and current dollars. As with all other regions, FMS deliveries to the Latin American Republic are substantially fewer than agreements. Indeed, for the entire thirty-one-year period examined,

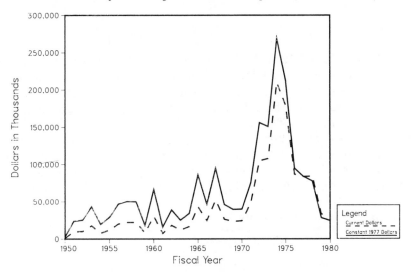

Figure 5.9. FMS agreements with Latin American republics.

deliveries to the region have exceeded $100 million only for fiscal years 1975, 1976, and 1977. For most of the period, deliveries have ranged from 20 to 50 million constant dollars per year.

Figure 5.10. FMS deliveries to Latin American republics.

Africa

Tables 5.11 and 5.12 and Figures 5.11 and 5.12 display FMS agreements and deliveries to Africa in current and constant dollars.[10] Foreign Military Sales agreements and deliveries to Africa throughout the thirty-one-year period have been a minor portion of worldwide agreements and deliveries. Throughout the 1950s and 1960s, sales to Africa were inconsequential. For 18 of the 21 years from FY 1950 through FY 1970, agreements and deliveries were less than a million constant dollars per year. Since FY 1970, however, FMS agreements and deliveries have increased substantially, reflecting the concern of successive U.S. admin-

Table 5.11. FMS Agreements with Africa

In Current and Constant 1977 Dollars

Fiscal Year	Current Dollars	Constant 1977 Dollars
1950	$ 0	$ 0
1951	0	0
1952	98,000	246,000
1953	81,000	198,000
1954	358,000	906,000
1955	107,000	261,000
1956	654,000	1,528,000
1957	255,000	579,000
1958	160,000	360,000
1959	96,000	215,000
1960	300,000	660,000
1961	83,000	181,000
1962	133,000	285,000
1963	410,000	866,000
1964	2,494,000	5,134,000
1965	81,000	163,000
1966	1,230,000	2,335,000
1967	188,000	343,000
1968	230,000	403,000
1969	101,000	170,000
1970	118,000	194,000
1971	16,328,000	25,397,000
1972	2,694,000	4,009,000
1973	2,606,000	3,646,000
1974	12,327,000	15,828,000
1975	22,306,000	26,460,000
1976	163,553,000	178,551,000
1977	115,798,000	115,798,000
1978	166,592,000	153,541,000
1979	134,577,000	114,534,000
1980	45,248,000	34,072,000

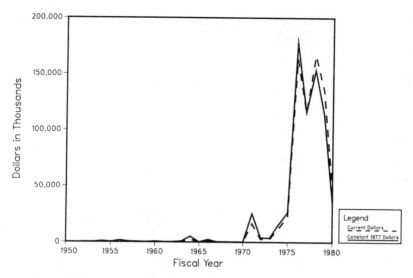

Figure 5.11. FMS agreements with Africa.

istrations about increasing Soviet aid activities, power projection capabilities, and penetration into sub-Saharan Africa, as well as about Cuban involvement there. The most dramatic increase occurred in FY 1976, when agreements with nations in the region reached 179 million

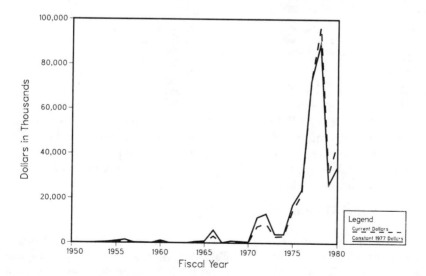

Figure 5.12. FMS deliveries to Africa.

Table 5.12. FMS Deliveries to Africa

In Current and Constant 1977 Dollars

===============================

Fiscal Year	Current Dollars	Constant 1977 Dollars
1950	$ 0	$ 0
1951	0	0
1952	16,000	40,000
1953	76,000	186,000
1954	145,000	367,000
1955	354,000	862,000
1956	591,000	1,381,000
1957	72,000	164,000
1958	42,000	95,000
1959	21,000	47,000
1960	485,000	1,067,000
1961	14,000	30,000
1962	18,000	39,000
1963	20,000	42,000
1964	286,000	589,000
1965	418,000	840,000
1966	3,000,000	5,696,000
1967	73,000	133,000
1968	501,000	878,000
1969	397,000	670,000
1970	265,000	435,000
1971	7,345,000	11,425,000
1972	8,754,000	13,027,000
1973	2,819,000	3,944,000
1974	3,048,000	3,914,000
1975	14,459,000	17,152,000
1976	21,764,000	23,760,000
1977	72,638,000	72,638,000
1978	96,723,000	89,146,000
1979	30,952,000	26,342,000
1980	45,247,000	34,072,000

constant dollars. By FY 1980, however, agreements with the region had decreased to $34 million. Actual deliveries of FMS weapons and services to Africa have always been extremely small compared to any other region. At their peak, FMS deliveries to African nations did not exceed 90 million constant dollars.

International Organizations

International organizations have been minor but not insignificant participants in the United States FMS program. For the thirty-one-year period from 1950 through 1980, agreements have totaled more than 1.5 billion constant dollars. However, actual deliveries to international organizations have totaled only less than half that amount.

FMS Financing

Most FMS deliveries are financed by the recipient. For example, in FY 1980, FMS deliveries worldwide exceeded 5.7 billion constant dollars. Of this total, more than $1.4 billion was accounted for by U.S. government-assisted financing, either debt waiving or guaranteeing or subsidizing credit provided by U.S. commercial financial institutions. This financing represents 25 percent of the total dollar amount of deliveries to recipients for that year.

Table 5.13 provides a worldwide and regional perspective on trends in FMS direct financing. The program grew sporadically from about 36 million constant dollars in FY 1955 to $1.1 billion in FY 1974. It then declined precipitously to less than $7 million by FY 1979. This decline was accompanied by the expansion of the financing guarantee program. Table 5.14 provides a perspective on the direction and growth of the FMS financing guarantee. By FY 1976, financed guarantees for FMS deliveries had reached $2 billion constant dollars. The program reached a new high in FY 1979, at almost 4.4 billion constant dollars. In FY 1980,

Table 5.13. FMS Direct Financing, by Region

Fiscal Year	East Asia & Pacific	Near East & South Asia	Latin America	Africa	Europe & Canada	Worldwide
1950	0	0	0	0	0	0
1951	0	0	0	0	0	0
1952	0	0	0	0	0	0
1953	0	0	0	0	0	0
1954	0	0	0	0	0	0
1955	0	0	36,532,000	0	0	36,532,000
1956	0	0	159,000	1,712,000	0	1,871,000
1957	0	95,757,000	24,220,000	0	0	119,977,000
1958	73,165,000	4,313,000	44,647,000	0	82,211,000	204,338,000
1959	0	9,855,000	18,296,000	0	0	28,148,000
1960	0	0	17,490,000	700,000	0	33,740,000
1961	23,150,000	0	3,735,000	0	0	47,131,000
1962	61,230,000	1,824,000	17,165,000	0	110,692,000	205,319,000
1963	99,738,000	42,895,000	19,607,000	0	37,105,000	199,345,000
1964	46,315,000	22,258,000	22,921,000	690,000	8,960,000	101,145,000
1965	13,872,000	46,848,000	850,000	0	0	61,570,000
1966	16,865,000	127,380,000	13,702,000	0	0	157,948,000
1967	14,783,000	120,621,000	21,505,000	0	0	156,908,000
1968	56,708,000	91,475,000	37,134,000	0	0	185,406,000
1969	33,503,000	274,868,000	35,976,000	0	33,744,000	378,090,000
1970	65,671,000	49,253,000	0	0	0	114,924,000
1971	90,230,000	880,849,000	68,865,000	0	27,988,000	1,067,942,000
1972	67,783,000	277,333,000	62,707,000	6,024,000	74,362,000	488,207,000
1973	67,021,000	223,590,000	82,461,000	0	76,955,000	450,028,000
1974	54,667,000	883,621,000	77,521,000	18,618,000	93,092,000	1,127,519,000
1975	0	0	47,805,000	35,943,000	74,733,000	158,482,000
1976	0	0	10,917,000	33,843,000	0	44,760,000
1977	0	0	0	28,000,000	0	28,000,000
1978	0	0	0	16,129,000	0	16,129,000
1979	0	0	0	6,809,000	0	6,809,000
1980	0	0	0	0	0	0

Table 5.14.   FMS Financial Guarantee, by Region

Fiscal Year	East Asia & Pacific	Near East & South Asia	Latin America	Africa	Europe & Canada	Worldwide
1950	0	0	0	0	0	0
1951	0	0	0	0	0	0
1952	0	0	0	0	0	0
1953	0	0	0	0	0	0
1954	0	0	0	0	0	0
1955	0	0	0	0	0	0
1956	0	0	0	0	0	0
1957	0	0	0	0	0	0
1958	0	0	0	0	0	0
1959	0	0	0	0	0	0
1960	0	0	0	0	0	0
1961	0	0	0	0	0	0
1962	0	0	0	0	0	0
1963	0	29,586,000	0	0	0	29,586,000
1964	0	0	47,345,000	0	0	47,345,000
1965	0	127,171,000	26,938,000	0	0	154,107,000
1966	1,682,000	381,175,000	55,531,000	0	0	438,386,000
1967	24,722,000	373,090,000	28,647,000	2,423,000	0	428,884,000
1968	59,636,000	182,658,000	24,164,000	0	0	266,458,000
1969	8,794,000	71,706,000	0	0	0	80,499,000
1970	0	0	0	0	0	0
1971	0	54,110,000	10,110,000	20,580,000	0	84,800,000
1972	37,202,000	223,214,000	29,018,000	0	37,202,000	326,637,000
1973	41,976,000	209,878,000	0	8,714,000	32,181,000	292,749,000
1974	134,769,000	385,208,000	65,871,000	0	70,621,000	656,469,000
1975	201,348,000	295,374,000	110,913,000	5,931,000	116,251,000	729,817,000
1976	488,216,000	1,078,057,000	159,715,000	34,607,000	306,769,000	2,067,364,000
1977	296,525,000	655,000,000	39,000,000	25,500,000	367,000,000	1,383,025,000
1978	371,429,000	588,940,000	66,359,000	31,797,000	400,922,000	1,459,447,000
1979	263,915,000	3,722,979,000	23,149,000	15,489,000	370,213,000	4,395,745,000
1980	189,759,000	479,669,000	13,878,000	56,152,000	352,410,000	1,091,867,000

however, only about 1 billion constant dollars' worth of equipment and services were financed through the guarantee procedure. The major recipients of guaranteed financing have been states in the Near East and South Asia.

Finally, the U.S. government provides financial assistance through waived credit, although this instrument has been applied only to Israel. Over the seven-year period of the program, Israel has been absolved of debt repayments on FMS in excess of 4.7 billion constant dollars.

COMMERCIAL SALES

Until 1970 arms transferred from the United States were in the form of government-to-government sales or grant assistance. In FY 1971, however, industries and U.S. commerical firms who had acquired the necessary export licenses were permitted to negotiate directly with defense industries or defense ministries of other countries. In the first five years, as revealed in Table 5.15, these commerical arms transfers

Table 5.15. Commerical Sales, FY 1971-FY 1980

Fiscal Year	Worldwide	East Asia	Near East	Latin America	Africa	Europe & Canada	International Organizations
1971	665,026,000	126,142,000	140,376,000	24,096,000	6,065,000	351,916,000	16,430,000
1972	715,216,000	129,935,000	246,494,000	47,458,000	7,064,000	256,382,000	27,882,000
1973	506,613,000	85,344,000	72,027,000	27,817,000	1,934,000	309,432,000	10,059,000
1974	644,795,000	119,078,000	138,649,000	22,748,000	7,196,000	355,214,000	1,909,000
1975	648,340,000	121,581,000	145,216,000	24,785,000	3,019,000	350,470,000	3,269,000
1976	1,530,567,000	301,719,000	453,099,000	70,023,000	33,141,000	661,181,000	11,403,000
1977	1,523,403,000	321,567,000	451,748,000	46,082,000	19,785,000	663,283,000	20,938,000
1978	1,544,707,000	373,907,000	441,010,000	52,102,000	13,557,000	643,812,000	20,320,000
1979	1,299,568,000	367,878,000	316,963,000	49,890,000	5,431,000	508,900,000	50,505,000
1980	1,332,709,000	374,791,000	303,656,000	49,481,000	5,465,000	599,316,000	0
Total	10,410,944,000	2,321,942,000	2,709,238,000	414,482,000	102,657,000	4,699,906,000	162,715,000

ranged from about $500 million to just more than $715 million in constant dollars. From 1976 on, such transfers have amounted to an average of about $1.45 billion per year. Many government officials believe, though, that the actual unrecorded level of commercial transactions is twice the recorded amount.

Table 5.15 depicts commercial deliveries in constant dollars for the period FY 1971 to FY 1980 which have amounted to 10.4 billion constant dollars. The bulk of these have been to Europe and Canada, although there have been significant deliveries to the Near East and East Asia. Europe has received 45 percent of all commercial deliveries, the Near East 26 percent, and East Asia 22 percent. Commercial deliveries to Latin America and Africa have been insignificant, representing 4 percent and less than 1 percent, respectively.

MILITARY ASSISTANCE PROGRAM

The Military Assistance Program (MAP) has drastically changed since 1950, declining from the primary U.S. security assistance instrument of the 1950s to a relatively minor instrument by FY 1977. For example, MAP deliveries peaked at more than 8.8 billion constant dollars in FY 1953 and declined irregularly to 246 million constant dollars in FY 1980. Table 5.16 displays the constant dollar amounts of arms and services authorized and delivered throughout the period FY 1950 through FY 1980; Figure 5.13 displays the actual value in constant and current dollars of worldwide MAP deliveries.

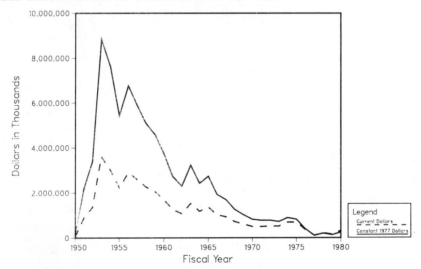

Figure 5.13. MAP deliveries worldwide.

Table 5.16. MAP Authorizations and Deliveries

In Constant 1977 Dollars

=====================================

Fiscal Year	Authorizations	Deliveries
1950	$ 2,901,358,000	$ 128,208,000
1951	9,584,143,000	2,195,983,000
1952	10,419,466,000	3,389,977,000
1953	5,834,760,000	8,839,290,000
1954	5,400,251,000	7,622,349,000
1955	3,586,985,000	5,443,400,000
1956	5,077,391,000	6,765,882,000
1957	4,055,276,000	5,884,992,000
1958	2,720,450,000	5,090,705,000
1959	4,091,000,000	4,604,560,000
1960	4,097,981,000	3,745,781,000
1961	3,691,571,000	2,719,811,000
1962	2,830,538,000	2,301,573,000
1963	3,028,755,000	3,228,352,000
1964	1,880,187,000	2,428,051,000
1965	1,770,322,000	2,737,195,000
1966	1,711,954,000	1,929,962,000
1967	1,506,384,000	1,705,636,000
1968	975,049,000	1,263,052,000
1969	703,768,000	1,020,666,000
1970	572,822,000	818,854,000
1971	1,121,607,000	775,783,000
1972	764,979,000	779,045,000
1973	783,012,000	720,770,000
1974	907,541,000	893,078,000
1975	607,125,000	820,874,000
1976	288,154,000	397,638,000
1977	241,169,000	108,679,000
1978	201,415,000	203,041,000
1979	182,596,000	134,428,000
1980	111,834,000	246,155,000

The largest volume of equipment and services under the Military Assistance Program was delivered to Europe during the 1950s as shown in Figure 5.14. Map deliveries to Europe and Canada were as high as 7 billion constant dollars in FY 1953, then declined precipitously to less than $1 billion by FY 1961. Major European countries such as Great Britain, France, and West Germany were phased out of the grant program in the late 1950s and early 1960s. Although Spain, Portugal, Turkey, and Greece remained sizable recipients throughout the late 1960s and early 1970s, by FY 1976 grant military assistance to Europe had become insignificant.

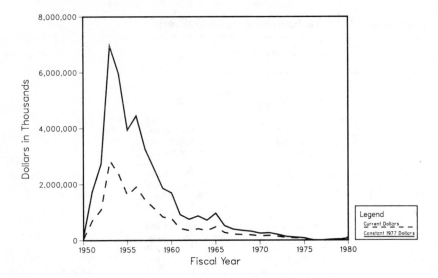

Figure 5.14. MAP deliveries to Europe and Canada.

Figure 5.15 depicts MAP deliveries to East Asia and the Pacific. In constant dollars, MAP deliveries to this region ranged from $1 to $2 billion through the period FY 1953 to FY 1965. From FY 1966 to FY 1976, MAP deliveries averaged about $500 million a year, but after FY 1976 became insignificant.

Figure 5.15. MAP deliveries to East Asia and the Pacific.

Throughout the period FY 1955 to FY 1965, several nations in the Near East and South Asia were substantial MAP recipients—Israel and Jordan were among the largest recipients. Figure 5.16 reveals that by FY 1958, MAP deliveries to the region had reached 450 million constant dollars. By 1970, however, this grant assistance program had declined to limited levels for the Near East and South Asia, although beginning in FY 1974 Israel began to receive grant assistance through the FMS financial waiver program, which by FY 1981 totaled 4.7 billion constant dollars.

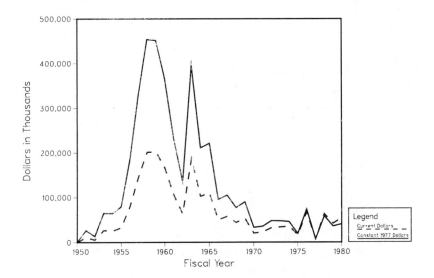

Figure 5.16. MAP deliveries to the Near East and South Asia.

MAP deliveries to Latin America have never exceeded 100 million constant dollars, as is shown in Figure 5.17. Reflecting the general decline in MAP, deliveries to Latin America were quickly reduced to insignificant levels early in the 1970s.

MAP deliveries to Africa have also been minimal when compared to other regions. Indeed, at their height, MAP deliveries to Africa were never more than 35 million constant dollars, as shown in Figure 5.18.

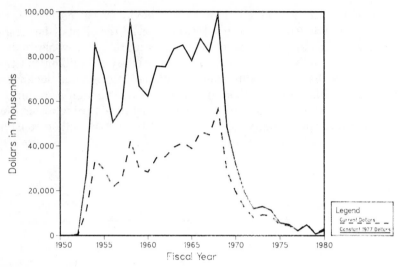

Figure 5.17. MAP deliveries to Latin American republics.

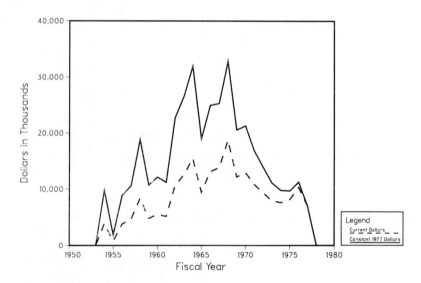

Figure 5.18. MAP deliveries to Africa.

Other Grant Programs

Other grant programs by which the United States provides security assistance include the Military Assistance Service Fund (MASF) program, the Excess Military Assistance Service Fund (EXMASF) program and the Excess Military Articles Program (EXMAP). MASF and EX-

MASF were grant programs entirely for nations involved in the Vietnam conflict (Korea, Laos, Philippines, Thailand, and Vietnam) from FY 1966 to FY 1975. (These nations also received U.S. security assistance through other grant and sales programs.) During this period, equipment and services valued at more than $24 billion in constant dollars were delivered to these countries through MASF alone. The value of these deliveries must be recognized in any analysis of U.S. arms transfer. Beginning in FY 1966, MASF deliveries in constant dollars rose from $874 million to a high of more than $5.9 billion in FY 1973. From the fall of the South Vietnamese government to North Vietnamese forces in FY 1975 through 1980, MASF deliveries totaled less than $17 million. Throughout the FY 1966–FY 1975 period, MASF deliveries constituted more than 35 percent of all U.S. military deliveries worldwide. Table 5.17, which shows MASF deliveries in constant dollars and the percentage of U.S. arms transfers that these accounted for, underscores the Vietnam conflict's impact on U.S. arms transfer activities. This impact is similar to that resulting from rearmament of Europe in the 1950s and to the emerging economic and strategic importance of the Near East and South Asia in the latter half of the 1970s. Although these vital U.S. interests were supported by MAP deliveries to Europe, and FMS deliveries to the Near East and South Asia, the net effect on U.S. security assistance was the same—a large dollar volume of arms transfers to support perceived vital, specific U.S security interests.

Finally, throughout the period FY 1950 to FY 1980 significant amounts of equipment were delivered to other nations through the Excess Military Articles Program.

Table 5.17. MASF Deliveries (to Korea, Laos, Philippines, Thailand, and South Vietnam)

FY	MASF Deliveries	Total U.S. Military Deliveries (%)
1966	$ 874,864,000	18.4%
1967	1,113,254,000	21.8
1968	1,871,419,000	32.6
1969	1,984,949,000	32.4
1970	2,929,601,000	42.5
1971	3,413,153,000	43.9
1972	3,936,818,000	48.0
1973	5,954,591,000	59.8
1974	1,459,093,000	19.4
1975	1,325,435,000	18.6

IMET and Other Military Training

The International Military Education and Training (IMET) program represents one of the least expensive military assistance activities of the United States in terms of dollars. Nevertheless, IMET has provided military training for thousands of foreign personnel. Reflecting the U.S. military assistance priorities for the post-Korean War period, IMET was greatest in the 1950s for European nations. During the 1960s, however, IMET shifted activity to East Asia, the Near East, Latin America, and Africa. In FY 1962, the value of IMET to all nations had reached nearly half a billion dollars. Since FY 1969, the program has experienced a steady and sizable decline from $64 million in that year to only $18 million by FY 1980.

The Military Assistance Service Fund (MASF) also provided for student training. This training was directed mainly to states involved in the Vietnam conflict between FY 1966 and FY 1975. Military personnel from Korea, Laos, Thailand, and Vietnam were trained under MASF on a grant basis, the worth of which amounted to 327 million constant dollars from FY 1966 to FY 1975.

Altogether, nearly 500,000 military personnel have been trained under IMET, MASF, and other programs. The largest proportion of personnel trained have been from nations in East Asia. The training program has been quite insignificant in Africa. Since FY 1960, about 3,500 military personnel per year have been trained in Latin America.

MILITARY ASSISTANCE AGREEMENTS AND MILITARY DELIVERIES: A SUMMARY CONCLUSION

Finally, it is useful to consider the magnitude of all military assistance—military services and equipment—provided by the United States to the rest of the world. This may be done by examining the dollar value of all these services and equipment either authorized by Congress or agreed to with other nations; or by examining the dollar value of all military services and equipment actually delivered to other nations by the United States. Moreover, each can be assessed in terms of current and constant dollars. It is necessary to examine all arms transfers from the United States from these four perspectives because of the extent of confusion concerning the trends in conventional arms transfers from the United States. It is also important to realize that much of the debate concerning how rapidly arms transfers have expanded is fueled by the use of different measures of arms transfer activity.

Table 5.18 presents worldwide military assistance agreements both in current and constant dollars; Figure 5.19 displays these data in graphic form. Military assistance agreements are a summary variable and here include FMS agreements, authorized MAP, MASF, EXMASF, IMET authorization, and authorized MASF training.

Table 5.18. U.S. Military Assistance Agreements Worldwide

In Current and Constant 1977 Dollars

Fiscal Year	Current Dollars	Constant 1977 Dollars
1950	$ 1,406,393,000	$ 3,652,969,000
1951	4,153,521,000	10,268,284,000
1952	4,512,145,000	11,308,634,000
1953	2,634,225,000	6,446,953,000
1954	2,374,259,000	6,009,261,000
1955	1,708,344,000	4,160,604,000
1956	2,475,923,000	5,783,516,000
1957	2,297,069,000	5,217,054,000
1958	1,835,216,000	4,131,508,000
1959	2,571,948,000	5,751,225,000
1960	2,335,216,000	5,136,859,000
1961	2,414,366,000	5,252,047,000
1962	2,485,050,000	5,325,868,000
1963	2,463,589,000	5,206,232,000
1964	2,520,092,000	5,187,509,000
1965	2,952,198,000	5,935,259,000
1966	3,243,639,000	6,158,419,000
1967	3,134,166,000	5,723,459,000
1968	3,508,495,000	6,146,628,000
1969	3,992,508,000	6,736,137,000
1970	3,913,917,000	6,425,738,000
1971	4,897,066,000	7,617,151,000
1972	6,879,630,000	10,237,545,000
1973	9,521,620,000	13,322,541,000
1974	12,021,715,000	15,436,203,000
1975	17,165,780,000	20,362,728,000
1976	15,046,627,000	16,426,449,000
1977	8,571,356,000	8,571,356,000
1978	11,285,671,000	10,401,540,000
1979	13,265,556,000	11,289,835,000
1980	15,650,484,000	11,785,003,000

When assessed in terms of current dollars, worldwide, military assistance agreements expanded rapidly to $4.5 billion by FY 1952, then declined to less than $4 billion until FY 1971, when they jumped to almost $4.9 billion. By FY 1975 they reached $17 billion. Since then they have ranged from $8 billion to $15.6 billion. When comparing military assistance agreements in the late 1950s and early 1960s with agreements in the 1970s, it is quite apparent that in terms of current dollars there has been a substantial increase.

These figures are misleading, however. When military agreements are measured in constant dollars, the increase has not been nearly as great.

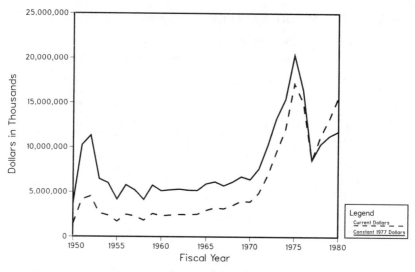

Figure 5.19. U.S. military Assistance agreements worldwide.

For example, when accounting for inflation, agreements were no greater in FY 1979 than they were in FY 1952, or in any subsequent year until FY 1973. Only in fiscal years 1973, 1974, 1975, 1976, and 1980 did military assistance agreements exceed FY 1952 levels. Indeed, in the nineteen-year period between FY 1952 and FY 1972, military assistance agreements remained fairly constant and averaged $5.7 billion per year for the period. Not until the mid-1970s did military assistance agreements with other nations again reach constant-dollar levels equal to those of the early 1950s.

As shown in Figure 5.20, in which regional portions of the total are portrayed cumulatively, the quantity of assistance involved in military assistance agreements across regions has varied widely. It is quite apparent that when all military assistance agreements with African nations are identified over the thirty-one-year period, a fairly constant and relatively insignificant pattern has existed. Indeed, not until FY 1976 did military assistance agreements for the African region exceed $50 million constant dollars per year. While military assistance agreements with Latin American nations have never been substantial, they began to decline drastically after FY 1974. By FY 1980, military assistance agreements with Latin American countries had reached their lowest level since FY 1951.

Military agreements with nations in the East Asian region have been large by comparison. Although fairly stable at 2 billion constant dollars until FY 1967, agreements with nations in the region began to expand

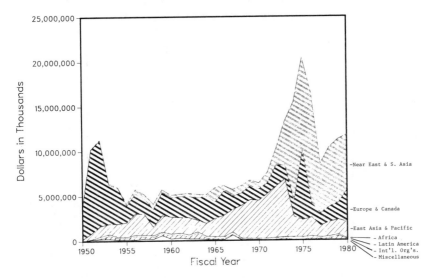

Figure 5.20. Worldwide and regional military agreements.

rapidly after that, reflecting American concern about Communist activities in Southeast Asia. During the period FY 1968 to FY 1973, the dollar value of these agreements were substantial, ranging from $3 to $6 billion in constant dollars. Military assistance agreements declined to pre-FY 1967 levels, reflecting the end of U.S. involvement in Vietnam after FY 1973.

Military assistance agreements with nations in the Near East and South Asia region involved substantial dollar amounts in the 1970s decade. In FY 1971 such agreements with nations in the region began to increase dramatically and over the decade reflected the most significant increase in the dollar value of agreements in the history of the U.S. security assistance program. In just three years, FY 1974, FY 1975, and FY 1976, military assistance agreements with nations in the region totaled $34 billion in constant 1977 dollars. After FY 1976, military assistance agreements stabilized at about $5.5 to $7.0 billion.

The value of military assistance agreements with Canada and European nations were at their highest levels in the early 1950s. For example, such agreements were valued at 9.3 and 9.5 billion constant dollars in FY 1951 and FY 1952, respectively. Not until FY 1975 did military agreements with European nations and Canada approach those early 1950s levels. In FY 1975, the worth of agreements reached 7.7 billion constant dollars. But for twenty of the thirty-one years considered here, the value of such agreements assessed in constant dollars was less than $2.5 billion a year.

Figure 5.21. U.S. military deliveries worldwide.

Military assistance agreements are a measure of U.S. bilateral relations. High values for such agreements are positive indicators of broad and continuing policy convergence between the recipient and the supplier. Hence, an assessment of security assistance cannot disregard military assistance agreements. However, a more accurate indicator of the extent and military impact of U.S. arms transfer activities is the actual deliveries of weapons systems, equipment, and services to other nations, that is, what was actually delivered to the recipient and not what was merely promised, authorized, or agreed.

Military deliveries is a summary variable for FMS deliveries, commerical export deliveries, MAP deliveries, MASF deliveries, EXMAP deliveries, IMET deliveries, and MASF training. It comprises all grants and sales of weapons and services that were delivered to recipients. Table 5.19 depicts military deliveries worldwide for the thirty-one-year period both in current and constant dollars. Figure 5.21 displays these data in graphic form. The data demonstrate the importance of assessing the U.S. security assistance program in terms of constant dollars. If worldwide deliveries are examined in current dollars, the conclusion to be reached is that U.S. arms transfers have substantially increased over the thirty-one-year period and that the dollar value of such deliveries was never greater than in FY 1980. This is a common assumption about arms transfers. But when worldwide deliveries are assessed in constant dollars, a quite different conclusion is evident: that the U.S. security assistance program has not significantly expanded since the 1950s.

Table 5.19. U.S. Military Deliveries Worldwide

In Current and Constant 1977 Dollars

Fiscal Year	Current Dollars	Constant 1977 Dollars
1950	$ 80,134,000	$ 208,140,000
1951	1,210,983,000	2,993,778,000
1952	1,669,645,000	4,184,574,000
1953	3,893,529,000	9,528,950,000
1954	3,272,320,000	8,282,258,000
1955	2,496,628,000	6,080,438,000
1956	3,170,841,000	7,406,776,000
1957	2,818,247,000	6,400,743,000
1958	2,852,510,000	6,421,679,000
1959	2,485,498,000	5,557,911,000
1960	2,321,730,000	5,107,193,000
1961	1,887,747,000	4,106,476,000
1962	1,839,248,000	3,941,809,000
1963	2,637,580,000	5,573,922,000
1964	1,881,420,000	3,872,828,000
1965	2,320,632,000	4,665,525,000
1966	2,500,129,000	4,746,780,000
1967	2,802,407,000	5,117,617,000
1968	3,272,797,000	5,733,702,000
1969	3,632,345,000	6,128,471,000
1970	4,200,027,000	6,895,464,000
1971	5,001,894,000	7,780,205,000
1972	5,516,735,000	8,209,427,000
1973	7,112,241,000	9,951,366,000
1974	5,848,242,000	7,509,299,000
1975	5,993,387,000	7,109,593,000
1976	7,636,732,000	8,337,044,000
1977	8,742,745,000	8,742,745,000
1978	9,338,927,000	8,607,306,000
1979	9,231,483,000	7,856,581,000
1980	9,849,385,000	7,416,706,000

Furthermore, those analyses which point to a U.S. arms transfer program growing by leaps and bounds as a phenomenon of the post-1970 Kissinger-Nixon-Ford foreign policy are based on faulty premises. For example, in FY 1953, the constant-dollar value of all weapons systems, equipment, and services delivered worldwide was $9.5 billion. Only in FY 1973 did the value of such deliveries ever exceed the FY 1953 level, and then by less than $430 million, or less than 5 percent of the FY 1953 total. What has changed has been the regional emphasis of U.S. arms transfer activity. This emphasis has changed from Europe, to East Asia and the Pacific, and finally to the Near East and South Asia, reflecting changes in U.S. Government perceptions of threats to its vital interests over the last three decades.

Moreover, rather than increasing rapidly over the ten years preceding FY 1981, military deliveries worldwide measured in constant dollars have remained relatively stable, and since FY 1977 have actually declined. Measured against the 1950s, the first decade following enactment of the Mutual Defense Assistance Act of 1949, the value of military deliveries in constant dollars for the decade FY 1971-1980 was less than $2 billion per year on the average. That this increase is so little is remarkable given the fact that the United States provides military assistance to more states through many more programs today than in the 1950s. And there is more pressure today on security assistance since the U.S. government can countenance neither direct military intervention nor mutual defense agreements as it could in the past. The changed international system and the recognition of the limits to U.S. powers have made security assistance one of the few foreign policy instruments currently available. Furthermore, even discounting for the effects of inflation, modern weapons systems such as sophisticated front-line combat aircraft like the F-15 and F-16 cost much more than their 1950s counterparts, as does the extent and cost of training and infrastructure to service these systems. Indeed, discounting a modest reduction in the late 1950s and early 1960s, military deliveries have remained relatively constant since FY 1954.

While the point has been established elsewhere throughout this chapter, it is critical to emphasize why there seems to be so much misperception about trends in security assistance. The trends are too often assessed in terms of the current dollar value of authorized, agreed, programmed, or promised military equipment and services. To demonstrate this point Figure 5.22 juxtaposes military agreements in current dollars with actual deliveries in constant dollars. As can be seen, military agreements in current dollars have increased substantially since the inception of the Nixon Doctrine, but military deliveries in constant dollars have not varied drastically since then and, with few exceptions, have been no greater than in the mid-1950s. Indeed, as stated above, only in FY 1973 did military deliveries exceed FY 1953 levels. However, military agreements valued in current dollars, the most common assessment, have increased substantially since 1970 after having remained relatively constant in the $3 billion-$4 billion range throughout the 1950s and 1960s. Such agreements expanded to over $15 billion in FY 1975. Military deliveries measured in constant dollars, however, did not increase drastically in the 1970s. The increase here was very gradual in the 1960s, ranging from $5 to $9 billion in constant dollars. Thus it is

Figure 5.22. Military agreements (in current dollars) and military deliveries (in constant 1977 dollars).

very difficult to substantiate claims that the increase in U.S. security assistance to the developing world has been a major cause of conflict and instability, or that the U.S. arms transfers program is accelerating out of control. The data simply do not show it.

Frequently, implementation of the Nixon Doctrine is cited as the cause for the increase in arms transfers. An examination of military agreements both in current and constant dollars reveals a substantial rise in agreements following its announcement. However, military deliveries in constant dollars have not substantially increased on a yearly basis following the Nixon Doctrine. In fact, since FY 1973 they have shown an average decline, and an absolute yearly decline since FY 1977. What has occurred is a regional change in the value of deliveries.

Table 5.20 presents trends in military deliveries on a regional basis in 1977 constant dollars, and Figure 5.23 presents these data graphically over the thirty-one-year period considered here. These data reveal that military deliveries to Africa have never been substantial. They remained stable throughout the 1960s and early 1970s in the range of $20 to $40 million. For three years, FY 1976, FY 1977, and FY 1978, deliveries increased, reaching $105 million in FY 1978, but then they declined to 1960s levels. The constant-dollar value of military deliveries to Latin America has also been stable over the thirty-one-year period and, measured against deliveries to Europe and the Near East and East Asia, has also been insignificant. Only in FY 1968, 1976, and 1977 have military deliveries to Latin America exceeded 200 million constant

Table 5.20. Military Deliveries by Region

Fiscal Year	East Asia & Pacific	Near East & South Asia	Latin America	Africa	Europe & Canada
1950	13,719,000	153,000	283,000	0	189,974,000
1951	280,492,000	28,843,000	2,690,000	0	2,515,498,000
1952	426,469,000	15,248,000	34,521,000	40,000	3,444,266,000
1953	1,374,846,000	91,826,000	192,376,000	186,000	7,301,202,000
1954	1,317,142,000	132,883,000	123,597,000	10,433,000	6,384,897,000
1955	1,244,747,000	117,428,000	129,394,000	3,242,000	4,288,475,000
1956	1,987,337,000	251,577,000	80,885,000	10,874,000	4,777,603,000
1957	2,063,770,000	363,691,000	113,227,000	11,869,000	3,519,067,000
1958	1,929,266,000	596,799,000	188,167,000	21,625,000	3,250,653,000
1959	1,820,304,000	496,782,000	99,671,000	12,442,000	2,301,055,000
1960	1,563,920,000	461,496,000	158,718,000	19,259,000	2,380,134,000
1961	1,487,775,000	313,354,000	153,035,000	23,896,000	1,575,408,000
1962	1,628,856,000	183,303,000	149,119,000	31,530,000	1,603,438,000
1963	1,586,264,000	446,902,000	174,419,000	31,325,000	2,591,574,000
1964	1,284,996,000	288,648,000	144,885,000	41,429,000	1,704,588,000
1965	1,685,414,000	348,014,000	147,668,000	33,221,000	2,203,536,000
1966	2,343,180,000	311,975,000	166,746,000	43,199,000	1,622,009,000
1967	2,096,174,000	340,530,000	160,489,000	34,114,000	1,568,448,000
1968	3,433,761,000	363,761,000	222,218,000	45,412,000	1,510,745,000
1969	3,453,032,000	530,167,000	128,249,000	25,839,000	1,851,733,000
1970	4,198,263,000	816,234,000	109,489,000	27,000,000	1,624,224,000
1971	4,665,741,000	930,888,000	114,038,000	40,025,000	1,936,282,000
1972	5,115,122,000	1,171,156,000	145,193,000	39,738,000	1,645,802,000
1973	7,210,486,000	1,085,171,000	140,049,000	20,838,000	1,410,028,000
1974	2,931,590,000	2,751,086,000	138,052,000	25,282,000	1,597,930,000
1975	2,565,337,000	2,646,203,000	181,033,000	32,095,000	1,604,632,000
1976	1,058,727,000	4,645,707,000	252,630,000	71,071,000	2,204,649,000
1977	901,716,000	5,620,203,000	219,466,000	102,477,000	1,784,191,000
1978	1,257,229,000	5,469,079,000	122,914,000	105,623,000	1,537,470,000
1979	1,222,408,000	4,549,097,000	106,092,000	34,386,000	1,823,646,000
1980	1,346,213,000	3,399,261,000	111,306,000	41,358,000	2,431,118,000

*Excludes deliveries to international organizations and general and regular costs.

dollars, and they have never exceeded $300 million in any fiscal year. It is important to note that deliveries to the Latin American republics were no greater in the 1970s than in the 1960s. The constant-dollar value of military deliveries to the region in FY 1980 was actually lower than in FY 1953.

Military deliveries to the Near East and South Asia have increased most dramatically relative to other regions. Throughout the 1950s and 1960s, with the exception of FY 1953, these deliveries ranged from $100 million to $500 million annually. In FY 1972 deliveries exceeded 1 billion

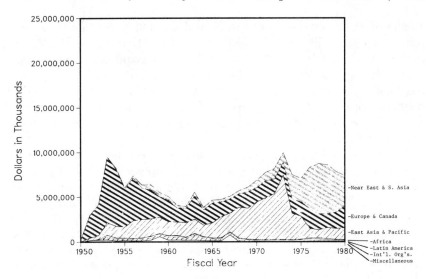

Figure 5.23. Worldwide and regional military deliveries.

constant dollars, rose to $5.6 billion in FY 1977, and then declined to $3.4 billion by FY 1980. As indicated earlier in the examination of specific programs, throughout the 1970s the Near East had become the major recipient of U.S. military equipment and services. A major and constant recipient of U.S. military deliveries has been East Asia, which since FY 1953 has received more than $1 billion per year in military assistance except in FY 1977. Deliveries to the region increased rapidly after FY 1965, reached a peak level of 7.2 billion constant dollars by FY 1973, then precipitously declined to levels between $0.9 billion and $1.4 billion after FY 1976. These trends reflected U.S. involvement in the Vietnam conflict, and its aftermath.

Table 5.20 and Figure 5.23 reveal that most arms delivered worldwide in the 1950s were to Europe and Canada. Throughout the 1950s, arms to the region ranged from 93 percent to 41 percent of all arms delivered worldwide. Throughout the 1960s and 1970s, however, arms delivered to Europe and Canada generally constituted less than one-third of all arms delivered worldwide. In the late 1950s East Asia and the Pacific became major recipients. By FY 1958 East Asia received 30 percent of all arms and services; the percentage of arms delivered to that region grew to 73 percent by FY 1973. Reflecting the withdrawal from Vietnam and the American rapproachement with China, deliveries to East Asia declined throughout the 1970s. By FY 1980, for example, deliveries to the region constituted 19 percent of all arms delivered throughout the world. The principal recipients of military deliveries during the latter half of the decade of the seventies were the Near East and South Asia. In some years, such as FY 1977 and FY 1978, deliveries to that region constituted two-thirds of all deliveries to the world. *A significant point to note with regard to regional trends is the relatively minor proportion of U.S. military deliveries to Latin America and Africa. There are over ninety political units in these regions, and yet U.S. deliveries have been relatively small, most often constituting less than 5 percent of the worldwide total.*

Over the thirty-one-year period considered here, the major recipients of U.S. security assistance have been the European friends and allies of the United States. Throughout this period, military deliveries measured in constant dollars averaged about $2.4 billion per year. While the value of military deliveries to Europe and Canada for this period has exceeded 75 billion constant dollars, most of these deliveries were in the ten-year period from FY 1951 to FY 1960, when Europe and Canada received over 50 percent of all the military equipment and services ever delivered to them. It is difficult to critize Congress or the Executive Branch for this type of national security support for U.S. European allies given the strategic position they have occupied since the close of the Second World War. Even the Carter administration, as it embarked upon its crusade to limit arms sales worldwide, was sensitive enough to exclude sales to NATO from its definition of an "arms transfer program run amok" and from its arms transfer ceiling.

NOTES

1 The Department of Defense has eighteen sets of deflators to measure budgetary total obligational authority. These deflators were current as of April 1981, but changes should affect only the budget "out years." The data presented in this chapter are from the Defense Security Assistance Agency *Fiscal Year Series*, the most complete collection of data on the current-dollar costs or value of U.S. security assistance activities. We converted these data to constant 1977 dollars.
2 United States, House, Committee on Banking and Currency, *Hearings on H.R. 6649, Export-Import Bank and Credit Sales of Defense Articles*, 90th Congress, 1st Session, 1967, pp. 65-66.
3 Ernest W. Lefevre, "Military Assistance Training Program," *Annals of the American Academy of Political and Social Science* (March 1976).
4 See Chapter 4.
5 United States General Accounting Office, *What Would Be the Impact of Raising or Repealing the Commercial Arms Sales Ceiling?* Report No. 1D-81-47, January 4, 1980, p. 2.
6 Afghanistan, Algeria, Bahrain, Bangladesh, Egypt, India, Iran, Iraq, Israel, Jordan, Kuwait, Lebanon, Libya, Morocco, Nepal, Oman, Pakistan, Qatar, Saudi Arabia, Sri Landa, Syria, Tunisia, United Arab Emirates, Yemen.

7 East Asia and the Pacific include the following recipients: Australia, Brunei, Burma, China, Fiji, French Polynesia, Gilbert Islands, Hong Kong, Indochina, Indonesia, Japan, Kampuchea, Korea, Laos, Macao, Malaysia, Nauru, New Caledonia, New Hebrides, New Zealand, Norfolk Islands, Papua New Guinea, the Philippines, Pitcairn, Singapore, Solomon Islands, Taiwan, Thailand, Vietnam, Western Somoa.

8 Military assistance to Vietnam and to other countries involved in that conflict was through grant programs that will be discussed later.

9 Latin America and the American Republics include the following nations: Antigua, Argentina, Bahamas, Barbados, Belize, Bermuda, Bolivia, Brazil, British Virgin Islands, Cayman Islands, Chile, Colombia, Costa Rica, Cuba, Dominica, Dominican Republic, Eduador, El Salvador, Falkland Islands, French Guiana, Greenland, Grenada, Guadeloupe, Guatemala, Guyana, Haiti, Honduras, Jamaica, Martinique, Mexico, Montserrat, Netherlands Antilles, Nicaragua, Panama, Paraguay, Peru, St. Christ-Nevis, St. Lucia, St. Pierre and Miquelon, St. Vincent, Trinidad-Tobago, Turks and Caicos, Uruguay, Venezuela.

10 Africa consists of the following nations: Angola, Benin, Botswana, Burundi, Cameroon, Central African Empire, Chad, Djibouti, Equatorial Guinea, Ethiopia, Gabon, Gambia, Ghana, Guinea, Ivory Coast, Kenya, Lesotho, Liberia, Madagascar, Malawi, Mali, Mauritania, Mauritius, Mozambique, Niger, Nigeria, Reunion, Rwanda, Senegal, Seychelles, Sierra Leone, Somalia, South Africa, St. Helena, Sudan, Swaziland, Tanzania, Togo, Uganda, Upper Volta, Zaire, Zambia.

Chapter 6

The Carter Experiment in Control and the Reagan Response

By 1976 two somewhat contradictory developments of great relevance to arms sales had emerged. The first was a growing domestic pressure to restrain the use of arms sales as a foreign policy instrument. As indicated in Chapters 2 and 3, Congress, in particular, had become increasingly critical of U.S. security assistance programs. Some members disapproved of grant aid, others voiced moral outrage about selling advanced weaponry to developing countries, and many felt that it was folly to provide arms in an effort to increase U.S. influence. Great concern was expressed that the Department of Defense was "pushing" arms worldwide, or that U.S. commercial firms were selling arms without adequate controls or concern for the long-range national interest.

The second development was the increasing dependence of the U.S. government on arms sales as an instrument of foreign policy. By 1976 arms sales served many purposes for U.S. foreign relations, including (1) resolving regional conflicts; (2) enhancing U.S. access to certain regimes; (3) influencing certain regimes to have resource export policies favorable to the United States; (4) attempting to balance military power among neighbors in regions critical to U.S. strategic interests; (5) improving the commonality or interoperability of equipment among America's major allies; (6) enhancing self-defense of friends and allies; (7) strengthening the internal position of regimes favorable to U.S. policies and interests; (8) limiting Soviet influence and penetration in certain areas by denying Soviet markets or strengthening the opponents of Soviet clients; (9) securing base rights and overseas facilities for U.S. military or intelligence personnel; and (10) moderating recipient weapons acquisition by offering either fewer weapons or less sophisticated weapons for sale than requested.

The arms transfer restraint policy of the Carter administration attempted to put aside many of these purposes and respond to the strong congressional distress about arms sales, a viewpoint that paralleled Carter's personal views. Upon assuming the presidency, Carter began a determined effort to check what he perceived as an ever-increasing worldwide flow of arms, and to alter the preeminent position of the United States as "the leading arms merchant." For the first three months of his administration Carter imposed a virtual moratorium on U.S. arms transfers pending an interagency review of arms transfer policies and procedures and the development of options for the procedural control of U.S. arms transfers, which would subsequently form the basis of the President's unilateral restraint policy.[1] This interagency review was headed by Leslie Gelb, who had become Director of the State Department's Bureau of Politico/Military Affairs.

Presidential Directive 13 (PD 13), which President Carter signed on May 13, 1977, was the final product of that review. It became the charter of the Carter administration's arms transfer policy, providing the guidelines for a set of controls to implement a unilateral policy of arms transfer restraint. These controls included the establishment of an $8.6 billion ceiling for the dollar volume of new commitments under the Foreign Military Sales and Military Assistance programs as well as a number of prohibitions against:

initial introduction into a region of newly developed or advanced weapons systems which would create a new or significantly higher combat capability, or the sale or coproduction of such weapons until they were operationally deployed with U.S. forces;

development or significant modification of advanced weapons systems solely for export;

coproduction agreements for significant weapons, equipment, and major components;

retransfers of certain weapons, equipment, and major components;

promotion of arms sales abroad by agents of the United States or commercial firms without prior policy-level authorization by the Department of State.

PD 13 declared that while arms transfers would still be utilized to promote U.S. security, and the security of the nation's closest allies, they would be used only in "instances where it can be clearly demonstrated that the transfer contributes to [United States] national security interests." In the future, arms transfers would be used only as an "exceptional" instrument of foreign policy.

The administration's unilateral restraint policy was premised on the development of multilateral restraint. As Carter stated when he announced the substance of PD 13 on May 19, "I am initiating this policy of restraint in the full understanding that actual reductions in the worldwide traffic in arms will require multilateral cooperation." In explaining the President's policy, officials of the administration stressed that continuation of U.S. unilateral restraint was predicated upon cooperation of other suppliers and establishment of a multilateral restraint regime.

By 1980, the Carter restraint policy was in tatters. The Carter administration itself had approved numerous sales of arms as exceptions to its own policy, beginning with the administration's public approval of the sale of AWACS to Iran a mere two weeks following announcement of the policy of restraint. Additionally, multilateral cooperation in restraint had gained no ground; the major effort to achieve agreement with foreign suppliers had been a series of negotiations with the Soviet Union, which ended in a deadlocked conference in Mexico City in December 1978. Finally, worldwide arms transfers had not been curtailed following America's example; rather, America's closest allies now competed for that share of the market from which the Carter administration had appeared to retreat.

The failure of the Carter administration's unilateral arms transfer policy is generally explainable in terms of the supply-demand that has been previously discussed, and will be further discussed in the following chapter. But the strategy was to seek multilateral agreement after adopting unilateral restraint. Had agreement with major West European suppliers, or with the Soviet Union—or more certainly with both—occurred, the Carter strategy could have been considered successful.

The failure of these negotiations may be overestimated. All suppliers find too many uses for arms transfers to expect them to restrain themselves. On the other hand, the Carter approach was intended to demonstrate that the largest supplier could act differently, and then negotiate in an atmosphere of newly established credibility for restraint. As much as we have emphasized the forces driving arms transfers, we cannot say that this strategy certainly could not have succeeded, for the Carter administration did not follow through with its implementation with single-minded determination. As is not uncommon within the U.S. government—a fact that the Carter restraint policy can be criticized for not anticipating—the Carter administration pursued several objectives in its foreign relations that generated divergent positions regarding arms transfer restraint negotiations. These divergent positions, combined with the pluralism characteristic of the complex structure of the governmental process involved, assured that the issue of the U.S. negotiating position at the four rounds of the Conventional Arms Transfer Talks (CATT)[2] with the Soviet Union would be subject to a considerable amount of buffeting within the U.S. government. As it happened, between December 1977 and December 1978, the CATT negotiating positions never received the high priority that would have assured the coherence of a directed solution. Relegated to a distinctly second-priority position, CATT survived only while the issues related to it were insubstantial.

The CAT negotiations were launched and initially supported by Secretary of State Cyrus Vance and ACDA Director Paul Warnke, but they were also left to the leadership of Leslie Gelb at the second echelon of the Carter administration, while the principals concerned themselves with the more pressing matters of the Strategic Arms Limitation Talks (SALT) and the search for peace in the Middle East. Although initiated with much bureaucratic fanfare at its inception, CATT became a secondary issue, a stepchild among the seven arms control initiatives given birth to or nurtured by the Carter administration. Probably as a result of this secondary status, CATT had an incredibly complex and interesting bureaucratic history. Issues divided agencies and departments from one another as might be expected, but they also split the relevant bureaus and offices within them. A major pattern in this dividing process was a split within the State Department, and to a lesser extent within the Defense Department, between those charged with functional responsibilities and those charged with regional responsibilities. There were also more than usually significant divisions between the political appointees and their own "permanent government" staffs. A more common characteristic of the factions involved—or at least a characteristic that remained within a more common dimension—was the linkage of factions across agencies. Parties often looked for allies in other departments and agencies as well as within their own. Factional differences also divided the National Security Council staff and played a role in CATT's demise, which occurred through the initiative of National Security Advisor Zbigniew Brzezinski.

CATT

Initial steps toward establishing multilateral arms transfers restraint were undertaken early in the Carter administration. Carter and his advisors discussed the issue at the first meeting of his National

Security Council; Vice President Walter Mondale discussed it with European leaders in January 1977 during a trip to Paris; and the President discussed it with his European counterparts at the London summit in May. In addresses before the United Nations General Assembly on March 17 and October 4, Carter reiterated his commitment to restraining multilateral arms transfer. He instructed Secretary of State Vance, during the March 1977 journey to Moscow, to discuss with the Soviet leadership the idea of restraining arms transfer to "troubled areas of the globe." All these initiatives met with little success.

Subsequently, a U.S. delegation went to Europe to explore supplier restraint to developing nations and to develop a coordinated allied posture. It also met with little success. The French declined to discuss the matter. The British were highly skeptical of the idea, but the Foreign Minister was willing to listen. Since Britain's primary competitor seemed intent upon limiting its own market advantage, Her Majesty's government had little to lose in exploring the subject. Although discouraging, the trip served a purpose for U.S. officials. They learned an important (though not altogether surprising) lesson: that allied cooperation would be predicated upon Soviet involvement. As Gelb related to the House Armed Services Committee, "They said 'why should we participate in this kind of exercise if the Soviets aren't going to cooperate? Go get the Soviets to cooperate first.'"[3]

The Soviets' initial reaction to Vance, scarcely two months after Carter became President, was obviously skeptical. The administration nonetheless pressed for formal U.S./Soviet discussions on the subject. The Soviet leadership agreed, and the first such meeting was held in December 1977 in Washington, D.C. The behavior of the Soviet delegates there indicates quite clearly that they viewed the talks as strictly exploratory; they came prepared to listen. The U.S. delegation, headed by Gelb, presented the general concept of negotiated multilateral restraint. The session was described as "procedural," the Soviet delegation "not very enthusiastic." Gelb described the meeting as "perfunctory," stating that "it was unclear whether [the Soviets] would agree to meet again."

After a five-month hiatus, however, the two governments held a second round of talks in Helsinki in May. In preparation for these discussions, the National Security Council's Special Coordinating Committee (SCC) decided that a tangible measure of Soviet seriousness about CATT, such as a joint communique, had to be produced at this round.

To achieve this objective, the U.S. delegation pursued a strategy that would give concrete meaning to the 1972 United States-Soviet Declaration of Basic Principles of Relations. Delegation members believed that this framework would appeal to the Soviet leadership because it would legitimate a Soviet role in and responsibility for easing worldwide tensions that might evolve from the international arms trade. The Soviet delegation, now headed by Ambassador L. I. Mendelevich,[4] was receptive and at the close of the round on May 11 the two delegations did issue a joint communique. The communique acknowledged that the problem of limiting international arms transfers was urgent, that the negotiations were a component of the U.S.-Soviet negotiations on "cessation of the arms race," and that they should be continued in accordance with the 1972 declaration. The communique further stated that:

> effective solution of the problem requires full consideration of the legitimate defense needs of recipients in accordance with the purposes and principles of the charter of the United Nations. They expressed their mutual desire that the efforts of the two sides would assist other international efforts to restrain the transfer of conventional arms, such as the opportunity offered by the forthcoming special session of the U.N. General Assembly devoted to disarmament, as well as possible regional arrangements.

At this session, and later at the third session (July 18-28) in Helsinki, the basic Soviet position was that multilateral cooperation in limiting arms transfers should be established on the basis of "political/legal" criteria, such as the U.N. Charter. This would mean, for instance, that the transfer of weapons to "aggressors" would be prohibited. The U.S. position was that a CATT regime could be constructed through selectively prohibiting the transfer of sophisticated or advanced weapons, using technical criteria to define these weapons by category. It was the U.S. position that a solid basis for this approach existed in the Arms Export Control Act. Thus, the U.S. delegation sought agreement on these "military/technical" criteria, and each side began to develop comparative weapons lists.

Gelb, however, had been pressing in Washington to focus the talks on specifics—regions and subregions. Other members of the administration agreed that the talks could go on forever if not specified in this way. This position reflected a concern that agreements on global criteria alone would not be an effective instrument for restraint because prohibiting specific arms transfers to unstable or problem areas either would be outside the applicable scope of such an agreement or would be interpreted differently by the U.S. and Soviet governments in specific situations. However, the perspective of most of the members of the SCC, which had become the focal point for generating negotiating postures for CATT, was that the talks should deal first with general principles.

Only after agreement had been reached on principles should agreement be sought on region-specific implementations. The problem with this approach was that it did not address the question of where negotiation ended and implementation began, a puzzle that promised to handicap any fledgling CATT regime. With this puzzle still unsolved, Gelb received an endorsement from the President, and "everyone fell into line." Operating with broad negotiating instructions, the U.S. delegation, in an effort to focus and move the May negotiations, introduced the concept of specific regions.

The May Helsinki discussions, perceived by the U.S. delegation as positive, generated an atmosphere of optimism that was reinforced by perceived progress at the United Nations Special Session on Disarmament (SSOD). It was commonly believed within the administration that the idea of supplier constraints or superpower limitations of arms deliveries to the developing nations would be viewed by these recipients with considerable suspicion. According to this belief, recipients would consider it "another example of the way the military 'haves' deny things to the military 'have nots'."[5] However, the Declaration of Principles of the SSOD proposed that the recipients and suppliers seek instruments limiting the export and import of arms. Gelb reflected U.S. optimism while testifying before Congress: "For the first time there was an international blessing for this idea. This will contribute to a psychological climate that will allow suppliers and recipients to get together and talk about what can be done on this subject."[6] In addition, the promoters of CATT were encouraged by signs of an emerging interest among Latin American nations in reaching a restraint agreement among themselves, limiting arms imports to the region.

By the end of the July round, the negotiations had turned to specifics. Both sides were close to agreement concerning each set of criteria—political/legal and military/technical—and had developed elaborate lists to govern which transfers might, and which might not, be approved under a CATT regime.

Although the Soviet delegation had expressed some initial skepticism about a regional focus, at the July round the negotiating teams convened a working group on regions. The U.S. delegates proposed discussions on Latin America and Africa and were prepared to proceed with substantive discussions on these regions—in fact, Latin American and African regional specialists were members of the U.S. delegation. While the Soviet delegates proposed no specific regions for discussion, they did propose consideration of the "neighbors" concept. Under this proposal, each superpower would refrain from transferring arms to a neighbor of the other. This suggestion was not well received within the U.S. government because, first, there was little likelihood that the

Soviets would transfer arms to neighbors of the United States, and second, the proposal had the potential of prohibiting the United States from providing security assistance to Iran, Turkey, Pakistan, and the People's Republic of China. The Soviet delegates, on the other hand, did not concede to the U.S. proposal that the agenda be limited to Africa and Latin America. While they proposed no specific regions for discussion, they did agree that regional discussions would be a significant agenda item for the next negotiating round.

While in Moscow in the early autumn on other business, Gelb was informed by Ambassador Mendelevich that the Soviets might want to discuss regions other than Latin America and Africa. He also raised the possibility of discussing China. Gelb responded that China was not a region, and that the United States would not be a party to the USSR's dispute with China. Upon Gelb's return, preparations were begun in anticipation of the Soviet agenda for the next CATT round scheduled for December 5 in Mexico City. The Saudis and Koreans were informed that the Soviet delegation might raise the issue of arms limitations to the Middle East and Far East, but that the discussion would be limited to a regional, not country-specific, focus.

Unknown to all but a few within the highest levels of the administration, however, normalization of relations with the People's Republic of China was proceeding rapidly toward conclusion under the leadership of National Security Advisor Zbigniew Brzezinski. Coincidentally, the crisis in Iran was assuming increased importance within the Carter administration. By November a rising crescendo of opposition to discussing the Far East or Middle East regions in CATT was emanating from offices with these regional responsibilities in several agencies, as well as from the NSC staff. Gelb himself was concerned about the Far East and Middle East questions, but he felt that the agenda agreed to at the previous negotiating round in Helsinki required that the U.S. delegates at least listen to Soviet statements if they raised the issue. The SCC eventually discussed the issue intensely. Although a compromise was initially reached at the November 27 meeting of the SCC, Brzezinski, who had until then not been actively involved with CATT, intervened. Concerned about the China issue and the deteriorating situation in Iran, and aware of the conflict already raging over the U.S. agenda for Mexico City, Brzezinski insisted that the delegation not discuss the Middle East or Far East if the Soviets broached the topic. Secretary of Defense Harold Brown, who did not want Korea discussed, supported Brzezinski. Gelb stood his ground. He understood through Secretary Vance, who with ACDA Paul Warnke was out of the country, that the President wanted regions discussed. With a cable from U.S. Ambassador Culver Gleysteen noting no objections to a "discussion" about Korea, and with the understanding conveyed that China would not be discussed, it appeared to Gelb's supporters that his position would prevail. It was a mistaken view, however, for CATT had little effective backing by then. Vance and Warnke had occupied themselves with the SALT negotiations and issues of peace in the Middle East, to the neglect of CATT. Vance in particular seemed unwilling to "go to the mat" over CATT negotiating strategy. Thus at both State and ACDA the support for the innovators was left to the deputies, Warren Christopher and Spurgeon Keeney, respectively. Although Christopher would later become famous for his role in negotiating the release of the hostages from Iran, in November 1978 neither he nor Keeney had the influence, access, or substantive involvement with high policy to provide the support Gelb and the remnants of his coalition needed either in the SCC or with the President.

At the eleventh hour the issue went to President Carter. At a meeting with Brzezinski and Brown, he decided that the delegation would discuss Latin America and Africa *only*, the "U.S. regions." If the Soviet delegation mentioned the Far East or Middle East, Gelb was to break off negotiations.

The Soviet delegation to Mexico City included a number of high-ranking Middle East and Far East specialists. At the very least, one can infer that they were prepared to discuss these regions. Gelb presented his position to his astonished counterpart. Conference procedures were immediately altered, and five days of head-of-delegation meetings ensued in an attempt to effect a compromise. Gelb and Brzezinski exchanged acrimonious cables about the immediate CATT agenda and the impending Indian Ocean negotiations. After five additional days of largely symbolic plenary meetings, the negotiations concluded.

Although President Carter and Soviet General Secretary Leonid Brezhnev mentioned CATT at the Vienna Summit, no further CAT negotiations were held. At a head-of-delegation meeting in July 1979, Ambassador Mendelevich and Reginald Bartholomew, Gelb's successor, restated old positions. A compromise within the U.S. government had been reached to permit an agenda item entitled "regions," with the question of which regions left to discussion between heads of delegations, but it never reached the negotiating table. The head-of-delegation meeting scheduled for September 1979 was cancelled in the midst of the "crisis" over the Soviet brigade in Cuba, and CATT became conspicuous only by its absence from the public State Department pronouncements on the U.S. arms control agenda.

A Domestic Coalition Explanation

CATT failed for more than one reason. The most obvious reason—although not the most fundamental one—was the disintegration of the coalition supporting it within the U.S. government. The Carter administration's effort at negotiation reflected a policy reversal. And that reversal occurred because one faction close to the President trumped the CATT faction, which by November 1978 was operating without a strong base of support. The central question concerning the breakdown of CATT is why the U.S. delegation went to Mexico City with negotiating instructions that appeared to contradict the earlier U.S. position— instructions that made any further negotiations futile. The primary reason is that the coalition supporting CATT came apart. Indeed, it appears that the major promoters of CATT as a policy innovation were operating with an illusory consensus or, at best, one that was highly vulnerable to shifts in assessments about the stakes perceived to be involved.

This explanation is underscored by an examination of the roles and perceptions of the principal types of U.S. actors involved in CATT decisionmaking. These actors may be differentiated in terms of their perceptions of several factors: (1) their perceptions of the consequences of unrestrained arms sales; (2) their perceptions of Soviet motives in the negotiations; (3) their expectations for the success of the CATT experiment; (4) their perception of the impact of an arms restraint regime on friends and allies; (5) their perception of the impact of a multilateral arms transfer restraint agreement on U.S. economic and strategic interests; and (6) their perception of the President's position on arms transfer restraint. An evaluation of the views of participants in the CATT negotiation process in terms of these perceptions and expectations revealed eight types of actors: (1) innovators, (2) principlists, (3) situationalists, (4) experimentalists, (5) reluctants, (6) diehards I, (7) diehards II, and (8) apathetics.

The data to support this argument were collected primarily from interviews conducted by the authors from August 1978 to January 1982, including interviews with most of the major actors involved in CATT decisionmaking. These were key personnel in the U.S. State Department, the Arms Control and Disarmament Agency, the Office of the Secretary of Defense, the Joint Chiefs of Staff, and staff members of the U.S. Congress.[7] This section conceptualizes domestic coalition-building problems for the negotiation of arms control agreements.

The *innovators*, best symbolized by the views of Gelb, were concerned about the lack of restraint in international arms sales and particularly a lack of restraint with regard to sophisticated weapons to certain regions. The restraint that had existed in the past was viewed as continually weakened by the fact that arms sales were used increasingly to solve a growing list of foreign policy problems during the Nixon and Ford administrations. They questioned whether the Soviet leadership had a serious interest in multilateral arms transfer restraint, except possibly to reduce U.S. sales to its neighbors, but they believed that multilateral restraint was a necessity given the administration's unilateral restraint policy. The innovators had fairly high expectations of success for CATT, while acknowledging that multilateral restraint was a tough political question and not merely an arms control negotiation. Concerning U.S allies who were also major arms exporters, the innovators assumed that these allies would have to get "on board." Had the negotiations progressed, they realized that "the Allies would have had to come along for if they did not, they risked having their interests perhaps adversely affected by an outcome which would have been for them a *fait accompli*." The innovators were not impressed by arguments that U.S. economic and strategic interests could be compromised through negotiated multilateral restraint regimes. Finally, they perceived that the President was highly motivated toward achieving agreement on this question.

Principlists, while not numerous within the bureaucracy, were fairly vocal in Congress. They expressed grave concern about unrestrained arms sales to the developing world. They viewed Soviet motives as similar to their own, and they held a significantly reduced perception of the "Soviet Threat." Their expectations for the success of CATT cannot be generalized, as principlists tended to bifurcate into optimists and pessimists concerning the success of any arms control regime. Like the innovators, they tended to deprecate the impact of arms sales restraint on the economic and strategic interests of the United States. Being outside the administration for the most part, they constantly sought reassurances that the President was seriously committed to this experiment. Their anxiety was revealed by the frequency with which administration officials were summoned to Capitol Hill to testify.

In and of themselves, arms sales were not viewed by *situationalists* as necessarily dangerous. Situationalists were, however, concerned about particular types of arms being transferred to developing nations, such as high-technology weapons systems or weaponry particularly suited to terrorist groups. They viewed arms transfers as positive or negative in terms of whether such transfers, in their view, stabilized or destabilized certain regions. As they perceived arms transfer issues as contextually determined, they rarely made general statements about Soviet motives. Regarding expectations of success for a multilateral arms transfer restraint regime, situationaists felt that progress could be realized if the negotiations remained at a technical level, that is, limiting the agenda to general prohibitions against the transfer of specific weapons and technologies. If negotiations remained at this level, they felt that "the Allies would go along," and that multilateral restraint would have minimal economic impact on European suppliers. The situationalists believed that the President could be persuaded that their position was the most practical application of his commitment to restraint.

The *experimentalists* viewed CATT as one among a number of instruments that might be useful for stabilizing U.S.-Soviet relations. Like the situationalists, however, they did not find arms transfers generally to be a major threat to international stability. They were highly skeptical of Soviet and European interests in multilateral restraint, and they had difficulty measuring areas of commonality between the United States and the Soviet Union. In particular, experimentalists observed that the superpowers tended to operate in mutually exclusve markets. They expressed doubts that the Soviet leadership would make any meaningful compromises unless the British and French agreed to limit their arms exports. Yet, they frequently noted that the United States and Europe were highly competitive in the Third World market, and that Europeans had serious economy-of-scale problems with respect to the manufacture of systems for their own forces. These problems provided frequent incentives for exporting such systems. Experimentalists did not have strong views about the impact of multilateral arms transfer restraint on economic and strategic interests of the United States. Their views can be summarized by one respondent, who said, "If the President wants it, let's try it and see where the hell it goes."

Reluctants represented a more diverse group than the others in terms of their perceptions of and expectations for CATT. While they were skeptical about arms sales restraint, they were unwilling to become basic opponents for fear that such action would compromise their positions on issues that they felt were more important. Reluctants perceived that the President was highly committed and thus that CATT was not worth the fight. Their distrust of Soviet motives was more fundamental, their expectations of success less, and their concern about the impact of CATT on U.S. allies more intense, than the experimentalist's.

Diehards I were openly hostile critics of both unilateral restraint and multilateral negotiations. They were not impressed with arguments stating the serious consequences of unrestrained arms sales. In fact, they argued that because of Soviet and European efforts, the United States should play a larger role in transferring arms. Diehards I derided the CATT initiative as naive and insisted that in its eagerness to obtain an agreement with the Soviets, the administration would "give away the store." The intensity of their criticism suggested a high expectation of some form of negotiated restraint which would be inimical to U.S. economic and strategic interests. Diehards I were particularly concerned about the adverse economic consequences for U.S. defense industries.

They perceived CATT as holding out great market potential for America's competitors, the Europeans.

Diehards II opposed the President's unilateral and multilateral restraint initiatives for essentially the same reasons as Diehards I; however, they differed markedly from Diehards I with regard to tactics. They openly supported the CATT initiative, hoping that if its proponents, whom they viewed as zealots, would exceed their mandate, they could then be "hoist with their own petard." On the other hand, they perceived that the President's unilateral policy depended on quick success, and that if it could be shown that success was not readily at hand, the entire restraint policy would collapse. Thus, their fundamental position was to support the initiative but constantly to stress the need for tangible indicators of progress in the negotiations.

The *apathetics* may be divided into groups. Those who felt CATT was "not an interesting subject" were willing to go along simply because they did not think the talks would go anywhere. Their position was rarely articulated in more specific terms. For the second group of apathetics, attention was a scarce resource. Faced with a large agenda of issues only marginally related to arms control, they were attentive neither to the negotiation nor to the coalition-building process behind it. The issue was obfuscated for them even more by the fact that at least in the early stages of the negotiations, CATT tended to be couched in technical arms control language. In most cases the apathetics reflected narrower regional or functional interests derived from their particular responsibilities.

Bureaucratic Perspectives on the Demise of CATT. Having identified the actors, we can now identify the initial consensus and how it evolved as CATT progressed. It appears that prior to the initial U.S.-Soviet discussions in Washington in December 1977, a broad coalition of support existed for multilateral restraint. The innovators had a President's enthusiastic support. Principlists had been pressing for this type of initiative for some time. Situationalists and experimentalists saw real opportunity to realize their own agenda within a continuing U.S.-Soviet arms control dialogue. As no agenda for CATT had been established, the reluctants saw no reason to oppose the initiative. Finally, diehards II were enthusiastic because a quick failure of this initiative would undermine the administration's unilateral restraint policies. Diehards I, who for the most part were not in the administration, constituted the only vocal opposition.

Although this coalition was maintained through the initial rounds in Washington and Helsinki, certain pressures became apparent. The primary promoters of the CATT initiative—at this point, the innovators, experimentalists, and situationalists—were aware that a time limit had been placed upon the negotiations. The principlists and diehards promoted the issue of a time limit. It was agreed at high levels within the administration that CATT must produce results within a year, although there was little discussion about what "results" meant. Members of the delegation believed that they had achieved tangible results when the Soviets agreed to the joint communique issued May 11. Elements of the coalition who supported the initiative because they felt that it would "not go anywhere" expressed surprise, voiced concerns, and cautioned that U.S. interests should be well understood in further negotiations. Concomitantly, as it became apparent that the Soviets found CATT a serious negotiating subject, discussion and debate over two issues emerged among the prime promoters of the talks. The first was over developing further tangible indicators of progress; the second was over developing the U.S. agenda for the third negotiating round, scheduled for July in Helsinki. These two issues became inexorably intertwined.

The first should be viewed in the context of a growing demand from several groups for "results within a year." The demands for early success came from several sources. First, the innovators felt they could enjoy the President's support for only a limited time, and besides, more was at stake than CATT. The innovators were committed to arms sales restraint, and the entire arms sales restraint policy depended on the development of "multilateral cooperation," as the President had said when he announced it. The President's support was essential. He could not be expected to provide such support without "tangible results." Moreover, the innovators perceived growing dissatisfaction with CATT and the Carter arms sales restraint policy from principlists, particularly those in Congress. Diehards I were adamant. They argued that security assistance was too critical for America's strategic needs, and too critical for U.S. relations with certain friendly governments, who were under internal and external pressures, to be subjected to delay. Moreover, they argued that the Soviets had everything to gain and nothing to lose through interminable negotiations. After all, only the United States had self-imposed restraints. There was general agreement within the other groups that time was a criterion for evaluation of success.

The situationalists did not agree. They believed it was a mistake to place this form of pressure on negotiations, for, as they argued, this was an experiment in an area central to U.S. foreign policy and international politics generally. The situationalists' view of time constraints converged with their views on criteria and their perception of what should be the initial goals of CATT: the establishment of procedures and mechanisms for long-term negotiations between the major suppliers, and then between suppliers and recipients. They felt that this could best be realized if the negotiations continued to focus on technical criteria from a global perspective. They argued that substantial progress had already been achieved in this area, and that this type of approach had the greatest chance of "spilling over" into broader political agreements. They warned that sufficient commonality did not exist between United States and Soviet interests to warrant expectations of early success if the agenda for negotiations were otherwise. The views of the situationalists, who were primarily in ACDA, did not prevail.

In preparation for the July meetings, it was decided to focus U.S. efforts on the issue of regions. The proponents of this view argued first that while Americans might find technical questions interesting, "the Soviets don't think that way." Second, the proponents of a regional focus believed that if any CATT agreement were to be meaningful, it had to address tough issues. This meant limiting transfers to particular regions since the purpose of the negotiations was to reduce the volume of transfers from the developed to the developing world, and not just to preclude sales of weapons that were not presently in demand. The President concurred with this view.

Operating under broad guidelines, the delegation that went to Helsinki in July was prepared to convince the Russians to discuss arms transfer restraint issues from a regional perspective. The diehards and the reluctants expressed great concern that because of these broad guidelines and the uncharacteristically quick pace of the negotiations, the delegation would "make policy in the field." At the July round in Helsinki, the Soviet delegation accepted the U.S. proposals for a regional focus. This progress had serious implications for the nature of the governmental coalition and preparations for the fourth round. In particular, progress between the delegations did not parallel progress in building or maintaining the internal U.S. government coalition supporting Gelb. The issue of which regions, present from the beginning, was accentuated at this point. The decision to specify the agenda through a concrete focus on regions became the blunt instrument by which the diehards, reluctants, and apathetics mortally wounded the CATT experiment.

A review of the perspectives of various regional interests within the bureaucracy reveals a wide spectrum of attitudes about where CATT was headed. The Latin American and African bureaus in both State and Defense saw in the talks a potential for limiting Soviet penetration into these areas. But they also had reservations. The Latin American bureaus did not want a Soviet-American agreement to undermine recent efforts by many Latin American governments to establish a regional regime. The African bureaus feared that a Soviet-American agreement would be "perceived by Africans as colonial or even racist." Gelb was able to defuse these issues, but he was not able to defuse the major opposition that emerged from officials with responsibilities related to the Middle East, Iran, the Far East and China.

Almost without exception, administration officials agreed that U.S. strategic and economic interests in the Middle East precluded discussion of a U.S.-Soviet restraint regime in that area. In addition, the emerging crisis in Iran sensitized Middle East region officials and specialists across agencies to a recognition that discussions related to the Middle East would accelerate the rapidly eroding position of the Shah. These concerns compelled the Middle East region officials and specialists to be cast as opponents of continued negotiations.

The prospect of a Far East regional agreement raised concerns about whether there was anything with which to bargain with the Soviets. The Soviet delegation was expected to raise the issue of limiting sales to Korea. But the United States, argued several participants, would gain little from any such restrictions, for South Korea is an important ally that depends on the United States for most of its arms. The Soviets, on the other hand, scarcely sell to North Korea. (Recently, in fact, North Korea has become relatively self-sufficient in armaments production, excepting advanced aircraft.) Said one participant with Asian responsibilities: "Our concern was that the Soviets would get everything and we would undermine an important ally. It seemed to us that we would get the short end of the deal." It was also expected that the Soviet delegation would raise the issue of China. This posed a serious problem at two levels—the operating levels within the bureaucracy, and within the NSC staff. The Far East specialists wanted to keep options open, while members of the NSC staff were actively and secretly working on the normalization of relations. The Far East specialists and policy officials advised Gelb that "he could not talk about sales to China, because we don't sell arms to China." The NSC staff perceived the China issue as one of major consequence. Those working the issue from the NSC were so concerned that they became the major opponents of CATT. In fact, as several participants noted, Brzezinski was so apprehensive about the normalization issue that he was determined "to eliminate anything which had a one one-thousandths chance of undermining it." NSC staff opposition was seen by the reluctants, the diehards, and the apathetics as a cue that the President no longer gave high priority to CATT. The growing defections from the original coalition in turn strengthened Brzezinski's opposition to CATT. He then convinced the President to send a delegation to Mexico City with narrow instructions—indeed, instructions that contradicted the earlier U.S. position.

In conclusion, the focus on regions had four major implications for the coalition. First, it opened a pandora's box by expanding the number of politically sensitive issues relevant to CATT. Second, it expanded the number of attentive actors or players in the policy-clearance process, making the group as a whole more diffused in its interests about and perspectives on arms transfers and the consequences of CATT for U.S. bilateral relations. Third, it mobilized the apathetics. Fourth, it gave the diehards and the reluctants ammunition to attack the restraint policy.

We will not speculate about whether the CATT negotiations would have succeeded had they not focused on regions. The coalition seemed to depend upon a regional focus since the conditions under which it was originally formed demanded a meaningful agreement secured in a timely fashion. Yet this approach contained the seeds of its own destruction because as the talks became more specific, they achieved high visibility and consequently greater opposition. As one participant noted, "CATT was allowed to bounce along until it bumped into China and the Middle East."

A "State-as-Actor" Explanation

In the last section we explained U.S. policy as the outcome of a factional process—of "bureaucratic politics," to use the fashionable term. As is common in the use of this explanatory method, we did not attempt to explain Soviet behavior by applying the bureaucratic model with equal fidelity, for the obvious reason that we know less about the particular Soviet factions in this case. An alternative way to explain the failure of CATT—in fact, a much simpler one, and one more commonly (if no more appropriately) applied to other less accessible governments than one's own—assumes that the Soviet Union behaved and would have continued to behave, if negotiations had continued, as if it were a single person, a unitary decisionmaker. One can then apply this explanatory premise to the United States as well. Accordingly, CATT failed because the United States perceived—finally recognized—that it had allowed the Soviet Union to negotiate in a cost-free environment, since the United States had initiated unilateral arms transfer restraint. Recognizing this situation was tantamount to admitting that the Soviets had not been serious about CATT and would not make the concessions and commitments necessary on their side to achieve a significant treaty.

The Soviet Union never stated its specific policy objectives with respect to CATT. At least by assumption, several motives for entering the negotiations can be ascribed to the Soviet leadership. For example, it is possible that they perceived CATT as an opportunity to extend the U.S. unilateral restraint effort. Even a limited CATT agreement might generate domestic pressures, particularly congressional pressure, for even more extensive unilateral initiatives. The Soviet Union may also have viewed CATT as a means of reducing U.S. and European arms sales to its neighbors, namely, Iran and Korea, and potentially China. Again, the Soviets may have thought an agreement could be reached to limit sales to countries that posed security threats to Soviet allies or client states, particularly in the Near and Middle East. Furthermore, as the United States and its allies possessed considerable access to oil-producing states (Saudi Arabia, Iran, etc.), the Soviet leadership may have believed that it would reduce U.S. leverage through a prolonged restraint regime. Since the Soviet Union was probably aware of the economy-of-scale problems of European arms suppliers and, as a consequence, the pressures within Europe to preserve export markets, it may have viewed a restraint agreement with the United States as an instrument for creating increased tension within the NATO alliance. Finally, the negotiations themselves could have been valued by the Soviet leadership for propaganda reasons, given the 1978 U.N. Special Session on Disarmament.[8] In summary, the Soviets had little to lose through preliminary discussions of arms transfer restraint.

The Soviet position throughout the four negotiating rounds varied widely, suggesting that perhaps for them also it was a secondary issue that was not subjected to as thorough clearance procedures as weightier issues evidently are. Their negotiating posture seemed reactive, without continuity, and excessively experimental and probe oriented. At various junctures this posture included lack of interest, promotion of political/ legal criteria, experiments with a "neighbors" concept, a proposal to prohibit arms transfers to certain specific countries (such as China), acceptance of U.S. suggested technical criteria as well as acceptance of a regional concept for negotiation, and limits on transfers to Latin America, excluding Cuba. It is not apparent that at any time the Soviets abandoned any of these positions—including lack of interest.

The Soviet position that was maintained most evidently throughout the talks was the development of political/legal criteria. The basic position was that these criteria must include restricting transfers to racist regimes, particularly states that have been sanctioned by the United Nations; states they considered aggressors; states they deemed militaristic or those they believed had unjust territorial claims; states that reject disarmament efforts; and states that they thought oppressed liberation groups. Working groups addressed the problem of defining mutually acceptable operational definitions of these proposed criteria at the second, third, and fourth negotiating rounds. Concomitantly, the Soviets experimented with approaches such as the prohibition of transfers to China, which surfaced outside the formal negotiations. Finally, they accepted the U.S. position that any criteria must be operationalized on a regional basis, but they insisted that the discussions not be limited to Latin America and Africa.

The objectives of the United States' multilateral effort were discussed earlier. Here the negotiating posture of the Soviets will be assessed. But it should be noted that the unilateral effort at restraint and the failure to reach agreement with the Europeans sharply constrained the Carter administration in its negotiations with the Soviets. The administration had announced a unilateral restraint policy before negotiations started, and continued to refer to this policy throughout the course of the negotiations. Thus it conspicuously affirmed that continued self-restraint depended on reciprocity from other suppliers. In effect, the President imposed a time limit on the negotiations. This time limit came to have an important effect on SCC deliberations over the CATT negotiating strategy.

The U.S. negotiating posture as it emerged after the Helsinki round rested on three points of potential agreement: (1) restriction of transfers to certain regions; (2) restrictions on transfers of certain types of weapons; and (3) restrictions of transfers according to certain political or legal criteria, the Soviet position.

Military/technical criteria were conceived to include prohibitions against transfers of certain types of weapons (such as surface-to-surface missiles and attack helicopters), and these criteria were to be operationalized on the basis of corresponding U.S.-Soviet weapons lists, on which the delegations were near agreement when the talks collapsed. The U.S. position also accepted the Soviet concept of political/legal criteria as a basis for negotiation, and working groups attempted to define concrete and enforceable criteria here. At a minimum, the United States was willing to discuss prohibitions on the transfer of weapons particularly useful to terrorist groups.

Soviet Negotiating Strategies and Constraints on U.S. Options. The U.S. position in CATT negotiations was vulnerable to a strategy of delay. The fourteen-month hiatus between March 1977 (when Cyrus Vance took the idea of CATT directly to the Soviet leadership) and May 1978 (when the joint communique was issued following the second round of negotiations) suggests that the Soviets did not take advantage of this vulnerability. This is especially noticeable when compared to the pace of other U.S.-Soviet arms control negotiations, such as SALT. The Soviet proposal that arms transfer restraint be negotiated on the basis of political/legal criteria, however, did impose a considerable obstacle to U.S. negotiators. The Soviet criteria were ambiguous: they lacked precision, and they could easily be unevenly applied and misinterpreted.

It was difficult for U.S. officials to assess whether the "neighbors" concept was a serious proposal because it was presented in such an incomplete form. Incomplete or not, however, the concept raised serious problems for the United States in relations with its allies, as well as in normalization of relations with China. It was scarcely reciprocal, as the Soviet Union does not sell arms to Canada or Mexico. In part to reassure U.S. allies, some of whom were on the defensive about arms transfer restraint anyway, the U.S. delegation indicated to the Soviets that the nature of the negotiations was not to enhance mutual security of the Soviet Union and the United States but to promote stability in troubled areas of the globe.

Given the reactive nature of the Soviets' negotiating behavior during the CATT process, their series of probes on issues seemingly irrelevant to the U.S. concept of the scope of the negotiations (the neighbors concept, the China issue, Soviet interest in Latin America, limitations with Cuba exempted, etc.), and the ambiguity of the proposed political/ legal criteria, it was difficult for U.S. planners to anticipate Soviet bargaining positions. This made preparations for each round extremely complex, and permitted extensive disagreement among participating departments and agencies in the Carter administration. Furthermore, when the administration moved the negotiations to a regional focus very early in the negotiating process, U.S. flexibility decreased. In effect, the United States opened the regional agenda and then became unable to close it off or limit it. This also had the effect of moving the negotiations from the bounded realm of arms control into a dialogue concerning global political issues.

Once the Soviets reacted to the U.S. proposal for a regional focus to apply the two sets of criteria (initially proposed at the May 1977 round), the U.S. became vulnerable to a "regional whipsaw." At the July 1977 round, the Soviets accepted a regional perspective and participated in regional working group sessions, but they left open the issue of which regions should be discussed at the next round. The United States was aware that at the next round the Soviets would introduce their own regions for negotiations, most likely the Far East, Middle East, and Near East. This compelled the U.S. to face the possible consequence for U.S. bilateral relations among friends and allies in these regions or to prepare to insist that only the originally proposed regions—Latin America and Africa—be discussed, and thus risk a possible collapse of the negotiations. There were few options for regional or subregional tradeoffs, and the risks to U.S. bilateral relations with allies in these areas of strategic and economic importance overshadowed possible gains from any foreseeable CATT regime. Not surprisingly, the U.S. government found that at that point it had little to negotiate, and the talks collapsed.

The Lessons of CATT

Several "lessons" emerge from the Carter administration's CATT experience, lessons that are relevant not only to the subject of negotiated multilateral arms transfer restraint, but also to other issues for future U.S.-Soviet negotiations. First, future arms control negotiations on subjects as complex as CATT should be given considerable time, so that the required substance and consensus of policy can be developed. Yet time had become costly. The requirement that tangible results had to be demonstrated in a timely fashion placed considerable pressure on the negotiations. Participants we interviewed stated that these results had to be demonstrated within one year. If they were not, the unilateral restraint policy would simply continue the opportunity for other arms suppliers to increase their market shares at U.S. expense. There was cause for concern that "the Soviets would drag the negotiations on forever." The unilateral restraint initiative was intended to demonstrate U.S. resolve to treat arms transfer restraint seriously, and it was at least a partial success in those terms. From another perspective, however, it was a serious bargaining error because of the time pressures that it imposed on the United States while providing no incentive for quick agreement by either the Europeans or the Soviets.

Second, future negotiations should focus initially on technical criteria. Arms transfers are too central to the defense and security objectives of both suppliers and recipients for the negotiations to progress significantly if cast initially along regional lines. It appears that early agreement could have been reached prohibiting the global transfer of certain types of weapons. A regional focus could then have been selectively introduced, perhaps with reference to least-sensitive regions. Early introduction of the regional focus without a clear way to limit which regions would be involved moved negotiations from the more bounded technical domain of arms control into a broader political realm which raised serious concerns within the administration about the threat the negotiations might pose for both U.S. bilateral relations and regional security objectives in certain regions.

Third, in future negotiations the U.S. approach should be incremental. While expectations of success varied greatly within the administration, the "tangible results" requirement tended to drive the process to unattainable objectives. Tangible results came to be defined as the region- or subregion-specific application of military/technical and political/legal criteria. Interviews with members of the U.S. delegation indicated that agreement on both sets of criteria had been nearly attained when the negotiations were suspended. It appears that these criteria could have served as a basis for global restrictions on the transfer of certain weapons such as long-range, surface-to-surface missiles or highly portable anti-aircraft missiles that terrorists could use against commercial airliners. While agreements of this type may not be significant in and of themselves, they would have had the effect of permitting a continuing negotiation dialogue. Alternatively, negotiations could have proceeded toward agreement on military/technical criteria and political/legal criteria before introducing the most difficult issue—regional application. This incremental strategy would have had the effect of accommodating a regional focus. Where weapons systems had to be accommodated on the basis of specific regions, the emphasis would have been on the weapons systems themselves, and not on the regions. The introduction of specific regional applications into the negotiations before a solid basis for negotiation had been established, or before the criteria to be applied had been agreed to, placed tremendous pressure on the negotiation process, and on the CATT decisionmaking process in the U.S. government. It had the unsettling effect of leaving the United States vulnerable to a regional whipsaw, of providing the Soviet Union the opportunity to suggest restrictions on U.S. arms transfer programs in areas of critical importance to it before the nature or extent of what these restrictions might be were codified, and of forcing the U.S. government into a reactive mode of evaluating virtually all of its arms transfer relationships so that Soviet regional initiatives at CATT could be countered. Again, this may be related to the self-imposed time constraint. The present analysis suggests that arms transfers are too central an instrument of bilateral relations for systematic political solutions to what are better defined as discrete arms control problems.

Keeping negotiations at the technical level could have entailed foreign policy management problems for the U.S. government, but none so severe as the ones caused by the early introduction of regional issues. Several considerations support this conclusion. Since the prospects for success at CATT were heavily discounted by most major U.S. allies and recipients, prolonging the negotiations and specific technical agreements would have provided a firmer basis for emergence of the issue of region-specific application through incrementally elevating the perception of probability of success among friends and allies and sensitizing them to the direction toward which CATT was headed. It can be expected that concerns for U.S. bilateral relations, which would have emerged as CATT became region-specific, could be sequentially identified and selectively managed. Finally, while the Soviet Union could have dragged out technical negotiations, it is unlikely that any Soviet position could have emerged at this level that would have created the concern within the U.S. government that anticipation of the Soviet proposals over the Far East, Near East, and Middle East did.

When regional issues did emerge, they could have been dealt with from a solid technical basis, perhaps within the context of a more completely defined and bounded agenda. While technical negotiations and agreement on technical factors would not have been sufficient for immediate attainment of U.S. objectives in the negotiations, they may have fractionized and made more manageable some of the negotiating problems encountered by the United States as it approached the regional issue.

Fourth, CATT perspectives within the U.S. government are likely to remain complex and multidimensional. Consensus-building efforts commensurate with their intractability are required if an effective negotiating posture with other suppliers or recipients is to be developed in the future. Some participants at high decisionmaking levels tended to conceptualize the foreign policy process within the government around CATT issues in terms of "hawks" and "doves." Yet analysis of interviews with CATT participants revealed that differences on policy issues could not be so easily displayed. Rather, central differences existed among the participants concerning perceptions of the consequences of unrestrained arms sales; perceptions of Soviet motives in the negotiations; expectations for the success of the CATT experiment; perceptions of the impact of an arms restraint regime on friends and allies; perceptions of the impact of a multilateral arms transfer restraint agreement on U.S. economic and strategic interests; and perceptions of the President's position on the issue. These dimensions are likely common to other arms control issues and generate a broad variety of options, issues, and positions within the government. "Hawk" and "Dove" differences tend to obfuscate this complex contextual detail.

Fifth, arms control issues must eventually make a smooth convergence with the main activities of the government. CATT, like many arms control negotiations, was a secondary issue for most of the bureaucracy, but its implications could be of primary importance for U.S. foreign policy. It was accorded this importance by the President and the Secretary of State early in the Carter administration, but Secretary Vance became preoccupied with SALT and the Middle East settlement and had neither the time nor the willingness to fight to save the CATT initiative. This greatly weakened Gelb's position in the final CATT strategy sessions.

The maintenance of bilateral relations and resource allocations constitute the primary focus of the daily business of the government in foreign affairs. It appears that if any functional innovation, such as CATT, is to be successful, it must converge with these specific daily concerns. It also appears that for arms control negotiations to succeed, the convergence can be implicit, but it must occur. Concerns about the implications of a regionally focused CATT regime and its impact both on agreements with friends and allies and on U.S. economic and strategic interests, remained latent as long as probabilities of a CATT agreement remained remote. In the future, greater attention must be given to the ultimate convergence of the arms control agenda if it is to be kept consistent with necessities of long-standing defense and foreign policy interests.

THE FAILURE OF THE UNILATERAL EFFORT

The failure of the unilateral effort for arms transfer restraint is not nearly as clear as the CATT failure, because it failed through erosion, not collapse. Partly as a result of the collapse of CATT negotiations, the unilateral restraint effort came under increasing pressure from within the government as well as outside it. The Soviet invasion of Afghanistan convinced almost all in the Carter administration that their initial assumptions about Soviet behavior were no longer valid. The unwillingness of America's allies to cooperate in a restraint regime, and the growing worldwide demand for arms, placed additional pressures on the unilateral effort. These pressures usually took the form of specific demands, for arms and other military equipment and services, or for relaxation of the pressure of U.S. diplomacy on allies' arms transfer activities.

While the ceiling was conceived by the administration to be an obvious signal to other arms suppliers that the United States was interested in limiting worldwide arms sales, and was a means of compelling recipient nations to plan more adequately for future weapons acquisitions, the ceiling process suffered major problems from the beginning. First, as the ceiling included many exemptions, it did not appear to the administration's critics as a genuine form of restraint, since commercial sales; sales to NATO members, Japan, Australia, and New Zealand; and military construction were exempted. These exemptions constituted a sizable proportion of total U.S. sales. For example, military construction sales in recent years have amounted to nearly $2 billion per year, and commercial sales annually amount to more than $2 billion. Second, and ironically, the ceiling did not permit the administration the flexibility to accommodate for the fact that arms requests from friendly nonindustrialized nations would vary from year to year according to perceptions of threat or need. In addition, major equipment replacement or initial acquisition may occur once in fifteen years, as with squadrons of advanced aircraft. Service, training, and infrastructure to support this can cause enormous variations in sales volume per year. These pressures forced the administration to string out major acquisitions to accommodate the ceiling. Third, the administration was already incredibly constrained in its ability to provide security assistance because of congressional cuts in the grant Military Assistance Program, International Military Education and Training Program, and Foreign Military Sales program credits.

Because of the impasse with CATT, the lack of support from allies, and the Soviet intervention in Afghanistan, President Carter decided not to reduce the FY 1980 ceiling further, as he had planned. In addition, the administration adjusted the FY 1979 ceiling for 8-percent inflation and then determined that the FY 1980 ceiling would be set at $9.2 billion. The collapse of sales to Iran, which had constituted about 30 percent of the space under the ceiling, in reality made the ceiling a meaningless instrument of restraint. Thus, the FY 1980 ceiling with its exemptions and its expansion scarcely appeared as restraint at all.

Another element of the unilateral restraint policy that quickly came into conflict with the realities of international politics was the prohibition against the production of advanced weapons solely for export. This aspect of the Carter policy denied the government a means by which to adapt flexibly to the unique geographical, technological, and developmental conditions existing in the Third World. With this prohibition, the administration forced itself to choose in many cases between U.S. weapons that either were too sophisticated for a recipient or did not meet the recipient's current perceived needs. As a consequence of this dilemma, as well as of the concern that this structure provided new sales opportunities for the Soviet Union and for Western European exporters (and thus decreased the U.S. government's ability to restrain worldwide sales rather than increase its capabilities for restraint), the administration found itself supporting the development of a jet fighter aircraft, the F-X, solely for export. Since the decision was made to develop the F-X, several companies have applied to the State Department for permission to discuss exporting it to twenty-one countries.

Similarly, the President's prohibition of coproduction arrangements was eroded by exceptions; more than seventeen exceptions were granted. The exceptions involved relatively less sophisticated weapons but they revealed recipients' growing demand that some form of coproduction arrangements be offered if they were to purchase U.S. weapons.

It can be said, then, that the Carter restraint effort was a victim of two conflicting demands; a demand for limited use of arms transfers as an instrument for U.S. foreign policy at a time when the international demand was for increased arms transfers. The Nixon Doctrine became a central element of foreign policy, even of Carter's foreign policy, because for a variety of reasons the United States was unwilling and incapable to respond to perceived threats to friendly governments in any way other than through arms transfers. Increasingly, the United States could demonstrate commitment to Iran, Saudi Arabia, Israel, Egypt, Jordan, South Korea, Pakistan, Taiwan, Spain, and Turkey, to name a few friendly countries, only through arms transfers. Similarly, the one way the United States could get agreement among conflicting nations was to promise arms as compensation for concessions made. Recall the aid promised Egypt and Israel after the Camp David accords and to Jordan for supporting them. A major way the United States could encourage moderation in oil-pricing policy was to deliver arms to those nations with the power to limit oil prices. Increasingly, arms transfers became a major means of countering Soviet penetration in Africa and Asia. And they also became a means for discouraging certain nations from developing nuclear weapons. In a troubled economy, arms transfers have become an important instrument for generating employment, a means of reducing developmental costs. Despite his desire for restraint and his public and diplomatic support for restraint, President Carter learned that because of the limited number of instruments available to him for dealing with international problems, arms transfers were simply too useful for too many purposes to be extensively curtailed.

INTERNATIONAL CONSTRAINTS ON ARMS TRANSFERS

Regardless of President Reagan's intentions, it is unlikely that security assistance can be greatly expanded, for several international and domestic factors prohibit it. In the international environment, these factors include the limited funds available to most recipients; high interest rates that reduce the feasibility or at least the attractiveness of credit sales; concern of international lending institutions about growing Third World indebtedness; and expanded sales efforts of European competitors. Domestic restraints on the expanded use of arms transfers include continued congressional skepticism about the advisability of arms transfers; congressional and administrative interest in limiting foreign aid costs; industry opposition to increased use of coproduction arrangements; and opposition of the Army, Navy, and Air Force to exports of top-line equipment until the procurement needs of the services are fulfilled.

International payments deficits, the need to generate jobs, the necessity of finding means to offset development costs, concerns about the length of production runs, and general economic pressures have compelled most industrialized nations increasingly to reduce military grant aid in favor of reimbursable assistance. Thus over the past few years, no matter how great the demand for arms, few nations have the resources to purchase vast quantities. With few exceptions, the largest importers of arms in 1978 were the oil-rich countries, Iran, Libya, Iraq, and Saudi Arabia. Moreover, OPEC nations have increased international payment pressures on poor nations that have to import oil. Soaring oil prices have been an enormous burden on developing nations, leaving them with precious little capital for either domestic services or enhanced defense readiness. The Morgan Guaranty Trust Company estimates that increased OPEC prices are the major contributor to the $85 billion international payments debts of non-oil-producing Third World countries.[9]

Related to the unavailability of capital for arms imports among Third World nations is the soaring cost of interest. The U.S. government is currently charging 12½ percent interest on loans processed through the Foreign Military Sales Finance Program. These interest rates make the procurement of major weapons systems a heavy burden for most developing economies. Increasingly, Third World borrowers are finding that higher interest rates are consuming more of their export earnings. Rimmer deVries, Senior Vice President at Morgan Guaranty Trust Company, estimated that ten years ago the twelve largest Third World borrowers needed only 6 percent of their export earnings to pay the interest owed on debts abroad, "but by 1980 interest took 16 percent of such earnings and this year could jump to 20 percent."[10]

A third financial constraint on expanded arms transfers to the developing countries is the fear among international banking experts that the Third World debt has grown to alarmingly dangerous levels. The Morgan Guaranty Trust estimates the developing countries' debt at $500 billion. Banking officials are concerned that any large default could, as a Lloyds Bank spokesman stated, "have a domino effect that could lead to a catastrophe."[11] While the Foreign Military Sales Finance Program does provide a guarantee for loans issued to developing countries by private institutions, lending officials believe that all indebtedness must be reduced in the near future.

An expanded arms transfer effort by the Reagan administration will also have to confront increased competitiveness from European suppliers. While the Carter administration was intent upon limiting the activities of U.S. industry and government representatives abroad, the European governments were intent on assisting their industries in expanding arms exports to the Third World. It was apparent by 1980, for example, that foreign military sales had become France's biggest growth industry. In 1970 the value of total arms deliveries abroad was only $600 million, but by 1979 the value of arms exports had grown to

$4.76 billion.[12] British sales efforts are no less ambitious. A comparison of U.S. and European exports to the Third World since 1974 reveals how rapidly and extensively the Europeans are capturing a sizable proportion of the Third World market.

Table 6.1 reveals the extent of European expansion of its exports to the developing world, especially since 1976. While U.S. arms exports to the developing nations have remained fairly constant at about $10 billion since 1976, European exports have more than tripled from $2.2 billion to $7.2 billion. European sales were expected to be even greater in 1981. Any expanded arms transfer program of the Reagan administration will confront, then, what one Defense Department official referred to as "fierce competition from our NATO allies."

Soviet aid activities should also be considered in a review of future arms transfer prospects. It should be noted that there are only a few recipients whom the United States and the Soviet Union compete to supply.[13] Moreover, a better argument could be made that Soviet aid activities stimulate arms transfers to a region rather than reduce such transfers. Yet, as Third World recipients attempt to reduce their dependence upon sole-supply relationships,[14] it may be expected that the United States and the Soviet Union will find themselves increasingly in competitive transfer situations. For example, while U.S. arms exports, measured in constant dollars, have remained fairly stable since the early 1970s, Soviet arms exports have expanded extensively, from only $1.7 billion in 1970 to $6.6 billion in 1978.

Finally, an expanded arms transfer program of the United States will confront an ever-growing number of major Third World arms producers. More than thirty developing nations now produce various weapons. The rapid growth of Third World producers may be illustrated by comparing domestic aircraft production in 1965 with such production in 1975: in 1965 only seven countries in the Third World produced a

Table 6.1. U.S. and European Arms Exports to Developing Nations

In Billions of Dollars

Year	United States	Europe*
1974	11.9	3.6
1975	11.6	5.4
1976	10.7	2.2
1977	9.9	6.5
1978	11.3	7.9
1979	10.4	7.2

*Note: Includes France, United Kingdom, West Germany and Italy

Source: Compiled from data provided in United States, Senate, Committee on Foreign Relations, U.S. Conventional Arms Transfer Policy (Washington, D.C.: USGPO, 1980).

military aircraft, but by 1975 seventeen countries did.[15] The U.S. Arms Control and Disarmament Agency has estimated that the value of armaments produced in the Third World, excluding China, has increased from less that $1 billion in 1970 to over $5 billion in 1977.[16]

Many of these weapons are produced under license or coproduction arrangements with industrial states, but it is quite clear that once a developing country acquires some indigenous production capability, it sees the same advantages to exports as do industrialized nations. Brazil, Taiwan, Argentina, Israel, and Yugoslavia have ambitious plans to export weapons. Generally, these weapons are at the intermediate level of sophistication and have relatively simple maintenance and operational requirements. There is a high demand for such equipment in Latin America and Africa. Reflecting that demand, Third World exports have increased from $49 million in 1969 to $707 million in 1978.[17] The proliferation of arms exporters, the expanded production facilities of such exporters, and the desire of many nations to avoid heavy dependence upon sole suppliers very probably will also limit the expansion of U.S. arms transfers.

Several domestic factors also constrain the expansion of arms transfers. Many members of Congress are still reticent about military assistance. Over a five-year period, culminating in 1977, Congress increasingly intervened in arms sales decisionmaking and imposed a variety of restrictions on the security assistance program, including the following: (1) specific lists of which nations could receive grant assistance, which could purchase weapons, and which could receive military credit assistance; (2) limitations on credit availability for weapons coproduction agreements; (3) prescriptions for how the United States could transfer weapons; (4) prohibitions stating that specific types of regimes, such as violators of human rights, could not receive security assistance; (5) restrictions on the dollar volume of total sales that could be made to Latin America and Africa; and (6) specific restrictions on the number of U.S. military personnel that could be assigned to security assistance functions in each recipient nation, and severe proscriptions on the activities of these personnel. Over the years Congress has established a lengthy list of restrictions,[18] and recent debates in Congress over aid to El Salvador or concerns about the possible expanded arms aid to Saudi Arabia and other Middle East nations reveal that Congress will remain a major restraining force.[19] The Reagan administration will be bound by law, as was the Carter administration, to implement congressional restrictions on the sale of arms.

As a consequence of limited capital and credit, only oil-rich nations will be capable of acquiring large amounts of equipment from the United States. Most other nations will need sizable grants (non-reimbursable aid) or very favorable credit to acquire major weapons systems.

Yet, Congress has a long history of opposing major military grant assistance programs. With the exception of Israel, which has been the beneficiary of about $4 billion in FMS through waived credit, Congress recently has been very reluctant to provide grant aid to arms recipients. The Military Assistance Program (MAP) has not exceeded $1 billion since 1964, and in 1979, Congress authorized only $213 million in MAP. As have past presidents, Reagan will find it extremely difficult to convince Congress to accept an expanded grant assistance program.

Another major domestic constraint on an expanded arms transfer program is industry and other opposition to coproduction arrangements. It is clear that, increasingly, Third World recipients will demand coproduction arrangements as a special condition for receiving arms from industrial suppliers. Some demand and obtain the same arrangement for civilian manufactured goods such as automobiles. Officials are concerned that if the United States does not agree, recipients will turn to Europe. Said a State Department official working on the issue, "We will have to be more flexible on this one. If we don't grant coproduction, France and Britain will. They won't want to, but I think they will see coproduction arrangements as a way of penetrating traditional U.S. markets." The pressures for coproduction agreements are revealed by the fact that of all the controls established by President Carter, this one had the most exceptions. In March 1980, Matthew Nimetz, Under Secretary of State for Security Assistance, Science and Technology, testified that there had been seventeen exceptions to the proscription against coproduction agreements with developing nations.[20] The Committee on Foreign Relations has recommended that the coproduction prohibition be reviewed and modified. Both industry and the services are alarmed by this trend. Industry is concerned about the possibility of creating new competitors by providing recipients technical data and construction skills which permit an export capability that such countries could not develop through an indigenous effort. This concern is specifically focused on the negotiation of coproduction memoranda of understanding (MOUs) by government officials without adequate coordination with industry.

The Defense Department also does not seem enthusiastic about the Third World nations' growing demand for coproduction agreements. The former Director of Technology and Arms Transfer Policy has stated that:

> . . . there is a growing concern from some quarters, particularly Defense, about where present and future coproduction agreements might take us. I see little enthusiasm among the Services, for example, for having major

components for U.S. systems produced by non-NATO countries, both for the effects that foreign coproduction is likely to have on the U.S. mobilization base and for the political risk of a disruption of supply in the event of political pressures, crisis or actual hostilities. And yet, to make any economic sense, coproducing recipients will probably have to find some markets for the items they produce beyond what are likely to be their small indigenous requirements. That leaves only two alternatives: either sell back to the U.S. or find Third country markets.[21]

Coproduction, then, leaves the Reagan administration with a variety of unacceptable options: the risk of alienating Third World nations by refusing to reach coproduction arrangements, with a possible loss of markets; the risk of dependence upon Third World production of items needed for the U.S. military inventory; and the risk of creating new competitors.

Finally, it should be noted that the armed services are not always as keen about arms exports as is often alleged. Even though arms exports often help offset development and procurement costs, and sometimes help clear inventories, many officers are distressed by long deployment delays that are caused by exports. As one officer in the air force sales office stated, "Each time we find a new buyer for the F-16, the requirements of the U.S. Air Force are delayed because we have to share limited production schedules with the new recipients." And a naval officer speaking of a U.S. arms sales program for Saudi Arabia said, "The Saudi Naval Expansion Program is marvelous. It is the kind of navy we could have if we just had the money and were allowed to get in line."

As the Reagan administration commits itself to a rapid expansion of U.S. conventional forces, it is likely that there will be growing conflict between that goal and the goal of providing major armament packages to other nations.[22]

New Directions for Arms Transfer Cooperation. Most likely the Reagan administration will invite discussions with the Europeans which can provide a framework for a more integrated Western posture to confront Soviet penetration in the Near and Middle East, and at the same time increase NATO's capabilities. These discussions will no doubt be encumbered by vestiges of the Carter restraint policy but, surprisingly, will embody many of the core objectives of the Carter program. For example, it appears that negotiations with the Europeans have a future potential for accomplishing the increased rationalization of arms transfers, the promotion of U.S. security objectives in the developing world through a controlled supply of armaments, and the improvement of NATO capabilities through enhanced rationalization, standardization, and interoperability (RSI). The Reagan administration and various European administrations should explore the following questions concerning more regularized and generalized procedures that could achieve coordinated allied security assistance as well as support efforts to rationalize weapons procurement within the NATO alliance:

What is the feasibility of cooperative security assistance?

What adjustments are necessary among NATO suppliers to engage in cooperative security assistance to Third World recipients?

Are there ways in which coordinated security assistance efforts might support RSI efforts in NATO, perhaps in the context of the family of weapons concept?

What countries or regions may be candidates for cooperative security assistance?

What instruments, including organizational structures, might be used for cooperative security assistance?

The present analyses suggest that these directions have the greatest potential for planned, rationalized, and coordinated Western supplier policies toward the developing world, which, after all, were major objectives of the Carter Presidential Directive 13. This form of cooperative arms transfers is an arms control regime that would have the greatest potential for generating incentives for cooperation from the Europeans, and for integration of tacit and explicit arms control policies with strategy and national security policy. The next chapter evaluates the prospects for progress in this area through a brief review of relevant NATO programs and through a discussion of major trends in the arms transfer policies of France, the United Kingdom, and West Germany.

NOTES

1 Presidential Review Memorandum (PRM)/NSC 12, January 26, 1977.
2 Commonly also referred to as the Conventional Arm Transfer (CAT) negotiations.
3 United States, House, Committee on Armed Services, *Hearings on Indian Ocean Arms Limitations and Multilateral Cooperation on Restraining Conventional Arms Transfers*, 95th Congress, second session, October 3, and 10, 1978, p. 13.
4 Mendelevich was also the Soviet's chief negotiator at the Indian Ocean negotiations; Gelb was Warnke's deputy on the U.S. side at those talks.
5 *Hearings on Indian Ocean Arms Limitations*, p. 14.
6 Ibid.
7 We express our gratitude for the candid responses given, which depended on our assurances of anonymity for specific opinions of our respondents.
8 Michael D. Salomon, David J. Louscher, and Paul Y. Hammond, "Lessons of the Carter Approach to Restraining Arms Transfers," *Survival* 23,5 (September/October, 1981), pp. 203-204.
9 Richard F. Jansen, "Third World Debts, Totaling $500 Billion May Pose Big Dangers," *Wall Street Journal* (January 28, 1981), pp. 1 and 19.

10 Ibid.

11 Ibid.

12 Felix Kessler, "French Arms Exports Mount as Paris Seeks to Counteract Oil Bills," *Wall Street Journal* (November 10, 1980), p. 1.

13 The exceptions from 1967 to 1978 include these cross-bloc recipients: Peru, Libya, Northern Yemen, Afghanistan, Pakistan, Nigeria, and Zambia. United States Arms Control and Disarmament Agency, *World Military Expenditures and Arms Transfers, 1969-1978* (Washington, D.C.: USGPO, December 1980).

14 See Michael Mihalka, "Supplier-Client Patterns in Arms Transfers," in *Arms Transfers in the Modern World*, edited by Stephanie G. Neuman and Robert E. Harkavy (New York: Praeger, 1979) pp. 49-77.

15 Michael Moodie, "Defense Industries in the Third World: Problems and Promises," in Neuman and Harkavy, *Arms Transfers in the Modern World*, pp. 294-314.

16 ACDA, *World Military Expenditures and Arms Transfers, 1969-1978*, p. 19.

17 Ibid., p. 21.

18 See United States, House, Committee on International Relations, *United States Arms Transfer and Security Assistance Programs*, 95th Congress, 2d Session, March 21, 1978.

19 See Bernard Gwertzman, "U.S. Said to Prepare Major Weapons Aid to Mideast Nations," *New York Times*, (March 8, 1981), p. 1.

20 Matthew Nimetz, Under Secretary for Security Assistance, Science and Technology, Statement before the Senate Foreign Relations Committee, March 6, 1980.

21 Robert H. Trice, "The Future of U.S. Arms Transfer Policy," speech, Columbus, Ohio, October 1980.

22 Salomon, Louscher, and Hammond, "Lessons of the Carter Approach," pp. 205-208.

Chapter 7

Transatlantic Arms Transfers:
The Search for Security,
Industrial Cooperation, and
Transfer Coordination

The United States confronts at least two major problems in dealing with transatlantic arms transfers. The first is the distribution of benefits in the form of sales among NATO allies. Europeans complain of inequity in sales and purchase ratios within the alliance that are to the United States' advantage. The second problem is U.S.-European competition in supplying arms to the Third World. This chapter is an effort to address these two problems, describing the factors that influence them and evaluating the prospects for potential solutions.

Intra-alliance sales ratios are an increasingly serious problem for the widely acclaimed goals of rationalization, standardization, and interoperability (RSI). U.S. weapons sales to NATO under the standardization banner have far exceeded U.S. purchases from the NATO allies. The ratio of the U.S. sales to U.S. purchases is on the order of ten to one and has been increasing in favor of the United States since 1974. These extreme ratios have generated increasing dissatisfaction from the NATO allies in Europe, which has, in turn, limited the effectiveness of the standardization program.

Not only are the Europeans becoming increasingly adamant about the asymmetry, but in 1981 they formed the Independent European Group (IEPG), which has the special objective of altering the existing situation. The IEPG favors specialization of the NATO allies along the lines of the "family of weapons" concept. The European allies have also taken steps to become more efficient and productive in arms procurement. These steps include consolidation, nationalization, and coproduction, as well as proposals to rationalize European defense industries through the framework of the European Community's industrial policy. A recent Senate Foreign Relations Committee staff report suggested that while these steps "invigorated the European arms industries and thus strengthened U.S. and NATO security," at the same time they resulted in a new European capability to compete for Third World markets.[1]

Given the heavy asymmetry favoring the United States in U.S.-European arms purchases and the size of individual national defense requirements in Europe, it should be no surprise that NATO procurement trends in conventional arms are related to perceptions of the nature of the market for sales in the Third World. European producers, in particular, consider the export of military hardware an important factor in maintaining a national defense industry. None of the European countries buy enough indigenously developed and produced weapons to cover the cost of production. Moreover, and particularly since the oil price increases of 1973 and 1979, European governments have been under pressure to offset unfavorable balances of trade through expanded arms sales, much of them to the Middle East.

In some cases, national armaments industries constitute the major source of growth in export earnings and strongly contribute to meeting at least short-term national employment requirements. With these points in mind, it is difficult to dismiss the intensity of governmental commitment in the major Western European countries to maintaining adequate external markets for the products of their defense industries. Rather than attempting to limit arms sales, European legislatures are more apt to criticize government arms sales offices for missed opportunities and lack of salesmanship.[2]

The deployment of weapons for which there is an external market is a necessary condition for several NATO members. Since the projected needs of Third World recipients became critical to Europeans, a consideration of RSI options must involve a consideration of what their market trends will be. In the case of major weapons systems currently being considered for NATO coproduction, acceptable non-NATO markets are a serious consideration in assessments by European nations. Several nations found the F-16 attractive as an RSI project because of its export potential.

As indicated in Chapter 6, this European drive for arms exports was in large measure responsible for the failure of recent U.S. efforts under the Carter administration to obtain multilateral restraint in arms transfers to the Third World. Indeed, the Soviet Union even appeared somewhat more interested in restraint than did the countries of Western Europe. Third World arms markets are too important to European economic well-being to be abandoned without adequate and effective offset arrangements. Moreover, as a review of supplier/recipient relationships with respect to arms transfers from 1967 to 1976 (the period before U.S. restraint efforts) reveals, the United States and Western European nations competed more extensively among themselves for sales to Third World countries than they competed with the Soviet Union.

With these considerations in mind, the remaining sections of this chapter will describe and document the general trends evident in transatlantic arms transfers and policy coordination. In doing so, it will examine the major problems involved in NATO RSI, in transatlantic and European industrial cooperation, and in the coordination of U.S. and European policy on arms transfers to the Third World. The inquiry will begin with a review of patterns of arms transfers, both transatlantic and those between the major producers and the Third World. It will then briefly review the record of transatlantic and European cooperation in arms procurement and arms transfer restraint. This will be followed by a discussion of the national arms sales policies of the major European producers—France, the United Kingdom and West Germany—in an effort to describe the pressures and constraints on arms exports that may have an impact on NATO RSI and on the prospect for future multilateral restraint or policy coordination. The final section will offer some preliminary recommendations for U.S. policy. It must be understood, however, that U.S. foreign policy options relating to arms transfers are seriously limited by the defense, cooperation, and procurement policies of its major European partners. Too many recommendations concerning arms transfer restraint, past and present, fail to understand the interrelatedness of European defense policies and the limits to U.S. options for arms transfers restraint.[3]

PATTERNS OF ARMS TRANSFERS

Reliable comparative statistics on arms transfer levels and on changes in them through time are difficult to obtain. Arms transfers are such a sensitive element of policy for most governments that adequate data are rarely made readily available to the public. When such data are supplied by national government sources, they are usually at a very general level. The criteria used for defining arms transfer levels are frequently unspecified and in any case vary from government to government. Nevertheless, it is important to begin this inquiry about supplier competition, distribution of benefits, and incentives to sell with an effort to note patterns in the arms transfers of major producers, both at a general level and in terms of transatlantic flows and arms transfers from the major producers to the Third World.

As the following tables indicate, most of the data used for this discussion were derived from the two major sources of comparative statistics on arms transfers, the U.S. Arms Control and Disarmament Agency (ACDA) and the Stockholm International Peace Research Institute (SIPRI). These sources are supplemented by national data sources, where available, as the arms transfer policies of France, the United Kingdom, and West Germany are discussed. (see Chapter 2 for additional data on global trends in arms transfers.)

Table 7.1 shows the rise in the total amount of arms transfers of the four major Western producers in recent years. While the United States still accounts for by far the largest amount of arms transfers, it is clear that the three major Western European producers, France, the United Kingdom, and West Germany (which now rank as the third, fourth, and fifth largest arms exporters in the world respectively, after the United States and USSR) have substantially expanded their arms exports in recent years, both in total amounts and, with some variation, in percentage of total exports. While the percentage of total exports is rather larger (though declining) for the United States than it is for Western European producers, one must keep in mind that foreign trade is a rather less important factor in the U.S. economy than it is for each of the three European economies.

A major focus of this chapter is the pattern and problems of transatlantic arms transfers. In this connection we need to "underline" a crucial point made in the previous section: the ratio of U.S. sales to U.S. purchases in transatlantic arms transfers was nearly ten to one in

Table 7.1. Value of Total Arms Transfers

	U.S.		France		U.K.		West Germany	
	Dollars	%	Dollars	%	Dollars	%	Dollars	%
1969	5,685	9.2	357	1.4	324	1.1	162	0.3
1970	4,788	7.2	308	1.1	123	0.4	293	0.6
1971	4,997	7.7	220	0.7	264	0.8	191	0.3
1972	5,787	8.2	1,023	2.7	663	1.9	465	0.7
1973	6,542	6.9	1,134	2.3	801	1.9	186	0.2
1974	5,489	4.6	853	1.5	671	1.4	256	0.2
1975	5,233	4.4	779	1.3	584	1.2	467	0.5
1976	6,242	5.1	1,058	1.7	820	1.7	687	0.6
1977	6,900	5.7	1,300	2.0	950	1.6	850	0.7
1978	6,237	4.7	1,256	1.7	1,024	1.5	814	0.6

Source: United States Arms Control and Disarmament Agency, *World Military Expenditures and Arms Transfers, 1969-1978* (Washington, D.C.: USGPO, December 1980).

favor of the United States for most years since 1974, and the ratio reached 23:1 in 1976. In an effort to fulfill the promise of a "two-way street," (e.g., the U.S. purchase of the Franco-German Roland missle and the British Harrier VTOL aircraft), but it is clear that the ratio is still dramatically in favor of the United States and is thus a source of significant discontent within NATO.[4]

According to data released by SIPRI in 1978, the four largest arms suppliers to the Third World for the period 1970-1976 were the United States, Soviet Union, United Kingdom, and France, respectively. United States arms transfers accounted for 38 percent of the world total and went primarily to the Middle East and the Far East. Iran and South Vietnam were the largest recipients. Soviet arms transfers accounted for 34 percent of the world total and went primarily to the Middle East and North Africa, particularly to Syria and Libya, but about 13 percent of Soviet transfers to the Third World went to the Far East. Here, the largest recipient was North Vietnam. The United Kingdom and France each accounted for 9 percent of the world total arms transfers to the Third World. Again, in each case, the countries of the Middle East and North Africa received by far the largest proportion of these transfers. Among recipients in this region, Libya offered perhaps the best example of a multiple supplier relationship, receiving arms in large quantities from both France and the Soviet Union.

Table 7.3 focuses more directly on the issue of competition between Western suppliers for Third World markets, and it illustrates a second major point made in the previous section: the United States and Western European nations competed extensively among themselves for sales to the Third World during the period from 1967 to 1976 (the period before the U.S. restraint efforts). Several important countries in the category of predominantly Western bloc recipients have not received more than 60 percent of their arms imports from any one producer.

Table 7.2. Major Arms Suppliers: Market Shares, 1968 and 1977

(percentage of total deliveries)			
1968		1977	
United States	50.3%	United States	39.2%
Soviet Union	29.8	Soviet Union	29.5
France	3.4	France	7.4
United Kingdom	3.0	United Kingdom	4.7
Poland	2.8	West Germany	4.5
China	2.6	Czechoslovakia	2.7
Others	8.1	Others	12.0
	100.0		100.0

Source: United States Arms Control and Disarmament Agency, *World Military Expenditures and Arms Transfers, 1968-1977* (Washington, D.C.: USGPO, October 1979), p. 18.

Table 7.3. Multiple Supplier Relations, 1967-1976

Western Bloc		Eastern Bloc		Cross-Bloc	
Predominant Recipients	Largest Supplier	Predominant Recipients	Largest Supplier	Recipients	Largest Supplier
Argentina	U.S. (50%)	Congo	USSR (50%)	Peru	USSR (25%)
Brazil	U.S. (43%)			Libya	USSR (54%)
Chile	U.K. (41%)			Northern Yemen	USSR (40%)
Colombia	U.S. (31%)			Afghanistan	USSR (32%)
Ecuador	U.S. (16%)			Pakistan	PRC (40%)
Honduras	U.S. (29%)			Nigeria	USSR (31%)
Mexico	U.K. (57%)			Zambia	Canada (19%)
Venezuela	France (33%)				
Lebanon	France (57%)				
Morocco	France (35%)				
Saudi Arabia	U.S. (47%)				
Indonesia	U.S. (51%)				
Ghana	U.K. (43%)				
Togo	Canada (40%)				
Zaire	France (46%)				
Singapore	U.S. (44%)				
Kuwait	U.K. (39%)				
Oman	U.K. (29%)				
Ivory Coast	France (50%)				

Source: United States, Arms Control and Disarmament Agency, *World Military Expenditures and Arms Transfers, 1967-1976* (Washington, D.C.: USGPO, 1978); and Michael Mihalka, "Supplier-Client Patterns in Arms Transfers," in *Arms Transfers in the Modern World*, edited by Stephanie G. Neuman and Robert E. Harkavy (New York: Praeger, 1979).

Year-to-year competition to supply twenty-one of these twenty-seven countries occurs among the Western producers and not between the West and the Soviet Union. There are few instances of cross-bloc arms transfers; for the most part, the Soviets have their own exclusive clients. Competition could also be said to occur between the Soviet bloc and Western suppliers over the logner term where the issue contested is bloc orientation. Ethiopia's switch to the Eastern bloc and Egypt's switch to the Western bloc during the mid-seventies illustrate this point.

From this brief presentation, we can begin to get a sense of two major problems for U.S. arms transfer policy. First, there is substance to European complaints about the balance of transatlantic arms transfers, a situation that has important implications for NATO RSI efforts. Second, there is evidence of growing competition between the United States and Western European suppliers for Third World markets which has important implications for efforts at multilateral restraint and policy coordination. As will be shown in the next two sections, these problems are not unrelated.

THE RECORD OF TRANSATLANTIC AND EUROPEAN COOPERATION IN ARMS PROCUREMENT, PRODUCTION, AND ARMS TRANSFER RESTRAINT

The Struggle for Rationalization, Standardization, and Interoperability in NATO

RSI in NATO has been promoted with varied intensity since the early years of the alliance. One of the most intense periods of its promotion was during the Carter administration.[5] It is clear that there is a needless and costly variety of weapons systems deployed by NATO members. In Central Europe NATO has fielded twenty-three different families of combat aircraft, twenty-two different anti-tank weapons, and seven different main battle tanks. In the words of Senator John C. Culver: "The end product is a hodge-podge of weapons making NATO appear to be a military museum."[6] When ammunition is not interchangeable and fuels, indeed even fuel nozzles, at some installations do not match some of the aircraft that might require refueling there in time of war, it is obvious that military efficiency is drastically reduced, not to mention the wasteful duplication in weapons research, development, and production programs,[7] and in spare parts inventories and maintenance facilities and training.

NATO officials have long expressed an interest in RSI. To the Western Europeans, however, it frequently appears that the U.S. drive for standardization is simply another way to say "Buy American." The ratios of U.S. weapons sales to purchases from NATO discussed earlier would seem to support this view, and President Carter's pledge to make transatlantic arms sales more of a "two-way street" was in response to this situation.

NATO competitive and cooperative research and development programs, coproduction, license production, and lead-nation specialization are all approaches to improving RSI through various levels of collaboration. Moreover, it is clear that the alliance has made progress in its efforts to collaborate in the production of defense equipment for NATO forces. One analyst recently identified some fifty collaborative projects successfully carried out or initiated by two or more members within the framework of NATO (see Table 7.4). However, formidable obstacles stand in the way of achieving the economies and operational flexibility promised as a collective good by NATO RSI. As we shall see, many of these obstacles are severe domestic political, economic, and industrial constraints, although some derive from differences in national military objectives, strategy, and tactics.[8]

European Cooperation in Arms Procurement and Production

One clear feature of NATO-sponsored cooperation in arms procurement and production programs is that many of the major ones (especially those involving cooperation through all phases of the procurement process) are composed of only Western European nations. Western Europe has reacted rather vigorously in recent years to avoid total domination of its defense and aerospace industry by the United States and to maximize the economic, political, and technological benefits accruing from a healthy European capacity to produce sophisticated (and marketable) weapons and defense equipment.

The Western European efforts in this regard received considerable impetus with the formation of the Eurogroup within NATO in 1968. Eurogroup collaboration in harmonizing tactical concepts for the 1980s in EUROLONGTERM and in equipment collaboration through EURONAD, the subgroup of National Armament Directors of Eurogroup countries, marked the real beginning of a European response to U.S. dominance and the imbalance in transatlantic arms transfers, as well as to the need for a European identity in NATO for effective joint discussions and bargaining with the United States.[9] Ever since the Eurogroup has operated within NATO, however, France has refused to become involved in the collaboration.

Table 7.4. NATO Collaboration in Weapons and Equipment

1. AIM-9L—SIDEWINDER air-to-air missile
2. ALPHAJET—ground attack trainer
3. AS-30—missile
4. BULLPUP—air-to-surface missile
5. CL-89 (AN/USD-501)—reconnaissance drone
6. CVR-(T)—armored fighting vehicle
7. European transonic wind tunnel
8. EXOCET—naval surface-to-surface missile
9. F 104-G—STARFIGHTER combat aircraft
10. FH70/SP70/RS80—towed and self-propelled howitzer and free-flight rocket
11. F-16—air combat fighter aircraft
12. G-91—tactical reconnaissance aircraft
13. General support rocket/missile system
14. HARPOON—anti-ship missile
15. HOT—anti-tank missile
16. JAGUAR—ground attack aircraft
17. KORMORAN—air-to-ship missile
18. LANCE—tactical ballistic missile
19. MARTEL—air-to-surface anti-radar and TV-guided missile
20. MARK 20—RH 202 rapid-fire gun
21. M72—light anti-tank weapon
22. MILAN—anti-tank wire-guided missle
23. Mutual logistics cooperative programs (12)
24. NATO acoustics communication with submarines
25. NATO Allied communications publications on common doctrine
26. NATO Allied technical publications on common doctrine
27. NATO fixed acoustic range in the Azores (AFAR)
28. NATO Air Defence Ground Environment (NADGE)
29. NATO Common Infrastructure—220 airfields, 31,000 miles of communications, 6,300 miles of pipeline
30. NATO ATLANTIQUE—maritime patrol aircraft
31. NATO AWACS—NATO Airborne Early Warning and Control System
32. NATO frigate for 1970s
33. NATO HAWK surface-to-air missile and HAWK improvement programs
34. NATO Long-Term Defence Program (LTDP)
35. NATO LYNX, PUMA, and GAZELLE helicopters
36. NATO Mark 44 and 46 torpedoes
37. NATO naval forces sensor and weapons accuracy check sites (FORACS)
38. NATO Integrated Ccmmunication System (NICS)
39. NATO patrol craft hydrofoil missile (PHM)
40. NATO SEA SPARROW—ship-to-ship missile
41. NATO SEAGNAT—ship defense system
42. NATO Standardization Agreements (STANAGS)
43. OTO MELARA—76mm compact gun
44. PATRIOT—air-defense missile system
45. SEA KING helicopter
46. SCORPION—Reconnaissance vehicle
47. TERRIER—sea-to-air missile
48. TOW—anti-tank weapons
49. TORNADO—multirole combat aircraft
50. TRANSALL C-160—medium-range military transport

Under Way

1. 10 major initiatives in the field of electronic warfare
2. NATO future identification system (NIS)
3. Joint tactical information distribution system (JTIDS)
4. NAVSTAR global positioning system (GPS)
5. Mobile acoustic communications study

Under Discussion

1. A short-range air-defense weapons system
2. Explosion resistant multi-influence sweep system for mines (ERMISS)
3. Electro-optical devices
4. NATO anti-surface ship missile (ASSM)
5. NATO small surface-to-air ship self-defense system
6. NATO defense research program
7. Coordination of national armaments schedules
8. Establishment of a NATO small arms test and evaluation program
9. Integration of national research, development, and procurement of weapons into the Long-Term Defence Programme
10. Establishment of a permanent NATO weapons planning program

Source: Alexander H. Cornell, "Collaboration in Weapons and Equipment," *NATO Review* 28, 5 (October 1980). Reprinted with permission of the *NATO Review*.

Some cooperation on background studies relating to European land armaments occurred in the context of FINABEL, an organization of Western European army chiefs of staff which included France, but it was the formation of the Independent European Programme Group (IEPG) in Rome on February 2, 1976, that marked the beginning of strong French participation in continuing Western European efforts to cooperate closely in arms procurement and production. The goals of the IEPG were to increase equipment collaboration in Europe; to increase standardization and interoperability of equipment; to strengthen the European factor in the equipment collaboration with North America; to adapt the structures and capabilities of the European armaments industries gradually to the overall demand of defense material; and to take into consideration the legitimate interests of nations not possessing any appreciable defense production capabilities.[10]

Western European collaboration in the IEPG has been relatively successful. Compared with efforts in the 1960s to develop cooperative arms production ventures, in which the United States played a large role and the products were mainly high-cost versions of U.S. weapons systems, the more recent effort at intra-European cooperation has resulted in cost-competitive products. This result holds promise for increased NATO security, but it also presents a challenge to the United States in terms of potential conflict and competition with the United States in arms transfers to the Third World. This kind of challenge may be even greater if initiatives within the European Community to rationalize the national defense and aerospace industries in Western Europe through the framework of an EC industrial policy gain more support from member governments.[11]

Multilateral Restraint and Coordination of Arms Transfers

In any case, recent trends in transatlantic arms transfer patterns, together with the closely linked NATO RSI efforts and European cooperation in arms procurement and production, have important implications for the prospect of multilateral restraint in, or coordination of, arms transfers to the Third World. Multilateral restraint was a major element in the arms transfer policy of the Carter administration. U.S. officials pursued this goal in the context of the Conventional Arms Transfer (CAT) negotiations with the Soviet Union and major European producers. As indicated in Chapter 6, the effort met with unambiguous failure. In fact, the Soviets even appeared more interested in restraint than did the governments of Western Europe. Third World arms markets appear too important to them at present, at least without some real prospect for an offset arrangement with the United States that would gain increased purchases of European arms in return for cooperation in restraining the marketing of European arms in the Third World.

Some suggestions of an offset arrangement during the latter part of the Carter administration stimulated a glimmer of interest in Western Europe, though certainly nothing approaching a commitment to restrain arms exports to the Third World. Nevertheless, it is precisely on this question that all of the elements of transatlantic arms transfers and policy coordination come together. At present, there is almost no coordination in NATO member military assistance and sales to the Third World. Given the present international environment, it appears that a careful consideration of the prospects for improved coordination is timely.

MAJOR EUROPEAN NATIONAL ARMS SALES POLICIES: PRESSURES AND CONSTRAINTS

What is behind the patterns of NATO arms procurement and transfers described above? What explains the continued lack of progress in NATO rationalization, standardization, and interoperability of weapons systems and in multilateral restraint of arms transfers to the Third World? Clearly, we are examining elements of policy that are the product of strong domestic and national security pressures, pressures that invariably make international cooperation and rationalization exceedingly difficult, and that in any case will shape any successful effort. A brief review of the arms sales policies of France, the United Kingdom, and West Germany since the mid-1960s should help illustrate the complexity of Atlantic arms procurement and transfers.

France

General Policies Toward Defense Cooperation. The administration of Charles De Gaulle, first President of the Fifth Republic of France, left a deep imprint on French defense policy in general, on French arms procurement and sales policy in particular and on NATO member cooperation that bears on multilateral cooperation and competition in arms sales. Elements of this impact remain important today.

De Gaulle's withdrawal of France from the NATO military command and planning structure in 1966 and his decisions to pursue an independent defense policy, which were part of a larger policy to assert French nationalism (in part to bring internal order to French politics), had important implications for defense procurement. The French defense and aerospace industry became a key priority for government support and expenditure in a period of limited economic growth for France. However, De Gaulle did not allow the disentanglement of the French military from NATO to affect French participation in the various defense production cooperation programs. France remained a member of the NATO HAWK missile development and production program, which involved industrial cooperation and some technology sharing between the U.S. Raytheon Corporation and the French Thomson Corporation. France continued full participation in the Conference of National Armaments Directors (CNAD) and continued its participation in bilateral procurement and production programs such as the effort with Britain on the Jaguar attack aircraft.

After the Soviet invasion of Czechoslovakia and the domestic turmoil in France in 1968, French defense policy became somewhat more cooperative, particularly in defense consultation and planning with NATO. In November 1968 French Foreign Minister Michel Debre signed a communique after a NATO meeting in Brussels which suggested that NATO was "of indefinite duration" and that "recent events had shown its existence to be more than ever necessary."[12] In particular, the French Navy showed interest in NATO's Mediterranean planning and strategy, given the growing Soviet strength and role in that region. There were also reports that the French had requested a return to the use of nuclear warheads under the "two-key" system in French tactical missiles in Germany, and that the French had offered to coordinate the targeting of the French nuclear force with the U.S. forces.[13] Finally, on December 5, 1968, Defense Minister Pierre Messmer stated strongly during a defense debate in the National Assembly that France was in the Atlantic Alliance and would remain there.[14] Several calls for European defense cooperation were also made during this debate, and J. F. Deniau, a French member of the European Economic Community (EEC) Commission, proposed increased Anglo-French defense cooperation as a means of defining a common European defense policy for an enlarged EEC.[15]

French strategy was also modified. The new Chief of Staff, General Michel Fourquet, moved from the massive retaliation strategy of his predecessor, General Ailleret, to an acceptance of flexible response. He also dropped Ailleret's notion of strategy in all directions in lieu of a concern solely for the threat from the East.[16] After De Gaulle's resignation on April 28, 1969, General Fourquet was reported to have placed official approval on a much closer level of consultation with NATO than De Gaulle had allowed.[17] There were certainly limits to this consultation and cooperation, however. When the representatives of ten European NATO countries met in November 1968 at the initiative of British

Defence Minister Denis Healey to form a European "identity" on defense questions, France declined to participate. Even though this group, which became institutionalized as the Eurogroup, took pains initially to make its ties with NATO ambiguous in the hopes that France might find participation easier, the situation did not change.

Under Georges Pompidou, who succeeded De Gaulle in 1969, French officials looked for alternative forums to NATO for European defense cooperation. As suggested above, France ruled out the Eurogroup because of its connection with NATO. Extending cooperation within the EEC to cover defense matters was a suggestion frequently made, but the WEU (Western European Union) was the organization most commonly (and seriously) proposed by the French. Such proposals were made even while the French were continuing their boycott of the organization, a boycott imposed by De Gaulle towards the end of his presidency. The boycott was in reaction to British efforts to establish new links with EEC members through the WEU after the French vetoes of British admission to the Community.

French Foreign Minister Michel Jobert made more serious and specific efforts for the use of the WEU in late 1973 and 1974.[18] Little came from these proposals, however; they were largely viewed as the product of Jobert's anti-Americanism and were suspected as less an instance of sincere French interest in defense cooperation than as an effort to sabotage the progress of the Eurogroup.

The Western European Union was proposed by Jobert (as well as other French officials) as a framework for European cooperation in the field of armaments production in particular; the organization's permanent weapons committee would serve as the specific structure. However, French Defense Minister Robert Galley qualified this possibility two months later, noting that French arms programs could not be affected for quite some time.[19] Little came from the proposal, but it appeared that at least the French Foreign Ministry was interested for a while.

Considerable interdepartmental and interministerial coordination takes place in the Fifth Republic form of cabinet government, but differences between the foreign and defense ministries do emerge and sometimes become public. Whether or not policy differences are successfully aired in public depends much on a cabinet minister's relationship with the President and on his own political strength. Jobert was in a strong position, at least for a time, in both areas, so his views on European defense cooperation could be articulated without great constraint; and he was outspoken. He appeared publicly to overshadow Defense Minister Galley for a time, but real progress in pursuit of Jobert's proposals (if indeed they were serious ones) could not be made without the cooperation of the Defense Minister and Defense Ministry.[20]

Cooperation in armaments production was problematic for the French, but it was less constrained by domestic politics than were other forms of defense cooperation. In July 1971, the Independent Republican Party proposed the creation of a European agency for armaments.[21] In December 1972, the ten members of the Eurogroup signed a joint declaration promising future cooperation in weapons procurement and production. The French initially declined participation, but by the end of 1973 there were reports that they might be willing to do so with the understanding that such a move did not represent the beginning of a French return to NATO's military structure. France did not actually join in these Eurogroup efforts during the Pompidou administration, but participation in the NATO Conference of National Armaments Directors (CNAD) was certainly maintained if not strengthened. Indeed, France was involved in decisions by this body to seek standardization in weapons produced and used by NATO countries: ammunition (1970) and tactical missiles (1974).[22] In January 1974, it was announced that France would participate in the second generation of the NATO HAWK missile development and production program.[23]

On the bilateral level, France continued cooperation with the United Kingdom in several major development and production programs: the Jaguar attack aircraft, three helicopters, the MARTEL TV-guided missile, and the EXOCET naval surface-to-surface missile. France and West Germany cooperated rather satisfactorily on the Roland missile.

After Pompidou's death in 1974, the presidential electoral process began that year with a wide field of candidates. Independent Republican Valery Giscard d'Estaing emerged as victor in a tight run-off ballot with the Socialist-Communist alliance candidate Francois Mitterrand. While defense questions were not determinative in the election, they were a part of the campaign debate. A prominent question raised during the campaign was the impact a Socialist President would have on defense policy and particularly on the policy toward NATO. Mitterrand sought to reassure the fearful by arguing that France must remain in NATO as long as there was no general disarmament and as long as the East and West blocs continued.[24] Giscard was more ambiguous and noncommittal about NATO, but he spoke in favor of more European defense cooperation.

Although Giscard's campaign statements did not portend great changes in defense policy, they generated speculation that his administration would bring significant change. By early 1976—two years later—a few important developments had occurred, and it was clear that the possibility of significant change had at least been given serious consideration.

This consideration process began shortly after Giscard took office, as he reviewed and participated in an organized debate among several experts on defense matters, including journalists and two generals,

Beaufre and Gallois, who had published widely their writings on nuclear strategy. Labeled by some as a "crash course" for a President whose knowledge of (and interest in) defense questions was slight, this briefing proved to be of little help because the advisors took contradicting positions on the major questions. Giscard thus did not announce his decisions on defense policy until March 25, 1975, in a televised address. Claiming that his conclusion was the same as that of General De Gaulle, he argued that security required an independent defense, and he sketched a policy that at least publicly followed Gaullist precepts.[25]

While Giscard's statements came as a surprise to some, they are not too difficult to understand, given the political pressures he had been subjected to from both the left and the right. The Communists as well as the Gaullists expressed concern over the possibility that his defense review might lead to a more cooperative and pro-Atlantic orientation. Gaullist Prime Minister Jacques Chirac initially served as a reminder to Giscard of the importance of Gaullist support for his government. Two months later, Chirac and Yvon Bourges, the new Minister of Defense, both stressed during debate in the National Assembly that there would be no change in the independence of French defense policy.[26] While in large measure this proved to be true, Giscard made subtle and cautious modifications in the more controversial (and characteristic) features of De Gaulle's defense policy legacy, particularly after Chirac left the government. He accepted changes in contested features of the defense budget and the nuclear "force de frappe." But these changes did not extend very far. De Gaulle had made the latter an important symbol of French nationalism, and the modifications in it did not destroy its symbolic weight. Nor did Giscard accept much change in French independence from Western European powers with respect to non-NATO cooperation where the challenge to French nationalism presumably would have been unavoidable. France, under Giscard, continued to decline participation in the Eurogroup's consultation and planning activities.

There were some small exceptions to this policy, as the government responded to Eurogroup initiatives. France did attend one meeting dealing with the problem of protecting North Sea oil fields, which was held at The Hague, and its connection with the Eurogroup was kept ambiguous. Giscard, like De Gaulle and Pompidou, had on occasion to restrain French bureaucrats from behaving more cooperatively than his policy permitted. On at least one occasion, French administrative officials expressed initial interest in a Eurogroup meeting, but declined after an intervention at the political level of Giscard's government. Giscard, again as his predecessors, permitted cooperation where issues of sovereignty were less conspicuous. French armed forces had been allowed to cooperate selectively and informally at the tactical operations and training level during the Gaullist years. Likewise, the Giscard government sent an observer to meetings of Eurocom, a subgroup on cooperation in tactical communications systems.

Armaments production cooperation advanced little from the Guallist era during the Giscard administration. Little resulted from Jobert's calls to use the Western European Union (WEU) as a focus for such cooperation, and bilateral cooperation did not greatly increase. France did, however, become more closely associated with the Eurogroup efforts along these lines. A growing movement within the EEC toward assurring the health and development of the European aeronautical and armaments industries was relevant to the French efforts.

When Jobert left office in 1974, French efforts for expanding formal European defense cooperation in the WEU were largely dropped. There still appeared to be French interest in cooperation regarding European economic matters through the EEC rather than through an Atlantic framework. When a report on the future of the EEC produced by Prime Minister Leo Tindemans of Belgium in late 1975 called for initiatives toward transatlantic cooperation, French Gaullists resisted, and Giscard backed off.[27] However, the French military did participate actively in FINABEL, the organization of NATO members army chiefs of staff, and French officials, including Giscard, also conferred with U.S. Secretary of Defense James R. Schlesinger in late September 1975, the first such consultations since France withdrew from NATO.[28]

A two-year competition beginning in 1974 to replace the F-104 Starfighters in the Belgian, Danish, Dutch, and Norwegian air forces— the so-called *contrat du siecle* that reached scandalous dimensions— demonstrated the inescapable nationalist components of NATO arms procurement and production issues. The stakes were very high. Since the four countries agreed to make a joint purchase for purposes of furthering arms standardization, the potential gains for the winner of the contract were substantial, and the competition was intense. Pitted against the French corporation Dassault-Breguet's Mirage F 1/M53 were the United States' General Dynamics YF-16 and the Northrop YF-17. The Swedish Saab-produced Viggen was also in the competition for a time, and at one point the British government and the British Aircraft Corporation tried to advance the Anglo-French Jaguar as a more "European" alternative. The Jaguar option died in the face of Dassault-Breguet's charges that the British were really trying to subvert the Mirage's chances.

In France, the competition became a highly political issue involving some scandal. In a letter to President Giscard d'Estaing, former French Air Force Chief of Staff General Paul Stehlin stated that the Mirage was inferior to both U.S. planes, even with the proposed (untested) modifications.[29] This letter eventually found its way into the French press, and Stehlin was forced to resign his position as Vice President of the National Assembly. The scandal was heightened later, when a subcommittee of the U.S. Senate revealed that Stehlin had apparently been receiving payment for serving as a consultant to Northrop.[30] Stehlin died a short time later of injuries received when he stepped in the path of a bus on the same day that the Senate disclosure was made. The competition was also clouded by charges of bribery on the part of both the French and the U.S. producers.

After some delay, all four countries decided in favor of the General Dynamics YF-16, the choice of the U.S. Air Force. This verdict seemed to make it clear to France that policy changes were in order if the European armaments market was to be in the reach of French producers. Serious French movement to a closer association with the countries of the Eurogroup began later that year. The members of the Eurogroup invited France to participate in a European Program Group, an organization designed to permit French collaboration without agitating French domestic political opponents of NATO. On French insistence, the name of the EPG was changed to the Independent European Program Group (IEPG); under this new designation, France has been active in the organization's development.

While bilateral cooperation policy in armaments production did not change greatly with the Giscard administration, the relative success of a few programs begun during earlier administrations became apparent as the weapons and aircraft became operational. The French-German Roland II missile was enough of a success to gain a contract for purchase and production from the U.S. Department of Defense. The completed Anglo-French Jaguar went on display at the 1975 Paris air show (along with the Anglo-French Concorde SST).

Arms Sales Policies and Patterns. French arms sales policy has undergone some change since the mid-1960s, but it has generally been a major priority for government interest and concern. From 1950 to 1960, arms exports averaged $85.8 million per year. By 1964, however, the rate had risen to $412.7 million per year. From there it skyrocketed. Despite a defense spending figure that represented approximately only one-fifteenth the amount spent on defense by the United States, France exported about one-fourth as much as the United States during the 1966-67 period, in large part because of the French government's nonrestrictive policy on the "end use" of military equipment sold.[31] French arms exports then increased dramatically, from $421.5 million in 1965 to $2,435.35 million in 1976.[32]

As a result, France became the third largest arms exporter, moving ahead of the United Kingdom but still lagging some distance behind the United States and the Soviet Union which rank first and second, respectively.

Under the De Gaulle administration, French arms sales were governed by some limited political or security criteria. For example, France imposed a general embargo on French arms exports to the Middle East on June 3, 1967, prior to the Six-Day War. However, France essentially ignored the 1962 United Nations embargo on arms sales to South Africa. Mirage III interceptors, tanks, submarines, helicopters, and Matra air-to-air and air-to-ground missiles were among the sales made, with the justification that only exports of external defense weapons (which could not be used in anti-guerrilla warfare) were permitted.

Since De Gaulle's resignation in 1969, French arms sales policy has become even less constrained by political or security criteria. In the Pompidou administration, Defense Minister Michel Debre initiated a major drive to expand arms sales, largely as an aid to financing French defense expenditures and procurement.[33] The largest relaxation of constraints and expansion in sales came in the administration of President Giscard d'Estaing.

Soon after his election, Giscard stated, "In contrast to other major powers, we avoid supplying arms to belligerent nations."[34] Moreover, on May 30, 1974, he stated in a message to Parliament, "France will reaffirm and emphasize the liberal mission of its diplomacy by supporting the cause of freedom and the right of peoples, I say peoples, to self-determination everywhere in the world. It will refrain from any arms sales that would run counter to the accomplishment of this mission."[35]

These declarations notwithstanding, on August 28, 1974, the general embargo on arms exports to the Middle East "battlefield" countries was lifted, and an unprecedented drive to increase arms exports, largely to help counter the tremendous financial impact of increased imported oil prices, was under way.[36] Perhaps the one major exception to this relaxation of arms export restrictions and the new willingness "to sell to almost anyone" was Giscard's decision to terminate sales of military ground and air equipment to South Africa, announced on February 14, 1977. Subsequently, the French government informed the Secretary-General of the United Nations that it had cancelled all arms contracts with South Africa.[37]

Along with the general expansion of French arms sales came a shift in the major recipients. The Arab countries of the Middle East, particularly the oil-producing ones, became major customers, and in general there was a shift from developed-country to developing-country recipients. In 1970, the United States and Western European countries accounted for 57 percent of French arms exports, but by 1976 this had dropped to 15 percent of deliveries.[38]

In addition to relaxing the restrictions of previous administrations on arms exports, the Giscard government frequently intervened in various ways to facilitate arms sales. Considerable emphasis was placed on French sponsorship of armaments exhibitions. The Paris Air Show, held every two years at Le Bourget airfield, has been the most prominent of several exhibitions. In 1977, the government established an interministerial commission to oversee the show but again retained Serge Dassault to serve as the exhibit's Commissioner General.[39]

Another effort to ease sales was the establishment of a service in the "Delegation Ministerielle pour l'Armement" (DMA) to provide technical, logistic, and operational assistance to recipient countries after arms deliveries are made.[40] France's competitive position as an arms supplier had suffered previously because of relatively poor availability of spare parts and other logistics requirements. The need to provide services competitive with U.S. logistics procedures in this regard would seem to explain this decision in part.

Decisionmaking structures for French arms sales provide the opportunity for strong executive control, even if Giscard or his government rarely exercised it to restrict a sale. A interministerial committee has the responsibility for assessing each arms sales situation; the government then is to base its decision on this assessment. In reality, the vast majority of sales are not impeded at all by this structure. Rather, government agencies, with their close ties to the defense and aerospace industries (only a few elements of which are not directly or at least largely, government controlled), served as active sales-promoting offices. The most prominent of these is the DMA with its export department, the Direction des Affaires Internationales (DAI). This agency organized demonstrations, exhibitions, and military sales missions abroad. However, the government itself does not sell armaments; rather, a series of agencies that are partly government-owned handle actual sales. These include the Office Francaise d'Exportation de Materiel Aeronautique (OFEMA) and the Office Generale de l'Air (OGA), which handle sales to Western allies and developing countries respectively. There are also agencies associated with individual military services: La Société Francaise d'Exportation des Armaments Navales (SOFREXAN) and La Société Francaise de Materiels d'Armament (SOFMA) for the army. The government also helps provide credit arrangements for recipient countries; its role in arms sales promotion and facilitation is strong—indeed, so much so that a major government-sponsored but confidential report on the issue warned of impropriety and financial overextension.[41]

Given the inclination in France at the time to expand arms sales and the general predisposition toward independence inherited from the De Gaulle period, it is hardly surprising that President Carter's call for multilateral restraint in arms transfers to the Third World was not received enthusiastically in France. Yvon Bourges, French Minister of Defense, publicly rejected the idea of a bilateral agreement with the United States to reduce arms sales in late 1977. Moreover, there is evidence to suggest that France was among the most active exporters in the scramble to pick up the slack in arms sales left by Carter's effort to restrain U.S. sales.[42] The French did not view the uncertain prospect of rewards for restraint in the form of promised U.S. responses to the demands for more of a "two-way street" in the transatlantic arms trade as an option worth pursuing. In part, this reaction doubtless reflected traditional suspicions about U.S. policy and fear of U.S. domination. More specifically, the French chose not to take up the U.S. option because they valued not only the foreign exchange and other economic benefits that arms sales bring, but also the cooperation from recipient countries such as oil suppliers in the Middle East. France had become dependent on large amounts of arms sales to the Third World.

Pressures and Constraints on Policy: Prospects for Change. It is clear that French arms sales policy is driven by strong forces—not only private interests, but also quite distinct public interests related to foreign and fiscal policy and, at another level, to French national politics. This makes it difficult for government decisionmakers to consider seriously anything approaching a restraint on sales. Prior to 1973, much of this pressure was in the form of direct arguments on the requirements for maintaining national defense and aerospace industries. These arguments were conditioned by the general framework of De Gaulle's emphasis on the need for an independent stance in foreign and defense policy, which in turn was rooted in his effort to solidify and stabilize France as a national state. Once De Gaulle rejected the idea that France should become an interdependent quasi-sovereignty in an integrated Western Europe that submerged national politics under layers of multinational agencies run by "Eurocrats," it was a foregone conclusion that France would become an aggressive arms exporter and competitor of the United States. The French national market was insufficient to make French weapons procurement and production economical; the production runs were just not large enough without a substantial external market. Extensive arms exports have indeed paid off in this regard; for example, a March 1976 report indicated that the economic return on exports of the Mirage III had by then amounted to fifty times the cost of the aircraft's research, development, and industrialization.[43] Similarly, the net cost of the AMX-30 tank was reduced significantly through exports, despite interruptions in French orders.[44]

The economy-of-scale factor continues to serve as an important motivation for sales. It has been powerfully reinforced since 1973 by the severe foreign exchange problem caused by the then fourfold increase on the international price of oil. As a result, as Edward Kolodziej has persuasively argued, since 1973 the French economy in general has become significantly dependent on high levels of arms exports.[45] OPEC oil imports are indispensable to France (and will be for the foreseeable future). The internal economic and external monetary impact of oil price increases has been dramatic. Expanded arms exports have provided an effective means of counteracting the tremendous balance-of-trade deficits that have resulted. A large percentage of French arms exports now go directly to Middle Eastern oil-producing countries; in effect, a barter arrangement is in operation.

The third main pressure on French arms exports is the short- and mid-term effect of arms manufacturing on employment. Estimates ranging to almost 300,000 have been given as the number of workers in the armaments industry and supporting government agencies.[46] Table 7.5 depicts the jobs directly generated by arms exports. As shown in the table, 28 percent of all the workers in that nation's armaments industry are employed in the production of equipment for export. Nearly 67 percent of naval construction workers are employed producing products for export. In the French aerospace industry 50 percent of all workers

Table 7.5. Percentage of Total Workers in French Armament Industry Employed in Export Market, 1976

Industry Sector	Total Workers	Export Workers	Per Cent in Exports
Ministerial Delegation for Armaments (DMA)	75,000	6,000	8%
Aerospace[a]	78,000	39,000	50%
Electronics	40,000	15,000	38%
Mechanics and Metallurgy[b]	40,000	11,000	28%
Naval Construction[c]	3,000	2,000	67%
Commissariat a l'energie atomique	12,000	—	—
Miscellaneous	23,000	2,000	1%
TOTAL	271,000	75,000	28%

Source: Adapted from data provided in Le Theule report on *Le Project de loi de finances pour 1976*, Assemblee Nationale, No. 1916 (1975).

[a] Excluding Delegation Ministerielle pour l'Armament (DMA).

[b] Excluding Direction technique disarmaments terrestres and Direction technique des constructions navales.

[c] Excluding Direction technique des constructions navales.

are export workers. Even arms sales critics in the French Communist and Socialist parties find it difficult to discount the employment impact costs of a restraint on arms exports in these terms, particularly given the severity of recent unemployment problems in France.

These three types of pressures, when taken together, have served as a major influence on the drive for expanded arms exports in France. In no other Western developed country are the pressures so strong. Indeed, critics of French policy have suggested that the pressures to export arms have been so strong that the French armaments and aerospace industries have become largely export-oriented, to the serious detriment of efforts to equip and support the French armed forces. French military leaders complain that they are forced to adopt less sophisticated weapons than they would like in order to encourage sales to the armed forces of Third World countries—for which the technology level is in fact more appropriate.[47] Whether this is altogether true or not, more clearly and easily demonstrated is the higher priority that export markets enjoy. Foreign customers receive French weapons often before French military forces do. A striking result of this priority order is that the re-equipment of the French air force fighter squadrons has been severely retarded in recent years. Since early 1977 few of the Mirage F1 aircraft have been delivered to French forces because export customers have taken precedence.[48]

Political and security-related pressures have remained somewhat important, at least as a justification for French arms sales. As Jean Klein argues, the drive for political independence and autonomous defense is strong, along with the need to maintain the well-being of the French defense industry, which is stimulated by the competition of the export program. Moreover, the government has announced its political commitment to aid countries in developing their abilities "to escape the hold of a powerful neighbor;" in the French view, the sovereign right of countries to defend themselves should be supported through arms sales.[49]

If the pressures for arms exports are strongest in France, it is also true that internal resistance to sales is perhaps the weakest and least effective there, in comparison to other Western producers. In part this stems from the structure of foreign and defense policy decisionmaking which permits the executive to act without significant impediment from the legislature, unlike in the United States. It is also true, however, that there appears to be little sentiment against large arms exports, either within the government or outside it in the form of domestic opinion groups actively objecting to the foreign arms trade.

Commentaries and editorials critical of the government's arms sales policy have appeared in the press from time to time,[50] and important religious leaders have occasionally attacked the government on the issue. The most dramatic instance of the latter occurred when Cardinal François Marty, Archbishop of Paris, denounced the growing "commerce of death" in a sermon at Notre Dame in January 1976. The attack was supported for a time by important figures of the political left, but it was defused when Prime Minister Jacques Chirac pointed out that the country's unemployment problems would be worsened if arms sales were reduced.[51] There are no organized interest groups campaigning against arms sales in France, and members of Parliament appear to have little or no interest in the issue, even setting aside the fact that Parliament could have little effect anyway.

Some change in French arms export policies seems likely under the new Socialist government of Francois Mitterrand. As part of a series of position statements and articles in reference to the 1978 parliamentary elections, Mitterrand, who was the Socialist party leader, openly criticized French arms sales policy. In doing so, however, he stressed the employment implications involved and noted that a change in policy would have to be very gradual.[52] The left was soundly defeated by the government coalition in those elections, but Mitterrand's subsequent election to the presidency in 1981 suggests potential for limitations on the emphasis on arms exports. By early 1982 it appeared that President Mitterrand would move only with caution because of the important economic pressures involved. During his first months in office, a major arms deal was concluded with Egypt, and new negotiations were initiated with Saudi Arabia, Jordan, and Iraq.

Moreover, to the chagrin of U.S. officials, just six months after Mitterrand took office, France concluded an arms sale with Nicaragua involving 7,000 air-to-surface missiles and other items. Similarly, British officials were dismayed to discover that France had decided to reinstate arms exports to Argentina shortly after the British victory in the Falkland Islands conflict. Indeed, the proven effectiveness of the EXOCET missiles purchased by Argentina led the French to increase the price of these missiles from $350,000 to more than $1 million each. France also now supplies Pakistan with submarines and has bested the U.K., Sweden and the Soviet Union in competition for a major aircraft sale to India. These sales notwithstanding, Defense Minister Charles Hernu stated in July 1981 that while present commitments would be honored, France would not sell arms to "racist and fascist" states in the future. It has not been specified which states are in those categories.[53]

The situation described above does not portend well for major changes in French arms sales policy. The pressures for sales are deeply rooted in French politics and commerce, and countervailing forces are weak. French participation in a strategy of multilateral restraint in transfers is no more likely in the near future than it was in response to the efforts of the Carter administration, at least as long as these efforts do not provide France with adequate alternative means for satisfying the pressures for arms sales. The possibility for increased international cooperation in arms procurement and production cannot be dismissed, but the constraints on some forms of defense cooperation imposed by De Gaulle's heritage remain.

The United Kingdom

General Policies Toward Defense Cooperation. Throughout the 1960s, the British faced a problem comparable to, though less obvious than, the one that De Gaulle was dealing with in France. De Gaulle adopted a flamboyantly nationalistic foreign and national security policy that catered to the right wing in French politics and to elemental popular nationalism while he brought the right under control and stabilized France. In the United Kingdom, the crisis of nationalism was more quiet, but persistent. At the beginning of the 1960s, the British still thought of themselves as a great power, next to the United States among the free-world powers, and with a special relationship to the United States. By 1968, they had to announce the withdrawal of all British forces east of Suez, and what had remained of their imperial splendor vanished. Britain's economic weakness was evident, and disappointments in military programs had shaken British expectations about maintaining great power status through high military technology. Britain's efforts to acquire an independent rocket force became an embarrassing failure, acknowledged with cancellation of the Bluestreak missile in 1960. Britain then counted on delivering nuclear weapons by missiles launched from stand-off bombers, only to be again disappointed when the Kennedy administration cancelled, without effective warning, further development of Skybolt, the U.S. stand-off missile on which the British were counting. Kennedy then made amends to the Macmillan government by offering it Polaris submarines, which the British government eagerly accepted. To maintain the posture of a major power, the British became ever more dependent on U.S. military technology for their claim to be a nuclear military power.

By the early 1960s, the contrast with France had already become stark. As De Gaulle was cutting off at least the outward forms of cooperation within Europe and across the Atlantic with NATO, allocating a substantial part of his military budget to the building of an independent nuclear military force, and pursuing independent diplomatic goals with Moscow, the United Kingdom had already adopted a different course. It emphasized cooperation—again, at least in the outward forms—in military and diplomatic activities, and finally even in trade and commerce, squaring its national aspirations with the realities of its limited economic, political, and technical prowess through multilateral and bilateral undertakings.

This general direction to British external relations might suggest that the British government would be responsive to appeals for cooperation in the control of arms sales. But in fact, the British have had a great deal of difficulty reconciling particular internal political and economic pressures with the general strategy of international cooperation in national security policy, and particular actions by British governments have not always been consistent with this general approach. While British governments have been publicly supportive of defense cooperation, in practice they have become ever more dependent upon U.S. military technology. As De Gaulle was pursuing an independent course by terminating the outward forms of cooperation within Europe and across the Atlantic with NATO, the United Kingdom was driven to reconciling its national aspirations with the realities of its limited economic and technical prowess through cooperation and joint undertakings.

Longstanding differences between the Conservative and Labour parties can, with some risk of oversimplification, be identified with questions relating to defense and foreign policy. The Labourites have been more critical of a nuclear defense force, less in favor of large defense expenditures and extensive commitments abroad, more supportive of aid to developing countries, and in general more concerned about domestic social welfare problems. Within the Labour party, the left wing traditionally takes a much stronger stand in each of the directions noted above—severely critical of the nuclear force, resistant to defense expenditures, intent on reducing foreign commitments (particularly those beyond Europe), and preferring economic over military instruments of foreign policy. Second, the British system of two major parties alternating between government and opposition has important implications for continuity in defense and foreign policy. It is common for the opposition party to be critical of policies that it later finds difficult to abandon due to international obligations and domestic constraints. In addition, much of the criticism is simply related to electoral goals and to holding the governing party accountable for its policies. Reversals in pre- and post-election policy stands are quite common.

The Labour victory in 1964, however, did lead to some moderate changes in policy toward defense cooperation. Prime Minister Harold Wilson left defense questions largely in the hands of Dennis Healey, the new Minister of Defence, and Healey's impact was substantial. The administration of British defense was rationalized; steps were taken to bring British commitments into line with limited economic resources by emphasizing forces in the NATO region, and there was some effort to help revitalize NATO in the wake of the French withdrawal. During the course of a June 1966 interview with Associated Press, Healey reportedly even suggested that France's withdrawal would make it easier for its fourteen partners to revise European defense strategy.[54]

In 1968, as a part of his revitalization effort, Healey proposed the creation of a "European identity" within NATO to provide for close cooperation among the West European powers. Helped by some American assurance, he maintained that such an effort would not weaken the alliance in its relationship with the United States. Rather, it would be welcomed and would enable expression of a collective European point of view to the United States. Part of the motivation arose from the expectation that the United States would withdraw a significant number of troops from Europe in the future, and thus greater European unity was required.[55] The Soviet action in Czechoslovakia was also cited as a reason for European cooperation. Healey invited the European NATO members to dinner discussions on the occasion of the ministerial session of NATO's Defense Planning Committee in November 1968. They met again on January 15, 1969, to discuss procedural details. By early 1970, they had established a permanent working group, or "Staff group,"[56] which was administered from Brussels by a permanent official ("the secretariat") supplied by the British government. The Eurogroup ministers continued to meet prior to each meeting of NATO's Defense Planning Committee. British officials also sought ways of promoting closer defense cooperation and consultation with the members of the EEC, particularly after and in response to the second French veto of the U.K. application to the EEC in late 1967. Nothing concrete developed from this effort, however.[57]

After a period of hesitancy, at least partially due to the organizational failures of NATO in this area, the United Kingdom became actively involved in several projects of European cooperation in the procurement and production of weapon systems. An important motivation here was clearly economic, though cooperative ventures often did not mean great (or perhaps any) savings in cost.[58] A series of expensive failures and cancellations in British procurement efforts also suggested the need for alternative approaches. The cancellation of the TSR2 aircraft, in particular, left the British without an adequate new aircraft for interdiction and put them in much the same position as the consortium of European countries who were seeking a replacement for the F-104 Lockheed fighters.[59] For a time, Britain and France had cooperated on a variable-geometry aircraft project, but financial problems led France to withdraw.[60] The British also tried to fill the void by ordering F-111s from the United States, but the order was eventually cancelled.[61] The United

Kingdom then joined the F-104 replacement consortium, and in 1969 began a project with Italy and West Germany to build the flexible Multi-Role Combat Aircraft (MRCA) under the auspices of NATO. The United Kingdom participated in several joint-procurement efforts with France during this period, most notably the Jaguar attack aircraft.[62] Like the French, the British displayed a strong interest in the activities of the Conference of National Armaments Directors, and they provided the site for the NADGE early warning system. An interest in cost-saving procurement cooperation was also an important motive for the British efforts to establish and begin to develop the Eurogroup.[63]

In June 1970, the Conservative party unexpectedly won a national election. The first Defence White Paper issued by the new government declared important changes in policy:

> The maintenance and improvement of our military contribution to NATO remains the first priority of defense policy.... But there are serious threats to stability outside the NATO area.... The Government intends in addition to contribute to 5-Power Commonwealth defense arrangements relation to Malaysia and Singapore and to continue discussions with leaders in the Gulf and other interested countries on how Britain can best contribute to the maintenance of peace and stability in the area.[64]

As implemented, the new policy reduced or at least slowed the withdrawal of forces from east of Suez and substantially increased defense expenditures, though less than the Conservative government had hoped.[65] As a result, the government claimed important improvements in Britain's forces, forces that were mainly committed to NATO.[66]

Like Jobert and other French officials at the same time, leading members of the Conservative government called for consultation among Western European nations (particularly the members of an enlarged EEC) in matters of defense and foreign affairs; Prime Minister Edmund Heath even spoke of the need for developing a common European defense policy.[67] The British probably were more genuinely interested in a common European policy than were the French, although the British interest may have been fueled in part by the prospect that it would ease Britain's admission to the EEC. While not actively opposing the French proposals for using the WEU as the forum for European defense cooperation, the British, sensitive to West German opposition to the WEU, favored the Eurogroup in the short term, and expressed interest in the EEC as the eventual appropriate forum.[68] Upon admission to the EEC, the British capitalized on the opportunity to pursue this interest to a degree, as Sir Christopher Soames was named to the EEC Commission as a vice president responsible for external relations.

Unlike the French, the British joined other NATO countries, albeit skeptically, in the initiative on Mutual and Balanced Force Reductions in Europe (MBFR). The British certainly were concerned about the domestic pressures in the United States for troop withdrawals, and they were active in the Eurogroup activities aimed at indirectly reducing the pressures. In response to President Nixon's suggestions on burden-sharing in the autumn of 1970, the Eurogroup adopted a European Defense Improvement Programme (EDIP) involving additional expenditures to improve NATO's infrastructure and conventional capabilities.[69] The EDIP required considerable consultation within the Eurogroup, and the United Kingdom played a leading role in the effort.[70] Together with the West Germans, the British were intent upon insuring that the EDIP had the appropriate "public relations" impact on the U.S. Congress and public. This goal was met quite successfully.

The Conservative government was active in and supportive of the Eurogroup in other areas as well. While Defence Minister Lord Carrington did not show as much interest in defense questions in general and in the Eurogroup in particular as his predecessor Dennis Healey had, he was clearly supportive of the program. He served as the first chairman of the Eurogroup's Ministerial Committee in 1971,[71] and the United Kingdom continued to provide the secretariat for the operation of the group.

The Eurogroup formed several subgroups (e.g., EUROCOM and EUROLOG) to deal with specific aspects of European defense cooperation. Of particular interest was the decision in 1972 to set up EUROLONGTERM, a subgroup for long-term planning aimed at developing tactical concepts for the 1980s. The intent was that a long-range view would facilitate collaboration in equipment before countries were committed to national programs.[72] The United Kingdom and West Germany cooperated for a time in EUROLONGTERM, for example, in trying to harmonize their views on the requirements for a new main battle tank. Indeed, some observers have suggested that advance agreement (or collusion) between the FRG and the United Kingdom enabled the two countries to prevail in the decisions of the full group, increasing the chances for successful equipment cooperation. Britain consulted with other European NATO members in both the Eurogroup and CNAD in order to avoid the duplication of expenditure on research and development and to promote arms standardization.[73] In 1972, it became a member of FINABEL, which performs a function similar to EUROLONGTERM and other Eurogroup subgroups, and is attended by the same British army personnel attending the relevant Eurogroup meetings.[74]

These consultation efforts may have been useful. Cooperation in the procurement and production of defense equipment seemed to grow in importance during the Heath administration. Collaborative projects begun during the Wilson administration—such as the Anglo-French Jaguar, helicopter, and MARTEL missile projects—were continued, and the government decided to enter into the initial stage of development of the MRCA in July 1970.[75] Full development began in December 1971. Britain also joined with Italy and West Germany in the development of two major artillery systems, and with Belgium in the development of combat reconnaissance vehicles.[76] Several other projects were identified and studied for future cooperation.

Progress in cooperative weapons procurement was driven by increasing economic constraints on purely national equipment development, but also improved the standardization of NATO weapons. During his tenure as U.S. Secretary of Defense from 1973 to 1975, James Schlesinger took a more flexible attitude than his predecessor on using European weapons for U.S. forces, and at the same time he aggressively promoted the adoption of U.S. aircraft (YF-16 and YF-17) to replace the aging F-104s in the Belgian, Dutch, Danish, and Norwegian air forces. It must be added, however, that there was a disposition for equipment cooperation among leading members of the Conservative government (at least in public expressions). With impending U.K. membership in the EEC, it was frequently suggested that the EEC countries should greatly increase their cooperation in this area.

Faced by industrial strife and the threat of economic chaos, Prime Minister Heath announced new parliamentary elections in February 1974. The election produced no clear winner, and, after some delay, on March 4 Queen Elizabeth asked Harold Wilson to form a minority Labour government. The new government set about to deal with severe labor unrest and to enact its program calling for, among other things, the renegotiation of British ties to the EEC. Wilson called for new elections that October in an effort to strengthen his government. He was not entirely successful. For the next years Labour governed with a wafer-thin majority in the House of Commons.

Defense matters did not provide the key issues in either of the 1974 national elections. But the spending cuts promised by the Labour party were at least indirectly important, and upon taking office, the Labour government, like the 1964 Wilson government, began a major defense review—this time under the direction of Roy Mason, the new Minister of Defence.[77] The government's support for cooperation in NATO remained firm, but it was clear from the start of the review that the British were working under increased economic constraints, as the following statement by Foreign Secretary James Callaghan indicates:

The maintenance of the Alliance's defence capabilty is a common concern for which we all share responsibility. We in Britain have always been prepared to play our part and our record in this respect is, I believe, credible. But we are bound inevitably by the constraints that our economic situation lays upon us.

Our persistent balance of payments difficulties, and our slow rate of growth compared with other major European countries carry serious dangers for our future economic prosperity. We have to deal with the balance of payments problem, and increase our investment in order to improve our growth rate. The Government have therefore been obliged to curtail public expenditure in all areas in order to release resources for improving our economic position.

Defence must play its part in this process. But we are determined not to make arbitrary cuts. That is why we have set in hand a major review of our defence expenditure and commitments, the most comprehensive for many years.[78]

The initial results of the review were published in a White Paper presented to Parliament in March 1975.[79]

As expected, the White Paper announced substantial, though not drastic, defense cuts, scarcely as severe as the demands expressed at the annual Labour party conference in 1973 would have led one to expect. The spending was to be reduced gradually over a period of ten years. It could indeed be argued that if reductions had to be made, this long-term approach was superior to the short-term cuts made by the previous Conservative government. In addition, the government's justification for the approach selected revealed both concern for the effects of the reductions and evidence of prior consultation with the NATO allies:

Our NATO allies have expressed sympathetic understanding of our economic difficulties. They have welcomed our assurance that NATO commitments will remain the first charge on our defence resources, and that no reductions are envisaged in the Central Region in advance of mutual and balanced force reductions, or in our nuclear contribution to the Alliance. Nevertheless they have expressed considerable disquiet at the overall scale of the reductions we propose and the weakening effect which they would have on NATO's conventional capability vis-a-vis the Warsaw Pact, if not offset by compensatory measures. They have also expressed concern lest these measures should be interpreted as weakening the solidarity of the Alliance (particularly in the Southern Region) and its deterrent value.

While the main process of consultation with our Allies has now been completed, we shall continue to keep in close contact with them about outstanding issues and the detailed implementation of our plans, taking account of developments in the economic, political and security situation as they arise.[80]

As this statement suggests, much of the spending cuts were reflected in force reductions in the non-European contingents. Indeed, by mid-1976 the U.K. government had withdrawn all forces from Singapore and the Middle East in fulfillment of a plan announced more than seven years earlier by the previous Labour government.

In addition to the usual criticism from the Conservative opposition, the government's proposed level of defense spending was attacked by the left wing of the Labour party. Demanding further defense cuts, left wing MPs sought without success to modify the budget in Parliament. They also failed in the attempt to pressure the government into abandoning the nuclear force.[81]

Once again British policy in defense planning and consultation did not change much with the change in government. Conservatives and Labourites alike found involvement in NATO a source of prestige and reassurance in the face of declining relative military strength and a means by which to fragment the opposition. Britain's military effort could be defended as an expression of nationalism, of course; but it was increasingly also a cooperatve venture with NATO allies, something that could reassure left-wing skeptics of nationalistic military powers. The 1975 Defence White Paper claimed that the government was playing a leading part in the prestigous Nuclear Planning Group. This claim amounted to saying that, with respect to strategic nuclear forces, Britain enjoyed a special relationship to the United States, since the main function of the Nuclear Planning Group was to review U.S. Nuclear targeting and nuclear operations plans. The White Paper also reported that the Eurogroup was perceived as "a valuable forum in which they [the defense ministers] can discuss the major defence issues facing the Alliance, and give direction to the practical work of cooperation that is carried out in the various Eurogroup subgroups."[82] Defence Minister Mason agreed to serve as the chairman of the Eurogroup for 1975, and he expressed special interest in the consultations of EUROLONGTERM:

In addition, I shall myself be looking with particular interest at the results achieved by EUROLONGTERM which I believe has a critical part to play. The useful work that it is now doing to develop tactical doctrines and concepts for the future will I am sure prove invaluable in easing the path towards future equipment collaboration and it is from such increased collaboration on equipment that further co-operation in the fields of training and logistics will be able to develop. I very much hope that this year will see solid achievements in EUROLOG, for which Britain provides the chairman; and indeed I will personally ensure that the UK plays a full role in contributing to the success of all the subgroups.[83]

Here one can see how British officials used defense cooperation to depict British defense policy in the most favorable light. Cooperation could offset declining relative natonal military power, and the United Kingdom could still buy strength—collective strength—and prestige, the prestige that came with a leadership role in European councils. It was a solution that proved attractive to both political parties, which was not surprising since they competed for a narrowly divided electoral majority.

Reflecting these conditions, members of both the Labour and Conservative Parties continued to demand consultation within the EEC on matters of defense, and the parliamentary members of the WEU adopted a report that called upon an EEC summit meeting to examine European defense policy.[84] However, the Labour government's efforts to "renegotiate" British ties with the EEC, where economic stakes were more tangible than in defense consultation arrangements, reduced or delayed any prospects for government initiatives in this area.

The government's process of defense review also reevaluated the cooperation programs in equipment procurement and production. The decisions reached here led to withdrawal from the RS 80 artillery project, but the other collaborative projects were retained. Indeed, the government continued to invoke a means to reconcile defense requirements with a grim economic situation now worsened by inflation and the energy crisis: "Severe restrictions on the resources available for defence will make collaboration even more important in the future, not only for the financial advantages to be gained but also for the military benefits to be derived from standardized equipment, which should facilitate common logistics, training and operations."[85] And again national security requirements were to be achieved through cooperation: "The Government attaches particular importance to European defence co-operation within the framework of the Alliance, especially over the joint procurement of equipment, in order to achieve economies and to increase fighting efficiency by enhancing the ability of Allied units to operate together."[86]

The government could point to some success in the past collaboration efforts, in procurement and production, as EXOCET and MARTEL missiles were installed on British ships and aircraft and the Jaguar strike aircraft came into service.[87] Work on the Multi-Role Combat Aircraft neared completion, but it was not without some controversy and criticism. The MRCA Toronado was pictured as too expensive and already out of date by some, but in March 1976 Defence Minister Mason announced the government's decision to order the 35 aircraft originally planned. The criticism and expense had cast doubt on this decision, but the desire to support the maintenance and further development of a European aeronautics industry appeared to have won out.[88] As noted earlier, collaborative efforts were supported by British participation in the consultations in EUROLONGTERM and FINABEL. Through these efforts, plans for cooperation on a new family of small arms and ammunition were developed. However, cooperation on a new main battle tank collapsed, in part as a result of Anglo-German differences in timetable requirements.

In April 1976, Harold Wilson turned over leadership of the government and the Labour party to Foreign Secretary James Callaghan, and a minor surprise occured in defense policy. Fred Mulley, who became Minister of Defence, turned out to be a strong opponent of further defense spending cuts. Indeed, in introducing the 1978 Defence White Paper, Mulley announced the government's decision to increase defense spending by 3 percent in real terms for 1979/80. However, the paper underlined the trend to gearing defense commitments almost totally to NATO; commitments outside the Atlantic Alliance region continued to decline.[89]

The Callaghan administration actively supported the IEPG during this period. Indeed, an IEPG working group under British chairmanship produced an extensive analysis of the equipment replacement requirements of member states for the next fifteen years.[90] Collaborative procurement planning should be facilitated by this effort.

The Labour government was defeated in a general election in May 1979; the election was necessitated by a vote of no confidence on the Scottish devolution issue. Margaret Thatcher, the new Conservative Prime Minister, moved quickly to increase defense spending further. In 1980 this included a cabinet decision to upgrade the nuclear deterrent with an expensive Trident nuclear missile submarine program. Defense cooperation policy did not change markedly under the Conservatives, but renewed interest in defense industrial rationalization and cooperation in the framework of the European Community was expressed by several prominent party spokesmen.[91]

Arms Sales Policies and Patterns. As in the case of France, arms exports have been a major interest of the British government. British arms exports have increased considerably since the mid-1960s, but not quite as dramatically as the French exports. Indeed, the United Kingdom has lost its third-place ranking among leading arms exporters to France in recent years. Reliable data comparable to those given for France are not readily available; there are, for example, considerable discrepancies between figures released by the Stockholm International Peace Research Institute (SIPRI) and those released by the U.S. Arms Control and Disarmament Agency (ACD). However, figures released by the British Ministry of Defence point to a rise in total receipts from British arms sales from £152 million for 1966/67 to £790 million in 1977/78.[92] Moreover, an important rise in British arms exports actually came just prior to the 1973 OPEC oil price increases whereas France's exports rose just after them. To some extent, this seems to reflect the effects of Britain's own version of the Nixon Doctrine in its withdrawal of forces from east of Suez. The withdrawal may have served as a stimulus to purchases by states faced with the need to be more self-sufficient in defense.

Other differences from France are also noteworthy. In 1965 approximately $150 million in British arms exports went to developing countries; the British viewed the Third World as a market of limited value because of the lack of economic resources.[93] However, Britain did develop an interest in the Middle East, particularly Saudi Arabia, prior to the OPEC economic turnaround in the 1970s. What is also distinct from the case of France is the degree of interest Britain has paid to the United States as a market for arms sales. One can trace this interest to certain British advantages flowing from the Anglo-American "special relationship," but in large measure it is a product of offset arrangements secured to help finance British purchases of U.S. high-technology armaments such as the Polaris missile—which is itself an artifact of the special relationship with the United States. Indeed, some have argued that early British success in penetrating the Saudi Arabian arms market was due to U.S. willingness to pull back on its efforts there, so that the United Kingdom could use resources gained from the Saudi deal to help finance planned purchases of the U.S. F-111 aircraft.[94] Whether or not there is truth in this, it is clear that the United Kindgom has had to struggle to obtain a favorable balance of trade in armaments. ACDA figures indicate that Britain's arms imports have been much larger than those of France (see Table 7.6). Indeed, in 1969 the United Kingdom imported arms worth over $200 million more than the arms it exported. The situation is even more serious for West Germany, which had unfavorable balances every year until 1976. France, in contrast, has not even approximated an unfavorable balance of trade in arms since 1967.

Part of Britain's difficulty with excessive arms imports is derived from national procurement problems experienced in the 1960s. As noted, several aircraft projects had to be cancelled, and the government was

Table 7.6. Arms Imports: France, Britain, West Germany

(in Millions of Constant 1977 dollars)

	France	Britain	West Germany
1969	$ 32	$ 568	$ 341
1970	15	77	324
1971	14	102	514
1972	28	141	952
1973	26	120	834
1974	24	109	701
1975	33	100	668
1976	52	253	555
1977	50	150	470
1978	37	139	269

Source: United States Arms Control and Disarmament Agency,
World Military Expenditures and Arms Transfers, 1969-1978
(Washington, D.C.: USGPO, December 1980).

forced to consider purchasing alternatives, leaving limited national aircraft possibilities to compete with other countries for arms exports.

While some may argue that the government has never presented a clear policy, British arms sales policy has undergone some variation under different political administrations since the 1960s.[95] In general, however, the government has taken political and security criteria into account in authorizing sales, at least to a limited degree. The United Kingdom has not had a policy of "selling to almost anyone," but the government has tended to permit sales unless adequate justification for disallowing the sale is provided. Over the years, this has led to a pattern of denying sales only to a select number of "pariah" states, such as South Africa, Chile, and to some extent Israel.

The exceptions to this trend are particularly instructive. Upon beginning his first term as Prime Minister in October 1964, Harold Wilson took a strong public stance in support of the U.N. ban on arms exports to South Africa. Existing orders would be filled, but new ones would be rejected. This position held up at least on the official level, even though the United Kingdom was under great pressure to sell arms for economic reasons during this period. South Africa was a willing and anxious market, as both the United Kingdom and the United States found when France quickly stepped into the breach left by them.

Despite considerable internal and external (U.S. and black Commonwealth) pressure, the Heath government reversed Wilson's policy in part because of concern about the strategic position of South Africa. It turned out, however, that by this time South Africa had a rather small shopping list with an emphasis on helicopters. In any case, when Wilson returned as Prime Minister in 1974, arms sales to South Africa were again forbidden. In addition, Chile was added to the select "pariah" list.

Generally, arms sales have not been used by the British government to achieve "positive" foreign policy goals. A possibly striking exception to this has been the recent consideration of arms sales to China—in particular the Harrier VTOL aircraft. Both Labour and Conservative governments have recently been inclined to make these sales, over the strong opposition of the USSR and considerable domestic controversy, suggesting certain possible strategic benefits as well as an effort to secure a large trade package, of which the arms sales would be a small part.[96]

Decisionmaking on arms sales policy and efforts to promote sales were primarily the responsibility of the Ministry of Supply. However, the Labour government's interest in maximizing the economic return on arms sales led Defence Minister Healey to establish a Defence Sales Organization (DSO). Initially headed by Raymond Brown, a business-man rather than a civil servant or politician, the DSO was jointly responsible to the Minister of Defence and the Minister of Technology. But with the demise of the Technology Ministry, it eventually became a part of the Ministry of Defence. The main function of the DSO was to promote arms sales, and its staff has been quite effective at times, prompting some to suggest that it should be given wider responsibility for "civilian" export promotion. The DSO has also been the target of criticism—for losing business by indecision (or slowness in coming to a decision) in the view of some and by being too demanding about credit arrangements for others.[97] It has not been criticized, as have its counterparts in the U.S. Department of Defense, for promoting sales too much or too successfully.

Arms sales are promoted by various means in the United Kingdom. This includes some effort at the top political level. For example, in a bid for more incentive for arms standardization and collaboration in NATO, Labour Defence Minister Mason in 1975 strongly urged that the United States make the transatlantic arms trade a "two-way street."[98] A Memorandum of Understanding (MOU) was signed between the two countries on the subject later that year. As another example, for a time various political leaders sought to push the Anglo-French Jaguar as a contender to replace the F-104 Starfighters in the "contrat du siecle." Despite such conspicuous cases of export promotion at the highest levels, a parliamentary inquiry into the welfare of the guided weapons industry suggested that top leaders, including the Prime Minister, should regu-larly play more of a role in arms export promotion during the normal course of their interactions with leaders from other countries.[99]

Not to be outdone by the French, the British opened their first international exhibition of armaments in 1976.[100] This has now become a regularized procedure in which potential foreign customers are invited to Aldershot to observe equipment and demonstrations sponsored by the Ministry of Defence and the British defense industry. In an instance of rather poor timing, the 1978 exhibition was scheduled to coincide with the sessions of the U.N. Special Session on Disarmament.

Arms export promotion reaches directly to other countries as well. The DSO, which produces a large *Defence Equipment Catalogue* annually, has offices in Washington, Bonn, Paris, and Ottawa, and makes use of defense attachés in British embassies for promotion. A novel effort along these lines has been the use of large naval vessels to serve as floating arms exhibitions, calling on the ports of various potential customers. British defense contractors are invited to participate in the trips and display their products. One such ship provoked some controversy by its plan to visit Tokyo; the pacifist mayor of Tokyo refused permission for it to berth.[101]

British policy was less openly negative than that of France to President Carter's policy to seek restraint of arms sales to the Third World, although Britain does not appear to have taken any concrete steps to support it. Carter's offer to push for a "two-way street" in transatlantic arms transfers was welcomed warmly in Britain, but it was not enough to provide an inducement for multilateral restraint; the British were not supportive participants in CATT. In preparation for the U.N. Special Session on Disarmament, the Foreign and Commonwealth Office drafted a guide to British arms control and disarmament policy. On conventional weapons exports, it summarized British policy as follows:

> Although the UK ranks fourth among arms suppliers it has only 4% of the world market. Unilateral action by the UK would make no impact on the problem. The British Government has always adopted a responsible policy on arms exports. The UN embargo on South Africa has been observed and sales to Chile have been stopped. We consider sales of defence equipment to other countries in the light of all the political, military, security and economic factors concerned, paying attention to our obligations to our Allies, to the end use of the equipment, and to the arms control implications.

> Overseas orders make an important contribution to the maintenance of a viable defence industry in the UK, which is necessary to fulfil the equipment needs of our own forces and reduces unit costs to our forces. There are also ancillary economic benefits; defence sales are likely to contribute £850 million to our balance of payments in 1977/78 as well as providing direct employment for 70,000 workers and indirectly for many more.[102]

Pressures and Constraints on Policy: Prospects for Change. The government statement just quoted provides an effective, though perhaps understated, summary of the major pressures on British arms sales policy. As in the case of France, a primary concern has been the maintenance of a viable defense industry in the country. This goal has been pursued since the early 1960s through a strategy of industrial concentration and rationalization; the policy continues as rationalization is extended to major components of the defense and aerospace industry. However, a major requirement for viability is adequate markets and thus long, economical production runs. A significant level of arms exports appears essential as a result. Britain's naval construction industry is severely threatened at present because of a lack of orders. British arms exports also make an important contribution to lowering military research and development costs. As Table 7.7 indicates, British arms exports from 1975 to 1979 were worth £1,557 million, while research and development costs for the period were £2,766 million. The earnings from exports thus made a major contribution toward offsetting costs. It should be noted, however, that British ground equipment is the most desirable to recipients and therefore the greatest export item, while the greatest research and development costs are accrued in producing combat aircraft. The British are less competitive in exporting combat aircraft.

Table 7.7. Relationship between British Research and Development Spending and British Military Exports, 1975-1979

Weapons Systems	Military Exports		R&D Budget	
	Millions of Pounds	% of Total	Millions of Pounds	% of Total
Combat Aircraft	£ 260.9	16.8	£ 1,532	55.4
Warships	322.0	20.7	436	15.8
Ground Equipment	869.6	55.8	323	11.7
Guided Missiles and Weapons	104.8	6.7	475	17.1
TOTALS	1,557.3	100.0	2,766	100.0

Source: Defence in the 1980's: Statement on the Defence Estimates 1980, Vol. 1, Cmnd. 7826-1 and 7826 (London: HMSO, April 1980), p. 81; and Trevor Taylor, "Research Note: British Arms Exports and R&D Costs," Survival (November–December 1980), p. 260.

Balance-of-payments problems have plagued Britain since the early 1960s, even after the 1967 devaluation of the pound sterling and before the 1973 OPEC increases in the price of imported oil. A contribution of £850 million toward a favorable balance cannot be ignored. It is true that given projected levels of North Sea oil production, the United Kingdom's foreign exchange situation is less serious than France's or perhaps West Germany's. On the other hand, British industrial production is less efficient and therefore less competitive than West Germany's and to a lesser extent France's. The British arms industry has been one of the few sources of growth in exports for an economy still heavily dependent on foreign trade.

We have noted that part of Britain's motivation for arms exports has been to provide a counterbalance to the high-technology arms imports that it has found necessary to purchase, particularly from the United States. This remains a consideration, and the need will certainly be heightened as the government follows through on its decision to acquire Trident nuclear missile submarines.

Finally, it is clear that the British government has been very much concerned about the benefits of healthy defense and aerospace industries to national employment requirements. Britain is probably even more vulnerable on this question than is France, but in any event it is clear that in Britain arms export/import questions are frequently viewed in these terms. This can be seen in the statements of defense officials and MPs almost continually, as well as in the concern expressed by trade union leaders every time it appears that the government is considering a purchase of arms from the United States or continental Europe. It was conspicuous whenever President Carter spoke of restraint.[103]

In sum, strong pressures for arms exports are present in the United Kingdom as well as in France, although they may indeed be more severe in the latter because of the energy crisis. On the other hand, domestic opposition to arms exports is somewhat stronger in the United Kingdom than in France and serves as a more important constraint. Unlike the situation in the United States, however, this opposition has not been voiced by members of the government or the parliamentary opposition.

In describing domestic opposition to arms sales, we should turn first to the most visible though perhaps not the most influential manifestation, the Campaign Against Arms Trade (CAAT), which was established in 1974. CAAT, which has no counterpart in France (or the United States and West Germany, for that matter) is a well-organized and active pressure group specifically devoted to ending arms sales. Although it is constrained by limited financial and staff resources, it has managed to collect and circulate a great deal of information on British arms sales policy and patterns. Occasionally, this information provides some embarrassment to the government, as it finds its way into the press or into the hands of sympathetic and interested MPs who may then raise sensitive questions to the government during parliamentary question periods.[104] CAAT has also been effective in mobilizing substantial protest demonstrations at various times, for example, on the occasion of the biennial armaments exhibitions at Aldershot.[105] This effort is complemented by several active religious groups such as Pax Christi (the international Catholic peace movement), the Quakers, and the Church of Scotland.[106]

Parliament is a focal point for the activities of these groups, and several left-wing Labour MPs, such as Frank Allaun, Robin Cook, Tom Litterick, Ian Mikardo, and Stan Newens have been quite sympathetic to their concerns. The extent of their impact on policy is questionable, though, given the fact that none of them has been able to secure seats on the Defence and External Affairs Sub-Committee of the House of Commons Expenditure Committee. In early 1979, Robin Cook raised challenging questions to the government during the question period on the proposed sale of Harriers to China. The debate received attention in the press but probably did not have much of an impact on policy. Parliament plays only a very limited role in defense decisions generally, and in the case of arms sales this has frequently been a supportive role, as MPs raise questions about the welfare of defense and aerospace industries and the employment and balance of payments implications of their work.[107] Much of the impact of parliamentary committees and subcommittees has been to criticize and suggest ways of improving the implementation of arms sales policies rather than the policies themselves.

MPs have at times been able to influence government policy on arms sales through the party machinery, particularly when their party wins an election after a period of opposition. In the case of the Labour party, the left-wing tends to dominate during the opposition period, and the party platform may thus be strongly influenced by the left. This kind of situation may have played a role in decisions to restrict arms sales to Chile and South Africa. Moreover, the political parties frequently sponsor or sanction study groups, the reports of which may have some influence on government policy.[108]

Labour MPs frequently have some difficulty with arms sales questions because their constituencies and particularly supporting trade unions are very concerned about the employment implications of arms sales decisions. Their moral or ideological position often conflicts with economic necessity. Nevertheless, considerable attention has been focused on the activities of some trade unionists and MPs in promoting industrial conversion strategies. The most prominent of these was the campaign of the shop stewards' committee at Lucas Aerospace, which developed a "Corporate Plan" for conversion of their plant to nondefense production. The plan has not been implemented, but it did provoke some critical examination of the concept in other contexts.[109]

The final element that has perhaps had some limited constraining effect on British arms sales policy is the Ministry of Defence and the British military itself. Sales have been curtailed to some states by the MOD, most notably to India, on the grounds of credit unworthiness or a record of debts on previous sales. Moreover, some effect has been seen as a result of complaints from military leaders similar to those expressed in France, namely, that foreign customers receive priority over British forces in deliveries. The British army for a time was not equipped with the newest Chieftain tanks because shipments to Iran took priority.[110]

Prospects for support of and cooperation in multilateral arms transfer restraint, or in coordinated Western supplier policies to the Third World and in the rationalization of weapons system procurement, appear marginally brighter in the United Kingdom than in France. The pressures for sales are slightly lower, the constraints on or opposition to sales are slightly more, and successive British governments have supported multilateral military planning, production, and procurement for their obvious advantages to a government needing prestigious support for its defense policies in a resource-stringent environment. Prospects for British arms export restraint remain dim, however. Pressures for export sales are real, remain strong, and greatly overbalance the tendencies toward restraint. The Conservative government of Prime Minister Thatcher is clearly interested in the economic benefits to be derived from an effective national arms sales program, as Thatcher's speech to the Farnborough air show in September 1980 indicated:

> Overseas sales of British defense equipment will this year earn £1.2 billion in foreign currency. That's a handy sum. That's quite a large sum. I want to pay tribute to those who earn it. But it is not enough. The procurement budget of government and the skills of our people, if used together to the best advantage, could bring the country far greater sums, greater benefits to both our armed services and to our industries, and more jobs at the same time.[111]

The British did push for multilateral restraint in one notable instance—sales to Argentina following the latter's invasion of the Falkland Islands. The British were able to secure an effective supplier embargo for the duration of the conflict, but there has been little evidence of sentiment for more general restraint. Rather, British arms manufacturers have begun to advertise "battle proven" weapons.

West Germany

General Policies Toward Defense Cooperation. Unique among the major Western arms suppliers, the Federal Republic of Germany must seek its national security by employing its armed forces in military alliances. Only by contributing to multinational military commands can the FRG legitimize its military efforts. After World War II, as a defeated nation, Germany was at first forbidden to rearm. The FRG was then, in the early 1950s, permitted to rearm only to contribute to the military strength of NATO. The weight of German history and the fact of Germany's division into two states assures that, in both the West and the Soviet bloc, any move by the FRG toward an independent military force, such as the course that De Gaulle took, would generate instant and profound resistance. It is no surprise, then, that a recent West German Defense White Paper states, "It is only in alliance with the North American countries that the security of Europe and the Federal Republic of Germany is assured."[112]

Defense cooperation with the United States is the main theme of West German security, but Bonn has also viewed close cooperation with other European governments, particularly in the context of the European Community, as an important foundation of its security. Given the predilections and goals of its closest European partner, France, it is not surprising that the FRG has continually found itself pulled in different directions at various points during its period of NATO membership. President De Gaulle, in particular, frequently attempted to force choices between Washington and Paris.[113] From Konrad Adenauer to Helmut Schmidt, West German Chancellors have handled this difficult situation with different styles and different points of emphasis, but NATO cooperation has always been given high priority.

In comparison with France and the United Kingdom, West Germany has been more consistently in favor of increased defense integration, whether it be in the form of new institutions, groupings, and forces, or in standardization of arms and equipment. Moreover, it has seemed to matter little whether the initiative for increased defense integration came from the United States or from a European government.

Obviously some explanation for West Germany's positive stance on defense cooperation lies in the country's peculiar position after World War II. In the late forties and early fifties, there was little potential for development of either a national defense establishment or a sound defense industry. However, when threats from the East were acute enough for NATO members to support West German rearmament and membership in the alliance, the government quickly welcomed this chance to prove itself worthy; moreover, it found purchasing arms, particularly from the United States, to be the most viable means for equipping its developing forces. From that time on, West Germany supported coproduction schemes, defense industry consortia, and new opportunities for shared responsibility whenever possible. The West German arms industry expanded quickly, and the FRG soon joined Britain and the United States as the most active supporters of NATO.

Denied nuclear weapons by treaty, not surprisingly the FRG has supported the several approaches to sharing decisionmaking about the disposition and use of nuclear forces, such as the U.S. proposal for a Multilateral Force (MLF), the British alternative proposal for an Atlantic Nuclear Force (ANF), and the reconciliation proposal for a Nuclear Planning Group. After the Soviet invasion of Czechoslovakia in 1968, the FRG joined the British in efforts to revive the Alliance and to develop the Eurogroup. West Germany was prominent in efforts to encourage the United States to continue to maintain its level of troops stationed in Europe (one such effort was the European Defence Improvement Programme, which promised increased defense spending); the FRG also agreed to pay the United States to offset troop costs.

West Germany's financial contribution to NATO defense efforts has not been without controversy. The offset payments to the United States (and the United Kingdom) have generally been subject to difficult negotiations between the governments. West Germany has generally ranked second only to the United States in its contribution to the aggregate defense effort of all the NATO nations in recent years; for example, in 1978 its portion of the total defense expenditure was 11.5 percent (the U.S. portion was 59 percent and France was third with 10 percent). West Germany also ranked second in both per capita defense expenditure and defense expenditure as a percentage of total central government expenditure.[114] However, the United States has often been unconvinced that the West Germans were doing as much as they could. This view was heightened in 1980 when Bonn announced that a reduction in planned defense expenditure was necessary, and it became clear that West Germany would not be able to live up to its NATO commitment for a 3-percent defense expenditure increase in real terms. West Germany had finally begun to experience the recession already plaguing other Western economies. In an election year, pressure from rising unemployment—then expected to climb past the 1 million mark— and balance-of-payments difficulties attributable to high OPEC oil prices led Chancellor Schmidt, after several revisions, to propose a defense budget with a real growth of less than 1 percent.

Nevertheless, Bonn has a strong record of contributing to NATO defense cooperation efforts. For one thing, the West German armed forces have been termed the most "standardized" of all the NATO members' military forces, an understandable result of the early years of participation in the Alliance, when equipment was obtained through purchase from other members, particularly the United States. In addition, Bonn has also been more willing to engage in joint procurements and in multinational industrial consortia than have the other members. Government policy in this regard has been stated as follows:

> About 60 percent of the expenditure of defence research and development and approximately 50 percent of the expenditure on military procurements is related to equipment projects implemented in collaboration with other allies.

> The Federal Government does not seek self-sufficiency in the field of defence production; nor does it want an independent branch of industry solely employed on arms contracts. On the other hand, due to military-logistic and technological-economic considerations the Federal Republic of Germany cannot do without a defence production capacity of her own. She must be concerned with being able to play her part in the Alliance as a suitable partner in collaborative efforts. Partnership in the Alliance calls for independent achievements.[115]

As to specific examples of collaboration, the Franco-German Roland missile program and the TORNADO Multi-Role Combat Aircraft program (with Italy and the United Kingdom) have been noted earlier. Other programs include Franco-German collaboration on the ALPHA-JET ground-attack trainer and the HOT anti-tank missile. Work is now in progress in cooperation with France and the United Kingdom on an advanced version of the MILAN anti-tank missile, and there are still efforts under way to salvage U.S.-German cooperation in the deployment of partially "standardized" tanks.

While it seems that some of the momentum in West German procurement collaboration efforts has been lost in recent years, Bonn has been one of the strongest proponents of a sound European defense industry. As noted earlier, initial efforts along these lines were proposed by France, in some respects as a challenge to U.S. dominance, and the Western European Union was proposed as the most appropriate locus for European cooperation in this area. West Germany even seemed willing to support this approach despite obvious negative views toward the WEU relating to the fact that the organization had been originally designed in part to "regulate" German rearmament. Moreover, along with the United Kingdom, West Germany was active in Eurogroup efforts to establish the IEPG, which could bring France into a concentrated program of planned defense production collaboration and industrial development. In addition, the FRG has been active within the European Community to ensure the viability of a European defense and aerospace industry. A major report on the subject was prepared for the European Parliament by Dr. Egon Klepsch, a West German member, and the West German government has supported proposals by the

European Commission to develop a European industrial policy that would encourage effective European arms procurement and support the IEPG's efforts.[116]

Arms Sales Policies and Patterns. One consequence of West Germany's arms procurement policy and defense cooperation efforts within NATO and Western Europe has been a strong interest in exporting arms and defense equipment to other NATO member states. A large proportion of West Germany's arms exports has been focused on the NATO market; not surprisingly, the government has thus been a very strong supporter, along with the U.K. government, of efforts to develop a "two-way street" in transatlantic arms sales.

This NATO focus for Bonn's arms exports can be attributed in part to the nature of the military equipment produced in West Germany, which in most cases was designed for the country's own needs in its NATO defense role.[117] However, the emphasis also reflects a longstanding official West German restrictive policy on exports to other parts of the world. Speaking before the Tenth Special Session of the U.N. General Assembly on Disarmament in May 1978, Chancellor Schmidt reaffirmed a policy that has been in place throughout much of West Germany's recent history as an arms exporter:

> Regulating the international transfer of armaments must feature prominently in our efforts to achieve arms limitation . . . We refuse as a matter of principle to grant aid for the export of weapons. Only in exceptional and on the whole very limited cases do we allow any weapons at all to be supplied to countries outside our own alliance . . . We strictly do not allow weapons to be exported to areas of international tension.[118]

Indeed, in contrast to France and the United Kingdom, Bonn's policy on exports to the Third World has been restrictive and as a matter of stated official policy has been to avoid "areas of international tension." Commercial interests are to yield to this policy, and exports of military weapons have never exceeded 0.7 percent of the total amount of West German exports.[119] However, there have been some variations in both Bonn's policy and its efforts to enforce the policy on West German industry, and there are growing pressures for a relaxation of official policy.

Some restriction on the government's arms policy is provided in the Paris Accord of October 23, 1954, which established the Western European Union and included West Germany and Italy as members. According to Protocol 3 of the Accord, West Germany was not to manufacture nuclear, chemical, or biological weapons, long-range missiles, guided missiles (excluding anti-aircraft and anti-tank missiles) and warships in larger numbers and tonnage than what was stipulated for the West German navy by the WEU's Agency for Control of Armaments. At least tacit consent was generally given for West German exports, however, and it is difficult to point to an instance in which WEU restrictions hindered arms export.

Further authority for restricting arms exports is provided in Article 26:2 of the Federal Constitution. The War Weapons Control Act of April 20, 1961, and the Foreign Trade and Payments Act of April 18, 1961, added more detailed provisions to this authority. The legislation resulted from problems with arms shipments to Morocco and Algeria and followed Bonn's decision in 1960 to enter into a program of military assistance to certain developing countries. Despite this explicit authority to restrict, there was no clear policy of restriction in the early to mid-1960s. There were secret military assistance agreements to supply surplus tanks, aircraft, and missiles to Israel (at the urging of the United States), and substantial assistance was provided to Nigeria, the Sudan, and Tanzania.[120] The recipients of West German arms sales and military assistance were limited to some extent during this period by the "Hallstein Doctrine," which prevented the FRG from approving exports to countries recognizing East Germany. For example, military assistance to Tanzania was cancelled in 1965 when its government exchanged diplomats with the East German government.[121]

In 1966, the Merex Company received permission from the West German government to sell aircraft to Iran and Italy—the aircraft involved ended up in Pakistan and India instead. Embarassed by this and criticism over the aid to Israel, Chancellor Ludwig Erhard decided that military assistance would no longer be provided to areas of international tension.

The rise of the Social Democratic party in the late 1960s had a further restricting effect on West German arms sales policy. The government's involvement in providing military assistance to the Third World was greatly reduced; private firms were left with the ability to make commercial arrangements in this respect, but in a somewhat constrained environment. Non-NATO sales during this period went mostly to countries in Africa and Latin America.

The culmination of the Social Democrats' efforts to restrict arms sales to non-NATO or non-"Western" countries was a clear statement of opposition in principle to such sales, on June 16, 1971. Exceptions could be made by the German National Security Council, but no exceptions were to be made to Warsaw Pact countries or to areas of international tension. In addition, the government required that final user clauses had to be written into all arms sales contracts.

In practice, however, the FRG has not always conformed to its statements of policy and principle. First, there have been signs of a weakening in the party and thus of government resolve on the issue in recent years, as industrial, financial, balance-of-payments, and employment pressures are brought to bear, and it is always up to the existing members of the National Security Council to define what constitutes an area of international tension. Second, private firms (and public officials) have devised a number of strategies for circumventing restrictions in a number of cases. These include licensing arrangements; the sale of complete arms manufacturing plants; foreign assembly of exported segments and parts; threats to simply shift production (and thus employment, etc.) to a subsidiary in another country if a deal is not permitted; maintaining fewer than 2,000 employees in West Germany so that the firm is technically too small to come under legislation requiring data on corporate activities (including exports); and exports through partners in multinational procurement consortia which were developed under the banner of NATO standardization or as an assurance of the competitive strength of the European defense and aerospace industry. At various times, West German experts have also emigrated to Third World countries to help develop defense plants.[122]

While important economic forces are at work in West German arms sales patterns, it does seem clear that the government has not sought to use arms sales or military assistance as an instrument of positive policy or in general for political purposes, at least not since the mid-1960s. The emphasis is on control and limitation, and the War Weapons Control Act provides a list of weapons subject to the restriction criteria. The Ministries of Defense, Foreign Affairs, and Economics are the government organs involved in the control of sales and in updating the list of weapons. Military assistance agreements (at present with Greece and Turkey) are administered by the Ministry of Defense.[123] There is no government office or structure for encouraging arms exports, in contrast both to the United Kingdom, which uses its Defence Sales Organization for this purpose, and to France, which uses several government and quasi-government organs of this type.

Nevertheless, West German arms sales have clearly increased since the early 1970s, as shown by Table 7.1. Complete statistics and information on individual arms deals are not released by the government. If released at all, sales figures are usually expressed in terms of the small percentage that arms exports constitute of total West German exports; the Federal Statistics Office is not permitted to publish specific statistics. However, researchers at Hamburg University's Institute for Peace Research and Security Policy claim that arms sales nearly doubled between 1972 and 1978[124] and a study by Dr. Eckehard Ehrenberg of the University of Bonn claimed that West Germany's arms exports between 1967 and 1977 amounted to more than $3.3 billion, based on 1975 prices. These studies verify the ACDA data reported in Table 7.1. Of the arms exports for the period from 1973 to 1977, approximately 30 percent went to NATO and other Western countries. Nearly half of the remaining 70 percent (going to the Third World) went to the Middle East (mainly Iran and Egypt); Africa, especially Libya and Algeria, received about one-quarter of the exports to the Third World.[125]

Some sources suggest that the percentage of arms exports to NATO and other Western countries is somewhat larger that 30 percent, but is is clear that the percentage of exports going to the Third World is increasing. Moreover, the Middle East is likely to remain the dominant recipient region for West German arms exports because the West German government has been under considerable pressure to conclude a major arms deal with Saudi Arabia. At present, most sources rank West Germany as the Fifth largest arms exporter, after the United Kingdom; West Germany accounts for approximately 2 percent of worldwide arms exports.

Pressures and Constraints on Policy: Prospects for Change. The debate over sales to Saudi Arabia demonstrates the pressures on Bonn to relax restrictions on West German arms exports. Proponents of the arms sales point to West Germany's recent balance-of-payments difficulties brought on by the continuing increases in the price of oil imported from OPEC. Since Saudi Arabia is now West Germany's principal oil supplier, the prospect of offsetting the oil payments with major arms exports is difficult to resist. Moreover, Saudi Arabia granted West Germany loans of $2.25 billion in 1980 and a substantial level of funding in 1981. In a period of recession, the loans have been a welcome means of covering budget deficits. This provides some relief to increasing constraints on West Germany's own defense expenditures and thus should not be jeopardized by a negative decision, but supporters of the sales to Saudi Arabia also note the direct earnings and reductions in weapon unit costs derived from a major arms export program. The decision was negative, however, at least for the time being; Chancellor Schmidt's soft refusal in April 1981 did not preclude a future arrangement, and Foreign Minister Hans-Dietrich Genscher has stated that Saudi Arabia is not at present considered an area of tension.

Similar economic pressures motivated Bonn to expand arms exports to Iran in the mid-1970s. Indeed, a major submarine deal had been concluded and construction begun when the Shah was deposed. West German officials found a partial replacement customer in India, and took the extraordinary step of permitting the sale of two submarines to the Pinochet regime in Chile. This action outraged left-wing members of Schmidt's Social Democratic party, but the government received strong support in the decision from workers in the Kiel shipyards.

In general, support from labor unions and the pressure of unemployment considerations have apparently not been crucial determinants of the FRG's arms export policy. The German Institute for Economic Research estimates that approximately 200,000 workers earn their livelihood in the defense industry (about the same number are involved in the steel industry), but a much smaller number, perhaps 36,000, presently depend on arms exports.[126] Nevertheless, in the environment of recession and increasing unemployment, the pressure for a relaxation of restrictions on arms exports is expected to heighten. An organization to represent workers in the arms industry, the Arbeitskreis Arbeitnehmer Wehrtechnischer Unternehmen, was formed in the mid-1970s to provide focus to such pressure.[127]

Quite understandably, the strongest pressure for relaxation has come from the German defense and aerospace industry itself. Leaders in the industry have waged an active press and lobbying campaign recently, arguing that Bonn's restrictions prevent firms from expanding or even working to full capacity and thus hinder competition with the United States, France, and the United Kingdom.[128] The industry cannot afford to maximize or take full advantage of technological developments; economies of scale cannot be attained with the limited production runs necessary to satisfy the needs of the West German military forces. Bonn has responded to concern about the soundness of the aerospace industry by urging the merger of its two leading firms, Verenigte Flugtechnische Werke (VFW) and Messerschmitt-Boelkow-Blohm.[129] An increasingly flexible attitude toward the restrictions appears likely.

As to constraints on West German arms sales, the greatest ones, aside from the formal legislative restrictions, may be Chancellor Schmidt and Foreign Minister Genscher themselves. Neither man seems to favor arms exports except to NATO and other Western countries. The Chancellor has made his position clear, at least in principle, in various speeches and messages. The Foreign Minister, while criticizing the arms sales policies of the four leading exporters, has recently called for the establishment of a U.N. registry office to which industrialized countries would submit detailed information on their arms exports.[130] While they have obviously permitted specific arms sales to the Third World throughout their periods of government service, Schmidt and Genscher seem to stand in marked contrast to other European leaders, who actively support arms sales for commercial reasons. By way of explanation, despite West Germany's recent economic deterioration and balance-of-payments difficulties, the country has enjoyed a strong industrial base and has generally been able to offset its expensive oil import bill with a very successful performance in its non-arms industrial exports. As noted earlier, arms exports have never accounted for a large percentage of West Germany's total exports.

From time to time, left-wing members of the Social Democratic party (SPD) have sought to constrain West German arms sales. In addition to mobilizing against the submarine sales to Chile, SPD members were outraged in 1980 by charges that the German firm Rheinmetall had been illegally selling arms and munitions to South Africa. This episode served to stimulate SPD and Free Democrat candidates in the 1980 parliamentary elections to step up their insistence on the need to tighten export restrictions. Defense Minister Hans Apel, for example, called for a more effective means of enforcing a "final use clause" for arms exports. Schmidt's coalition increased its majority in the elections, but it is not at all clear whether Parliament will adopt proposed legislation that would require it to be informed specifically each time the German National Security Council approves sales to non-NATO countries.

SPD members of Parliament have been supported in their efforts to restrict arm sales to the Third World by a group of German academics and researchers. The most active of these are Ulrich Albrecht, Peter Lock, and Herbert Wulf, all of the University of Hamburg. Position papers are written for MPs, and briefing sessions are conducted to apprise members of specific facts and figures for use in speeches and in questioning government officials.

Finally, concern about West Germany's foreign image still seems to serve as an important constraint at times. Bonn's decision not to join the bandwagon in supplying arms to China—perhaps partially in response to a personal intervention by Soviet President Brezhnev—was a source of satisfaction to many when China soon afterward launched its invasion of Vietnam.[131]

The prospects for a major change in West German arms export policy are uncertain. Much will depend on whether the economy and the balance-of-payments problems continue to worsen. It is clear that there is very strong pressure on Bonn from the defense and aerospace industry for a relaxation of restrictions on arms sales, and there is a very willing market for German arms, particularly in the Middle East. It is fair to say that the pressures for increased arms sales are strong, but perhaps less so than in the United Kingdom and certainly much less so than in France. Meanwhile, the opposition to and constraints on arms sales appear slightly stronger than in the United Kingdom and therefore much stronger than in France. A first cautious step toward increased arms sales was taken on May 3, 1982, when new guidelines were announced that appeared to relax the "areas of tension" restriction. The government now has greater flexibility on sales, but whether it will in practice permit sales to grow rapidly remains unknown.

The prospects for West German support of multilateral arms transfer restraint, however, still appear brighter than in France and the United Kingdom. Indeed, the 1979 Defense White Paper even suggests government support for such efforts, at least in principle: "Arms exports will continue to be handled restrictively. Such a restrictive stand on arms exports, however, can be effective internationally only if both private and government trade in arms is substantially curbed through universal national self-restraint, or regional or world-wide agreements. The Federal Government therefore supports every political approach pointing in this direction."[132] One can also expect continued support from the West German government for NATO RSI efforts. The government in general is predisposed to close cooperation in NATO, but there is also increasing interest in close collaboration with other European governments, through both the IEPG and the European Community, in arms procurement. In any case, it appears that the days of standardization through large arms purchases from the United States or other NATO members are past. West Germany's defense and aerospace industry is now too well developed and too entrenched politically to permit it. Moreover, the government seems to indicate a connection between cooperation on weapons procurement and multilateral arms export restraint or coordination, by suggesting that "any expansion of equipment collaboration may necessitate increased endeavors to harmonize national policies on the exportation of defence material."[133]

IMPLICATIONS AND RECOMMENDATIONS

In sum, in this chapter we have discussed the internal political and economic factors that are associated with the arms sales policies of the three major Western European arms suppliers: France, the United Kingdom, and the Federal Republic of Germany. France remains heavily committed as a matter of state policy to the full exploitation of its position as a producer of arms, and to export arms as a means of generating foreign exchange and as an essential part of a policy of maintaining a national arms industry. Britain exports for similar reasons, although successive British governments have been less single-minded than French governments over the past twenty years in promoting and protecting designated industries as a matter of national economic policy. Britain has abandoned the development and production of several important weapons systems in that period as a response to competitive pressures from allies. Britain is willing to purchase arms from allies, particularly the United States, whereas France is not. This has increased the pressure on Britain to export what arms it does produce to generate foreign exchange, but that pressure has been reduced in recent years from the favorable foreign exchange effects of developing its North Sea oil fields—reduced demand for imported oil and increased export earnings from selling oil. In neither country however, is there much opposition to selling arms abroad; in both, political spokesmen with rare and so far relatively insignificant exceptions accept arms exports as an essential part of the economy's vital activities. In both, arms exports are a feature of the economy that as a matter of conventional wisdom are seen as a source of foreign exchange, as well as a source of employment, expressed in terms of the number of jobs these exports create or sustain.

The Federal Republic of Germany is another matter. Its economic position has been more competitive. At least until the end of the 1970s, West Germany maintained a strong foreign exchange position based on a highly productive private sector. Its economic strength has worked to its disadvantage in one respect, however. The NATO allies have persistently sought ways for Bonn to assume more of the burden of NATO defense. The United States and the United Kingdom in particular have demanded that the Federal Republic commit itself to purchase goods and services from them to offset the costs of U.S. and British forces stationed in the country, which is the forward area of NATO defense. To some extent these offset arrangements are a charade; many of the purchases counted in the offset agreements would occur anyway. It would be difficult for Bonn, given its free-market national economic policies, either to deny or generate all the imports counted as offsets without changes in its economic policies that neither Bonn nor the Americans or British expect.

Given the strong international trading position of the West German economy, one might expect the FRG to be the most successful competitor in arms exports. But this would be to ignore the legal and political constraints that have slowed the development of the German arms industry, that still prohibit the development and production of certain weapons, and that exercise a real inhibition on Bonn's arms export policies. West Germany has not been an aggressive promoter of arms exports, and in fact it still exercises strong restraints on such exports— at least the strongest among the three European exporters.

The FRG may now be in a transition in its basic economic position in the world which portends a more uninhibited arms export policy. West Germany has been hit hard by the oil price increases of the last decade. While it is less dependent on imported fuels and feed stocks than is France, its less regulated economy is more directly vulnerable. Given the limited tools of state economic policy available to the Bonn government, the fact that time is on the side of more acceptance of the Federal Republic as an arms exporter, and the competitive position of the German economy generally, the prospects are that the FRG will become increasingly competitive with France, the United Kingdom, and indeed the United States as an arms supplier.

This speculation requires one major qualification. Among the three main European arms suppliers, the Federal Republic encounters the most internal opposition to arms exports. Were this opposition to grow much, it could influence the growth or even the maintenance of present levels of exports. This is not a wholly remote possiblity. The flaring of disarmament sentiments in Western Europe during late 1981 could reinforce it, although by this writing in late 1982, the two similar viewpoints do not seem to have come together to make any significant difference in long-term attitudinal trends.

The predilections of France, the United Kingdom, and the Federal Republic to export arms take on added significance when they are considered in terms of what may be an increased need to provide effective security assistance to friendly countries in the Third World, especially South Asia, the Persian Gulf region, and possibly Africa. Serious problems in providing effective security assistance may emerge from arms export competition in NATO.

First, the present situation is not economical for recipients, many of whom have very scarce resources (e.g., Pakistan); it is possible a larger production run of a particular weapon system (rather than individual efforts by several countries to offer similar systems produced on necessarily short runs) would lower the cost of security assistance for all friendly nations. Second, recipients who purchase weapons from a variety of European and U.S. sources will end up with a logistician's nightmare: incompatible hardware and costly space requirements. Third, competition may lead suppliers—France is the most conspicuous example at present—to give little consideration to political factors in selling arms. Stability or regional security goals may thus be confounded as sales from the West to a region (and perhaps to active enemies) reflect lack of coordination and strategy. A lack of coordination of arms sales policies by NATO members can result in a worsening of relations between states in a particular region, each of whom may have interests that are friendly both to the United States and to NATO.

Multiple sources of supply, when combined with delayed delivery schedules characteristic of high-demand items, can complicate a supplier's efforts at control and restraint. Moreover, a decision made by the United States might be cast in a new light by the recipient government's purchase of a complementary weapons system from a competitive supplier before the U.S. delivery actually takes place. The new purchase may completely alter the rationale for the U.S. sale. The potential problem of competitive arms transfers by NATO nations to the Third World is exacerbated by the significant time lapse between initial negotiation of an arms transfer deal and the production and delivery of arms and services. The value of the pipeline of undelivered but scheduled U.S. arms and services is more than $65 billion and is growing at an estimated $1 billion per month. This large pipeline in a competitive supplier environment is a serious challenge to planned security assistance for friendly Third World nations. Finally, with the exception of a few weapons such as the F-16, little attention has been devoted to the relationship between a successful RSI project and the procurement trends of Third World nations.

While the foregoing analysis suggests that any effort at multilateral restraint in arms transfers to the Third World, such as the restraint policy pursued by the Carter administration, is unlikely to be successful while the strong pressures on European suppliers to export prevail, there may be some limited potential for more coordination of security assistance among arms-supplying governments. More specifically, a program of coordinated security assistance might support RSI efforts in NATO, perhaps in the context of the family of weapons/lead nation specialization concept. It may indeed be possible to add an effective transatlantic component to the efforts presently under way in the IEPG and the European Community, in order to rationalize security assistance to the Third World through offset arrangements and market sharing. Unfortunately, "buy American" attitudes in the Congress have placed the U.S. government in a weak position to secure commitments from European suppliers on this type of proposal. Efforts to counteract these attitudes and promote an "alliance-wide defense industrial system," as proposed by Senators Roth, Glenn and Nunn must gain additional support in the Congress and in the executive branch if there is to be any hope of coordinating security assistance among Western Suppliers.

NOTES

1 United States, Senate, Committee on Forengin Relations, *Prospects for Multilateral Arms Export Restraint,* staff report prepared for the use of the Committee on Foreign Relations (April 1979), p. 29.

2 For example, see: United Kingdom, House of Commons, *Seventh Report from the Expenditure Committee, Session 1975-76: Guided Weapons* (July 22, 1976).

3 See, for example, Andrew Pierre, *The Global Politics of Arms Sales* (Princeton, N.J.: Princeton University Press, 1982), p. 298.

4 See *Aviation Week and Space Technology* (special issue on NATO weapon collaboration, July 3, 1978). This point is also supported in data collected during the course of a major inquiry conducted by the Institute for Defense Analyses. See Herschel Kanter and John Fry, "Why NATO Doesn't Standardize Arms," *Astronautics and Aeronautics* 19, 5 (June 1981), pp. 34-40.

5 For example, see: United States Department of Defense, *Rationalization/Standardization Within NATO: A Report to the United States Congress* by Harold Brown, Secretary of Defense, January 31, 1979; and U.S. Department of Defense, *Written Statement on NATO-Improved Armaments Cooperation* by the Honorable William J.

Perry, Under Secretary of Defense for Research and Engineering to the Research and Development Subcommittee of the Committee on Armed Services of the U.S. Senate, April 4, 1979.

6 Speech before the Senate, July 2, 1976.

7 On some of the economic aspects of this problem, see Thomas A. Callaghan, Jr., *U.S./ European Cooperation in Military and Civil Technology: An Issues-Oriented Report* (prepared for the Department of State by EX-IM Tech, Inc.), August 1974.

8 See Eliot Cohen, "NATO Standardization: The Perils of Common Sense," *Foreign Policy* 31 (Ssmmer 1978), pp. 72-90. See also United States General Accounting Office, *No Easy Choice: NATO Collaboration and the U.S. Arms Export Control Issue*, Report No. ID-81-18, January 19, 1981; and Herschel Kanter and John Fry, *Cooperation in Development and Production of NATO Weapons: An Evaluation of Tactical Missile Programs* (Arlington, Va: Institute for Defense Analysis, 1980), and Martin Edmonds, ed., *International Arms Procurement: New Directions*, (New York; Pergamon Press, 1981).

9 See *The Eurogroup* (Brussels: Van Muyscwinkel/The Eurogroup; issued by the NATO Information Service, 1979).

10 See D. C. R. Heyhoe, "*The Alliance and Europe: Part VI, The European Programme Group*," Adelphi Papers No. 129 (London: International Institute for Strategic Studies, 1977).

11 See Egon Klepsch, *Future Arms Procurement: USA-Europe Arms Procurement (The Klepsch Report)* (New York: Crane Russak, 1979).

12 For the full text of the communique, see *NATO Letter* (December 1968), pp. 18-19.

13 Wilfrid L. Kohl, *French Nuclear Diplomacy* (Princeton, NJ.: Princeton University Press, 1971), p. 264.

14 *Le Monde* (December 7, 1968).

15 Ibid. (December 5, 1968).

16 Ibid. Ailleret presented his "tous azimuths" strategy in an article in the December 1967 issue of *Revue de Defensc Nationale*. It was subsequently confirmed in a speech by De Gaulle in January at L'Ecole Militaire (see *L'Aurore*, January 30, 1968) and in an interview with Pierre Messmer published in *La Nation* (February 23-24, 1968), p. 1.

17 *The Times*, (London) (December 17, 1969).

18 Ibid. (November 22, 1973); *New York Times* (November 22, 1973); and *Le Monde* (April 22, 1974).

19 *The Times* (London), (January 26, 1974); and *The Economist* (February 23, 1974).

20 For an effective analysis and description of this interdepartmental and interministerial coordination, as well as of the relationships among ministers and between them and the Prime Minister and President, see Jack Hayward, *The One and Indivisible French Republic* (New York: W. W. Norton, 1973), pp. 85-99.

21 *Le Monde* (July 2, 1971).

22 Ibid. (April 29, 1974).

23 Ibid. (January 22, 1974).

24 *New York Times* (May 1, 1974).

25 *Le Monde* (March 27, 1975), pp. 8-10.

26 *Quotidien de Paris* (May 22, 1975); *La Croix* (May 22 and 23, 1975); and *Le Monde* (May 23, 1975).

27 See *The Economist* (January 10, 1976), p. 27; and *Le Monde* (January 9, 1976), p. 3.

28 *Le Monde* (September 30, 1975), p. 9; and *New York Times* (September 30, 1975), p. 9.

29 For the text of this letter, see Paul Stehlin, *La France Desarmee* (Paris: Calmann-Levy, 1974), pp. 159-181.

30 *Le Monde* (June 8, 1975), p. 8, and *Le Monde* (June 24, 1975), p. 20.

31 Lewis A. Frank, *The Arms Trade in International Relations* (New York: Praeger, 1969), p. 57.
32 A careful analysis of this growth in French arms exports is provided by Edward A. Kolodziej, "Determinants of French Arms Sales: Security Implications," in *Threats, Weapons and Foreign Policy Behavior: Volume 5, Sage International Yearbook of Foreign Policy Studies*, edited by Patrick J. McGowan and Charles W. Kegley, Jr. (Beverly Hills, Calif.: Sage, 1980). This effort is complemented by his article on data problems relating to French arms transfers, see Edward A. Kolodziej, "Measuring French Arms Transfers: A Problem of Sources and Some Sources of Problems with ACDA Data," *Journal of Conflict Resolution* 23, 2 (June 1979), pp. 195-227.
33 See Michel Debre, *Livre Blanc sur la Défense Nationale*, Volume 1 (Paris, June 1972), pp. 54-56.
34 *Financial Times* (June 10, 1975).
35 French Embassy (New York), Press and Information Division, PP/77/12, "France's Position on the Sale of Arms."
36 The impact of the 1973 OPEC oil embargo and price increase is persuasively described in Kolodziej, "Determinants of French Arms Sales," pp. 138-162.
37 *Diplomatic World* (November 6, 1978), p. 6. See also *New York Times* (November 9, 1977), p. A.7.
38 Kolodziej, "Determinants of French Arms Sales," p. 146.
39 *Aviation Week and Space Technology* (April 25, 1977), pp. 74-80.
40 *Le Monde* (June 3, 1975).
41 See *Le Monde* (September 29, 1976, and November 9, 1976).
42 *Le Monde* (November 25, 1977). See also Chapter 6 and *Aviation Week and Space Technology* (June 6, 1977).
43 *Le Monde* (March 20, 1976).
44 Jean Klein, "France and the Arms Trade," in *The Gun Merchants: Politics and Policies of the Major Arms Suppliers.* edited by Cindy Cannizzo (New York: Pergamon Press, 1980), p. 144.
45 Kolodziej, "Determinants of French Arms Sales." On the continued importance of arms exports to maintaining the defense and aerospace industries, see *Le Monde* (November 22, 1975); and *Aviation Week and Space Technology* (March 21, 1977, pp. 47-50, and June 6, 1977, p. 46).
46 France, Assemblee Nationale, Commission des Finances, *Rapport sur le projet de loi de finances pour 1977*; *Defense: Depenses en Capital*, No. 2525 (1976).
47 See Beau Morris, "Why France's Arms Exports Make It a Paper Tiger," *Armed Forces Journal International* (October 1978), pp. 19-23.
48 *Air International* (October 1979), p. 158.
49 Klein, "France and the Arms Trade," pp. 129, 134, 145-146. See also Georges Pompidou, letter to Bishop, March 8, 1973, reprinted in *Entretiens et Discours (1968-1974)* (Paris: Plon, 1975).
50 See, for example, Francois-Henri de Virieu and Paul Thibau, "La Mort 'Made in France'!" *Le Nouvel Observateur*, No. 551 (June 2, 1975), pp. 21-23; and Jacqueline Grapin, "Les effets pervers de l'exportation des armes," *Le Monde*, (November 9, 1976), pp. 19-20. See also chapters 1 and 2 of *La France Militarisee* by Olivier Brachet, Christian Pons, and Michel Tachon (Paris: Les Editions du Cerf, 1974) and *Que penser du commerce des armes?* (Paris: Cadres Chretiens, Responsables No. 85, 1977).
51 See *Le Monde* (January 14, 1976, p. 12, and January 15, 1976, p. 7).
52 Ibid. (December 15, 1977).
53 Ibid. (July 11, 1981).
54 *Financial Times* (June 6, 1966).

55 Sir Bernard Burrows and Christopher Irwin, *The Security of Western Europe: Towards A Common Defence Policy* (London: Charles Knight, 1972), p. 52.
56 *The Eurogroup* (Brussels: NATO Information Service, 1972), pp. 24-25.
57 See reports of speeches by Chancellor of the Exchequer Jenkins (*Guardian*, January 30, 1969) and Foreign Secretary Stewart (*The Times*, February 7, 1969 and *International Herald Tribune*, February 17, 1969).
58 Michael J. Brenner, "Strategic Interdependence and the Politics of Inertia: Paradoxes of European Defense Cooperation," *World Politics* 23, 4 (July 1971), pp. 660-661.
59 A. H. C. Greenwood, "MRCA—The Future System of Military Procurement," *RUSI* 117, 3 (September 1972), p. 8.
60 *Survey of British and Commonwealth Affairs*, February 3, 1967, p. 134; and Cmnd. 3701, *Supplementary Statement on Defense Policy: 1968*, p. 11.
61 Cmnd. 2901, *Statement on the Defense Estimates: 1966, Part I, The Defence Review*, pp. 11-12; and *The Times* (London) (February 23, 1966), p. 7.
62 Cmnd. 3927, *Statement on the Defence Estimates: 1969*, p. 44.
63 See Defence Minister Healey's speech to the American Chamber of Commerce lunch, April 16, 1969 (London Press Service, Verbatim Service 101/69).
64 Cmnd. 4521, *Supplementary Statement on Defence Policy: 1970*, p. 4.
65 Cmnd. 4592, *Statement on the Defence Estimates: 1971*, pp. 64-69.
66 Cmnd. 5891, *Statement on the Defence Estimates: 1972*, p. 3.
67 *The Guardian* (January 8, 1974).
68 Lord Carrington, "British Defence Policy," *RUSI* 118, 3 (September 1973), p. 10.
69 Richard Neff, "Europe Joins on Defense," *European Community* 146 (June 1971), pp. 14-16.
70 British Information Services, *Fact Sheets on Britain: Defence* (July 1972), p. 3.
71 See Lord Carrington, "The Eurogroup," *NATO Review* 20, 1-2 (January/February 1972), pp. 10-11.
72 Eurogroup, "Eurogroup and European Defence," EG/75/74, p. 3 (mimeographed). See also NATO information Service, "The Eurogroup," *Atlantic Community Quarterly* 14, 1 (Spring 1976), p. 85.
73 Cmnd. 5231, *Statement on the Defence Estimates: 1973*, pp. 3 and 37-38.
74 Interview with Colonel C. R. J. Pitcairn, British army delegate to those meetings May 5, 1975. See also *Daily Express* (London) (March 28, 1973).
75 Cmnd. 4521, *Supplementary Statement on Defence Policy: 1970*, p. 8.
76 Cmnd. 4891, *Statement on the Defence Estimates: 1972*, p. 41.
77 Parliamentary Debates, Volume 870, March 21, 1974, Cols. 153 and 154.
78 James Callaghan, "Britain and NATO," *NATO Review* 22, 4 (August 1974), p. 14.
79 Cmnd. 5976, *Statement on the Defence Estimates: 1975*.
80 Ibid., p. 7. See also pp. 1-6.
81 *The Times* (London) (July 4, 1974).
82 Cmnd. 5976, p. 29; see also pp. 28-30 and 53-54.
83 Roy Mason, "The Eurogroup in 1975," *NATO Review* 23, 2 (April 1975), p. 8.
84 See Assembly of Western European Union, Document 646, *European Union and W.E.U.* (December 1974); *Daily Telegraph* (October 16, 1974); and Assembly of Western European Union Recommendation No. 20 on European Union and the W.E.U., May 1975. See also: *The Times* (London) (March 18, 1975), p. 4 (article by Julian Critchley, Chairman of the Defence and Armaments Committee of the WEU Assembly).
85 Cmnd. 5976, p. 20.
86 Ibid., p. 29.
87 Ibid., pp. 42-43 and 48-49.
88 *The Economist*, March 13, 1976, pp. 55-56.

89 Cmnd. 7099.

90 Lawrence Freedman, *Arms Production in the United Kingdom*: Problems and Prospects (London: The Royal Institute of International Affairs, 1978), p. 23.

91 See, for example, Julian Critchley, "A community Policy for Armaments," *NATO Review* 27, 1 (February 1979), pp. 10-14.

92 United Kingdom, Ministry of Defence, *Defence Estimates*. For a detailed presentation on this, see Freedman, *Arms Production in the United Kingdom*, pp. 28-38.

93 Frank, *Arms Trade in International Relations*, p. 81.

94 Anthony Sampson, *The Arms Bazaar* (London: Hodder and Stoughton, 1977), pp. 157-163.

95 For Example, see Martin Edmonds, "The Domestic and International Dimensions of British Arms Sales, 1966-1978," in Cannizzo, *The Gun Merchants*, pp. 68-100.

96 *New York Times*, (November 6, 1977, p. 19; November 7, 1978, p. 9; November 24, 1978, p. A3); and interviews with British defense officials and MPs in January 1979.

97 *Daily Express* (London) (April 14, 1975); *The Times* (London) (April 18, 1975); and *Daily Telegraph* (London) (November 16, 1976).

98 *The Times* (London) (May 23, 1975), p. 1.

99 U.K., House of Commons, *Guided Weapons*, pp. 207-209.

100 *Le Monde* (June 23, 1976), p. 12.

101 See *The Times* (London) (February 9, 1977, and April 12, 1977); and *Financial Times* (July 26, 1978).

102 United Kingdom, Foreign and Commonwealth Office, Arms Control and Disarmament Department, *British Arms Control and Disarmament Policy: A Short Guide* (London, January 1978), pp. 8-9.

103 U.K. House of Commons, *Guided Weapons*. See also *The Times* (London) (June 30, 1975); *Daily Express* (London) (July 14, 1975); *The Guardian* (Manchester) (May 21, 1977); and *Daily Telegraph* (London) (July 26, 1978).

104 CAAT publishes a periodic newsletter containing information on arms sales made and pending as well as registers of British corporations involved in the arms trade such as a pamphlet entitled *British Military Exporters*.

105 See, for example, *The Guardian* (June 16, 1976 and September 19, 1978).

106 See *Sunday Times* (London) (June 27, 1976), and *The Guardian* (May 7, 1978). See also Joseph Camilleri, *Britain and the Death Trade* (London: Housemans for Pax Christi, 1971).

107 This is discussed in some detail in Norman A. Graham and David J. Louscher, "The Political Control of Weapons System Acquisition: A Comparative Analysis of the Legislative Role in the United Kingdom and the United States," in McGowan and Kegley, *Threats, Weapons and Foreign Policy Behavior*.

108 For example, see *Sense About Defence: The Report of the Labour Party Defence Study Group* (London: Quartet Books, 1977).

109 David Elliott, *The Lucas Aerospace Workers' Campaign*, Young Fabian Pamphlet 46 (London: Fabian Society, 1977).

110 Freedman, *Arms Production in the United Kingdom*, p. 31.

111 As quoted in *Aviation Week and Space Technology* (September 15, 1980), p. 13. See also the June 8, 1981, issue, p. 93.

112 Federal Republic of Germany, Ministry of Defense, *White Paper 1979: The Security of the Federal Republic of Germany and the Development of the Federal Armed Forces* (Bonn, September 4, 1979), p. 19.

113 See Wolfram F. Hanrieder, "West German Foreign Policy, 1949-1979: Necessities and Choices," in *West German Foreign Policy: 1949-1979* (Boulder, Colo.: Westview Press, 1980), pp. 15-36. See also Catherine McArdle Kelleher, "Germany and NATO: The Enduring Bargain," pp. 43-60 in the same volume.

114 *White Paper 1979*, pp. 270 and 276-278.
115 Ibid., pp. 35-36.
116 The report and the resulting resolution by the European Parliament is contained in Klepsch, *The Klepsch Report*.
117 See Hans Rattinger, "West Germany's Arms Transfers to the Nonindustrial World," in *Arms Transfers to the Third World: The Military Buildup in Less Industrial Countries*, edited by Uri Ra'anan, Robert L. Pfaltzgraff, Jr., and Geoffrey Kemp (Boulder, Colo.: Westview Press, 1978), pp. 242-246. See also *White Paper 1979*, pp. 163-185.
118 United Nations, General Assembly, Tenth Special Session, *Summary Records*, May 26, 1978.
119 United States Arms Control and Disarmament Agency, *World Military Expenditure and Arms Transfers 1969-1978* (Washington, D.C.: USGPO, December 1980), p. 133.
120 See Helga Haftendorn, *Militarhilfe und Rustungsexporte der BRD* (Dusseldorf: Bertelsmann, 1971), Chapter 4.
121 Frank, *Arms Trade in International Relations*, p. 65.
122 For a detailed discussion and examples of some of these strategies for circumventing the restrictions, see Rattinger, "West Germany's Arms Transfers," pp. 248-251 and Ulrich Albrecht, Peter Lock, and Herbert Wulf, *Arbeitsplatze durch Rustung? Warmung vor falschen Hoffnungen* (Hamburg: Rowohlt Taschenbach, 1978), pp. 147-172.
123 For a description of the government's arms sales decisionmaking and control apparatus, see Mike Dillon, "Arms Transfers and the Federal Republic of Germany," in Cannizzo, *The Gun Merchants*, pp. 105-108.
124 *Frankfurter Rundschau* (October 18, 1980).
125 Eckehard Ehrenbert, *Rustungs-Export-Studio* (Bonn: University of Bonn, 1980).
126 *Frankfurter Rundschau* (October 18, 1980).
127 Dillon, "Arms Transfers and the Federal Republic of Germany," p. 123.
128 Albrecht, Lock, and Wulf, *Arbeitsplatze durch Rustung?* p. 46.
129 See *New York Times* (October 13, 1980), p. D1; and *World Business Weekly* (December 15, 1980), p. 13. See also *Aviation Week and Space Technology* (June 8, 1981), pp. 94-95.
130 *Die Zeit* (January 16, 1981).
131 *Frankfurter Allgemeine Zeitung fur Deutschland* (February 19, 1979).
132 *White Paper 1979*, p. 39.
133 Ibid., p. 32.

Chapter 8

Summary and Conclusion

Previous chapters have identified the aggregate contours and detailed the major elements of recent U.S. government experience with arms transfers. These contours outline a major instrument of foreign policy. The U.S. government has, over the last three decades, used arms transfers often—indeed, persistently—to achieve a considerable variety of foreign policy objectives. Even the Carter administration—which began its tenure with the President and many of his top advisors explicitly committed to limiting and reducing arms transfers—came to rely on arms transfers as a major instrument of its foreign policy.

Arms transfers are a valuable tool of foreign relations because of a great worldwide demand for arms. Most governments that do not produce modern arms want to buy them on some concessionary terms. This global demand for arms is in all likelihood quite durable. Worldwide, national policymakers in most countries acquire and maintain arms as a means of promoting national objectives. On the average (although with considerable regional and national variation), both developed and developing nations spend more than 5 percent of their gross national products on military equipment and manpower. Whether to enhance national security in the face of border disputes and other conflicts with foreign states, or to seek regime stability in the face of civil war, subversion, terrorism, or domestic unrest, governments continue to regard arms as indispensable. Their demand for arms in turn fuels regional arms races. In most cases that demand cannot be satisfied by indigenous production. Hence, the demand for arms transfers is massive; any policy that denies the pervasiveness, persistence, and deep political roots of this demand is illusory.

The pressure from several independent sources to sell arms is also strong and difficult to restrain. Aside from global and regional security objectives, the governments of supplier states are beset with a variety of serious economic, social, and national security pressures that predispose them to satisfy the global demand. Always present, the economic pressures were felt most keenly by Western supplier governments when the skyrocketing price of imported oil after 1973 had to be offset to relieve the economic consequences of severe balance-of-payment deficits. National employment pressures during a worldwide recession have motivated the governments of developed states to ensure the maintenance of economically healthy defense industries through export of arms. National defense costs also may be reduced by arms exports, through longer production runs of weapons systems that relieve fixed and capital costs and offset or reduce the burden of research and development expenditures.

The governments of France, the United Kingdom, and West Germany have endured more of these pressures to sell than has the United States, but as Chapter 3 indicated, the search for relief from balance-of-payment pressures was an important ingredient in the U.S. government's decision in the 1960s to expand foreign military sales and reduce the grant Military Assistance Program. Foreign exchange earnings remain a prominent motive for U.S. arms exports to the oil-rich countries of the Middle East, the region where the greatest proportion of arms have been delivered recently.

The forces that induce the supply, marketing, and demand for arms transfers are strong and multiple; but there are also discontinuities in the market, including variations from supplier to supplier in the prime motives that drive arms transfers. Formerly an arms supplier for political reasons, the Soviet Union increasingly holds a commercial interest in its arms transfers, seeking precious foreign exchange earnings, preferably in hard Western currencies. France—and, to a lesser degree, the United Kingdom—is unashamedly commercial in its pursuit of arms transfer clients. Israel and, recently, Brazil and other new or small suppliers are quite clearly driven by commercial imperatives. For these three larger suppliers, and for the lesser ones as well, arms transfers are increasing. In the separate case of the United States, the trends are less clear-cut, the motivations for arms transfers are complex, and, despite the relative size of the U.S. effort, the reluctance to sell is greatest.

As Chapter 5 demonstrated, the popular perception that U.S arms transfers have grown dramatically in the last decade is simply false. The United States remains the largest supplier of defense equipment and services, but when actual deliveries (as opposed to agreements) of weapons systems, equipment, and services are measured in constant dollars, it is clear that there has been little real growth in U.S. arms transfers. Furthermore, substantial portions of U.S. arms exports were directly related to three key periods in post-World War II U.S. foreign policy. In these periods, arms transfers were used to support vital U.S. national interests that were perceived to be threatened. As Figure 5.23 portrays, during the 1950s the majority of U.S. arms exports were to Western European nations in accordance with rearmament plans to meet the Soviet threat. From the late 1960s to early 1970s, U.S. interests in Southeast Asia accounted for a substantial portion of U.S. arms exports. Indeed, in 1973 more that 63 percent of all U.S. arms exports were to Southeast Asia. More recently, transfers to other regions have declined substantially in favor of a focus on the Middle East, which involves a set of complex and sometimes contradictory economic, political, and security factors. Taking account of the pressures induced by America's world role in the post-World War II era, the United States has been a substantial, albeit reluctant, supplier of defense equipment and services.

An elaborate decisionmaking machinery and approval process now involves both the Congress and the Executive Branch actively in and approving arms transfer agreements. This clearance system represents the culmination of more than thirty years of official reluctance to transfer arms. Congressional reluctance is long-standing and conspicuous. The main congressional opponents to arms transfers have made a formal record of their opposition in legislation and legislative deliberations. The Carter administration also made its opposition a matter of record, but Executive Branch reluctance is scarcely limited to the Carter administration, or to presidential administrations as distinct from elements of the permanent government. Other recent administrations, specific agencies, and even specific offices in the military services have all shown reluctance to transfer some specific arms or weapons technologies, or have opposed transfers to certain recipients. A comparison of the Reagan and Carter administrations illustrates the difficulty of accurately characterizing U.S. policy stances, given their complexity. These two consecutive presidential administrations appear at first glance to be as different as night and day on the issue of conventional arms transfers. Yet the approval process and requirements instituted by Carter and inherited by Reagan remain largely intact, and the Reagan administration has demonstrated its recognition of the inherent limitations on its ability to expand arms transfers dramatically, as well as the dangers and dilemmas that will accompany their increased use as an instrument of U.S. foreign policy. The Falkland Island incident, a recent conflict between an industrial supplier and a Third World recipient, will probably generate greater reluctance—particularly among the military services of the United States and the major Western European suppliers—to disperse high-technology weapons systems.

DILEMMAS OF ARMS TRANSFERS AS AN INSTRUMENT OF U.S. FOREIGN POLICY

As demonstrated in Chapter 2, successive administrations since 1940 have overcome their reluctance about arms transfers because they found them to be a valuable foreign policy instrument for use in a wide variety of circumstances. During the early Cold War years, arms transfers were important to the building of NATO, and later, to the multilateral alliances in the Middle East and Asia that the United States promoted. More recently, in an era when key instruments of statecraft, such as bilateral and multilateral alliances, have waned, U.S. officials have relied on arms transfers as a substitute for alliance commitments. The reasons for this reliance are obvious. First, arms transfers are deemed (not always correctly) as crucial instruments of influence. They are often used to support diplomatic efforts, to influence the political orientation of foreign elite policymakers, or to exert political or diplomatic leverage. Perhaps the most conspicuous use of arms transfers has been as a substitute for stationing U.S. troops on foreign soil to demonstrate a U.S. commitment to the security of friendly states.

Second, arms transfers are used to help strengthen friends and allies by improving a state's external and internal security. Arms transfers to NATO countries have been used to promote standardization of weapons systems in the alliance in order to strengthen NATO as a whole and thus provide more effective mutual defense.

Third, U.S. policymakers have often believed that arms transfers were essential for promoting or maintaining a regional balance of power. In addition to the example of NATO, U.S. policy toward the Middle East has clearly been guided by this perception, and transfers to South and Southeast Asia have often reflected it.

I liked don't examples

Fourth, conventional arms transfers aim to limit the proliferation of nuclear weapons. Policymakers have frequently thought that the offer of sophisticated conventional equipment was a means of dissuading certain recipients, such as Pakistan, from acquiring nuclear capabilities.

Finally, beginning with the Truman administration, successive administrations have used arms transfers as an instrument in the global competition with the Soviet Union. From direct efforts to contain the expansion of Soviet dominance over other states to more subtle efforts to compete for influence in the Third World, U.S. policymakers have relied (sometimes unsuccessfully) on arms transfers and the attendant support and training ties to limit Soviet influence and strengthen pro-Western sentiment.

While U.S. decisionmakers have often felt compelled to use arms transfers for the reasons listed above, many also have recognized the dangers. Over the past thirty years, significant opposition has emanated from the Congress, within the Executive Branch, and from a limited but articulate and attentive foreign policy public, which has sensitized the U.S. political process to the dangers of the increased uses of arms transfers.

As is argued, influence gained through arms transfers can be ephemeral; it is difficult if not impossible to measure and can disappear quickly. Additionally, even when the objective conditions for U.S. leverage and influence have been present, U.S policymakers have not always been effective in utilizing them. On the contrary, they have often been manipulated and misled by recipient governments that have been more intent on acquiring American arms than on conferring influence over their affairs, raising serious concerns about who is influencing whom. The U.S. government has found it increasingly difficult to exert substantial leverage on arms transfer recipients in today's competitive supplier environment. Policymakers have complained to the authors that in areas where the United States has attempted a serious policy of restraint—namely, in Latin America and Africa—France, the United Kingdom, or the Soviet Union has been too willing and too able to meet the local demands for arms.

Similarly, supplying arms may not even enhance military capabilities, narrowly defined. There is an awareness within the government that the mere delivery of U.S. equipment does not guarantee that a recipient's military capability will be strengthened. Inadequate manpower, poor training, poor morale, inadequate equipment maintenance, inappropriate strategies and tactics, corruption, and regime instability are among the main factors that can diminish the contribution of security assistance to a recipient's national security.

Even the most ardent proponents of the uses of arms transfers for broad geopolitical reasons—to strengthen recipient governments to contain Soviet influence and limit Soviet expansion, or to sustain the recipient against some other external threat—have acknowledged that the containment effect of a given arms transfer is difficult to measure and may even be negative. Arms transfers often reduce the pressure on a regime to eliminate the underlying conditions that weaken it; the existence of an arms transfer program may establish a dependence on the supplier that adds to the recipient's internal political woes and sustains its administrative maladies. As with economic aid, military assistance may indeed strengthen a recipient government, but it also may have quite the opposite effect.

As has been also realized by each administration since World War II, promoting or maintaining regional power balances through arms transfers is a tricky task. What constitutes "balance" is never altogether clear. It has often been recognized by the implementers of arms transfer programs as well as by critical observers that arms transfers may in fact prove to be a stimulus for a regional arms race, rather than a deterrent.

Finally, while arms transfers may relieve the nuclear ambitions of certain regimes, the connection between the two is by no means direct or readily predictable. The purpose for which national policymakers strive to acquire nuclear weapons may be substantially unrelated to the security problem for which conventional arms are acquired. Given the prominence of national prestige motivations, the purpose may not be security-related at all.

DILEMMAS OF ARMS-TRANSFER RESTRAINT

Efforts to restrain global arms transfers, unilateral or multilateral, have thus far failed to live up to their promise. The Carter administration's attempt to set an example through unilateral restraint was naively conceived. Multilateral restraint never materialized; discussions with Western European governments produced no agreement, and the CATT negotiations with the Soviet Union collapsed. The complexity of interests and views on arms transfers held within the U.S. government was impossible to translate into a consistent and useful position that could form the basis for negotiations with the Soviet Union. Negotiations on arms export restraint with Western European suppliers have not progressed. The immediate economic and political effects of restraint would be too costly for them. As Chapter 7 demonstrates, sentiment for arms transfer restraint is at present limited in France and in the United Kingdom, and it appears to have weakened recently in West Germany. When one weighs these attitudes against the strong and growing economic pressures in each of these countries in favor of extensive arms sales, the future prospects for multilateral restraint appear dim indeed.

In earlier chapters we presented some options available to the U.S. government as it attempts to deal with the dilemmas related to the increased use of arms transfers. It must be stated categorically that the worldwide dispersal of high-technology weaponry is a very complex phenomenon that presents numerous and continuing policy issues and choices for government. Yet, little progress will be made in dealing with arms transfer issues if critics misstate their dimensions or conceive of the problems involved in formulating policy as simple. Many of the solutions presented thus far by popular critics of U.S. arms transfer activities have been either naive or pedestrian, more a product of sentiment and preference rather than one reflecting analysis guided by a careful regard for the motivations of suppliers and particularly recipients, and for the real marketplace choices.

Since the early 1970s, prevailing sentiments have been to make the United States an even more reluctant supplier. This has been expressed in numerous legislative proposals and enacted laws. Popular and learned journals have also featured proposals designed to limit arms transfers. Almost without exception, this literature has failed to acknowledge the serious purposes of suppliers, the strength of the demand from recipients, and the Hobson's choices faced by both groups. European and American critics seek to eliminate one of the few instruments of foreign policy that remain available to their governments. At the same time, they deny the demands of recipient governments seeking the traditional means of acquiring power and independence.

In our introduction, we identified and discussed the need for more accurate explanations of arms transfers as they fit within the overall framework of U.S. foreign and national security policy. The list of standard misperceptions about arms transfer activities is long. The remainder of the book presented a more accurate picture of U.S. arms transfer activities than has usually been displayed.

The main source of error has been to examine arms transfer trends in terms of the current-dollar valuation of arms sales agreements reached between the United States and a recipient. As we have demonstrated, such data are misleading. In particular, arms transfers consitute more than sales, cannot be correctly assessed in terms of current dollars, and represent something other than agreements. Analysis and recommendations based on such measures exaggerate trends, and generate a sense of urgency that impels the search for once-and-for-all solutions. To be plausible, such analyses and recommendations divorce arms transfer activity from the foreign policy that it must serve and that the U.S. government practices in its relation wtih other governments. It is no wonder that recommendations by scholars and analysts outside of government concerning the future of arms transfers have had so little impact: they are alien to the needs and experiences of foreign policy practitioners.

Proponents of arms transfer proposals often talk past each other because they are guided by a systematic difference in values. In his excellent book, *The Arms Debate*, Robert A. Levine discusses the nuclear debate of the late 1950s in terms that are highly relevant to the present discussion of arms transfers.[1] Accordingly to Levine, every policy argument consists of value judgments or statements of preference, analyses, and recommendations. Policy arguments involve an effort to connect values and analyses coherently to provide recommendations for the future. But as Levine indicates, these connections are made in two different ways: by optimizing or by maximizing.

> Optimizing systems of choice attempt to resolve conflicts among competing values by weighing the relative subjective importance of the values, measuring analytically the relative objective probabilities of their fulfillment by different policies and then arriving at a policy recommendation which provides a "best" combination of value fulfillments. Maximizing systems concentrate on a few non-competing values and, without having to resolve any conflicts, choose policies which are best in relation to these values.[2]

The centrality of arms transfers to U.S. foreign policy since World War II, the many uses of arms transfers, and the limited number of alternative foreign policy instruments available constantly confront policymakers with conflicts among values. Uncertain estimates of the probabilities of success of different policies, and decisions that reflect the constraints of the domestic and international environments in which policy is made further complicate the decisionmaking process, permitting decisions to be made that most often reflect optimizing or suboptimizing choices. However, there is an inclination toward value-maximizing among those wishing wholesale reform in the arms transfer decision process or extensive limitation of the use of arms transfers. Not surprisingly, these recommendations exist largely outside the practioners' domain and have received little or no attention within the policymaking community. Indeed, one can claim that even the Carter arms transfer restraint experiment—initially based on maximizing premises—lasted a scant four weeks following its May 19, 1977, annoucement—until President Carter sent Congress the notification of his administration's decision to sell the AWACS to Iran.

Future arms transfer restraint as a foreign policy strategy for the U.S. government is unlikely given the lack of substitutible foreign policy instruments, the availability of substitute suppliers, and the "demand-pull" aspect of the arms transfer phenomenon. We do not have a practical option—at least not in this world—of stopping arms transfers by saying "no" ourselves. Advocates of extensive curtailment do not have to be reminded that the problem is more basic than the argument that "if we don't sell, others will." There are also positive stakes. If we wish to be a major power, we must exchange in the commodities desired by friends and allies to address their perceived security needs (as well as our own), or we must seek alternative instruments to do so. Arms transfers often substitute for U.S. intervention, for U.S. overseas bases, for a greater U.S. military presence throughout the world, and for U.S. government bilateral security guarantees and treaties. Compared with these alternatives, arms transfers are the "Hobson's preference." (Of course, some critics of arms transfers intend to limit or eliminate this whole class of foreign policy activities.)

The U.S. government cannot expect to be able to influence events in other countries and regions without cultivating the power to do so. In the course of cultivating that power, it can make mistakes or lose the capacity to influence others; but it can also generate and sustain the capacity to influence and exercise that capacity constructively. Arms transfers have often been oversold as a source of assured influence for the supplier, although the risks faced by suppliers are rarely strong enough to assure that they will do what is necessary to protect their interests. At best, arms transfers increase the probabilities that the influence that favors our interests will be generated.

In the course of implementing arms transfer programs, leverage can be lost or reversed. What started out as a U.S. option became a commitment, while the recipient government preserves its options. Without close attention to the pursuit of U.S. objectives in the implementaion of arms transfer programs, the direction of U.S. policy is likely to become confused; and, even if it remains relatively clear, the capacity to pursue it can be lost or much diminished. Friendly influence is an exchange process, the balance of which cannot be taken for granted.

There is not doubt that the U.S. government has too often taken for granted that, once an arms transfer program was in place, its objectives would be realized. Yet the reaction against the use of arms transfers to acquire influence has generated at least as many problems as it has avoided. Arms transfers continue. As a practical matter, we may be able to shape them, but we are unlikely to end them for some time. Much of the effort by opponents of arms transfers throughout the 1970s was in the direction of limiting U.S. capabilities, and therefore U.S. options and U.S. potential to maintain influence over recipient governments. Given the fact that arms transfers are going to continue, the main question should be how to assure (as much as possible) that they will serve the ends of U.S. policy. The remainder of this chapter will summarize what we have said that answers this—the main question about arms transfer policy.

First, refusing to sell or otherwise provide arms is unlikely by itself to gain us much leverage with potential recipients. Unless our terms are highly concessionary, the recipient, as has often been demonstrated, will go elsewhere to satisfy his needs. We may of course refuse to sell for other reasons, such as disinterest in the customer, doubt that the equipment or services he seeks would be much help to him or us, concerns about the reactions of other states in the recipient's region whose interests are important to us, or for a variety of other reasons, including legal restrictions (such as those discussed in Chapter 4).

Second, the recipient government will have an intense interest in assuring that our influence does not get in his way. If any government ever suffers from a surfeit of choices, it is not a government that must acquire from a major power. Recipient governments have good reason to take our arms and try to minimize our influence. Hence, the implementation of U.S. arms transfer programs should seek to maintain U.S. options and leverage against a presumed effort by the recipient to reduce both.

The United States needs to adopt policies that reflect the limits of its influence, that cultivate its influence, and that prevent recipients from taking the initiative away from the U.S. These are not easy things to do. Arms do not by themselves provide influence. Recipient governments have demonstrated remarkable capabilities to insulate themselves from the influence that our involvement with them would seem to provide. Further, the permeability of the U.S. government makes it easy at times for recipient governments to practice effective reverse influence. As already noted, in the process of gaining clearance with the U.S. government for an arms transfer program, such as the AWACS to Saudi Arabia, and in the annual grant military appropriation requests, these programs are often oversold. This overselling is a further source of potentially weakened leverage over the recipient.

Third, the relationship among the major Western suppliers is complex and competitive; a cartel is a practical impossibility and limited cooperation is at present only a hope. As we have demonstrated in Chapters 2, 6, and 7, the competition for economic and political influence among the suppliers is intense, a situation that requires more elaborate proposals for generating cooperation than those presented by the reformers.

The problem of generating a cooperative arms transfer policy among suppliers is illustrated by the dilemmas confronted by the United States following the Argentine defeat in the Falkland Island conflict. During the conflict, Great Britain's greatest casualties were the result of French weapons (even French-British jointly designed weapons) evidently loaded onto Argentine warplanes in the presence of French technicians—weapons sold primarily for economic reasons. Moreover, the Argentines may have been emboldened to create the conflict as a result of heavy arms deliveries from France, an ally of Great Britain. An ally of all these nations, the United States for over twenty years attempted to limit its transfers to Argentina as well as to other Latin American countries.

The strains of the Falklands crisis, the considerable damage inflicted on the British navy, the potential weakening of the British contribution to NATO and the resultant economic strains on the United States as it addresses this European problem, and the political differences that erupted between Britain and France seem to argue for more cooperation among Western suppliers. But much cooperation is unlikely. The Reagan administration confronts the prospect that the Argentines may turn to the Soviet Union for arms if they cannot be acquired from the West in the quantities desired. This may enhance Soviet influence in the region. It is questionable, given the climate of present U.S.-Argentine relations, that the Argentines would seek to purchase arms from the United States. As a consequence, the U.S. government may be compelled to support, or even help finance, major arms purchases by Argentina from France.

Fourth, much fault can be found with arms transfers as an instrument of U.S. foreign policy, but that does not justify abandoning the instrument. The default position is irresponsible. The transfer of the weapons of war as an instrument of foreign policy is a sometimes dangerous business with ambiguous effects. It is unquestionably in need of constant evaluation and assessment. And, as imperfect as they are, however, arms transfers are still a practical, available and potentially effective foreign policy instrument. Critics have not yet proposed new or effective lower-cost, lower-risk substitutes.

Fifth, the public debate over arms transfers has exhibited a misplaced focus on the seeming growth of the volume of arms transfers represented by sales agreements, and not on the more appropriate measure—total actual military exports or deliveries. Agreements to sell or buy arms reflect the more symbolic or diplomatic attributes of policies, much as any international agreement does. As we demonstrate in Chapter 5, U.S.

arms export deliveries have been fewer, and the rate of increase slower, than the critics contend. More than a substantial portion was directed to the protection and promotion of vital U.S. interests in Europe, Vietnam, and the Middle East as these interests were perceived threatened during separate periods by no less than five different administrations over the last three decades. Furthermore, the level of Third World indebtedness, and the diminishing availability of credit for arms purchases, will serve as an additional brake on increases in U.S. arms exports.

Finally, the central point for U.S. foreign policy is how much effort we put toward participating in and influencing international affairs. Of course, we can have some effect on the quantity of arms sold, and on what kinds of arms are sold. We can see to it that American arms are *not* sold. If we believe that all arms are equally bad, that it is morally degrading for us to be involved in arms transfers—or at least that our involvement will accomplish no useful purpose—then the case is clear enough for us not to sell arms. In the end, the issue is one of confidence in government. The authors believe that although the U.S. arms transfer policy has seldom been optimal, it has usually been responsible. The Executive Branch and Congress have devoted extensive attention to correcting errors and improving performance. We do not believe that other suppliers could do better or would have the inclination to do so.

Arms transfers are an imperfect instrument for achieving foreign policy objectives. Now that it is quite clear that we are going to live with this instrument, it behooves the U.S. government and its critics to improve the way that instrument works. Most recently, the U.S. government has attempted two improvement strategies. The first, promoted by the Carter administration and Congress, has employed negative means, for example, control over the activities of U.S. military advisors in recipient countries to the point of eliminating their capacity to do much of anything. This has removed an important and direct level of contact with recipients whose requests for arms we should seek to influence. There have been many past failures of the U.S. military advisory system. Nonetheless, field personnel were the element of the U.S. government's security assistance apparatus that could, as one State Department official told us, "make sure their [the recipient's] army had boots and transport before they asked us for Vulcan guns." Force planning with recipients, oriented toward managing their requests for the equipment and services that we want them to have, is one important function a reconstructed military advisory system could perform. The second strategy, control of the process of program review and approval, was initiated by the Carter administraion and continues, more or less intact, under President Reagan. The successes of this strategy have been obvious, and have included more systematic and regular reviews of arms transfers requests, more inputs to arms transfer decisions, and more concerned actors within the Executive Branch involved in the decision-making process. While these factors do not in themselves guarantee that the quality of U.S. arms transfers policy will be improved—that is, the means will be made more appropriate to the objectives we seek, at acceptable cost—they have produced a policy environment where this is more likely to occur. Contrary to much popular opinion, the U.S. government has managed this aspect of its foreign and national security policy adequately. While the appropriateness of those conceptions of the national interest promoted by successive Republican or Democratic administrations since Franklin Roosevelt's administration is a continuing feature of the public political debate in this country, each administration has managed its arms transfer programs consistent with its own definition of that national interest.

NOTES

1 Robert A. Levine, *The Arms Debate* (Cambridge: Harvard University Press, 1963).
2 Ibid., p. 33.

Selected Bibliography

GENERAL WORKS

I. General Works on Arms Transfers and Efforts to Control Them

"Tomorrow's Pterodactyls: A Survey of the Aerospace Industry," *The Economist*. 30 May 1981.

Adams, Gordon. *The Iron Triangle: The Politics of Defense Contracting*. New York: Council on Economic Priorities, 1981.

Albrecht, Ulrich, D. Ernst, P. Lock, and H. Wolf. "Militarization, Arms Transfer and Arms Production in Peripheral Countries," *Journal of Peace Research* 12,3 (1975) 195-212.

Beaton, Leonard. "Economic Pressures in the Arms Trade." *Occasional Papers*. Ottawa: Carleton University, School of International Studies, 1971.

Beaton, Leonard, et al. "Arms Trade and International Politics." *Occasional Papers*, No. 13. Ottawa: Carleton University, School of International Studies, 1971.

Bloomfield, Lincoln P., and A. C. Leiss. "Arms Transfer and Arms Control." *Proceedings of the Academy of Political Science* 29,3 (March 1969) 37-54.

Cahn, Anne Hessing. "Have Arms, Will Sell." *Arms Control Today* 4,10 (October 1974).

Cahn, Anne Hessing, Joseph J. Kruzel, Peter M. Dawkins, and Jacques Huntzinger. *Controlling Future Arms Trade.* New York: McGraw-Hill (1980s Project/ Council on Foreign Relations), 1977.

Cannizzo, Cindy (ed.) *The Gun Merchants: Politics and Policies of the Major Arms Suppliers.* New York: Pergamon Press, 1980.

Carter, Barry. "What Next in Arms Control?" *Orbis* 17,1 (Spring 1973) 176-196.

Cyr, A. "Arms Sales and the Major Western Powers." *Vanderbilt Journal of Transnational Law* 10 (Winter 1977) 109-120.

Englemann, Bernt. *The Weapons Merchants.* Translated by E. Detto. New York: Crown, 1968.

Frank, Lewis A. *The Arms Trade in International Relations.* New York: Praeger, 1969.

Freedman, Lawrence. "The Arms Trade: A Review." *International Affairs* 55,3 (July 1979) 432-437.

Gelb, Leslie H. "Arms Sales." *Foreign Policy* 25 (Winter 1976-77) 3-23.

Gellnor, J. "The Developing Countries and the Control of the Arms Trade." *Occasional Papers,* No. 12. Ottawa: Carleton University, School of International Studies, 1971.

Gillingham, Arthur. *Arms Traffic: An Introduction and Bibliography.* Los Angeles: Center for the Study of Armament and Disarmament, California State University Political Issues Series Vol. 4, No. 2 (1976).

Gray, Colin S. "The Arms Phenomenon: Definitions and Functions." *World Politics* 24 (October 1971) 39-79.

Griffiths, Franklyn. "Transnational Politics and Arms Control." *International Journal* 26,4 (Autumn 1971) 640-674.

Harkavy, Robert E. *The Arms Trade and International Systems.* Cambridge, Mass.: Ballinger, 1975.

Harkavy, Robert E. "Comparison of the International Arms Trade in the Interwar and Postwar Periods." *Michigan Academian* 4,4 (1972) 445-460.

Kemp, Geoffrey. "The International Arms Trade: Supplier, Recipient and Arms Control Perspectives." *Political Quarterly* 42 (October-December 1971) 379-389.

Leiss, Amelia C., et al. *Arms Transfers to Less Developed Countries.* Cambridge, Mass.: MIT, Center for International Studies, 1970.

Neuman, Stephanie G., and Robert E. Harkavy (eds.). *Arms Transfers in the Modern World.* New York: Praeger, 1979.

Perlo, Victor. *Militarism and Industry: Arms Profiteering in the Missile Age.* New York: International Publishers, 1963.

Ra'anan, Uri, Robert L. Pfaltzggraff, Jr., and Geoffrey Kemp (eds.) *Arms Transfers to the Third World: The Military Buildup in Less Industrial Countries.* Boulder, Colo.: Westview Press, 1979.

Rothschild, Emma. "The Boom in the Death Business." *New York Review of Books* 22 (2 October 1975) 7-12.

Sampson, Anthony. *The Arms Bazaar—The Companies, the Dealers, the Bribes: From Vickers to Lockheed.* London: Hodder and Stoughton, Coronet Books, 1977, 1978; New York: Viking Press, 1978.

Sivard, Ruth L. "Let Them Eat Bullets." *Bulletin of the Atomic Scientists* 31 (March 1975) 6-10.

Stanley, John. "The International Arms Trade and Its Control." *Army Quarterly and Defense Journal* 103 (January 1973) 210-220.

Stanley, John, and Maurice Pearton. *The International Trade in Arms.* New York: Praeger (International Institute for Strategic Studies), 1972.

Taylor, T. "The Control of the Arms Trade." *International Relations* (May 1971) 903-912.

Thayer, George. *The War Business: The International Trade in Armaments.* New York: Avon Books, 1969.

Vayrynen, Raimo. *Arms Trade, Military Aid, and Arms Production.* Basel: Verlag, 1973.

II. Trends in Arms Transfers

Barnaby, Frank. "Arms Industry—A Seller's Market." *The Bulletin of the Atomic Scientists* 37,5 (May 1981) 10-12.

Leiss, Amelia C. *Changing Patterns of Arms Transfers: Implications for Arms Transfer Policies.* Cambridge, Mass.: MIT, Center for International Studies, 1970.

Sivard, Ruth Leger. *World Military and Social Expenditures, 1979.* New Brunswick, N.J.: Transaction Books, 1979.

SIPRI (Stockholm International Peace Research Institute). *Armaments or Disarmaments? The Crucial Choice.* Stockholm: SIPRI, 1978.

SIPRI (Stockholm International Peace Research Institute). *Arms Trade Registers: The Arms Trade with the Third World.* Cambridge, Mass.: MIT Press, 1975.

SIPRI (Stockholm International Peace Research Institute). *The Arms Trade with the Third World.* London: Paul Elek, 1971.

SIPRI (Stockholm International Peace Research Institute). *SIPRI Yearbook of World Armament and Disarmament.* New York: Humanities Press (annual).

SIPRI (Stockholm International Peace Research Institute). *World Armaments—Abundance Amid Scarcity.* Stockholm: SIPRI, 1976.

Sutton, John L., and Geoffrey Kemp. *Arms to Developing Countries, 1945-1965.* Adelphi Paper No. 28. London: International Institute for Strategic Studies, 1966.

United States. Arms Control and Disarmament Agency. *World Military Expenditures and Arms Transfers, 1969-1978.* Washington, D.C.: USGPO, December 1980. (Latest volume in an annual series.)

United States. Arms Control and Disarmament Agency. *World Military Expenditures and Arms Transfers, 1968-1977.* Washington, D.C.: USGPO, October 1979.

United States. Central Intelligence Agency, National Foreign Assessment Center. *Arms Flows to LDC: U.S.-Soviet Comparisons, 1974-1975.* November 1978.

United States. Department of Defense. *Foreign Military Sales and Military Assistance Facts.* Washington, D.C.: USGPO (published annually).

United States. Department of Defense. *Fiscal Year Series.* Washington, D.C.: USGPO (published annually).

United States. General Accounting Office. *Statistical Data on Department of Defense Training of Foreign Military Personnel.* Report No. FGMSD-80-48. 15 April 1980.

III. Economic, Military, and Political Effects of the International Arms Trade

Albrecht, Ulrich, et al. "Armaments and Underdevelopment." *Bulletin of Peace Proposals* 3,2 (1972) 173-185.

Barrett, Raymond J. "Arms Dilemma for the Developing World." *Military Review* 50 (April 1970) 28-35.

Bloomfield, Lincoln P., and Amelia C. Leiss. *Controlling Small Wars: A Strategy for the 1970's.* New York: Knopf, 1969.

Chaudhuri, Gen. J. N. "International Arms Trade: The Recipient's Problem." *Political Quarterly* 43 (July-September 1972) 261-269.

Cook, Fred J. "Deadly Contagion: Arms Sales to the Third World." *Nation* 214 (24 January 1972) 106-109.

Deutsch, R. "African Arms Race." *African Report* 24 (March-April 1979) 47-49.

Fitch, John S. *The Political Consequences of U.S. Military Assistance to Latin America.* Carlisle Barracks, Pa.: Strategic Studies Institute, 1977.

Francis, Michael J. *Military Assistance and Influence: Some Observations.* Carlisle Barracks, Pa.: Strategic Studies Institute, 1977.

Gutteridge, William F. "The Political Role of African Armed Forces: The Impact of Foreign Military Assistance." *African Affairs* 66 (April 1967) 63-101.

Hoagland, John H. "Arms in the Developing World." *Orbis* 12 (Spring 1968) 167-184.

Hoagland, John H., and John B. Teeple. "Regional Stability and Weapons Transfer: The Middle Eastern Case." *Orbis* 9 (Fall 1965) 714-728.

Hughes, Col. David R. "The Myth of Military Coups and Military Assistance." *Military Review* 47 (December 1967) 3-10.

Jasami, Bhupendra. "Arms Race in the Third World." *Africa* (January 1979) 46-48.

Kemp, Geoffrey. "Arms Traffic and Third World Conflicts." *International Conciliation.* No. 577 (March 1970) 1-81.

Kemp, Geoffrey. "Arms Transfers and the "Back-End" Problem in Developing Countries." In *Arms Transfers in the Modern World,* edited by Stephanie G. Neuman and Robert E. Harkavy. New York: Praeger, 1979, pp. 264-275.

Kemp, Geoffrey. "Dilemmas of the Arms Traffic." *Foreign Affairs* 48 (January 1970) 274-284.

Kemp, Geoffrey. "Strategy, Arms and the Third World." *Orbis* 16 (Fall 1972) 809-815.

Kennedy, Edward M. "The Persion Gulf: Arms Race or Arms Control?" *Foreign Affairs* 54,1 (October 1975).

Klare, Michael T. "The Political Economy of Arms Sales." *Society II* (September-October 1974) 41-49; and *The Bulletin of the Atomic Scientists* (November 1976) 11-18.

Klare, Michael T. "White-Collar Mercenary and Repressive Technology." *USPCI News Letter*, No. 1 (Spring 1978) 18-19, 38-39.

Oberg, Jan. "Arms Trade with the Third World as an Aspect of Imperialism." *Journal of Peace Research* 12,3 (1975) 213-234.

Pryor, Leslie M. "Arms and the Shah." *Foreign Policy* 31 (Summer 1978) 56-71.

Quigg, Lieutenant Colonel Stuart M. *Latin American Military Expenditures: Some Implications for the United States.* Carlisle Barracks, Pa.: Strategic Studies Institute, 1977.

Qureshi, Khalida. "Arms Aid to India and Pakistan." *Pakistan Horizon* 20,2 (1967) 137-150.

Simon, Sheldon W. (ed.). *The Military and Security in the Third World: Domestic and International Impacts.* Boulder, Colo.: Westview Press, 1979.

Smith, Colonel Norman M. *Conventional Arms Transfers to Latin America.* Carlisle Barracks, Pa.: Strategic Studies Institute, 1977.

United Nations. Department of Political and Security Council Affairs, Center for Disarmament. *Economic and Social Consequences of the Arms Race and of the Military Expenditures: Updated Report of the Secretary-General.* New York: United Nations, 1978.

United Nations. Office of Public Information. *Economic and Social Consequences of the Arms Race and Military Expenditures.* New York: United Nations, 1977.

United States. Congress, House, Committee on International Relations. *Impact of Cuban-Soviet Ties in the Western Hemisphere.* Washington, D.C.: USGPO, 1978.

United States. Congress, House, Committee on Foreign Affairs. *The International Transfer of Conventional Arms.* Washington, D.C.: USGPO, 1974.

United States. General Accounting Office. *Critial Factors Affecting Saudi Arabia's Oil Decisions.* Report No. ID-78-32. 12 May 1978.

United States. U.S. Military Academy, 1976 Senior Conference [Final Report]. *Arms Transfers.* West Point, N.Y.: 10-12 June 1976.

Victor, A. H. "Military Aid and Comfort in Dictatorships." *U.S. Naval Institute Proceedings* 95 (March 1969) 42-47.

Weaver, Jerry L. "Arms Transfers to Latin America: A Note on the Contagion Effect." *Journal of Peace Research* 11,3 (1974) 213-220.

Wolf, Charles, Jr. *Economic Impacts of Military Assistance.* Rand Report P-4578. Santa Monica, Calif.: Rand Corporation, February 1971.

IV. Arms Transfers Between Advanced Industrial Countries and NATO RSI Issues

Bajusz, William D. "Advanced Technology and Public Policy: Multinational Weapons Acquisiton." *Policy Sciences* 11,1 (February 1980) 263-284.

Berry, Clifton, Jr., and Benjamin F. Schommer. "How Europe Sells." *Armed Forces Journal International* 114 (August 1977) 15 ff.

Bray, Frank T. J., and Michael Moodie. "Defense Technology and the Atlantic Alliance." *Atlantic Community in Crisis: A Redefinition of the Transatlantic Relationship*, edited by W. F. Hahn and R. L. Pfaltzgraff, Jr. New York: Pergamon Press, 1979, pp. 149-190.

Callaghan, Thomas A., Jr. *US/European Economic Cooperation in Military and Civil Technology*. Washington, D.C.: Georgetown University, Center for Strategic and International Studies, 1975.

Callaghan, Thomas A., Jr. "Standardization—A Plan for U.S./European Cooperation." *NATO Review* 23,4 (July-August 1975) 11-15.

Cohen, Eliot. "NATO Standardization: The Perils of Common Sense." *Foreign Policy* 31 (Summer 1978) 72-90.

Cornell, Alexander H. "Collaboration in Weapons and Equipment." *NATO Review* 28,4 (August 1980) 14-20; and 28,5 (October 1980) 14-19.

Critchley, Julian. "A Community Policy for Armaments." *NATO Review* 27,1 (February 1979) 10-14.

Edmonds, Martin (ed.). *International Arms Procurement* New York: Pergamon Press, 1981.

Edmonds, Martin. "International Collaboration in Weapons Procurement: The Implications of the Anglo-French Case." *International Affairs* 43 (April 1967) 252-264.

Facer, Roger. *The Alliance and Europe: Part III, Weapons Procurement in Europe—Capabilities and Choices*. Adelphi Paper No. 108. London: International Institute for Strategic Studies, 1975.

Fouquet, David. "To Compete and/or to Cooperate? The Atlantic Arms Race!" *European Community* (August-September 1976).

Franko, Lawrence G. "Restraining Arms Exports to the Third World: Will Europe Agree?" *Survival* 21,1 (January-February 1979) 14-25.

Hagen, Lawrence S. "Twisting Arms: Political, Military, and Economic Aspects of Arms Cooperation in the Atlantic Alliance." *Queen's University National Security Series* No. 3/80 (1980).

Heyhoe, D. C. R. *The Alliance and Europe: Part IV, the European Programme Group*. Adelphi Paper No. 129. London: International Institute for Strategic Studies, 1977.

Holst, John Jorgen. "The Independent European Programme Group: Cooperation and Western Security." *NATO Review* 29,2 (April 1981) 6-9.

Kanter, Herschel, and John Fry. *Cooperations in Development and Production of NATO Weapons: An Evaluation of Tactical Missile Programs*. Report prepared for the Office of the Under Secretary of Defense for Research and Engineering. Arlington, Va.: Institute for Defense Analyses, December 1980.

Kanter, Herschel, and John Fry. "Why NATO Doesn't Standardize Arms." *Astronautics and Aeronautics* 19,5 (June 1981) 34-40.

Latour, Charles. "Armaments Sales." *NATO's Fifteen Nations* 18 (April-May 1973) 74-76 ff.

Port, A. Tyler. "Co-operation on Arms Production: The Task Ahead." *NATO Review* 21 (May-June 1973) 13-17.

Schutze, Walter. *European Defense Cooperation and NATO*. Paris: Atlantic Institute, 1969.

Simpson, John, and Frank Gregory. "West European Collaboration in Weapons Procurement." *Orbis* 16 (Summer 1972) 435-461.

Stone, John. "Equipment Standardization and Cooperation." *NATO Review* 22,4 (August 1974) 26-28.

United States. Congress, House, Committee on Foreign Affairs. *NATO Mutual Support Act of 1979*. Washington, D.C.: USGPO, 1979.

United States. Congress, Senate, Committee on Foreign Relations. *Proposed Sale of AWACS to NATO*. Washington, D.C.: USGPO, 1976.

United States. Department of Defense. *Rationalization/Standardization within NATO: A Report to the United States Congress*. By Harold Brown, Secretary of Defense, 31 January 1979.

United States. General Accounting Office. *No Easy Choice: NATO Collaboration and the U.S. Arms Export Control Issue*. Report No. ID-81-18, 19 January 1981.

United States. General Accounting Office. *Standardization in NATO: Improving the Effectiveness and Economy of Mutual Defense Efforts*. Report No. PSAD-78-2, 19 January 1978.

United States. General Accounting Office. *Transatlantic Cooperation in Developing Weapon Systems for NATO—A European Perspective*. Report No. PSAD-76-26, 21 March 1979.

United States. General Accounting Office. *The Multinational F-16 Aircraft Program: Its Progress and Concerns*. Report No. PSAD-79-63, 25 June 1979.

V. International Efforts to Curb or Regulate Arms Transfers

Alcock, Norman. "UN Special Session on Disarmament." *Peace Research* 10,4 (1978) 135-140.

Bloomfield, Lincoln P., and Amelia C. Leiss. "Arms Transfers and Arms Control." *Proceedings of the Academy of Political Science* 29,3 (March 1969) 37-54.

Culver, Sen. John C. "Need for an International Conference on Arms Sales." *Congressional Record* 121 (23 September 1975), p. 516510.

Gray, Colin S. "Traffic Control for the Arms Trade?" *Foreign Policy* 6 (Spring 1972) 153-169.

Huntzinger, Jacques. "Regional Recipient Restraints." *Controlling Future Arms Trade*, edited by Anne Hessing Cahn, et al. New York: McGraw-Hill, 1977.

International Peace Research Association. "Recommendations to the Special Session of the General Assembly on Disarmament." *Bulletin of Peace Proposals* 9,2 (1978) 1-15.

Kemp, Geoffrey. "Regulating the Arms Trade." *Disarmament* 16 (December 1967) 11-15.

Klein, Jean. "Les Aspects Actuels de la Reglementation du Commerce des Armes." *Politique Etrangere* 34,2 (1969) 161-189.

"Regional Arms Control Arrangements for Developing Nations: Arms and Arms Control in Latin America, the Middle East and Africa." Cambridge, Mass.: MIT, Center for International Studies, 1964.

"Socialist International on Disarmament." *Socialist Affairs* No. 4/78 (July-August 1978) 79-95.

The Stanley Foundation. *Multilateral Disarmament and the Special Session*. 12th Conference of the U.N. of the Next Decade, San Juan del Rio, Mexico, 19-25 June 1977.

United Nations. *The Arms Race and Development.* OPI/609; CESI.E57. New York, 1978.

United Nations. *Disarmament: A Periodic Review by the U.N.* New York (three times a year).

United Nations. Department of Political and Security Council Affairs, United Nations Centre for Disarmament. *Status of Multilateral Arms Regulation and Disarmament Agreements: Special Supplement to the United Nations Disarmament Yearbook, Vol. 2, 1977.* New York, 1978.

United Nations. Department of Political and Security Council Affairs, United Nations Centre for Disarmament. *The United Nations Disarmament Yearbook.* New York (annual since 1976).

United Nations. Department of Political and Security Affairs. United Nations Centre for Disarmament. *The U.N. and Disarmament: 1945-1970.* New York, 1970.

United Nations. Department of Political and Security Affairs. United Nations Centre for Disarmament. *The U.N. and Disarmament: 1970-1975.* New York, 1976.

United Nations. General Assembly. *A Guide to the Final Document to the Special Session on Disarmament, 23 May-1 July 1978.* OPI/619. New York, August 1978.

United Nations Associations-USA. *Controlling the Conventional Arms Race.* New York: UNA-USA, 1976.

United States. Congress, Senate, Committee on Foreign Relations. *Prospects for Multilateral Arms Export Restraint.* Washington, D.C.: USGPO, 1979.

United States. General Accounting Office. *United Nations Special Session on Disarmament: A forum for International Participation.* Report No. ID-79-27, 3 July 1979.

Wainhouse, David W., and Associates. *Arms Control Agreements.* Baltimore: The Johns Hopkins University Press, 1968.

Weeks, Dudley. "The U.N. Special Session on Disarmament: Successes and Failures." *Prioritas* 2,2 (October-November 1978) 3-4.

NATIONAL ARMS TRANSFER POLICIES: DIMENSIONS AND MEANS OF CONTROL

VI. United States

Anderson, Sally. "U.S. Military Assistance and Sales (U.S. is Number One!)." *The Defense Monitor* 3,5 (May 1974) 1-12.

Arms Transfers and U.S. Foreign and Military Policy. Washington, D.C.: Georgetown University, CSIS, 1980.

Avery, William P. "Domestic Influences on Latin American Importation of U.S. Armaments." *International Studies Quarterly* 22,1 (March 1978) 121-142.

Baines, John M. "U.S. Military Assistance to Latin America: An Assessment." *Journal of Inter-American Studies and World Affairs* 14 (November 1972) 469-487.

Baldwin, William L. *The Structure of the Defense Market, 1955-1964.* Durham, N.C.: Duke University Press, 1966.

Betts, Richard K. "The Tragicomedy of Arms Trade Control." *International Security* 5,1 (September 1980) 80-110.

Bleckman, Barry M., Janne E. Nolan, and Alan Platt. "Pushing Arms." *Foreign Policy* 46 (Spring 1982).

Corbett, Colonel Charles D. *Inter-American Security and U.S. Military Policy.* Carlisle Barracks, Pa.: Strategic Studies Institute, 1977.

"The Crisis in Iran." *Armed Forces Journal International* (January 1979).

Duscha, Julius. *Arms, Money, and Politics.* New York: Ives Washburn, 1964, 1965.

Einaudi, Luigi, et al. *Arms Transfers to Latin America: Toward a Policy of Mutual Respect.* Rand Report No. R-1173-Dos. Santa Monica, Calif.: Rand Corporation, June 1973.

Farley, Philip J., Stephen S. Kaplan, and William H. Lewis. *Arms Across the Sea.* Washington, D.C.: The Brookings Institution, 1978.

Ferrell, Robert H. "The Merchants of Death, Then and Now." *Journal of International Affairs* 26,1 (1972) 29-39.

Gansler, Jacques S. *The Defense Industry.* Cambridge, Mass.: The MIT Press, 1980.

Gervasi, Tom. *Arsenal of Democracy: American Weapons Available for Export.* New York: Grove Press, 1978.

Gordon, Michael R. "Competition with the Soviet Union Drives Reagan's Arms Sales Policy." *National Journal* (16 May 1981) 868-873.

Gray, Colin S. "What Is Good for General Motors . . . " *Royal United Service Institution Journal* 117 (June 1972) 36-43.

"Growth of U.S. Arms Sales Abroad and Its Effect on Political and Business Institutions" (3-part series). *New York Times*, 19-21 October 1975.

Haddaway, George. "Crisis in Persia: A Postmortem." *Government Executive* (April 1979) 29-32.

Hammond, Paul Y., David J. Louscher, and Michael D. Salomon. "Controlling U.S. Arms Transfers: The Emerging System." *Orbis* 23,2 (Summer 1979).

Hammond, Paul Y., David J. Louscher, and Michael D. Salomon. "Growing Dilemmas for the Management of Arms Sales." *Armed Forces and Society* 6,1 (Fall 1979).

Hammond, Paul Y. "Military Aid and Influence in Pakistan: 1954-1963." Rand Report No. RD-5505/1-ISA. Santa Monica, Calif.: The Rand Corporation, June 1971.

Harrison, Stanley L. "Congress and Foreign Military Sales." *Military Review* 51 (October 1971) 79-87.

Hout, Marvin J. "Munitions Export Control Policies and Procedures." *Defense Management Journal* 8 (July 1972) 49-52.

Jordan, David C. *U.S. Foreign Policy and a Military Regime in Argentina.* Carlisle Barracks, Pa.: Strategic Studies Institute, 1977.

Kaplan, Stephen S. "U.S. Arms Transfers to Latin America, 1954-1974: Rational Strategy, Bureaucratic Politics, and Executive Parameters." *International Studies Quarterly* 19,4 (December 1975) 399-431.

Katzenbach, Nicholas de B. "U.S. Arms for the Developing World: Dilemmas of Foreign Policy." *U.S. Department of State Bulletin* 57 (December 1967) 794-798.

Kemp, Geoffrey. "U.S. Military Policy: Dilemmas of the Arms Traffic." *Foreign Affairs* 48 (January 1970) 274-284 [reprint in *Military Review* 50 (July 1970) 2-31].

Kincade, William H. "U.S. Disarmament Policy: Post Special Session." *Nineteenth Strategy for Peace Conference Report* (5-8 October 1978).

Klare, Michael. "The Politics of U.S. Arms Sales to Latin America." *Latin American Report* 9 (March 1975) 12-17.

Langer, William L., and S. Everett Gleason. *The Challenge to Isolation, 1837-1940.* New York: Harper & Bros. for the Council of Foreign Relations, 742-776.

Leonard, James F. "U.S. States View on Conventional Arms Restraints." *U.S. Department of State Bulletin* 65 (20 September 1971) 309-315.

Ligon, Walter B. "Foreign Military Sales." *National Defense* 60 (July-August 1975) 30-32.

Lincoln, George A. "Forces Determining Arms Aid." *Academy of Political Science Proceedings* 25 (May 1953) 263-272.

Louscher, David J. "Constancy and Change in American Arms Sales Policies." *Selected Papers of the Mershon Center.* Columbus: Ohio State University Press, 1978.

Louscher, David J. "The Rise of Military Sales as a U.S. Foreign Assistance Instrument." *Orbis* 20,4 (Winter 1977) 933-964.

Louscher, David J., and Michael D. Salomon. "New Directions and New Problems for Arms Transfers Policy." *Naval War College Review* 35,1 (January/February 1982).

Louscher, David J., and Michael D. Salomon. "Conflicting Trends for Arms Transfer Restraint." *Naval War College Review* 33,6 (November/December 1980) 82-88.

Pierre, Andrew J. *The Global Politics of Arms Sales.* Princeton, N.J.: Princeton University Press, 1982, p. 298.

Pierre, Andrew J. (ed.). *Arms Transfers and American Foreign Policy.* New York: New York University Press/Council on Foreign Relations, 1979.

Platt, Alan, and Lawrence D. Weiler (eds.). *Congress and Arms Control.* Boulder, Colo.: Westview Press, 1978.

"Potential Military Sales Blocked." *Aviation Week & Space Technology* (26 March 1979) 68-73.

Pranger, Robert J., and Dale R. Tahtinen. *Toward a Realistic Military Assistance Program.* An Enterprise Institute for Public Policy Research, Foreign Affairs Study No. 15. Washington, D.C., December 1974.

Refson, J. S. *U.S. Military Training and Advice: Implications for Arms Transfer Policies.* Cambridge, Mass.: MIT, 1970.

Roosevelt Papers. Secretary's File, Box 59, Franklin D. Roosevelt Library.

Rubin, Barry. *Paved with Good Intentions: The American Experience and Iran.* New York: Oxford University Press, 1980.

Salomon, Michael D., David J. Louscher, and Paul Y. Hammond. "Lessons of the Carter Approach to Restraining Arms Transfers." *Survival* 23,5 (September/October 1981).

Salomon, Michael D., and David J. Louscher. "Conventional Arms Sales in the Carter Administration: Dilemmas of Restraint." *Arms Control Today* 10,8 (September 1980).

Snider, Lewis W. *Arabesque: Untangling the Patterns of Supply of Conventional Arms to Israel and the Arab States and the Implications for United States Policy on Supply of "Lethal" Weapons to Egypt.* Denver: University of Denver, 1977.

Solarz, Stephen J. "Arms for Morocco?" *Foreign Affairs* 58,2 (Winter 1979-80) 278-299.

Taylor, Trevor. "President Nixon's Arms Supply Policies." *Year Book of World Affairs* 26 (1972) 65-80.

The U.S. Military in Saudi Arabia: Investing in Stability or Disaster?" *The Defense Monitor* 10,4 (1981).

"U.S. Weapons Exports: Can We Cut the Arms Connection?" *The Defense Monitor* 7,2 (February 1978) 1-8.

"U.S. Weapons Exports Headed for Record Level." *The Defense Monitor* 11,3 (1982).

U.S. Arms Control and Disarmament Agency. *The International Transfer of Conventional Arms.* (Report to Congress.) Washington, D.C.: USGPO, 12 April 1974.

U.S. Congress. Senate, Committee on Foreign Relations. *U.S. Conventional Arms Transfer Policy.* Washington, D.C.: USGPO, 1980.

U.S. Congress, House, Committee on Foreign Affairs. *Changing Perspectives on U.S. Arms Transfer Policy.* Washington, D.C.: USGPO, 1981.

U.S. Congress, Senate, Committee on Foreign Relations. *Arms Transfer Policy.* Washington, D.C.: USGPO, 1977.

U.S. Congress, House, Committee on International Relations. *Conventional Arms Transfer Policy.* Washington, D.C.: USGPO, 1978.

U.S. Congress, House, Conference Report. *International Security and Development Cooperation Act of 1980.* Report No. 96-1471, 20 November 1980.

U.S. Congress, House, Committee on International Relations. *United States Arms Transfer and Security Assistance Programs.* Washington, D.C.: USGPO, 1978.

U.S. Congress, House, Committee on Foreign Affairs. *U.S. Policy Toward El Salvador.* Washington, D.C.: USGPO, 1981.

U.S. Congress, House, Committee on Foreign Affairs. *U.S. Security Assistance and Arms Transfer Policies for the 1980's.* Washington, D.C.: USGPO, 1981.

U.S. Congress, House, Committee on Foreign Affairs. *Proposed U.S. Arms Sales to Saudi Arabia.* Washington, D.C.: USGPO, 1980.

U.S. Congress, House, Committee on Foreign Affairs. *Supplemental 1979 Middle East Aid Package for Israel and Egypt.* Washington, D.C.: USGPO, 1979.

U.S. Congress, House, Committee on Foreign Affairs. *Proposed Arms Transfers to the Yemen Arab Republic* Washington, D.C.: USGPO, 1979.

U.S. Congress, House, Committee on Foreign Affairs. *Proposed Arms Sales for Countries in the Middle East.* Washington, D.C.: USGPO, 1979.

U.S. Congress, House, Committee on Foreign Affairs. *Crisis in the Subcontinent: Afghanistan and Pakistan.* Washington, D.C.: USGPO, 1980.

U.S. Congress, Committee on International Relations. *Prospective Sale of Airborne Warning and Control System (AWACS) Aircraft to Iran.* Washington, D.C.: USGPO, 1978.

U.S. Congress, House, Committee on International Relations. *United States' Arms Policies in the Persian Gulf and Red Sea Areas: Past, Present, and future.* Washington, D.C.: USGPO, 1977.

U.S. Congress, Senate, Committee on Foreign Relations. *Latin America.* Washington, D.C.: USGPO, 1979.

U.S. Congress, Committee on International Relations. *United States Military Installations and Objectives in the Mediterranean.* Washington, D.C.: USGPO, 1977.

U.S. Congress, Senate, Committee on Foreign Relations. *U.S. Military Sales to Iran.* Washington, D.C.: USGPO, 1976.

U.S. Congress, Senate, Committee on Foreign Relations. *International Security and Development Cooperation Act of 1980.* Washington, D.C.: USGPO, 1980.

U.S. Congress, House, Committee on International Relations. *International Security Assistance and Arms Export Control Act of 1976.* Washington, D.C.: USGPO, 1976.

U.S. Congress, Senate, Committee on Foreign Relations. *Implications of President Carter's Conventional Arms Transfer Policy.* Washington, D.C.: USGPO, 1977.

U.S. Congress, House, Committee on International Relations. *Review of the President's Conventional Arms Transfer Policy.* Washington, D.C.: USGPO, 1978.

U.S. Congress, House, Committee on Foreign Affairs. *International Security and Development Cooperation Act of 1980.* Washington, D.C.: USGPO, 1980.

U.S. Congress, House, Committee on Appropriations. *Foreign Assistance and Related Programs Appropriation Bill, 1978.* Washington, D.C.: USGPO, 1977.

U.S. Congress, House, Committee on International Relations. *Foreign Assistance Legislation for Fiscal Year 1978.* Washington, D.C.: USGPO, 1977.

U.S. Congress, House, Committee on International Relations. *International Security Assistance Act of 1977.* Washington, D.C.: USGPO, 1977.

U.S. Congress, Senate, Committee on Foreign Relations. *U.S. Missile Sale to Jordan.* Washington, D.C.: USGPO, 1975.

U.S. Congress, Senate, Committee on Foreign Relations. *The International Security Assistance and Arms Export Control Act of 1977.* Washington, D.C.: USGPO, 1977.

U.S. Congress, House, Committee on International Relations. *International Transfer of Technology.* Washington, D.C.: USGPO, 1979.

U.S. Congress, Senate, Committee on Foreign Relations. *Proposed Sale of C-130's to Egypt.* Washington, D.C.: USGPO, 1976.

U.S. Congress, Senate, Committee on Foreign Relations. *International Security Assistance and Arms Export Control Act of 1976-1977.* Washington, D.C.: USGPO, 1976.

U.S. Congress, House, Conference Report on *International Security Assistance and Arms Export Control Act of 1976*. Washington, D.C.: USGPO, 1976.

U.S. Congress, House, Committee on International Relations. *United States Arms Sale Policy and Recent Sales to Europe and the Middle East*. Washington, D.C.: USGPO, 1979.

U.S. Congress, Senate, Committee on Foreign Relations. *International Security Assistance*. Washington, D.C.: USGPO, 1976.

U.S. Congress, House, Committee on International Relations. *Proposed Aircraft Sales to Israel, Egypt and Saudi Arabia*. Washington, D.C.: USGPO, 1978.

U.S. Congress, House, Committee on International Relations. *International Security Assistance and Arms Export Control Act of 1976*. Washington, D.C.: USGPO, 1976.

U.S. Congress, House, Committee on Foreign Affairs. *International Security Assistance Act of 1979*. Washington, D.C.: USGPO, 1979.

U.S. Congress, House, Committee on Foreign Affairs. *Military Assistance Training*. Washington, D.C.: USGPO, 1971.

U.S. Congress, Senate, Committee on Foreign Relations. *International Security Assistance Programs*. Washington, D.C.: USGPO, 1978.

U.S. Congress, House, Committee on International Relations. *Foreign Assistance Legislation for Fiscal Year 1979 (Part 1)*. Washington, D.C.: USGPO, 1978.

U.S. Congress, House, Committee on International Relations. *Foreign Assistance Legislation for Fiscal Year 1979 (Part 2)*. Washington, D.C.: USGPO, 1978.

U.S. Congress, House, Committee on Foreign Affairs. *Foreign Assistance Legislation for Fiscal Years 1980-81 (Part 2)*. Washington, D.C.: USGPO, 1979.

U.S. Congress, House, Committee on International Relations. *Foreign Assistance Legislation for Fiscal Year 1979 (Part 7)*. Washington, D.C.: USGPO, 1978.

U.S. Congress, House, Committee on International Relations. *Foreign Assistance Legislation for Fiscal Year 1979 (Part 3)*. Washington, D.C.: USGPO, 1978.

U.S. Congress, House, Committee on International Relations. *Foreign Assistance Legislation for Fiscal Year 1978 (Part 1-9)*. Washington, D.C.: USGPO, 1977.

U.S. Congress, Senate, Committee on Foreign Relations. *Fiscal Year 1980 International Security Assistance Authorization*. Washington, D.C.: USGPO, 1979.

U.S. Congress, Senate, Committee on Foreign Relations. *Foreign Assistance Authorization*. Washington, D.C.: USGPO, 1976.

U.S. Congress, Senate, Committee on Foreign Relations. *Implications of President Carter's Conventional Arms Transfer Policy*. Washington, D.C.: USGPO, 1977.

U.S. Congress, Senate, Committee on Foreign Relations. *The Conventional Arms Transfer Policy of the United States*. Washington, D.C.: USGPO, 1980.

U.S. Department of Defense. *Foreign Military Sales and Military Assistance Facts*. Washington, D.C.: USGPO, 1966 (annual report).

U.S. Department of State. *International Traffic in Arms Regulations (ITAR)*. Title 22, Code of Federal Regulations, Parts 121-128.

U.S. General Accounting Office. *Profiles of Military Assistance Advisory Groups in 15 Countries*. Report No. ID-78-51, 1 September 1978.

U.S. General Accounting Office. *Management of Security Assistance Programs Overseas Needs to Be Improved*. Report No. ID-78-27, 21 April 1978.

U.S. General Accounting Office. *Financial and Legal Implications of Iran's Cancellation of Arms Purchase Agreements*. Report No. FGMSD-79-47, 25 July 1979.

U.S. General Accounting Office. *The Roles and Functions of Overseas Security Assistance Offices Need to Be Clarified*. Report No. ID-81-47, 29 May 1981.

U.S. General Accounting Office. *What Would Be the Impact of Raising or Repealing the Commercial Arms Sales Ceiling?* Report No. ID-80-9, 4 January 1980.

U.S. General Accounting Office. *Foreign Military Sales—A Potential Drain on the U.S. Defense Posture*. Report No. LCD-77-440, 2 September 1977.

U.S. General Accounting Office. *Assessment of Overseas Advisory Efforts of the U.S. Security Assistance Program*. Report No. ID-76-1, 31 October 1975.

U.S. General Accounting Office. *Opportunities to Improve Decisionmaking and Oversight of Arms Sales*. Report No. ID-79-22, 21 May 1979.

U.S. General Accounting Office. *Arms Sales Ceiling Based on Inconsistent and Erroneous Data*. Report No. FGMSD-78-30, 12 April 1978.

U.S. General Accounting Office. *U.S. Munitions Export Controls Need Improvement*. Report No. ID-78-62, 25 April 1979.

U.S. General Accounting Office. *Forging a New Defense Relationship with Egypt*. Report No. ID-82-15, 5 February 1982.

Wood, Gen. Robert J. "Military Assistance and the Nixon Doctrine." *Orbis* 15 (Spring 1971) 247-274.

Wood, Gen. Robert J. "Military Assistance Program." *Armed Forces Management* 11 (November 1964) 105-106.

VII. U.S.S.R.

Alexander, Arthur J. *Decision-Making in Soviet Weapons Procurement*. Adelphi Papers No. 147-148. London: International Institute for Strategic Studies, 1978.

Alexandros, L. "Sowjetische Rakentenschiffe im Mettelmerraum." *Wehr and Wirtschaft* 10 (15 April 1966) 257-259.

Baker, Ross K. "Soviet Military Assistance to Tropical Africa." *Military Review* 48 (July 1968) 76-81.

Checiniski, M. "Structural Causes of Soviet Arms Exports." *Ostteuropa Wirtshaft* 22 (1977) 169-184.

Cordesman, Anthony H. "Facing the New Soviet Threat: U.S. and Soviet Competition in Arms Exports and Military Assistance." *Armed Forces Journal International* (August 1981) 65-72.

Dalin, Alexander. "Domestic Factors Influencing Soviet Foreign Policy." *The U.S.S.R. and the Middle East*, edited by M. Confino and S. Shamir. Jerusalem: Israel Universities Press, 1973.

Donaldson, Robert H. (ed.). *The Soviet Union in the Third World*: *Successes and Failures*. Boulder, Colo.: Westview Press, 1981.

Einbeck, Eberhardt. "Moskaus Militarhilte on die Dritte Welt." *Assempolitik* 22 (May 1971) 300-313.

Gallagher, Matthew P., and Karl F. Speilman, Jr. *Soviet Decision-Making for Defense*: *A Critique of U.S. Perspectives on the Arms Race*. New York: Praeger, 1972.

Gasteyger, Curt. "Moscow and the Mediterranean." *Foreign Affairs* 46 (July 1968) 476-487.

Gilbert, Stephan P. "Soviet-American Military Aid Competition in the Third World." *Orbis* 13 (Winter 1970) 1117-1137.

Gilbert, Stephan P. "Wars of Liberation and Soviet Military Aid Policy." *Orbis* 10 (Fall 1966) 839-858.

Gilbert, Stephan P., and Wynfred Josua. *Arms for the Third World*: *Soviet Military Aid Diplomacy*. Baltimore, Md.: Johns Hopkins University Press, 1969.

Glassman, Jon D. *Arms for the Arabs*: *The Soviet Union and War in the Middle East*. Baltimore, Md.: Johns Hopkins University Press, 1975.

Herold, Robert C., and Shane E. Mahoney. "Military Hardware Procurement: Some Comparative Observations on Soviet and American Policy Processes." *Comparative Politics* 6,4 (July 1974) 571-600.

Husbands, Jo. "Soviet Weapons Exports: Russian Roulette in the Third World." *The Defense Monitor* 8,1 (January 1979).

Jacobsen, C. G. *Soviet Strategy—Soviet Foreign Policy*: *Military Considerations Affecting Soviet Policy-Making*. Glasgow: Robert Maclehose, The University Press, 1972.

Kapur, Ashok. "Soviet Arms Supplies and Indian Ocean Diplomacy." In *The Indian Ocean in Global Politics*, edited by Larry W. Bowman and Ian Clark. Boulder, Colo.: Westview Press, 1980.

Novosti Press Agency. *Disarmament*: *Soviet Initiatives*. Moscow, 1977.

Pajak, Roger F. "Soviet Arms Transfer as an Instrument of Influence." *Survival* 23,4 (July-August 1981).

Pye, Lucian. "Soviet and American Styles in Foreign Aid." *Orbis* 9 (Summer 1960) 159-173.

Ramazani, R. K. "Soviet Military Assistance to the Uncommitted Countries." *Midwest Journal of Political Science* (November 1959) 356-373.

Ra'anan, Uri. *The USSR Arms the Third World*: *Case Studies in Soviet Foreign Policy*. Cambridge, Mass.: MIT Press, 1969.

Rajasekhariah, A. M., and V. T. Patil. "Soviet Arms Supply to Pakistan: Motives and Implications." *Modern Review* 123 (October 1968) 706-710.

Sharma, B. L. "Soviet Arms for Pakistan." *United Service Institution of India Journal* 98 (July-September 1968) 223-238.

Smolansky, Oles M. "The Soviet Setback in the Middle East." *Current History* 64 (January 1973) 17-20.

Thayer, George. "The Communists as Arms Traders." Ch. 8 in *The War Business*. New York: Avon Books, 1969, pp. 319-352.

U.S. Central Intelligence Agency, National Foreign Assessment Center. *Communist Aid Activities in Non-Communist Less Developed Countries: 1978*. Report No. ER79-10412U (September 1979).

Wagner, Charles. *The Impact of Soviet Arms Introduction into the Middle East: A Missed Opportunity*. Santa Monica, Calif.: Arms Control and Foreign Policy Seminar, March 1972.

Weinstein, Warren, and Thomas H. Henriksen (eds.). *Soviet and Chinese Aid to African Nations*. New York: Praeger, 1980.

Yodfat, A. Y. "Arms and Influence in Egypt: The Record of Soviet Military Assistance since June, 1967." *New Middle East* 10 (July 1969) 27-32.

VIII. France

Alia, Josette. "Les Marchands de Mort." *Nouvel Observateur* 313 (19 November 1970) 24-25.

Brachet, Olivier, Christian Pons, and Michel Tachon. *La France militarisée: ventes d'armes*. Paris: Les Editions du Cerf, 1974.

Butler, A. "Commerce des armes: le jue de la France." *Realites* 298 (November 1970) 80-85.

"Le commerce des armes avec le Tiers-monde: la France." *Parole et Societe* 80,1 (1972) 53-77.

Crocker, C. A. "France's Changing Military Interest." *Africa Review* 13 (June 1968) 16-24.

Defourneaux, Marc. "France and a European Armament Policy." *NATO Review* 27,5 (October 1979) 19-25.

Delvolve, P. "A propos d'une décision d'embargo: le régime juridique francais de l'exportation des materiels militaires." *Actualité Juridique* 25,10 (20 October 1969) 528-545.

"Entretien avec Jean Laurent Delpech, delegue ministeriel pour l'Armement." *Défense Nationale*. 31 (June 1975) 15-37; also 30 (October 1974) 17-40.

"Entretien avec le général Maurin, chef d'état major des armées." *Défense Nationale* 30 (July 1974) 7-27.

Erven, L. "France in the Mediterranean." *Review of International Affairs* 21 (5 March 1970) 10-13.

Evron, Yair. "French Arms Policy in the Middle East." *World Today* 26 (February 1970) 82-90.

Faveris, J. "Le controle des industries d'armement." *Défense Nationale* 29,2 (February 1973) 49-69.

"France Woos Libyans with Aid." *Africa Report* 15 (June 1970) 20-21.

"France's Aerospace Industry." *Flight International* (17 November 1979) 1675-1703.

Friedrich, P. J. "Defence and the French political left." *Survival* 16,4 (July-August 1974) 165-171.

Huntzinger, J. "Le P.S. et la défense." *Project* 104 (April 1976) 450-458.

Klein, Jean. "Commerce des armes et politique: le cas francais." *Politique Entrangère* 41,6 (1976) 567-586.

Klein, Jean. "Désarmement: continuité et novations." *Regards sur l'Actualité*, No. 42 (June 1978) 3-12.

Klein, Jean. "France and the Arms Trade." In *The Gun Merchants: Politics and Policies of the Major Arms Suppliers,* edited by Cindy Cannizzo. New York: Pergamon Press, 1980.

Kolodziej, Edward. "Determinants of French Arms Sales: Security Implications." In *Threats, Weapons and Foreign Policy Behavior: Volume 5, Sage International Yearbook of Foreign Policy Studies,* edited by Patrick J. McGowan and Charles W. Kegley, Jr. Beverly Hills, Calif.: Sage, 1980.

Kolodziej, Edward. "France and the Arms Trade." *International Affairs* 56,1 (January 1980) 54-72.

Kolodziej, Edward. "Measuring French Arms Transfers: A Problem of Sources and Some Sources of Problems with ACDA Data." *Journal of Conflict Resolution* 23,2 (June 1979) 195-227.

Kolodziej, Edward. "Les Ventes d'Armes Conventionnelles." *Le Monde Diplomatique* (October 1978) [reprinted in *Problemes Economiques,* No. 1.599 (29 November 1978) 30-32].

Lachaux, Claude. "La réglementation des exportations des matériels de guerre." *Défense Nationale* (December 1977) 35-41.

Lamarche, Rene. "Death At Any Price—France: The Hard Sell." *Agenor* (October 1974) 22-25.

Lammers, L. "La fortune des armes." *Economie* (Paris) 1072 (2 September 1968) 22-26.

Lambert, Mark. "France's Aerospace Industry." *Flight International* (19 November 1977).

Lambert, Mark. "France's Aerospace Industry." *Flight International* (4 November 1978).

Lennart, Edith. "France: 'Merchanct of Death'." *Far Eastern Economic Review* (7 May 1976).

Leroy, Daniel. "La France Exportatrice de missiles." *Science et Vie* 120 (November 1971) 112-119.

Manor, Y. "Does France Have an Arms Export Policy?" *Res Publica* (Bruxelles) 16,5 (1974) 645-661.

Michel, R. "La France vend des armes." *Project* 49 (November 1970) 1098-1112.

Morice, G. "France troisième exportateur mondial d'armement." *Science et Vie* 119 (643) (April 1971) 92-100.

Morris, Beau. "Why France's Arms Exports Make It a Paper Tiger." *Armed Forces Journal International* 100 (October 1978) 19, 22-23.

Nallet, T. "La France marchand de canons." *Croissance des Jeunes Nations* 169 (March 1976) 19-26.

"Le Parti socialiste et la Défense nationale." *La Nouvelle Revue Socialiste* 6 (1974) 4-57.

Ramsden, J. M. "France's Aircraft Industry." *Flight International* 100 (28 October 1971) 685-700.

"Record French Arms Exports in 1970." *International Defense Review* 4 (April 1971) 113-114.

"Rencontre nationale sur le désarmement." *Les Cahiers de Combat pour la Paix* 294 (June 1978) 1-52.

Ribes, B. "La France et les ventes d'armes à l'étranger." *Etudes* (Paris) (January 1972) 5-26.

Rochebrune, R. de "Le commerce de l'armement: la France a fait mouche." *Entreprise* 833-834 (27 August-8 September 1971) 41-49.

Roulleaux Dugage, H. J. "Du bon usage de la coopération interalliée in mattère d'armement." *Défence Nationale* (August-September 1976) 85-94.

Rouquie, A. "Les ventes d'armes francaises en Amerique latine." *Politique Aujourd'hui* 1-2 (January-February 1974) 139-142.

Sallon, Andree. "La règlementation de la fabrication et du commerce des armements." *L'Actualité Juridique* 34,2 (20 February 1978) 67-81.

"L'univers des marchands de canons." *Preuves* 15 (3rd Trimester, 1973) 38-47.

Vermont, Jacques. "Relance francaise sur le désarmement." *Défense Nationale* (July 1978) 105-110.

Veyrard, P. "A propos d'un colloque: menaces et perception des Menaces." *Défense Nationale* 30 (April 1974) 11-15.

Virieu, Francois-Henri de, and Paul Thibau. "La Mort 'Made in France'!" *Le Nouvel Observateur*, No. 551 (2 June 1975) 21-23.

France. Ministere de la défense. *Livre Blanc sur la Défense Nationale*. Volumes 1 and 2. Paris, June 1972.

France. Ministere de la défense. Service d'information et de relations publiques des armées. *Vrai, faux: la défense de la France*. Paris, 1978.

IX. United Kingdom

"Arms and Sadat." *Economist* (20 December 1975) 13.

Beale, Albert. "Machiavelli's Reps." *Peace News* 16 (June 1978) 8.

Camilleri, Joseph. *Britian and the Death Trade*. London: Housmons (for Pax Christi).

Campaign Against Arms Trade. *British Military Exporters*. London: CAAT, 1977.

Cook, Robin. *Britian and the Arms Trade*. London: Labour Party International Department, 1976.

Defense Policy and Arms Sales. London: Royal United Services Institution for Defense Studies, December 1976.

"The Defense Sales Organization." *State Research Bulletin*, No. 6 (June-July 1978) 115-121.

Edmonds, Martin. "The Domestic and International Dimensions of British Arms Sales, 1966-1978." In *The Gun Merchants: Politics and Policies of the Major Arms Suppliers*, edited by Cindy Cannizzo. New York: Pergamon Press, 1980.

Elliot, David. *The Lucas Aerospace Workers' Campaign*. Young Fabian Pamphlet No. 46. London: Fabian Society, 1977.

Franklin, Gloria. "UK Arms Transfer Policy: A Defense." In *The Control of Arms Transfers: Report of a FCO/BISA Seminar*, edited by J. Simpson. London: ACDRU, 1978.

Freedman, Lawrence. *Arms Production in the United Kingdom: Problems and Prospects*. British Foreign Policy to 1985 Occasional Paper. London: The Royal Institute of International Affairs, 1978.

Freedman, Lawrence. "British Foreign Policy to 1985 IV: Britain and the Arms

Trade." *International Affairs*. 54,1 (July 1978) 377-392.

Graham, Norman A., and David Louscher. "The Political Control of Weapons System Acquisition: A Comparative Analysis of the Legislative Role in the United Kingdom and the United States." In *Threats, Weapons and Foreign Policy Behavior: Volume 5, Sage International Yearbook of Foreign Policy Studies*, edited by Patrick J. McGowan and Charles W. Kegley, Jr. Beverly Hills, Calif.: Sage, 1980.

Hickmott, J. R. "We Must Have Conventional British Weapons." *Contemporary Review* 210 (April 1967) 171-172.

"If We Don't Sell Those Arms." *Economist* 237 (21 November 1970) 13-14.

The Labour Party. *Sense about Defence: The Report of the Labour Party Defence Study Group*. London: Quartet Books Limited, 1977.

Lloyd, Lorna, and Nicholas A. Sims. *British Writing on Disarmament from 1914 to 1978: A Bibliography*. New York: Nichols, 1979.

Lucas: An Alternative Plan. Nottingham, England: Institute for Workers' Control, IWC Pamphlet No. 55.

Manistry, Peter. "Selling British Naval Equipment Worldwide." *Navy International* 84,9 (September 1979) 14-17.

Martin, Lawrence (ed.). *The Management of Defence: Papers Presented at the National Defence College Seminar, Latimer in September, 1974*. London: Macmillan, 1976.

Owen, David. "Speech to the Socialist International on Disarmament." *Socialist Affairs*, No. 4/78 (July-August 1978) 85-88.

Pajak, R. "French and British Sales in the Middle East: A Policy Perspective." *Middle East Review* 10 (Spring 1978) 45-54.

Ramsden, J. M. "EEC and British Aerospace." *Flight International* 101 (20 January 1972) 89-92.

Watt, D. C. "Britain Stirs It Up." *Spectator* (16 September 1966) 339-340.

Watts, Anthony J. "The Defense Sales Organization." *Navy International* 84,9 (September 1979) 4-8.

United Kingdom. Foreign and Commonwealth Office, Arms Control and Disarmament Department. *British Arms Control and Disarmament Policy: A Short Guide*. London, January 1978.

United Kingdom. Parliament. *Export of Surplus War Material*. Cmnd. 9676. London, HMSO, 1956.

United Kingdom. Parliament. House of Commons. *Seventh Report from the Expenditure Committee, Session 1975-76: Guided Weapons*. 22 July 1976.

X. West Germany

Albrecht, Ulrich. *Politik und Waffengeschafte: Rustungsexporte in der BRD*. Munich: C. Hanser, 1972.

Albrecht, Ulrich, Peter Lock, and Herbert Wulf. *Arbeitsplatze durch Rustung? Warmung vor falschen Hoffnungen*. Hamburg: Rowohlt Taschenbach, 1978.

Albrecht, Ulrich, and Birgit A. Sommer. "Deutsche Waffen fur die Dritte Welt." *Militarhilfe und Entwichkungspolitik*. Hamburg: Rowohlt, 1972.

"Arms Industry Sceptical about 'Areas of Tension' definition." *Süddeutsche Zeitung*, 21 January 1976.

"Arms Orders Make Industry Increasingly Dependent on Defence Spending Spree." *Süddeutsche Zeitung*, 24 February 1979.

"Bonn Doesn't Sell Arms to South Africa!" *German International* 20,12 (December 1976) 9-12.

Dillon, Mike. "Arms Transfers and the Federal Republic of Germany." In *The Gun Merchants: Politics and Policies of the Major Arms Suppliers*, edited by Cindy Cannizzo. New York: Pergamon Press, 1980.

Ehrengerg, Eckehard. *Rustungs-Export-Studio*. Bonn: University of Bonn, 1980.

Federal Republic of Germany. Ministry of Defense. *White Paper 1979: The Security of the Federal Republic of Germany and the Development of the Federal Armed Forces*. Bonn, 4 September 1979.

Haftendorn, Helga. *Militarhilfe und Rustungsexporte der BRD*. Dusseldorf: Bertleman, 1971.

Manchester, William. *The Arms of Krupp, 1587-1968*. Boston: Little, Brown, 1969.

Rattinger, Hans. "West Germany's Arms Transfers to the Nonindustrial World." In *Arms Transfers to the Third World: The Military Buildup in Less Industrial Countries*. Boulder, Colo.: Westview Press, 1978.

"To Sell or Not to Sell Arms? That Is the Question." Deutsches *Allgemeines Sonntagsblatt*, 14 March 1976.

XI. Other Arms Producers and Suppliers

Cahn, Anne Hessing. "Have Arms, Will Sell." *Bulletin of the Atomic Scientists* 31 (April 1975) 10-12.

Cobban, William. "Dealing out Death Discreetly: The Traffic in Canadian Arms." *Saturday Night* 86 (November 1971) 23-26.

Daniels, Jeff. "Swedish Strike Power from SAAB." *Flight International* 101 (9 March 1972) 360-362.

"Die Illegole Waffenausfuhr aus der Schweiz." *Flugwehr und Technik: Arms et Technique de l'Air* 31 (January-February 1969) 15-18.

Jacob, A. "Israel's Military Aid to Africa, 1960-1966." *Journal of Modern African Studies* 9 (August 1971) 165-187.

Kurz, H. R. "Die Durch-und Ausfur von kreigsmaterial aus der Schweiz." *Osterreische Militarische Zeitschrift* 2 (March-April 1966) 109-116.

Nagashima, Shusuke. "Japan's Defense Rests on U.S. Technology." *Technology Week* 19 (6 December 1966) 32-33.

"Schweiz: Rustungsproduktion und Waffenausfuhr." *Wehrkunde* 19 (February 1970) 104-105.

Scott-Stokes, Henry. "It's All Right to Talk Defense Again in Japan." *The New York Times Magazine* (11 February 1979) 18 ff.

"In Self-Defense of Jobs." *The Economist* (Japan) (22 April 1978) 94.

"Sweden's Arms Export Policy: Tight but Easing." *Armed Forces Journal* 110 (February 1973) 56-57 ff.

Weller, Jac. "Israeli Arms Production." *Ordinance* 55 (May-June 1971) 540-544.

"Who Has Been Arming the Middle East?" *Business Week* (18 July 1970) 72-73.

Index

About the Authors

Paul Y. Hammond has been Edward R. Weidlein Professor of Environmental and Public Policy Studies at the University of Pittsburgh since 1976. He teaches in the Graduate School of Public and International Affairs and until recently served as Co-Director of the Energy and Environment Center and the Energy Policy Institute at the University of Pittsburgh. Previously he had been Head of the Rand Corporation's Social Science Department as well as Director of its National Security Studies Program and its Program in Soviet, China, and Third Country Studies. Dr. Hammond had been a senior staff member at Rand since 1964. Before that, he served on the research staff of The Johns Hopkins University's Washington Center of Foreign Policy Research and taught at Yale University, Columbia University, and Harvard University. Dr. Hammond has published mainly in the field of national security policy and foreign policy. He is author of a classic work on Defense Department organization. Some recent publications also have dealt with energy policy.

David J. Louscher is an Associate Professor of Political Science at the University of Akron. He has worked as a consultant for Analytical Assessments Corporation and The Futures Group. Dr. Louscher also has been a consultant to the Department of Defense and the House of Representatives. Professor Louscher is the author or co-author of numerous articles on arms transfers and other security issues.

Michael D. Salomone is Associate Dean, College of Humanities and Social Scences, Carnegie-Mellon University, Pittsburgh, Pennsylvania. Before coming to Carnegie-Mellon, he was with the International Division, U.S. General Accounting Office, and served on the faculties of the University of Pittsburgh and Bethany College. Mr. Salomone is the author or co-author of articles and studies on various national security policy issues including arms transfers, command and control, and arms control, and serves as a Senior Consultant to the Analytical Assessments Corporation, Marina del Rey, California, on defense issues.

Norman A. Graham is Senior Research Associate at The Futures Group of Glastonbury, Connecticut. He holds a Ph.D. degree in international relations from Columbia University, and his research interests include problems of national security and defense, international economic relations, and economic, demographic, and security trends in Western Europe and the Third World. Prior to joining The Futures Group, Dr. Graham served as a Research Associate with the Institute on Western Europe of Columbia University and the United Nations Institute for Training and Research. He has taught at both Columbia and Michigan State Universities and has been a consultant to the Department of State, the Department of Defense, the Agency for International Development, and the United Nations. Dr. Graham is currently principal investigator on a major research project involving forecasts of various social, economic, resource use, and security trends for seventeen countries in the Caribbean Basin, and has recently completed similar studies for Morocco, Pakistan, and Egypt.

—